C000130216

Studies on the European Union

Series Editor:

Wolfgang Wessels
Jean Monnet Chair *ad personam* for Political Science
CETEUS | Centre for Turkey and European Union Studies
University of Cologne

Volume 18

Aline Bartenstein

The Concept of Solidarity

Energy Policy in the European Union

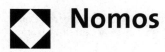 **Nomos**

The Deutsche Nationalbibliothek lists this publication in the
Deutsche Nationalbibliografie; detailed bibliographic data
are available on the Internet at http://dnb.d-nb.de

a.t.: Köln, Univ., Diss., 2021

ISBN   978-3-8487-8419-6 (Print)
         978-3-7489-2795-2 (ePDF)

British Library Cataloguing-in-Publication Data
A catalogue record for this book is available from the British Library.

ISBN   978-3-8487-8419-6 (Print)
         978-3-7489-2795-2 (ePDF)

Library of Congress Cataloging-in-Publication Data
Bartenstein, Aline
The Concept of Solidarity
Energy Policy in the European Union
Aline Bartenstein
318 pp.
Includes bibliographic references.

ISBN   978-3-8487-8419-6 (Print)
         978-3-7489-2795-2 (ePDF)

Onlineversion
Nomos eLibrary

1st Edition 2021
© Nomos Verlagsgesellschaft, Baden-Baden, Germany 2021. Overall responsibility
for manufacturing (printing and production) lies with Nomos Verlagsgesellschaft mbH
& Co. KG.

Acknowledgments

When I drafted the first ideas of my thesis in 2017, I was far from imagining how this rambling path will develop over time. In 2020, – when the Covid-19 health crisis hit hard – I wondered if it was possible to complete the thesis without childcare, without or only limited access to libraries and without the possibility to meet in person with my supervisors.

Writing the thesis was certainly an eventful journey which only succeeded thanks to the different fellow travellers who accompanied me. I would like to thank my supervisors Prof. *Wolfgang Wessels* und Prof. *André Kaiser* who have both encouraged my work and research angle.

I thank also my colleagues at the Jean Monnet Chair and at CETEUS at the University of Cologne who provided the opportunity to discuss my research in an inspiring and challenging environment. Even more important was the friendly and humorous atmosphere. My thanks go in particular to Dr. *Claudia Hefftler*, Dr. *Andreas Raspotnik* and *Leonie Völker*.

I am very grateful to have had the moral support of a group of exceptional and brilliant women who share the pleasure and burden of having kids in the academic world. I want to thank *Mirjam Dickmeis*, Dr. *Ursula Gießmann* and Dr. *Nicole Hiekel*. *Heidi Fritze*, Dr. *Friederike Strack* und *Susanne Wolfmaier* have been great friends during this time! Thank you so much for your precious help.

But who am I without my family? Merci, *Thierry Albrecht*, for all your understanding and support. You always reminded me of my strength and motivated me in difficult times. *Louise* and *Emile*, you brought me back down to earth, when I was lost in thought. There is nothing more rewarding than exploring the world together with you.

Thank you, dear sisters, *Julia Bartenstein*, *Hanna Gallus* and *Liane Leske*, for always being there when I need you. Mein größter Dank geht aber an meine Eltern *Birgit und Otto Bartenstein*. Ihr habt mich immer darin bestärkt meinen eigenen Weg zu gehen, mutig zu sein und das Leben selbst in die Hand zu nehmen.

Köln, July 2021   Aline Bartenstein

Table of Contents

List of Figures   11

List of Boxes   13

List of Abbreviations   15

1. Introduction: European solidarity – a chameleonic term   17
    1.1. Research interest   21
    1.2. Research question   25
    1.3. Research design   28
    1.4. Outline of the book   29

2. Research framework   32
    2.1. Concept formation   32
        2.1.1. The evolution of solidarity over time: reflections of
        the pioneers   35
        2.1.2. Sources of solidarity   41
        2.1.3. Delineation of solidarity from neighbouring terms   55
        2.1.4. Analysis of the features of solidarity   60
        2.1.5. Concept formation of solidarity between Member
        States   72
        2.1.6. Definition and concept of solidarity   86
        2.1.7. Results   89
    2.2. Theoretical framework   90
        2.2.1. Drivers for solidarity explained by neofunctionalism   90
        2.2.2. Variables and Hypotheses   96
        2.2.3. Operationalisation of variables   99
    2.3. Methodological framework   105
        2.3.1. Case Selection and Analysis   105
        2.3.2. Data Collection and Analysis   111

3. The principle of solidarity as political commitment and legal
    norm   118

    3.1. Solidarity is running through the EU's bloodlines   118
         3.1.1. From Maastricht to Nice: inclusion of solidarity as a
                legal principle   121
         3.1.2. The new impetus by the Treaty of Lisbon   122
         3.1.3. Solidarity as legal norm and binding commitment   126
         3.1.4. European energy policy and the effects of solidarity as
                a legal principle   128
    3.2. The different stages of European energy policy   132
         3.2.1. Phase I: Energy policy under pressure to reform
                (2005 – 2008)   133
         3.2.2. Phase II: Changing old patterns (2009 – 2013)   143
         3.2.3. Phase III: The Energy Union (as of 2014)   148
         3.2.4. Results and discussion   152

4. Solidarity in secondary law: only cosmetic improvements?   154

    4.1. Case 1: SoS – solidarity in case of emergency   156
         4.1.1. Times of crisis – solidarity in crisis   161
         4.1.2. The stony way to Regulation 2017/1938   181
         4.1.3. Results and discussion   200
    4.2. Case 2: The integration of the gas market: the pursuit of
         solidarity   204
         4.2.1. Regional solidarity as answer to the gas crisis   204
         4.2.2. Results and discussion   209
         4.2.3. Lex Nord Stream 2   211
    4.3. Case 3: Intergovernmental agreements under European
         scrutiny   213
         4.3.1. Decision (EU)2012/994: solidarity should guide our
                actions   214
         4.3.2. Solidarity? We are not so sure about it: Decision (EU)
                2017/684   219
         4.3.3. Results and discussion   224
    4.4. Case 4: Making solidarity work: investments in
         infrastructure   226
         4.4.1. The TEN-E Regulation: Did pipe dreams come true?   229
         4.4.2. Results and discussion   236

4.5. The Court Case: Speaking with one voice? Nord Stream 1 as
solidarity quest   237
    4.5.1. The development of Nord Stream 1   238
    4.5.2. The OPAL Case T-883/16 and Case C-848/19 P   243
    4.5.3. Results and discussion   248

5. Conclusions   251

    5.1. Theoretical reflections on solidarity   252
    5.2. Synopsis of work: synthesis of findings   259
    5.3. The solidarity concept and further research avenues   268

List of Literature   273

Annex   309

    Annex 1: Definitions of Solidarity   309
    Annex 2: Code Book – Concept of Solidarity   313
    Annex 3: List of interviews and personal communications   315
    Annex 4: Major policy trends in energy policy with a focus on
solidarity   316

List of Figures

Figure 1: Values in European Council Conclusions 2004–2019   19

Figure 2: References to solidarity in European Council
conclusions   27

Figure 3: Causal mechanism – functional spillover   110

Figure 4: Causal mechanism – cultivated spillover   111

Figure 5: Frames in Commission Communication on Security of
Supply 2002   157

Figure 6: European Parliament Debate on Security of Gas Supply
2010   178

Figure 7: Framing of solidarity by Commission   192

Figure 8: Frames used by European Parliament   260

Figure 9: Frames used by Commission   263

List of Boxes

Box 1:   The Solidarity Discourse   17

Box 2:   Research Questions   25

Box 3:   Conceptualisation   34

Box 4:   Solidarity actors   65

Box 5:   Forms of solidarity   67

Box 6:   Ensuring Solidarity   71

Box 7:   Solidarity actors on the EU level   76

Box 8:   Forms of solidarity between EU Member States   81

Box 9:   Ensuring solidarity between EU Member States   85

Box 10:   Definition of solidarity between EU Member States   86

Box 11:   Features of solidarity   87

Box 12:   Legislation on gas policy containing references to
           solidarity   107

Box 13:   Examples of interview questions   117

Box 14:   Gas crisis 2006   134

Box 15:   Presentation of variance of solidarity   155

Box 16:   Solidarity features named by the Commission   184

List of Abbreviations

ACER	Agency for the Cooperation of Energy Regulators
AFET	Committee on Foreign Affairs
ALDE	Alliance of Liberals and Democrats for Europe
BNetzA	Bundesnetzagentur
CEAS	Common European Asylum System
CFSP	Common Foreign and Security Policy
CJEU / ECJ	Court of Justice of the European Union
COM	European Commission
Council	Council of the European Union
DG	Directorates-General
DV	Dependent Variable
ECON	Committee on Economic and Monetary Affairs
EEAS	European External Action Service
ENTSOG	European Network of Transmission System Operators for Gas
EP	European Parliament
EPE	Energy Policy for Europe
EPP/PPE	European People's Party
EU	European Union
EUCO	European Council
GCG	Gas Coordination Group
HR	High Representative of the Union for Foreign Affairs and Security Policy
IA	Impact Assessment
IEA	International Energy Agency
IGA	Intergovernmental Agreement
INI	Own-initiative procedure
ITRE	Committee on Industry, Research and Energy
IV	Independent Variable
LNG	Liquified Natural Gas
MEP	Member of European Parliament
NATO	North Atlantic Treaty Organization
NEL	Nordeuropäische Erdgasleitung
NS	Nord Stream
OECD	Organisation for Economic Co-operation and Development
OPAL	Ostsee-Pipeline-Anbindungsleitung
PCI	Project of Common Interest
PEES Act	Protecting Europe's Energy Security Act
PSE	Party of European Socialists
PT	Process Tracing

RC	Rational Choice
RQ	Research Question
SEA	Single European Act
SoS	Security of Supply
TEN-E	Trans-European Networks for Energy
TEU	Treaty on the European Union
TFEU	Treaty on the Functioning of the European Union
TPA	Third-Party Access
TSO	Transmission System Operator
UEN	Union for Europe of the Nations
UK	United Kingdom
Verts/ALE	The Greens/European Free Alliance
WP	Working Party (Council)

1. Introduction: European solidarity – a chameleonic term

Solidarity has evolved as a vibrant notion during the last two decades in European Union politics as it has been invoked in different crisis situations: Solidarity was a controversial issue during the Euro crisis when trust between Member States eroded. Solidarity triggered redistributive measures as shown by the European Solidarity Fund, which was introduced in response to natural emergencies in 2002. In the face of the coronavirus pandemic, solidarity is currently the order of the day.

> „However, there is a yawning gap between the rhetorical commitment to solidarity and member states' practices of solidarity: Even though the EU and its members regularly refer to solidarity as one of their fundamental values, the concept regularly fails to translate into concrete and common action" (Grimmel 2020).

The refugee crisis of 2015 is one example where solidarity between Member States was weakened. The gas crises of 2006 and 2009 also testify the unwillingness of Member States to act in solidarity (Andoura 2013: 34). Juncker emphasised the lack of solidarity in 2017, when he declared that „(l)e grand absent européen, c'est la solidarité" (Juncker 2017). Over time, solidarity was called on for different purposes and objectives in various political fields: Solidarity unites, solidarity stabilises and solidarity reconciles.

Box 1: The Solidarity Discourse

„Europe will not be made all at once, or according to a single plan. It will be built through concrete achievements which first create a de facto solidarity" (Robert Schuman 1950 on the integration of Europe).

„Le modèle économique européen doit se fonder sur trois principes: la concurrence qui stimule, la coopération qui renforce et la solidarité qui unit" (Jacques Delors 1995 on the principles of the Single European Act).

„There is no stability without solidarity and no solidarity without stability" (Jose Manuel Barosso 2010 on the financial crisis in Greece).

„Noch nie waren Zusammenhalt und Solidarität so wichtig wie heute" (Angela Merkel 2020, government declaration on EU Council Presidency referring to coronavirus pandemic).

But „(s)olidarity is sometimes used as *a nebulous concept* that is not defined at all. Its use may be a subterfuge in political rhetoric to hide the fact that the phenomenon of solidarity is missing or on the decline in the real world" (Stjernø 2005: 2, emphasis added).

Solidarity is an integral part of the story of the European Union. Schuman's declaration shows that he believed in the coming of existence of solidarity among Member States. However, the implementation of solidarity in different policy fields is neither precise nor self-evident although Commission President Juncker referred to solidarity also as „the glue that keeps our Union together" (Juncker 2016) in the State of the Union speech in 2016. Juncker listed policy fields where solidarity has been successfully implemented (emergency aid), and that some policy fields (e.g. Euro, the budget) are an expression of solidarity, and that solidarity is lacking in other policy fields (e.g. the so-called refugee crisis). Juncker also believes that „(…) solidarity must be given voluntarily. It must come from the heart. It cannot be forced" (Juncker 2016).

The EU spends up to a maximum annual total of € 500 million with help of the EU Solidarity Fund, which supports Member States in case of natural disasters as expression of solidarity (Commission n.d.). Cohesion and solidarity are both mentioned in Art. 3 of the Treaty on the Functioning of the European Union (TFEU). Cohesion policy aims at decreasing regional disparities between EU Member States and is as such reflecting financial solidarity (Bachtler and Mendez 2020: 121). Since 2015, € 2.6 billion were distributed to third countries as emergency funding to address large-scale humanitarian needs in order to demonstrate solidarity in action (Commission 2019c).

Providing Member States or third states with assistance in times of need is one interpretation of solidarity. Alternatively, the European Court of Justice declared already in 1973 that solidarity is to be interpreted as obligation to follow the common rules of the community. Neglecting the common rules would result in a disturbance of the balance of duties and responsibilities (CJEU 1973), which underlines the federal character of solidarity (Arban 2017).

These different political and legal interpretations and expectations of solidarity stress the complexity of talking about solidarity without clarifying its meaning. Solidarity is flexible in its application, which is why it is so difficult to grasp as political concept. Solidarity is present in the political discourse, in particular in times of crisis. At the same time, it is a legal obligation, which penetrated EU primary law. Solidarity is a core concept in the history of European integration, and it is invoked in the central documents of the European Union (Immerfall 2016: 49). Even though the term is fluid in its meaning, European discourse on solidarity underlines the high relevance of this value for the EU. Solidarity is the most mentioned value in the European Council Conclusions[1], which were published between 2004 and 2019, covering 71 % of those Conclusions.

> „The Union is founded on the values of respect for human dignity, freedom, democracy, equality, the rule of law and respect for human rights, including the rights of persons belonging to minorities. These values are common to the Member States in a society in which pluralism, non-discrimination, tolerance, justice, solidarity and equality between women and men prevail" (Art. 2 TEU).

The listed values are all values or describing qualities of the European society, which are mentioned in Art. 2 TEU:

Figure 1: Values in European Council Conclusions 2004–2019

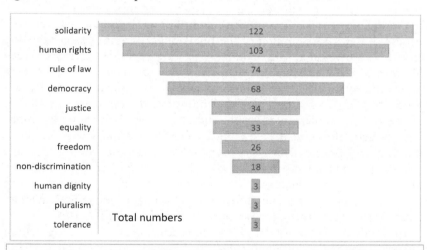

Own compilation; based on 69 European Council conclusions between 2004 - 2019

---

1   Multiple entries were counted once per paragraph. Freedom and justice were not counted when they were mentioned under the 'area of freedom, security and justice'. Solidarity was mentioned in 49 out of 69 documents. The documents don't include all extraordinary summits, such as the summits on Art. 50.

Although solidarity seems to be of great significance for the European project, the concept remains under-theorised. „Solidarity is a commonly used expression in the European discourse and yet it remains a somewhat neglected concept in the literature on European integration" (Ferreira-Pereira and Groom 2010: 596). This statement exemplifies the difficulty to fully grasp the notion of solidarity. Solidarity is multicoloured, obviously a chameleonic term, which implies various characteristics and provokes mixed feelings when it is invoked. This observation led me to the question how to grasp the meaning of solidarity. Which characteristics determine that an act can be understood as solidarity action? And how can we be sure that an action, which is purportedly an act of solidarity, can be evaluated as solidarity action? In the end „it can be all too easy to agree that there is a need for solidarity while remaining vague about what kind of solidarity one is referring to" (Thielemann 2018: 79).

This book examines the concept of solidarity between Member States and its application in secondary law and therefore sheds light on the concept of solidarity within the political, legal and institutional framework of the EU. Only a clarification of solidarity in the legislative acts can contribute to our understanding of the final application of *de facto* solidarity by the Member States. The book presents a concept of solidarity between Member States, which enables the measurement of the presence or absence of ‚institutionalised solidarity' in secondary law (as opposed to ‚declarative solidarity') and, in a second part, to demonstrate the influence of spill-over effects on the implementation of solidarity in legislative acts. By applying my definition and the developed conceptualisation I will capture if the measures promised by secondary law can be understood as genuine solidarity (institutionalised solidarity) or if they are only cosmetic improvements (declarative solidarity). The concept of solidarity is applied in five case studies, presenting four different legal acts and one complementary recent legal case on the determination of solidarity as legal norm.

The study finds that solidarity is scarcely institutionalised in the field of European gas policy although solidarity has increasingly become part of the discussion and a catchword of the Energy Union. Nevertheless, two forms of solidarity can be observed. First, solidarity serves as an insurance mechanism between Member States. Second, solidarity is a behavioural norm that prescribes certain behaviour between the Member States. Both forms of solidarity imply that *group members are expected to make a sacrifice in order to serve the interest of the group*. Solidarity unfolds certain pressure as a norm; however, the exclusion of free riders and the acceptance of responsibility are decisive for the institutionalisation of solidarity.

The research is carried out through the lens of neofunctionalism (Haas 1958; Niemann 2006) in order to shed more light on the causal mechanisms, which lead to the varying outcomes of solidarity. Reflections from federal theory are also taken into account, but without teleological determinism (Burgess 2006; Arban 2017). This book offers an explorative study whether any particular reasons led to the introduction of solidarity in secondary law. The research contributes to our understanding of the role supranational actors played in formulating solidarity in legislative acts and the extent to which functional pressures asserted influence. Additionally, the concept of solidarity is further refined through empirical analysis. The first chapter of the book provides an overview of the research project and introduces further reflections on solidarity. Based on a literature review, the introductory part covers trends in research on solidarity and demonstrates how this thesis contributes to tackle the research lacuna on Member State solidarity. The chapter closes with a comprehensive outlook on the scope and purpose of the study.

1.1. Research interest

The quote of Schumann of 1950 emphasises the expectation, that the institutionalisation of solidarity is not only of national societal concern, but that de facto solidarity can emerge on the European level. This is both intriguing and puzzling, since solidarity usually refers to a group of individuals at the national level – the nation state is since the beginning of the 19th century the spatial reference point for solidarity (Beckert et al. 2004) – or it points to a cosmopolitan understanding but not to a group of states as solidarity group (with the exception of international law, compare Hilpold 2007). Solidarity has acquired additional political significance since it has increasingly appeared in the EU Treaties. The Treaty of Lisbon mentions solidarity 22 times (including the Charter of Fundamental Rights) referring to solidarity between people, between generations, between Member States and between Member States and the EU. Additionally, solidarity between Member States is mentioned regarding different policy fields, such as migration, energy, foreign policy and emergencies including terrorism and natural disasters. The discourse on European solidarity also indicates that solidarity played a particular role concerning the Euro crisis and the refugee crisis in the last ten years (Schmale 2017; Wallaschek 2019). As solidarity was heralded as a necessary behaviour in response to the various crises the EU faced, the relevance of solidarity between Member States as research object grew. This development puts the state as research unit at the centre of interest (among others Knodt and Tews 2016; Hilpold 2015; Bast 2014; Grimmel and Giang 2017).

The focus of the book is on solidarity between Member States, as my research concentrates on policies that implement solidarity or are an expression of solidarity between Member States. I will only deal with other solidarity relations in passing as they are of minor relevance for my research endeavour: solidarity between generations touches on questions of social contract or the long-term effects of climate change. Solidarity between people focuses on the question how people perceive the quality of solidarity with others and the limits to it.

International relations research works primarily on issues of cooperation, reciprocity or burden sharing (Keohane 1986), while in social sciences solidarity serves usually as research object regarding social movements and the cohesion of society (Kapeller and Wolkenstein 2013; Stjernø 2005; Engler 2016). Nevertheless, it cannot be denied that solidarity has become an important concept in legal studies and political science – also with regard to studies on the EU (Knodt and Tews 2016; Grimmel and Giang 2017; Biondi et al. 2018). First, authors cover the normative dimension of the term discussing what the EU should do, what kind of value solidarity is, and in how far solidarity is a global (legal) norm (Karagiannis 2007; Ferreira-Pereira and Groom 2010; Konstadinides 2013; Sangiovanni 2013 and 2015; Thielemann 2018). Second, authors look into the effects of the euro crisis on solidarity relations, social cohesion, transnational solidarity, public discourse and voters' support to solidarity (Baute et al. 2019; Rebhahn 2015; Federico and Lahusen 2018; Viehoff and Nicolaidis 2015; Closa and Maatsch 2014; Kleider and Stoeckel 2019; Wallaschek 2019; Loh 2016). This dimension concerns particularly the relation between transfer payments and the acceptance of those payments by citizens. The individual citizen or politician (compare Closa and Maatsch 2014) is in the focus of the analysis. And third, research is concentrating on how solidarity influences the implementation and design of institutions in order to resolve collective action problems (Kapeller and Wolkenstein 2013; Kleger and Mehlhausen 2013; Mau 2008; Stjernø 2005). The authors analyse at which level solidarity is implemented, which actors are involved and what kind of philosophical understanding informs the solidarity action.

Additionally, the literature reveals that there are three perspectives to look at solidarity relations: Bottom-up describes how the solidarity community creates and legitimises solidarity between Member States (Keating 2009; Federico and Lahusen 2018; Gerhards et al. 2020). Top-down illuminates how solidarity (crises) at the Member State level influences the society and/or the solidarity between European societies (Siebold 2017; Börner 2014; de Witte 2012). The last perspective concerns solidarity between Member States identifying legal and political aspects of solidarity at EU level only (Hilpold 2007; Calliess 2011; Nettesheim 2018 and 2020; Küçük 2016; Boutayeb and Laurent 2011; Härtel 2014; Knodt and Tews 2016; Fernandes and Rubio 2012; Steinvorth 2017; Saracino 2019; Trein 2020; Grimmel 2020). However, this last perspective is strongly dominated by legal scholars. „(…) (T)here are only isolated contributions analyzing conflicts over solidarity between Member States" (Holesch 2021). Despite all these research endeavours there is no clear-cut concept of solidarity between Member States. There is hardly any literature in EU studies, which is breaking up the term, in order to clarify what it means for a structure beyond the nation state. Saracino (2019) worked on the development of the concept of solidarity in the field of asylum policy, but the concept lacks clarity since the features of solidarity remain abstract. Additionally, the process of conceptualisation does not reveal any particular reflections about intergovernmental solidarity. Also, Grimmel (2020) provides an analysis of the features of solidarity which include voluntariness, selflessness and identification. He concludes that solidarity is only a rhetorical phenomenon. This result is no surprise looking at the chosen features, which correspond to spontaneous solidarity only. Knodt and Tews (2016) uncover the different solidarity relations within the EU based on the actors involved. Even though this approach is helpful, the authors hardly elucidate the consequences. In general, few authors illuminate why solidarity was actually under discussion and how it is exactly implemented.

Although the body of literature comprises many different facets of solidarity, theoretical reflections remain limited. „„Solidarity' seems to have been confined to the realm of rhetoric while serious theoretical work has concentrated on other aspects of political association such as democracy, nationalism, community, multiculturalism and human rights" (Wilde 2007: 171). Solidarity has been mostly discussed within the framework of the nation state or as moral obligation as regards the international community (Lahusen and Grasso 2018: 4), where solidarity is often interpreted as a „(…) political act of resistance" (Scholz 2008: 53). But the European Union does not correspond to these two types. Another problem is that solidarity is used differently in each policy field or even from case to case, which is why „(…) the multi-dimensional character of this concept may result in the fragmentation and inconsistent application of 'solidarity' (…)

" (Bauder and Juffs 2019: 2). This is, however, also true for other concepts, such as democracy, justice or equality.

The concept of ‚solidarity between Member States' lacks a general agreement on its attributes. The basic question, therefore, is, how can we detect solidarity between Member States? Since the subject of interest – solidarity – is not only fluid in its meaning but also in its scope of application, this book offers a concept of ‚solidarity between Member States' in order to make solidarity measurable as well as comparable at the European Union level and to detach it from the national level.

Even though solidarity is part of the treaties there is no definition of its meaning:

> „Since its codification in the Treaties, however, the concept of solidarity has raised an interpretative conflict, inherent in the very nature of value, which places itself between the legal obligation and the moral obligation. In this regard, the Treaties do not help to identify their legal nature, since the notion of solidarity is not defined at any point in the Treaties" (Circolo et al. 2018: 171).

Solidarity can only be further interpreted by the European Court of Justice (CJEU), if it is written down in secondary law. Therefore, the political implementation is of huge relevance for its legal interpretation. Solidarity is present in different forms in secondary law (solidarity funds, solidarity mechanism, spirit of solidarity, principle of solidarity), which leaves much room for speculation concerning its meaning, purpose and consequences. The term under scrutiny is used both in the treaties as well as rhetorically to make demands on the way how European Member States should work together. Actors use solidarity usually in the discourse to make normative demands. Solidarity is either applied as means of pressure to claim help or solidarity is refused out of fear that certain actions could overstretch solidarity (Calliess 2011: 65; Rittberger et al. 2017: 920). Solidarity is in many minds closely linked to empathy, altruism or charity. For this reason, the study offers an analysis of how solidarity is used by the different institutions and how they conceptualise the term. This research process also clarifies the question which different expectations can be generated by solidarity and which obligations result from it therefore taking into account its normative dimension.

Solidarity is often used without any further definition or conceptualisation, which can have a significant impact on research (Talus 2013; Hayward and Wurzel 2012). The results are vague and can be only used to a limited degree for generalisation. Due to moral expectations, which are shared but not questioned by many researchers, research results conclude that solidarity between Member States has not been realised or only to a very limited extent (Beutler 2017: 21; Grimmel 2020). Kneuer even observes a solidarity crisis (2017: 20). Moreover, the papers raise high expectations on the output of solidarity even in policy fields that are hardly integrated at the EU level and although competing solidarity relations exist. This has been demonstrated during the coronavirus pandemic, when EU Member States were not willing to share materials for health care in the beginning of the crisis, which was criticised as a *lack of solidarity* (Ondarza et al. 2020). Therefore, the developed concept of solidarity contributes to this discussion between high hopes and false expectations. This is significant for both academia as for politics.

1.2. Research question

These observations and trends in academic research demonstrate the importance of a concept of solidarity between Member States. The concept should not only outline the features of solidarity, but also be able to measure whether solidarity is actually present. The concept of solidarity is only effective if solidarity is implemented in secondary law, otherwise it would only be part of political rhetoric. Additionally, the reasons for the implementation of solidarity in secondary law are unclear. Why would it be necessary to implement solidarity in secondary law? The following questions build thus the centre of my research interest:

Box 2: *Research Questions*
RQ1: How to conceptualise solidarity between European Member States?
RQ2: Why and how was solidarity implemented in secondary law?

The first research question concentrates on the conceptualisation of solidarity, which I consider as a necessary endeavour due to the lack of a thorough conceptualisation of solidarity between Member States. Therefore, I chose to focus on the actual characteristics of solidarity in my conceptualisation process. This process aims to make the concept measurable. Solidarity plays a major role in discursive studies on EU migration and refugee policies, however, the implementation of solidarity in secondary law is hardly part of the analyses (compare e.g. Wallaschek 2019). This is striking, since the shear statement of solidarity is no proof of its applicability. This book focuses therefore on the question why solidarity is institutionalised and how the institutionalisation of solidarity is designed.

In the conceptualisation process, I encapsulate both normative-based and rational choice-based arguments (compare Habermas 2014 and Tranow 2012). Even though the characteristics of solidarity might not be measurable on a numerical scale, they can be observed with help of qualitative criteria. The final concept is following a *wide version of rational choice theory* (RCT), which takes into account the role of norms, but considers in particular the argument that the avoidance of free riding is essential for the institutionalisation of solidarity. The chosen features are (1) ‚group cohesion', (2) ‚reciprocity and rules for implementation' and (3) ‚monitoring and self-responsibility'. If the examined so-called solidarity action/policy does not show all identified features, I call it ‚declarative solidarity'. Solidarity, which fulfils the characteristics, is called ‚institutionalised solidarity'. Since solidarity serves apparently different purposes being either ‚declarative' or ‚institutionalised', I cast my net to identify secondary legislation, which stipulated solidarity. Secondary law includes solidarity in different policy areas, such as migration, budget, energy and regional policy. For the analysis, I chose four legal acts and one Court case concerning gas policy, which represent my case studies. The reasons for this choice are detailed in chapter 2.3, but in the following I briefly discuss why energy solidarity is a promising research topic.

Energy policy has been one of the policy fields where solidarity is up and trending. Energy policy has been – just as solidarity – a cornerstone of the development of the European Union. However, it lagged usually behind other policy fields since energy policy is highly relevant for security questions and as such of particular national interest. Additionally, energy policy lacked a specific Treaty provision until 2009. Until the Treaty of Lisbon came into force, energy policy legislation was usually based on harmonisation measures.

Treaty Art. 194 TFEU implemented shared competences in energy policy, but Member States emphasised that decisions on the national energy mix (i.e. the choice of energy sources) remained exclusively a national competence. The Treaty of Lisbon contains two references to energy solidarity. The first reference can be found in Art. 122, where solidarity concerns supply difficulties „notably in the area of energy" (Art. 122 TFEU). The second solidarity reference concerns Art. 194 TFEU, where solidarity characterises the general development of European energy policy. Solidarity thus obviously fulfils two tasks, relating to the implementation of energy policy in general and as a specific response to emergencies.

Moreover, an analysis of the European Council conclusions between 2004 and 2019 demonstrated that solidarity in relation to energy was mentioned second most often after solidarity in relation to migration. This observation underlines that energy solidarity is a relevant issue for the heads of states and governments.

Figure 2: References to solidarity in European Council conclusions

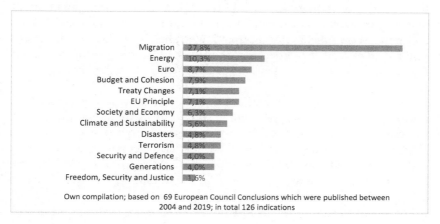

Migration 27,8%
Energy 10,3%
Euro 8,7%
Budget and Cohesion 7,9%
Treaty Changes 7,1%
EU Principle 7,1%
Society and Economy 6,3%
Climate and Sustainability 5,6%
Disasters 4,8%
Terrorism 4,8%
Security and Defence 4,0%
Generations 4,0%
Freedom, Security and Justice 1,6%

Own compilation; based on 69 European Council Conclusions which were published between 2004 and 2019; in total 126 indications

The market integration of the gas and electricity sectors progressed only slowly, although the process started in the late 1990s. The security aspect played only a marginal role in the beginning. Security issues mainly concerned the electricity sector, which had to go through some changes in the integration process. The stability of the electricity grid was an important security issue, which was of technical and internal importance at the same time. The security dimension changed with the accession of the Eastern Member States to the EU, the gas crises caused by the Russian-Ukrainian gas conflict and the changing internal gas supply structures by the UK. Solidarity became a key word in order to resolve all kinds of security concerns in the gas sector and to respond to the consequences of market failures. The notion of solidarity was featured as a cornerstone of energy policy in key strategic policy papers. The Energy Security Strategy (COM(2014) 330 final), a hallmark of the EU, is based on eight pillars, which are all underpinned by solidarity and also the Energy Union's (2015) first dimension is entitled „security, solidarity and trust – diversifying Europe's sources of energy and ensuring energy security through solidarity and co-operation between EU countries" (Commission 2017d). The integration of the gas market made the EU as a whole vulnerable. So why was solidarity proposed as a solution in a policy field where usually national interests prevail?

A closer look at secondary law reveals that solidarity was differently used over time. It played no prominent role in legislation until the gas crisis of 2009. Solidarity as a principle was avoided by the Member States: „The visible nationalization of energy policies, and the consistent overlooking of the principle of solidarity (…), lead to internal cracks in the union and a tendency to overlook neighbors' interests and the impact of our decisions and policies on others" (Szulecki and Westphal 2014: 45). Solidarity was inserted in several legislative acts as of 2009. The security of gas supply regulation (1938/2017), which was published in 2017, makes even 104 references to solidarity.

The Eastern enlargement and Polish influence have clearly changed the European energy landscape. There is consensus in the literature that the gas crises of 2006 and 2009 led to increased energy policy integration (Maltby 2013). However, although the gas crises could be a cause, they do not explain why solidarity started to play a more prominent role. Therefore, my research interest culminated in the question „why was solidarity implemented in secondary energy law"?

Following the logics of neofunctionalism, the implementation of solidarity depends on the successful entrepreneurship of supranational institutions and/or on functional pressures, which could force the Member States to move towards solidarity as policy outcome in secondary law. This book concentrates on the questions why solidarity was introduced and how solidarity is implemented. This procedure uncovers not only a detailed understanding of solidarity as policy outcome but reveals also how the institutions designed solidarity over time.

1.3. Research design

The book is divided into two parts. The first part concentrates on the conceptualisation of solidarity. The conceptualisation process is influenced by different authors, such as Sartori (1984), Gerring (1999) and Goertz (2006) who provide the researcher with different instructions how to make a ,good concept' (Gerring 1999). Based on the instructions, I have developed a thorough conceptualisation process that takes into account the specific aspects of solidarity. The overall process takes the form of a rigid literature review starting with the historical roots of solidarity. The process culminates in a definition and a clear-cut concept. Main aspects of the process include an analysis of the semantic history of solidarity, a discussion and clarification of the sources of solidarity and in how far those are applicable to the EU level, a reconstruction of the concept and the final presentation of the definition as well as the outline of the specific features that form the concept.

Secondly, in order to capture my dependent variable (= implementation of solidarity) I use a process tracing research design. This research framework is particularly useful since I assume that there is a variance of the dependent variable (institutionalised and declarative solidarity). The population of cases consists of all legal acts which include solidarity. Since I aim to clarify the influence of the independent variables of interest, it is the most promising way to use rather similar cases at this point (Gerring 2006). This is why I chose a set of cases from the same policy field (energy), which all have been implemented or last revised under the ,ordinary legislative procedure' after the Treaty of Lisbon came into force. At the same time the selected cases are least likely since the policy field under discussion (gas policy) is highly securitised and as such the explanations provided by neofunctionalism are contested. To recall, my concept of solidarity is newly formed and might need further clarification. This is why the research process is also exploratory and I take into consideration the practical understanding of solidarity of the different institutions.

Getting to know the cases in detail and thus unveiling the causal mechanisms is crucial for process tracing. A rigid data collection process and dense content analysis is therefore expedient to come closer to the research aim. The main documents of analysis were the legislative acts applying the concept and all kind of preparatory documents published by the EU institutions to outline the causal mechanisms at work. This analytical process has been accompanied by semi-structured expert interviews.

1.4. Outline of the book

The most challenging aspect is that there is no clarity about the components of solidarity between EU Member States (Chapter 2). While Baurmann (1999) elaborates that solidarity can only be based on a voluntary will to contribute to a public good (people act out of fairness), Hechter (1988, 1990) stipulates the necessity to monitor and control group members in order to guarantee solidarity and to avoid free riders. The two concepts show that there are different theoretical approaches to solidarity.

In order to develop my concept, I first delve into the semantic history and ideational meaning of solidarity. Since I am not developing a completely new concept but changing the level of analysis, I reconceptualise solidarity by analysing the prevailing definitions from different disciplines. From these definitions I derive the attributes for my conceptualisation. To clarify the concept, I distinguish the term from synonyms (e.g. loyalty) and define its opposite pole (subsidiarity). The conceptualisation process culminates in a definition and concept of solidarity between Member States based on a wide version of rational choice theory. The concept corresponds to 'institutionalised solidarity'. If the features are not sufficiently present I call the outcome „declarative solidarity". My outcome (=dependent variable) refers as such not to an overall implementation of solidarity in energy policy, but to single legislations.

My research provides not only a tool to make solidarity empirically observable but examines also in how far spill over effects affect the implementation of solidarity. This sub-chapter on the conceptualisation, being part of the research framework, is complemented by the theoretical assumptions based on neofunctionalism as well as the methodological part. Neofunctionalism has been revised by Niemann in 2006 and provides us with specific assumptions about EU integration processes. Central aspects for my research are functional spill-over effects as well as the importance of supranational institutions in the integration process. The second chapter concludes with the methodological framework explaining in detail the case selection and the application of process-tracing. Additionally, I present how I collected and analysed my data with help of document analysis, qualitative content analysis and expert interviews.

Chapter 3 starts with an exploration of EU law concerning solidarity and energy solidarity in particular, which is followed by a brief retrospective of the development of European energy policy with a specific focus on solidarity in gas policy and a short explication of the gas crises and its consequences for the functioning of the internal gas market. An important development over the last 25 years was the implementation of the internal gas market. A market, where all Member States are interconnected and where national decisions have consequences for all other EU market participants, would consequently lead to interdependence in questions of security of supply and choice of energy sources. As already mentioned, the gas crises seem to be a part of the answer, but do not explain why and how solidarity was implemented.

The interests of the Member States played certainly a role for the overall development of the policy field, which is sufficiently presented in the literature (Fischer 2017a; Benson and Russel 2015; Haghighi 2008; Kanellakis et al. 2013). Starting with the European Council at Hampton Court in 2005, the European Council instructed the Commission to present further steps for the development of an ‚Energy Policy for Europe‘. The gas crises and the push by the Eastern Member States towards more integration (e.g. the proposal of the energy NATO) drove the process of further integration of energy policy (Maltby 2013: 436). To complete the picture, however, three more actors need to be mentioned. First, the European Commission inserted solidarity in its policy papers and legislative proposals and emphasised the importance of solidarity in the internal energy market. Second, I delve into the discussions within the European Parliament regarding solidarity. In general, the Parliament started to embrace solidarity as of the moment when Eastern MEPs entered the stage. Third, I take a closer look at the attitude of the CJEU, and how it influenced the build-up of solidarity as a legal principle. The aim of the study is to analyse whether and to what extent these institutions have played a particular role in shaping solidarity.

In chapter 4, I present the relevant cases and group the cases according to the variance of the dependent variable. I apply my concept of solidarity to the chosen cases with help of content analysis and analyse the different cases employing process tracing. Furthermore, I assess the ruling of the General Court concerning the OPAL pipeline. The CJEU interpreted solidarity as a legal obligation, which is why the case reveals how solidarity between Member States is legally interpreted. Overall, it is puzzling that the principle of solidarity emerged so extensively (at least on paper) although Member States did originally not intend to fully endorse the principle. Solidarity was interpreted as an attempt of window-dressing when it was introduced (Fischer 2017a: 137). I analyse – relying on neofunctional arguments – if and in how far the supranational actors succeeded in the implementation of solidarity using strategically their capacity as policy entrepreneurs. Additionally, I shed light on the question if the perception of policy makers to agree on solidarity mechanisms changed due to the gas crises as well as the Russian-Ukraine conflict.

The final chapter (Chapter 5) summarises the research results with two foci. First, I reflect on the usefulness and challenges of my concept, identify shortcomings and corrections and propose prospective research areas. Second, I outline the results concerning the role and influence of spill-over effects and evaluate the causal mechanisms. The dissertation is topped off with an outlook on research opportunities for my concept of solidarity within and beyond the field of energy policy.

2. Research framework

2.1. Concept formation

A clear concept is necessary in order to conduct valuable research. „Die Bildung von Konzepten ist deshalb so wichtig, weil sie der Einordnung von Fällen, ihrer Messung und Bewertung vorgelagert ist" (Eising 2006: 388). Concepts are necessary elements of research because they help to create logical structures and to evaluate the object of interest. Additionally, concepts give researchers the opportunity to understand better the reality, which is why it is necessary to critically assess and – if necessary – reformulate concepts. On the one hand, academic and day-to-day language can differ widely in the definition of a term and, on the other hand, new concepts can occur and enter the academic debate (Hartleb 2011: 109).

This thesis conceptualises solidarity between Member States, in order to make solidarity empirically observable. Sartori underlines the importance of concept formation. „We cannot measure unless we know first what it is that we are measuring" (Sartori 1970: 1038). Sartori's approach to concept formation has influenced my conceptualisation of solidarity, however, I am not strictly following his recipe but interlock different methods of concept formation. Sartori supports the idea to concentrate on specific observations. It would be misleading to expect a concept which could cover any forms of solidarity (Sartori 1970: 1035). The main focus of this study is on solidarity between Member States, which is why my concept aims to be applicable to any form of solidarity between Member States.

Although there are a number of ways to generate a concept, Gerring presents a common understanding on three aspects of concept formation:

> „‚Concept formation' conventionally refers to three aspects of a concept: (a) the events or phenomena to be defined (the extension, denotation or definiendum), (b) the properties or attributes that define them (the intension, connotation, definiens, or definition), and (c) a label covering both a and b (the term). Concept formation is thus a triangular operation; good concepts attain a proper alignment between a, b, and c" (Gerring 1999: 357).

Point (c) refers to the fact that if points (a) and (b) change, it is also necessary to change the term which describes the other two aspects. The concept must thus be aligned with the research object. A number of different strategies exist how to create or evolve a good scientific concept, which have been developed by Giovanni Sartori (1970), Gary Goertz (2006), Collier and Levitsky (1997) and John Gerring (1999). However, these authors do not agree on how to do it right. Sartori is criticised since he spends a large part of his conceptualisation by explaining the semantic background of état (state, government). Goertz elucidates that a semantic analysis is too far away from real world phenomena, which is why definitions become arbitrary (Goertz 2006: 4).

Aware of the critique, I follow partly Sartori's approach, because looking back at the ideational history of a term provides the researcher with insights about its roots, its meaning over time and unveils the influences on the development of the term. „Whatever we know is mediated by a language, if not by the language in which we know it" (Sartori 2009: 97). Gerring also underlines the importance of language for the understanding of a term (1999: 359). However, „ordinary usage may be an appropriate place to begin, it is not usually an appropriate place to end the task of concept formation" (Gerring 1999: 362). Gerring points out that it is of importance to make the process of conceptualisation transparent. In the end, it depends on the research goal, how a concept is established (Gerring 1999: 367). Sartori formulated in his oeuvre on social science concepts that his method is open for change. Rules can be adapted or dismissed, but he points out that it is necessary to have a method (Sartori 1984: 57). Sartori's rigidity of concept formation might limit possible comparisons. But according to Mair, the concept has to be changed in order to make more comparisons possible. If the aim of the research is for instance to compare a democracy and a non-democracy, it is a comparison between regimes and not between democracies (Mair 2014: 77f.).

Gerring offers eight criteria for conceptual goodness but he argues, that concept formation consists of trade-offs and that there is no best solution (Gerring 1999: 367). I am considering four criteria of Gerring as particularly helpful, which are familiarity, parsimony, differentiation and internal coherence (Gerring 1999: 368). I also take into account Sartori's instructions on the reconstruction of concepts. Sartori stipulates that „concept reconstruction is a means whose ultimate purpose is to provide a cleaned-up basis for construction – that is, for the formation of concepts" (Sartori 1984: 46).

1) Familiarity tells us if the characteristics of a concept are in line with our expectations. As example serves the conceptualisation of Kotowski, who identifies five common characteristics of revolution (Kotowski 2009:

208). He then compares the conceptual approaches of several authors regarding the identified characteristics. Kotowski demonstrates also „how disciplinary and theoretical contexts affect the characterization of the concept" (Kotowski 2009: 210). The procedure by Kotowski is helpful since he compares the definitions of the different authors in order to find a common core of the term and to create awareness for the differences. This is why it is important to look at the context of each concept.

2) Differentiation: I consider it as helpful to reflect upon the question which terms are used as synonyms and what might be the opposing term. Discovering synonyms clarifies further the core of the term under scrutiny and the differences between those terms. Gerring calls this point differentiation: „useful definitions define a term against related terms, telling us not only what a concept is, but also what it is not" (1999: 377). I connect this point with the assumption of Goertz that the reflection of the negative pole (the opposite) can further specify the features of the positive pole (Goertz 2006: 33).

3) Parsimony: A concept, which is overloaded by many attributes and an endless definition is hardly helpful. „A concept is an abbreviation, just as sequences of words (sentences, phrases, books) are abbreviations of things" (Gerring 1999: 372).

4) Internal coherence: The main characteristics of a concept should not be contradictory. „Attributes may be logically or functionally related" (Gerring 1999: 374).

The process of conceptualisation is not a sequential endeavour but a going back and forth on different aspects. My approach of conceptualisation looks as follows:

Box 3: Conceptualisation

A. Ideational development of the term:
  - Semantic history and ideational development
  - Sources of solidarity
B. Reconstruction of concept:
  - Familiarity: Analysis of definitions from lexicons and other authors
  - Differentiation: Clarification of synonyms and finding the opposite pole
  - Parsimony: Extraction from characteristics
  - Coherence: Attributes which describe the concept should not be conflictive

---

C. Definition of concept and explanation of features:
  - Presentation of definition
  - Determination of features

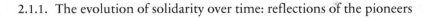

2.1.1. The evolution of solidarity over time: reflections of the pioneers

Solidarity between Member States is at the centre of my research as one particular phenomenon. Even if there might be definitions which are sufficiently abstract to cover this relation, it is necessary to reflect upon a specific concept which can capture this phenomenon more properly for the following reasons: 1) The process aims to reduce confusion with other forms of solidarity, such as transnational or international solidarity. 2) Definitions are no concepts. The features of solidarity between EU Member States are yet to be clarified.

In order to approach the concept of solidarity, I start by delving into the history of solidarity, which is part of the examination of the semantic term and the ideational history. This endeavour entails also examples of the disparate forms and understandings of solidarity intending to clarify how solidarity was interpreted differently depending on time and context.

The history of solidarity is complex, since the term had gone through different metamorphoses, which still inform our understanding of the term:

- The concept of solidarity goes back to Roman law, where it has been understood as legal obligation.
- After the French Revolution solidarity was used in concordance with fraternity (civic friendship) correlated with social struggle and a strong connotation of us versus them.
- Also, the church used the term, however, as 'obligation to help' as understood by charity and social justice.
- Another form of the concept can be found in relation to the class struggle of the working class. Solidarity is since then connected to welfare and interpreted as leftist social thought (Bayertz 1998: 11; Kim and Schattle 2012: 476f.).

The principle of solidarity originated in Roman language – *obligatio in solidum* – meaning that a group is responsible for the individual debt. Therefore, solidarity is originally a legal term, referring to obligations arising from joint liability. „So bindet schon die *obligatio in solidum* im Medium abstrakten Rechts *fremde* Personen, *komplementäre* Rollen, *heterogene* Interessen zusammen" (Brunkhorst 2002: 10; emphasis by author). In a very similar way this interpretation of solidarity was used in French law in the 16th century (Stjernø 2005: 26). And still today, the legal interpretation of solidarity plays an important role „(...) in most civil law systems today as obligations solitaires in the French Code Civil or as Solidarhaftung, Solidarschuld, Haftung zur gesamten Hand, Solidarobligation or Gesamtschuldnerschaft in German, Austrian and Swiss civil law" (Ottmann 2008: 38).

At the end of the 18th century, solidarity was extended beyond the financial obligations (Engler 2016: 28). The transition of solidarity as legal obligation to a social/political concept is located between 1750 and 1840. Next to the ideas of socialism and communism, solidarity found its way into common language due to social struggles (Wilde 2013: 20). Stjernø points out that the terms brotherhood and fraternity are the forerunner of solidarity. They manifest voluntary relations within groups or between individuals which exist outside of the family. Solidarity is a modern term coined by the French revolution and as such connected to the legal reference of equality but also the political dimension of democracy. However, during the French revolution it was fraternity which dominated the discourse. Solidarity superseded fraternity progressively after the French Revolution: the term spread continuously on to other societies and languages (Engler 2016: 28f.; Brunkhorst 2002: 9). Solidarity became a distinct term after the European revolution in 1848. At the end of the century, solidarity was also introduced to sociology and jurisprudence (Brunkhorst 2002: 9).

There is a general agreement in the literature that Pierre Leroux (1797–1871) was the first author who conceptualised solidarity systematically, although Charles Fourier (1772–1837) already referred to solidarity in his oeuvre *Theorie de l'Unité* (Stjernø 2005; Wilde 2013). But also the work of Auguste Comte (1798–1857) made solidarity „a standard linguistic term" (Metz 1999: 194). Leroux elaborated his concept of solidarity as critique of Christian charity, the social contract and the understanding of solidarity as organism. According to Leroux, these concepts were lacking equality, a genuine interest in community and justice (Stjernø 2005: 29). Leroux defined solidarity as a mutually supportive relationship sourced from the love to god (the source of charity would be the duty to god). „The goal of solidarity was universal social inclusion through peaceful means" (Wilde 2013: 21). Metz concludes from Leroux's conceptualisation that solidarity „is a right, a claim, and not mercy; and, as right, it forms the basis for a new form of socialization, which Leroux terms ‚socialistic'" (Metz 1999: 194). This is, however, contested by Wildt, who argues that Leroux is making only a remark to rights and that there are no political and social implications. Accordingly, Leroux talks about solidarity as an expression of love, harmony and identity between men (Wildt 1999: 212).

The term solidarity was constructed at the same time as modern societies. ‚National solidarity' evolved when the nation states in Europe were created (Wilde 2013: 43). This evolvement explains why solidarity became a political term in response to social struggle in a world based on human and not divine law (Engler 2016: 29). Karl Marx did not make any theoretical contributions to solidarity; however, the term was vitally important for his thoughts on class-struggle and on how to overcome class rule. Marx interpreted solidarity as basic principle which should unite all workers in order to reach their common goals (Wilde 2013: 31).

Solidarity continued to expand to other areas; at the end of the 19th century, it was no longer only a term referring to the working class, but it entailed also economic, political and judicial variations (Engler 2016: 29). One of the most influential authors on the concept of solidarity is Emile Durkheim (1858–1917), who developed a vision of liberal solidarity (Wilde 2013: 35). Durkheim dissolved solidarity from social struggle and developed the concept as solution for the individual, which found itself between ever more autonomy and ever-growing interdependence due to division of labour. Durkheim interpreted the unfair conditions, under which the working class had to suffer, as abnormalities. For this reason, the society would not have to change fundamentally, but the institutions would need to adapt in order „to regulate the economy and remove the injustices" (Wilde 2013: 39). Although Durkheim underlined that nationalism spurred particularly strong solidarity relations, he did not exclude the existence or development of solidarity beyond the borders. However, his thoughts remained vague on the universal conceptualisation of solidarity (Wilde 2013: 40f.). The philosophical approach to solidarity, which was developed by Durkheim, was partly „put into political practice in a series of social laws between 1892 and 1910. ‚Solidarity' had become the most important term within the political language (…)" (Metz 1999: 196). Social policies, such as medical care for the poor, were introduced in France at the end of the 19th century and cemented solidarity as a legal right and no longer just as an optional principle (Metz 1999: 197).

In the 20th century, the term solidarity was used by trade unions in Communist regimes. ‚Solidarność' (a Polish trade union) demanded both political changes (e.g. release of political prisoners) but also the implementation of social welfare (e.g. extended maternity leave) (Wilde 2013: 51). Durkheim's vision of evolved institutions, which would level out the abnormalities produced by the inequalities between the capital-owners and working class, came partly true with the insertion of the Welfare State, which is „(...) at least in its most egalitarian form (...) the embodiment of social solidarity" (Wilde 2013: 54). The rights and obligations of citizens were formed over time. Social rights were finally introduced as reaction to the demands of groups, who felt socially and politically excluded. One important lesson of the time was that liberty meant not only the right to do something but also the protection from something (ibid.).

The concrete configuration of these rights and liberties differs in each country. In contrast to the French vision of solidarity, the British focus was on deservingness. People were expected to practice self-help. If they were not fulfilling certain conditions, social laws would not protect them. This was reflected in the poor law of 1834 (Metz 1999: 197). The conditions for granting public aid included that the situation was not self-inflicted and that there was a willingness to improve the situation independently (ibid.).

The German welfare system developed under completely different circumstances. The introduction of different insurance mechanisms by Bismarck in the end of the 19th century was no expression of social solidarity but a political move by the government to detain the increasing support to the left. The particular German understanding of solidarity was influenced by Christian thoughts. The Church emphasised that social responsibility was a matter of conscience and as such a moral question. The source of this responsibility was the „common transcendental connection with god" (Metz 1999: 204). Consequently, the term was no longer in use by a confident working class, but changed its meaning to „an acknowledgment of the mutual dependency of human beings living within a society, extending from a factual to a moral relationship" (Metz 1999: 204). Due to this development, solidarity became consensual within the state.

Solidarity is a key term in social theory as it is important in both social democracy and Christian democracy. While the latter claims that solidarity is even more important than charity, the former puts solidarity as leading motive of class struggle, which led to the different formations of the welfare state (Stjernø 2005: 1). Discussions on solidarity within the modern welfare state concern „the limits of social and individual responsibility and the principles on which the society is based" (Wilde 2013: 58).

> „Als die spezifisch moderne Form der Solidarität gilt der Sozial- oder Wohlfahrtsstaat, der in dem Maße, wie er sich nun als zerbrechlich erweist, auch neuartige Erfahrungen des Angewiesenseins auf Andere nach sich zieht; vor allem da, wo die mit dem Sozialstaat einhergehenden Prozesse der Verrechtlichung institutionalisierter Solidarität

ältere, meist als ‚traditional' eingestufte Formen des Sichverlassenkönnens auf den Beistand Anderer verdrängt haben" (Liebsch 2007: 149).

Gelissen (2000) identifies affectionate and emotional motives, culturally based convictions and self-interest as main reasons for the support of institutionalised solidarity at the welfare state level (Gelissen 2000: 288). Others argue that solidarity emerged within states due to the institutions which were brought to life by social policy (Kuhn and Nicoli 2020: 12).

The globalised world led also to other forms of solidarity beyond the national state. Transnational solidarity has been called for by different grass root organisations, such as Greenpeace or Amnesty International. Solidarity can be extended to strangers; however, these different forms of solidarity might be conflictive with the original tight interpretation of solidarity. Therefore, new forms of solidarity can, on the one hand, be a helpful tool to integrate polities and, on the other hand, overstrain original forms of solidarity (Liebsch 2007: 160f.). These considerations underline the possibly exclusive character of solidarity.

Global solidarity is also an international political topic within the structures of the United Nations, which underlined solidarity as one of its main principles. Solidarity unites its members „to maintain international peace and security" (UN n.d.). Additionally,

> „(s)olidarity is identified in the Millennium Declaration as one of the fundamental values of international relations in the 21st Century, wherein those, who either suffer or benefit least deserve help from those who benefit most. Consequently, in the context of globalization and the challenge of growing inequality, strengthening of international solidarity is indispensable" (ibid.).

Nonetheless, solidarity structures not only societal relationships, it is also a principle of political order in federal states next to the principles of pluralism and subsidiarity. In this regard, solidarity is also an inherent principle of federal systems such as Austria, Belgium and Germany. Even though it is highly contested that the EU corresponds to a federal system, Burgess declares that the Union takes a hybrid form, which corresponds to „a new kind of federal-confederal union" (Burgess 2006: 239). For this reason, federal systems provide some insights into the interpretation of solidarity between its constituent units (compare also ch. 2.1.2 on the political allegiance source and the discussion on loyalty in ch. 2.1.3).

In general, federal solidarity underlines the importance that central and peripheral governments need to work together and support each other (Arban 2017: 249ff.). In contrast, horizontal solidarity, as solidarity relationship between co-equal governments, is going beyond the concept of federal solidarity: Horizontal solidarity implies the „(…) duty not to frustrate each other but rather to collaborate for the ultimate benefit of the federation" (Arban 2017: 259). Solidarity means not only that stronger constituent units are obliged to support weaker constituent units, but also that a balance between the plural units of the community must be ensured (Detterbeck 2011: 34).

> "The principle of federal solidarity thus creates certain positive duties of assistance, and in prohibitions against imposing certain negative externalities on other federal partners. Cooperative federalism is thus normatively justified by the need for each level of government to protect and promote the interests of a shared citizenry forming a common body politic" (Cyr 2014: 21).

The 'EU in crisis' discourse concentrates on the question of "how much solidarity members of the community owe to each other under which conditions" (Börzel and Risse 2018: 102). Solidarity has thus become a major term in the European discourse over time:

> „'European solidarity' is probably one of the most frequently used words in public discourse and media. Appeals to 'European solidarity' have multiplied as a consequence of financial crises, the refugee crisis and several other crises that have hit the Continent in recent times" (Schmale 2017: 855).

Horizontal solidarity relations exist in different federal systems. As practical example serves the distribution key (Königsteiner Schlüssel) in Germany, which informs the distribution of asylum seekers between the German Länder based on regional wealth (Bast 2014: 155). Another aspect concerns the redistribution of financial means (e.g. the Länderfinanzausgleich in Germany), which represents not only a visible expression of horizontal solidarity but illustrates also the possible problem of distribution and justice (Kneuer 2017: 19). The EU entails similar federal solidarity arrangements: Vertical solidarity between the EU and the Member States and horizontal solidarity between the EU Member States (ibid.). While the constituent units are important

> "to be closer to the citizen, to achieve better democratic participation, to respect collective identities and to better react to demands from markets and societies. A strong central level is needed to deal with externalities, provide collective goods, assure credible commitments and realize economies of scale" (Jachtenfuchs and Kasack 2017: 559).

This sub-chapter dealt with the question how solidarity developed seman-tically and ideationally over time. The term did undergo a number of transformations, however, without losing any former meaning. This obser-vation demonstrates the complexity of the term. The possible meanings of solidarity were inflated over time. One important transformation is the change from solidarity as a very limited and exclusive concept between individuals towards a morally motivated cosmopolitan form. Additionally, depending on the socio-cultural context there are various characteristics of solidarity of varying importance (e.g. deservingness) and ways of imple-menting solidarity. Last but not least, federal solidarity indicates an explic-it political order. This underlines my claim that a concept for solidarity between Member States is necessary, since Member States as constituent units of the EU need to cooperate. This chapter illustrated that there are wide discrepancies on what solidarity is based on. Therefore, I outline in the next sub-chapter the different sources of solidarity in order to reflect on the possible motivations of Member States to act in solidarity.

2.1.2. Sources of solidarity

Based on the ideational and semantic history of solidarity, I identified five main lines of theoretical assumptions as important drivers for solidarity, which are: 1) interdependence, 2) self-interest, 3) morality, 4) political allegiance and 5) identity.

The source of solidarity has a direct effect on the configuration of the group but might also have an effect on the strength and perseverance of solidarity. The source determines the composition of the group: either the group is exclusive, since group members share some specific common ground. „Man ist ‚solidarisch' mit Menschen, deren Geschichte, Überzeu-gungen oder Interessen man teilt (...)" (Bayertz 1998: 21). Or solidarity is a general value connecting all people: humanity results in global (cos-mopolitan) solidarity. Consequently, there might be differences in the strength of solidarity depending on the motivation for it. Related to this question is the level of solidarity under scrutiny: Solidarity can exist on the micro level (family), the meso level (civil society organisations) and macro level (national and transnational). This means also that different levels of solidarity co-exist, which can be competitive (Lahusen and Grasso 2018: 5f.). This sub-chapter provides an overview of the sources of solidarity by briefly outlining which sources exist and what they mean for the configu-ration of solidarity at both the individual and the European level.

1) Interdependence

The authors using this source only refer to the individual level, which does not mean that the assumptions could not be transferred to the EU level. The interdependence source describes a functional understanding of solidarity. Emile Durkheim proves to be one of the most influential thinkers on the development of solidarity (Durkheim 1964: The Division of Labour in Society). His ideas on solidarity are closely connected to the question what form of society developed in the modern world. The main driver for Durkheim's interest was the evolution of the individualised society. Solidarity was his key explanation for the cohesion of society. Also, Comte was referring to solidarity as something which holds the society together, however, it was Durkheim's work that was more explicit on the concept of solidarity. Durkheim wanted to analyse the reasons, which hold a society together, in a world, where people have more freedoms and at the same time more social responsibilities (Große Kracht 2017: 109).

No longer, small communities and families were the providers of security and stability for the family, but the system changed towards a more individual society. This change from community to society was – according to Durkheim – accompanied by an adaption of solidarity. *Mechanical solidarity*, which is a form of solidarity based on the resemblance of ideas and emotions, works only within small communities, where the individuals are close to each other. The community – even though it may still exist – provides no longer the only bond between humans. Due to economic specialisation and division of labour solidarity developed in larger structures such as the city and the nation (Allen and O'Boyle 2017: 48; Große Kracht 2017: 112). Organic solidarity reflects a community of interdependence and not a community of similarity. Division of labour leads to the development of solidarity since individuals conceive the group as community of faith. In a modern society social inequality exists (just as before natural inequality) because every individual has different chances of success. „Dialektisch vereint Solidarität Gegensätze, Widersprüche, Differenzen. Die ‚*noch zusammenhaltbare*‛ Verschiedenheit, Heterogenität und Fragmentierung ist das ‚Maß der Solidarität‛" (Brunkhorst 2002: 15, emphasis by author). Therefore, in order to guarantee a stable and safe society, it is necessary to equal out major differences within a society. The necessary regulations (market or state interventions) establish relations of solidarity (Miller 2017: 72). The individual is forced „(...) to act in view of ends which are not strictly his own, to make concessions, to consent to compromises, to take into account interests higher than his own (Durkheim, 1966/1893: 227) " (Van Oorschot and Komter 1998: 6). Rules (or law) are the objective crystallisation of solidarity. However, Durkheim's ideas about the content and effect of those rules are not sufficiently developed, also with regard to their effect of generating feelings of solidarity (Große Kracht 2017: 123).

Kleger and Mehlhausen (2013) base their concept of organic solidarity also on Durkheim's thought that solidarity is the cement of society. Since division of labour leads to specialisation, no individual is easily replaced which makes solidarity necessary due to the growing interdependence. Rational actors support distributive measures when they are needed to guarantee the functioning of the system. In the end, solidarity serves the self-interest. The authors claim that this kind of solidarity can be found as regards the negative integration of economy. The interdependence of the single market leads to organic solidarity (Kleger and Mehlhausen 2013: 59 f.).

The *division-of-labour/esteem* source, as formulated by Loh and Skupien (2016), is close to Durkheim's „organic solidarity". Due to division of labour every individual has to contribute to the general prosperousness. If an individual does not support this system, the other contributions remain useless. The authors point out that – in order to be complete – *recognition* must be added to this concept. True solidarity emerges only, if each one acknowledges that each individual generates additional value for the community, even though the contributions are not of the same value. Due to this value dimension, this source of solidarity is often interwoven with the democratic-legitimacy source since the society needs to agree on a fair distribution of labour, which cannot be guaranteed by market mechanisms alone (Loh and Skupien 2016: 586).

2) Self-Interest

The difference between Durkheim's functional understanding and an interest-driven motivation for solidarity lies in interdependence. While functional motivation posits that individuals have no choice if they want to secure their survival, interest-driven motivation does not comprise this component. Individuals build a solidarity group (which is a voluntary act) „(...) by exchanging goods or services or by co-operation to achieve a common goal" (Van Oorschot and Komter 1998: 19). The interest-driven approaches are based on a rational choice understanding. All authors, which are part of this analysis, share the assumption that a common goal is necessary, that solidarity can take the form of an insurance scheme, and that emotional relations or altruism do not play any role. Some authors stress the necessity to put into place rules as well as control and sanctioning mechanisms (Hechter 1988). For others, trust plays a certain role regarding the implementation of more solidarity (Haversath 2012). Depending on the author, trust and the function of rules as well as sanction and control mechanisms interrelate to a greater or lesser extent.

Individual level

Baurmann (1999) inquires how individual benefits and contributions are related to individual and collective interests. This approach suggests that the individual is better off by contributing actively to the public good since the benefits are higher with its contribution. Therefore, the driver of solidarity is rational utility maximisation. Additionally, the interests of the group and the individual are overlapping. According to Baurmann, this constellation succeeds only in small homogenous groups, because usually stronger members are mainly responsible for the provision of a public good (Baurmann 1999: 243f).

Hechter (1988) explains solidarity from a rational choice approach. Individuals are interested in forming a solidarity group, because they want to produce a joint good, which they could not produce on their own. Emotional relations or altruistic behaviour are not important for this concept.

> „Es wird davon ausgegangen, dass Eigeninteressen unter dem Einfluss spezifischer Kontrollmechanismen in kooperatives Verhalten, das einem gemeinsamen Zweck dient, transformiert werden. Im Zentrum stellt (er) also die interessegeleitete Vermeidung unsolidarischen Verhaltens" (Kraxberger 2010: 7).

Also, Van Oorschot and Komter support the argument that role obligations are necessary to put solidarity in place. Voluntary, non-binding commitments can be rather understood as loyalty. However, enforced solidarity needs to be legitimised in order to be maintained (Van Oorschot and Komter 1998: 19f.).

Hechter is criticised for his narrow rational choice approach since his explanations on solidarity equal opportunistic behaviour. According to Tranow, a rational utility maximiser, as understood by Hechter, is not able to enter into a solidarity norm (Tranow 2012: 142). Tranow claims that a wider understanding of the rational choice approach is more useful to conceptualise solidarity. The wider rational choice approach entails that individuals do not consider how to behave on individual issues in their best interest but follow a certain conduct. Engagement of a certain conduct (Verhaltensbindung) influences „das Verhalten anderer zum eigenen Vorteil" (Tranow 2012: 143). Individuals evaluate overall gains and burdens rather than single events, which is why they agree to follow a certain conduct.

Member State level

Andrea Sangiovanni's interpretation of solidarity unites functional and interest-based motivations. He depicts solidarity between Member States as result from integration. In the integration process, Member States face profits and losses which are unequally distributed. On the one hand, the EU generates different collective goods, such as the internal market, regional stability and a stable legal system from which all states benefit to a certain extent. On the other hand, these collective goods create new disturbances, such as regional imbalances, tax evasion or unequal flow of workers (Sangiovanni 2013: 223ff.). Sangiovanni is referring to the welfare state, but these advantages and burdens can be also adapted to other areas: the abolition of internal borders creates higher risks in security questions (e.g. health, migration); an internal market leads to a common risk of market failures (e.g. electricity; gas). Hence, Member State solidarity can be understood as insurance to offset the possible risks (Sangiovanni 2013: 230).

Mau argues that interdependence emerges because labour is divided among the different countries in order to organise it more efficiently or to produce goods in general. Therefore, solidarity is depending on the level of necessary cooperation to make a good available. An example on the EU-level would be that richer Member States are willing to contribute financially to poorer Member States because they fear the negative side-effects for themselves. The interest to help others is thus dependent on the self-interest and not on common values (Mau 2008).

Hilpold underlines that solidarity is completely different from altruistic behaviour, since it is based on interest. A group or community forms because the members try to reach a certain goal, such as risk insurance. Reciprocity is a necessary element of this relationship, why Hilpold underlines that solidarity is a „cold and calculating instrument" (Hilpold 2015: 262). Being in a community of solidarity promises rights but also demands obligations. Hilpold further argues that solidarity has not been built in the European Union as of once but only step by step in order to create confidence and to ascertain that Member States behave according to the rules (Hilpold 2015: 264).

Haversath follows the idea that it is only self-interest which determines a community of solidarity. A social bond might be working for a close and small-sized community, but not when community members do not know each other. However, Haversath postulates that trust is an important aspect of solidarity, since solidarity *cannot* be legally demanded. If a member does not follow its solidarity obligations, it has to leave the community (Haversath 2012). Also, Küçük claims, that the strongest driver for solidarity is self-interest. She bases this argument on the human nature, which is naturally pursuing self-interest, and on the idea of insurance schemes, which clarify that cooperative action might benefit an individual even if it has to contribute to the benefit of others (Küçük 2016: 969f.).

Kleger and Mehlhausen (2013) develop a model of distributive solidarity based on John Rawls' interpretation of the egalitarian-liberal understanding of justice. On the one hand Rawls argues that nature is responsible for unequal talents, which is why compensation is necessary. On the other hand, Rawls posits that human beings are risk adverse. Hence, they would always tend to bolster even the weakest position in a community. These assumptions lead to vertical solidarity, resulting in a redistributive system. Rational actors support distributive measures when they are needed to guarantee the functioning of the system. In the end, solidarity serves the self-interest. But this means also that members of the community can be excluded when the costs of the member surpass the benefits (Kleger and Mehlhausen 2013: 59 f.). The authors argue that it is difficult to impose distributive solidarity in the EU, however, they show in how far the EU developed already beyond international cooperation by the agreement of common values (e.g. Copenhagen criteria). As examples of distributive solidarity serve the European social fund, the Globalisation fund and also Art. 222 on solidarity in case of natural catastrophes (Kleger and Mehlhausen 2013: 60f.).

3) Morality

Solidarity, which is based on morality, cannot be enforced since it depends on the moral motives of the individuals. Bayertz argues that global solidarity is based on universal morality, since the only reasons to act in solidarity is that we are all humans. However, he doubts that this solidarity based on morality is strong enough to be executed (Bayertz 1998: 21). Other authors underline that morality plays an important role for solidarity. If actors are not morally motivated to act in solidarity, they would not follow a collective interest. A „(...) motive for solidarity, distilled from the theories of Durkheim and Parsons, depends on culturally-based convictions, which imply that the individual feels a moral obligation to serve the collective interest and to accept existing relations of solidarity" (Van Oorschot and Komter 1998: 19). It depends on the moral motive how strong solidarity is implemented. Wildt argues that the minimal consensus on the meaning of solidarity is that it is a certain type of „connection" or „cohesion" (Wildt 1999: 216). He explains further that solidarity is always connected with a certain moral aspect. The obligation to help is based „on feelings of social union" (Wildt 1999: 217), which is why solidarity is voluntary. Therefore, he assumes, that there are two characteristics to solidarity, which are „first, a special form of moral motivation or altruism and secondly, a reference to cooperation, or at least reciprocity" (Wildt 1999: 216). This means by implication that solidarity is no legal obligation, and therefore no right (Wildt 1999: 217). Altogether, the moral source might be useful to explain cosmopolitan solidarity, which comprises solidarity with all human beings based on the principle of equality (Díez Medrano et al. 2019).

4) Political allegiance

Another source, which I could identify in the literature, lacks a common name. The source comprises solidarity relations which are based on a common feeling of belonging to the same (political and legal) system and to share political values.

Individual level

Müller and Scheppele (2008) centre their research on ‚constitutional patriotism', which would lead to solidarity based on common political values. Therefore, it is neither national identity nor cosmopolitan hopes that feed solidarity.

> „In general, the concept of constitutional patriotism designates the idea that political attachment ought to center on the norms, the values, and, more indirectly, the procedures of a liberal democratic constitution. Thus, political allegiance is owed, primarily, neither to a national culture, as proponents of liberal nationalism have claimed, nor to "the worldwide community of human beings," as, for instance, Martha Nussbaum's conception of cosmopolitanism has it. Constitutional patriotism promises a form of solidarity distinct from both nationalism and cosmopolitanism" (Müller and Scheppele 2008: 67).

Loh and Skupien argue that the *democratic-legitimacy* motivation is a by-product of democracy. The individual chooses to live in a certain political system and forms thus a political identity. Solidarity emerges because the individual wants to guarantee the integrity of the political system and believes in the reciprocity of obligations. If the source is legitimacy the individual believes in the rule of law. Since the individual can be ensured that the rule of law treats everyone equally, a will for solidarity develops (Loh and Skupien 2016: 584).

Miller claims that people will feel solidarity if they benefit from the same system. Thus, solidarity is not the reason for the establishment of the welfare system but the outcome. Universal welfare systems increase solidarity feelings because all people are treated equally and thus co-citizens consider each other also as fair. Selective welfare programs on the other hand create inequality and therefore reduce solidarity. Institutional coverage alone is not a sufficient tool to create solidarity as can be seen by separatist movements in democracies and the European Union (Miller 2017: 75f.).

Charles Taylor identified civic solidarity as driving force for the citizens to „participate in self-rule" (Smith and Laitinen 2009: 52). Additionally, citizens, who feel this attachment to the political community, share certain goals which are of importance for the majority. Citizen solidarity is about common rights and obligations of citizens of a state. The concept is detached from emotions or interests. Citizens feel solidarity because they are part of the same system which is creating reciprocal acknowledgment. On the EU-level this kind of solidarity is expressed by institutionalised rights and obligations such as the four freedoms, the right to vote on community and European level and diplomatic assistance. These rights and obligations are enshrined with the Union citizenship, which could lead – if upgraded – to a supranational community. However, the discrepancy between national welfare systems led to an intense discussion in how far Union citizens can have access to other national welfare systems (Mau 2008).

Also, Habermas argues that the source of solidarity can be found in the self-interest of the integrity of the common political form. „Was solidarisches Verhalten voraussetzt, sind politische, also rechtlich organisierte und in diesem Sinne artifizielle Lebenszusammenhänge" (Habermas 2014: 26). This interpretation of solidarity indicates that solidarity must be institutionalised to work. Hondrich and Koch-Arzberger understand this source as mechanical form of solidarity, as it was envisaged by Durkheim. However, the authors state that on the one hand this source of solidarity can refer to commonly understood convictions of religious kind or family-based togetherness. At the same time this source covers modern forms of collective convictions, such as human rights, equality and democracy (Hondrich and Koch-Arzberger 1992: 18). An extreme or very particular form of this form of solidarity takes place when solidarity is enacted due to conflict of value systems. People act out of empathy which is why they see the need to ameliorate the situation of others. Solidarity means thus the „(...) Bereitschaft, sich für gemeinsame Ziele oder für Ziele anderer einzusetzen, die man als bedroht und gleichzeitig als wertvoll und legitim ansieht, besonders die engagierte Unterstützung eines Kampfes gegen Gefährdungen, vor allem gegen Unrecht" (Härtel 2014: 227).

Member State level

Immerfall argues that responsibility for each other emerges from interdependence. Common identity is not necessary to bring solidarity to life. „Es handelt sich gewissermaßen um eine rechtlich verbürgte Solidarität zwischen Staaten, welche auf der sehr viel voraussetzungsreicheren Form der Solidarität zwischen Bürgerinnen nur indirekt rekurrieren muss" (Immerfall 2016: 49). Kim and Schattle share the idea that identity has its limits regarding the notion of solidarity. Solidarity is multi-layered and can thus function with different communities. Instead of identity, it is the will to belong to a constitution or a secular, civil notion, which forms the basis for solidarity. The authors define solidarity as follows:

> „we (...) define solidarity as an ethos of collective responsibility that sets up suitable background conditions for policy decisions that not only affirm pragmatic interests among a set of governments or stakeholders, but also, in some cases, extend from common normative values that can be identified among cooperating regional political and economic actors in an interdependent world" (Kim and Schattle 2012: 467).

Even though interdependence is here the key driver for solidarity, it is common responsibility which makes solidarity work. Member States work together in order to solve common problems jointly by cooperation or even sacrifice.

„The construction of the EU lies upon a de facto solidarity, as was once envisaged by Robert Schuman in his famous declaration. The concept of solidarity underpins the phenomenon of European Integration. To forget this is to forget the very essence of Europe" (Andreosso-O'Callaghan 2002: 362). However, there is no agreement how to fulfil this „fundamental imperative in the EU" (Kim and Schattle 2012: 482f.). Kim and Schattle argue further that the EU was from the beginning on propelled forward by the cosmopolitan approach to solidarity, which is now challenged to be reduced to ‚national' solidarity with the rising problems of immigration and very different prosperity levels in the EU. The advantage of this value-based approach for European solidarity is that solidarity is not determined by a social bond or friendship, but by a normative and pragmatic understanding of collective responsibility. Similar to this understanding of joint responsibility due to interdependence is the description of Blanquet: He explains that Member States' solidarity is based on the mutual understanding that, due to EU membership, Member States agree to the treaty obligations, which is the principle of communal fidelity, i.e. „une conscience de tous les partenaires qu'ils sont réunis par un même lien" (Blanquet 2009: 162). This communal fidelity is translated in legal principles and therefore solidarity goes beyond spontaneous help and emotional acts (Schiek 2020). Kleger and Mehlhausen base *federal solidarity* on Kant's oeuvre „Zum ewigen Frieden": democratic societies affiliate because they defend each other in a federalism of free states resulting in a union. Solidarity underpins federal communities since it informs the delicate relationship between the national and the European level. „Federalism is about dividing and sharing power at a territorial level and the relationship between those levels" (Keating 2017: 622). Federal solidarity allows as such an opening up of closed national solidarity relations based on identity by implying „(...) duties of reciprocity by the parties involved (...)" (Arban 2017: 243). Also, 'union' is strongly interwoven with fraternity, which is pointing not only to an alliance of defence but an even stronger alliance. The union members are internally connected by common values and externally by common enemies (Kleger and Mehlhausen 2013: 56).

The approach ‚logic of appropriateness' by March and Olsen (1989) deals with the influence of norms on actors. Norms are defined as institutions which determine over time the behaviour of actors, because actors' behaviour is based on the socio-cultural context. The institutional environment establishes norms and expectations which clarify what is appropriate behaviour. Therefore, actors do not automatically act only due to calculated risks and benefits but are strongly influenced by issues of identity and appropriateness (Thielemann 2003: 255). Solidarity plays a significant role in this approach, since it explains why actors are interested in sharing costs. First, if actors behave due to some solidarity obligation, the actors will adhere to a common solution. Second, actors demonstrate solidarity by refusing benefits which are not equally spread, or which could harm other members. „Actors choose among alternatives by evaluating expected consequences of their actions for the achievement of certain objectives, expecting other actors to do the same" (Thielemann 2003: 258). The resulting patterns of this motivation are also informed by the norm-based logic: Either states accept a certain distribution of burdens based on equity or to secure norms, such as human rights.

5) Identity

Lastly, the source of common identity presents a motivation for European solidarity. Even though this source refers to the individual level, and thus could be rather applied to transnational solidarity (which is solidarity between citizens of different states), it can have an effect on solidarity between Member States. Transnational solidarity can legitimise solidarity politics between Member States, and it has therefore an influence on Member State solidarity, which must not be underestimated. „Wenn (...) die Solidaritätsbereitschaft der Bürger überfordert wird, dann besteht die Gefahr, dass letztlich auch die EU selbst, das europäische Integrationsprojekt insgesamt, überfordert wird" (Calliess 2011: 64f.). The main argument of the identity source is, that people feel responsible for each other because they share a common identity, i.e. they perceive each other as alike. Experiments showed that individuals were more willing to help others if they were told that they had something in common (Miller 2017: 74f.).

Loh and Skupien explain that individuals decide to act in solidarity because they are part of a specific group, which is formed due to ethnic or language reasons. Individuals act in solidarity because there is an associative obligation due to the membership to the group. The *cultural-identity* source is interwoven with nationalism. Individuals feel as part of a nation-state because they identify themselves with the victims of the past (Loh and Skupien 2016: 583f.).

Also bonding solidarity (Verbundenheitssolidarität' by Mau (2008)) refers to the feeling of connectedness between members of a social group. Typically, these are rather small communities, however, as is proven by the national welfare regime, this concept can also be true for large groups. Until now citizens of the European Union feel still strongly connected with the national state, but this does not contradict that a European solidarity could also emerge. The degree of European identity depends on two categories: 1) length of membership and 2) transnational trust increases over time (Mau 2008). Recent research concentrates on the relationship between collective identities and core state powers in the EU (Kuhn and Nicoli 2020). Nicoli et al. conclude in their article on fiscal solidarity, that an exclusive national identity does not prevent European social policy, but the design of the policy influences the support of exclusive nationalists (Nicoli et al. 2020).

It is questionable in how far the identity source is helpful to understand solidarity between Member States. Solidarity can also develop due to other reasons, such as common values, a shared history or on the basis of common experience in a community of fate. However, the question arises if Europe displays any specific characterisations at all, or if it is only an appendix of the Asian continent (Martens 2008: 39). Wydra explains that political solidarity is a pre-condition for a stable EU. Identity is the keyword provoking the question for more or less solidarity. Due to the large heterogeneity in Europe the creation of one European identity seems impossible. However, particularly the idea of ,united in diversity' could eventually lead to solidarity, since it would trigger a process of democratisation and mutual appreciation. Therefore, solidarity would develop due to political will as well as the affiliation to the same legal community (compare political allegiance source) (Wydra 2010: 109). Bauböck claims that identity can indeed be a (even strong) source for solidarity, especially if we look at the nation-state level and nation-states, which fail to integrate minorities (e.g. Catalonia or Scotland) (Bauböck 2017: 3). Even though many scholars underline the importance of identity for solidarity also on the European level, I doubt that identity serves as valid explanation to explain the institutionalisation of solidarity between Member States (see also Steinvorth 2017: 49), but it might be a constraining factor.

6) The source of EU Member State solidarity

The former chapters demonstrated that theoretical implications refer mostly to the individual as the principal actor of solidarity. However, reflections on solidarity showed also that groups of solidarity go beyond the narrow circle of family or neighbours. The sources of solidarity explain how solidarity can exist beyond this close connectedness. Solidarity moves thus to another level of relationship. Calliess argues that Member States function as catalyst of citizens' solidarity:

> „Das Solidaritätsprinzip als Rechtsprinzip des Staaten- und Verfassungsverbunds bezieht sich somit hauptsächlich auf die Solidarität zwischen den Mitgliedstaaten im Hinblick auf die (Ziele der) EU; die Mitgliedstaaten fungieren insoweit als Medium ihrer Bürger als der originären Solidaritätsträger" (Calliess 2011: 17).

While the bond of solidarity exists between citizens, the member states must enforce the resulting obligations. An important claim in the literature on EU solidarity is that it is only possible to speak of solidarities in the EU because the application and intensity of solidarity varies according to the policy field. Instead of individuals, Member States as collective actors are the subjects of solidarity (Knodt and Tews 2014: 8). But there are two principal problems to conceptualise solidarity on the European level (or multi-level system). First, solidarity is usually applied to relations between individuals and not between Member States. However, this classical approach is not helpful to grasp the complex intergovernmental and multi-level governance character of the EU. And second, solidarity is supposed to need a source such as e.g. identity. Knodt and Tews develop their solution on Durkheim's concept of organic solidarity, which describes that the individuals do not act in solidarity due to personal contact but due to interdependence and the resulting self-interest, which could then be similarly applied to Member States, respectively the multi-level system (Knodt and Tews 2017: 49f.).

Steinvorth doubts that states are capable of being the bearers of solidarity. First, nations do not possess the same rights as individuals and second, nations and individuals do not pursue the same interests (Steinvorth 2017: 12; Mau 2008). It remains to be seen in how far solidarity can be further established on the EU-level especially because the risk remains that the fragile community is overburdened by solidarity demands. If the demands are too high, acceptance problems might occur leading to a fractured system of solidarity supporters and opponents (Mau 2008). Even though the critique might be reasonable, it cannot be excluded that states can be the bearers of solidarity. First, it is necessary to repeat that solidarity between Member States is not only a political demand but also a legal principle manifested in the treaties. Solidarity is therefore better understood as a federal principle. Solidarity moves as concept between political and legal aspects, which is why it is necessary and helpful to reflect further on its consequences for the Member States. Second, I comprehend states as collective actors, who can claim or reject solidarity politically but have at the same time legal rights and obligations. Additionally, I recall that solidarity between individuals touches upon different research fields, such as the legitimacy of political decisions.

This chapter demonstrated that there are different sources which stipulate solidarity. It is, however, necessary to select the sources which form the basis for solidarity between Member States since the sources hint at the features of solidarity. The moral understanding of solidarity implies that solidarity is a voluntary act based on a cosmopolitan perception of the group members. This source excludes the reciprocal character identified by other sources as well as the freeriding problem and stipulates spontaneous help based on emotions and the moral compass. But one basic feature of Member State solidarity is that solidarity concerns this group exclusively, which is why this source seems not suitable for the further conceptualisation of solidarity between Member States.

The view that the belonging to the group is based on a shared identity would point to the role of citizens. Identity might be a fruitful concept to discuss the legitimacy or the acceptance of policies, but it primarily serves as source for solidarity between individuals. This view, however, is not helpful regarding Member State solidarity as it remains highly contestable if the European identity is strong enough to be the basis for political solidarity actions (Verhaegen 2018). However, this does not mean that the feeling of belonging to a group has no influence on solidarity. To the contrary, the different sources have revealed that identification with the group is very relevant for solidarity – but this is not equal to identity.

I argue, that the source for solidarity in the EU is inspired by different sources. The most promising sources to explain the motivation of Member States are the sources based on *self-interest* and *interdependence* (rational choice approach) and on *political allegiance* (normative approach). First, interdependence plays a crucial role for the EU. The development of the internal market and other integrative measures led to an ever-growing interdependence between the Member States. Looking at Brexit, it becomes even more evident how difficult it is to untie the knot. Second, interests do certainly play a key role. Interests form due to particular features of a Member State, such as historical background, industry, welfare programmes to name just a few factors. However, Interdependence and self-interest are intertwined because even though the self-interest explains the original motivation to enter a solidarity group, interdependence explains why group members are willing to stay in long-term solidarity relations and might accept sacrifices. Interests alone lack sufficient argumentative potential to explain why group members would agree to measures where they would mostly bear the costs without insurance about positive feedback.

Additionally, I attribute particular value to the belonging to the political club, the community of law (Knodt and Tews 2014). The ‚political alignment' source promises to be helpful to understand the motivation for solidarity on the EU level. Political allegiance underlines the group's willingness to agree to rights and obligations resulting from group membership. The source entails that solidarity between Member States is based on the adherence to the common principles because Member States are part of the political and legal community. The normative implication comprises that this perception of the interrelation between interdependence and common values leads to joint responsibility. Trust is created because group members believe that they will be treated equally. Thus, for both approaches the possibility of sanctions plays a certain role. I follow the assumption that the key to the development of European solidarity lies not only in the functional assumption of division of labour but in the *integrative effect of belonging to and legitimacy through a political and legal community*. This allegiance creates a sense of responsibility and at the same time rights and obligations are ensured by institutions.

2.1.3. Delineation of solidarity from neighbouring terms

One important point in the process of conceptualisation is to reflect which neighbouring terms exist and how they differ from the term under exploration. Depending on the context, there are different neighbouring terms to solidarity.

> „Ultimately, it (solidarity) was also adopted by philosophical ethics, where until today it stands, largely unexplained, in relation to complementary terms such as „community spirit" or „mutual attachment", „social cooperation" or „charity", and – from time to time – „brotherly love" or „love of mankind" (Bayertz 1999: 3).

The closest term to solidarity can be found in its historical roots. In the 19th century, *fraternity* was synonymously used with solidarity. Over time both terms developed distinct meanings. Fraternity is very exclusive since it refers to a group of people who share something, or who have something in common (Stjernø 2005: 27). Even though fraternity today exceeds the relations of brotherhood, fraternities are clubs of people who are closely connected by sports, profession or the same college. This is why fraternity groups are bound by thick ties (like blood between siblings), which are united in destiny. Solidarity does neither imply such ties nor an indissoluble community of destiny.

Also, *charity* played a certain role in the development of solidarity as social term. However, the difference to charity is profound. To act out of charity means to give something. Charity entails no reciprocal expectation, it has more of an altruistic character. The relation between the giver and taker of charity is a vertical relation. A crucial difference between solidarity and charity is that „solidarity could be comprehended as cohesion amongst equals, i.e. horizontally" (Metz 1999: 191). Previous concepts, such as charité, describe a vertical relationship towards the poor who seek aid. This interpretation is influenced by the Christian understanding of serving God.

Looking at solidarity from a collective action perspective, the neighbouring term would be *cooperation*. Cooperation comprises a wide range of facets, such as: ‚balance of efforts', ‚burden sharing', ‚mutual assistance' and ‚responsibility sharing'. There are several differences between cooperation and solidarity. Cooperation can refer to a single interaction and to a series of interactions, however, it entails always a direct balancing of debts. Cooperation means not to help or to support but only to do something in the mutual interest. Cooperation usually exists because there is a club good (all members invest and harvest). „(...) (S)olidarity can (...) be distinguished from adjacent socio-political concepts such as cooperation (where mutuality is not as paramount to the achievement of the set goal) and loyalty (where common goals are pursued in such a way that equality is undermined)" (Badanova 2019: 114). Küçük (2016) underlines that solidarity entails the common will of all Member States to attain the greater objectives of the EU. This reasoning makes the difference to usual cooperation, since all Member States are attached to each other by following a greater goal beyond their interest.

In the following, I will focus on *loyalty* since it is used in close relation to solidarity, and even legal studies provide no coherent answer to the question on what constitutes the difference between loyalty and solidarity. The legal community conducts a lively debate about the differences between the principles of loyalty and solidarity. There is no common agreement on the importance of each principle and on whether both principles are legal principles at all.

Kappeler and Wolkenstein develop the concept of *counter-Enlightenment solidarity*, which is „understood as loyalty to a specific ethnic, national, religious, etc. group" (2013: 478). Freedom or reason do not play a role in this account, however, there is a comprehensive normative dimension. Loyalty not only implies duties and obligations but also points to the dichotomy of "us versus them" as it underlines the myths of nation or race (Kappeler and Wolkenstein 2013: 478). Loyalty in this case comes from belonging to a particular group, which is why members of the group deserve solidarity measures, while non-members are automatically excluded. Loyalty is thus based on a thick notion of identity and accompanying exclusivity (Kapeller and Wolkenstein 2013: 487). Even though this analysis reveals the entangled relationship between solidarity and loyalty, the difference between both concepts is not obvious. In search of a clearer answer to the difference between solidarity and loyalty, I address the legal discussion below.

Klamert observes that there have „always been claims that there is no difference between the legal concepts of solidarity and loyalty in EU law" (Klamert 2014: 40). The principle of loyalty was already initiated in Art. 5 of the Treaty of Rome expressing the obligation of the Member States to adhere to the commitments as set out in the Treaties.

> „Member States shall take all general or particular measures which are appropriate for ensuring the carrying out of the obligations arising out of this Treaty or resulting from the acts of the institutions of the Community. They shall facilitate the achievement of the Community's aims. They shall abstain from measures likely to jeopardise the attainment of the objectives of the Treaty" (Treaty establishing the European Economic Community).

This was repeated later in Article 10 of the Treaty establishing the European Community. Member States need to fulfil their obligations and also „facilitate the achievement of the Community's tasks" (Art. 10, TEC). Additionally, Member States shall refrain from actions that might endanger the realisation of the objectives.

This adherence to loyalty from both Member States as well as community institutions is also underlined by the CJEU (e.g. CJEU Case 230/81). Art. 10 TEC constitutes a legal norm that is an expression of a more comprehensive general principle of law of the community law. Art. 10 was also used by the CJEU to underline the necessity to fully implement Community law. This obligation to support the attainment of objectives of the Treaties is therefore necessary, so that the Community can function. However, Art. 10 cannot be used in order to create new obligations by the Member States but is an accompanying norm with the community loyalty as supplementing principle. Therefore, Art. 10 can only be seen as supporting element to a community competence. Art. 10 serves thus as benchmark function to evaluate the behaviour of Member States. Consequently, Art. 10 cannot serve for further development of law (Gussone 2005: 66ff.).

Community loyalty does not oblige member states to act in a particularly cooperative manner in the Council, nor are they obliged to take majority decisions if there is no common compromise. To the contrary, Member States shall act upon their own interest. However, community loyalty is demanded on the inter-institutional level in order to facilitate the application of the treaty provisions. Art. 10 TEC does not only oblige Member States to act upon the principle of loyalty as regards the Community, but also the institutions (Gussone 2005: 76f.).

Contrasting loyalty and solidarity, Gussone develops the following argument: loyalty is only used as means in order to shape obligations between the Member States, however, it constitutes not the obligation. This is done by the principle of solidarity, which is inherent to the community membership. The community is legitimised to wield power because its purpose is the attainment of the common good. The common good is not the sum of all single interests but it is the collective interest as established by the objectives and the preambles of the treaties. However, also Member States – and certainly in a less fragile way than the EU – possess this legitimacy. Therefore, there is a conflict between different sovereignties. This conflict is resolved by the solidarity principle, which is activated with the accession to the EU. The solidarity principle constitutes the obligation of the Member States to accept the equilibrium between burdens and benefits resulting from the community membership (e.g. CJEU case 39/72) (Gussone 2005: 84ff). Under Article 4(3) TEU the principle of loyalty was renamed in ‚the principle of sincere cooperation'.

Solidarity and loyalty share the feature that obligations need to be fulfilled although national interests might be different. „In these cases, the Member States have to allow the collective interest of the EU to prevail over their individual interests, and thereby show solidarity with other Member States" (Küçük 2016: 974). Van Elsuwege makes a difference between positive and negative obligations for Member States arising from loyalty. A positive obligation means e.g. that Member States represent the EU in front of the International Labour Organisation (ILO), since the ILO did not accept the EU as a member. A negative obligation means that Member States refrain from expressing their national opinion if this opinion endangers the implementation of the EU's goals (Van Elsuwege 2019).

The Court of Justice used the principle of solidarity in different court rulings as reason why Member States needed to adhere to the obligations arising from the Treaties in order to keep the equilibrium of burdens and benefits (Küçük 2016: 974; Klamert 2014: 40). Even though the principles were used interchangeably by the Court, Klamert analyses that solidarity refers to the relationship between Member States and *loyalty to the relationship between Member States and the EU*. Also, federal loyalty describes the "fundamental commitment of the constituent units and their representatives to the overall needs of the larger federal system" (Burgess 2013: 15). Member States act in solidarity because they have shared goals, why they are connected by a ‚bond of unity'. „Solidarity, thus, is a principle guiding the conduct of Member States in their relationship with each other. As such, it is rather a political than a legal concept, important exceptions aside" (Klamert 2014: 40). Härtel does not share this analysis by Klamert regarding solidarity as legal principle. Härtel claims that European loyalty expresses the adherence to the community values and goals. Loyalty emerges from the Treaty obligations and determines loyal actions. Solidarity differs from loyalty since it demands an active support of each other and mutuality. Due to its extension from the individual to the state level, solidarity obtains legal quality (Härtel 2012: 149). Solidarity is needed in order to ensure Union action if „Member States' expected loyalty in implementing EU policy appears not to be sufficient" (Vanheule 2011: 8). To sum up, the difference between solidarity and loyalty is that solidarity entails the obligation to support or not to harm each other, while loyalty refers to the adherence of Treaty obligations.

Subsidiarity as counter-principle to solidarity

For the further clarification of solidarity, it is also useful to look at the opposite term. Goertz calls it the ‚negative pole'. I consider this exercise as helpful to clarify further the term under scrutiny. Opposing poles to solidarity are manifold. It depends very much on the understanding of solidarity, what constitutes the opposition.

Habermas claims that the other side of the coin is justice. Solidarity and justice are opposing each other but are also inseparable like twins since solidarity has to be equalled out by justice (Habermas 2014). Knodt and Tews (2017) argue that also autonomy is an opposing pole to solidarity, since it reflects individuality vs. solidarity as collective principle.

The opposing pole depends on the research interest. Since my research examines the question, why solidarity was implemented, the question of more or less integration and the level of action play a significant role. Therefore, I consider that subsidiarity is the adequate counter-principle to solidarity. Also Knodt and Tews underline that subsidiarity is the opposing pole to solidarity (next to autonomy) since it „influences the distribution of competencies within the EU and serves as a source for legitimacy" (Knodt and Tews 2017: 52). Härtel develops a similar argument. While loyalty and solidarity stand for cooperation in the EU, subsidiarity shall prevent disproportionate centralism (Härtel 2012: 150).

Calliess argues that solidarity is necessary to implement the common good. The state is responsible to enforce solidarity in situations when the individuals and their associations cannot cope with the social problems or can no longer do so to the overwhelming satisfaction (Calliess 1996: 168). The principles of solidarity and subsidiarity are necessary to create a balance between the common good and the freedom of the individual (Calliess 1996: 169). The application of the subsidiarity principle is dependent on various elements: different units must be related in a hierarchal order; the units must have a joint range of duties with competing competencies and they must refer to the same goal. Same goals result in the solidarity principle but underline also the inner bond of smaller units in respect of the entirety, which presupposes the principle of subsidiarity.

> „Das Gemeinwohl entfaltet sich auf diese Weise im Solidaritätsprinzip einerseits und im Subsidiaritätsprinzip andererseits. Hierdurch entsteht ein Spannungsverhältnis, das dem Subsidiaritätsprinzip immanent ist und bei seiner Auslegung zu berücksichtigen ist. Beide Prinzipien werden in diesem Spannungsverhältnis einander zum gegenseitigen Korrektiv. Demnach bestimmen sich die konkreten Folgerungen aus dem Subsidiaritätsprinzip unter Berücksichtigung der Anforderungen des Solidaritätsprinzips" (Calliess and Ruffert 2016).

The solidarity principle emphasises the integrity of the entirety in contrast to the separate unit (Calliess 1996: 168). Solidarity and subsidiary are thus two sides of the same coin. Their relationship determines how collective and individual claims and competencies are distributed.

In order to further reflect on the different features of solidarity, I analyse in the following sub-chapter already existing definitions and concepts of solidarity. The different sources showed that there are various characteristics of solidarity, but the sources of solidarity focused on the motivation for solidarity and not on the implementation of solidarity. In the following, I examine definitions of solidarity from all kind of disciplines in a first step, and in a second step, I concentrate on specific EU-related definitions in order to identify the features of solidarity.

2.1.4. Analysis of the features of solidarity

To develop the concept, I started with the history of solidarity in order to come closer to its semantic history and application over time and space. In a second step, I drew a picture of the different sources of solidarity, which allowed me to reflect on the usefulness of application of each source for solidarity between Member States. This step contributed also to the theoretical considerations of solidarity, i.e. to clarify the implications which arise from the different sources. This was followed by a reflection on the neighbouring terms of solidarity and its opposite pole in order to further illuminate, which empirical phenomena can be grasped with help of the concept and to limit its implications. In the next step, I compile different definitions and concepts of solidarity and deduce the main aspects of solidarity (s. annex 1 for definitions of solidarity). Based on the developed categories, I identify the inherent features of solidarity between EU Member States. The analysis shows that there are two basic concepts of solidarity, which are normative-based and rational choice based. In the analysis, I will present the different features that emerge from the two theoretical approaches to illustrate why I have chosen to base my concept of solidarity on a wide version of rational choice theory[2]. This wide version of RCT follows Niemann's basic understanding of RCT in neofunctionalism: „(A)gents are more likely to enter into new relationships following an instrumental rationale, but tend to develop certain norms and identities and may change their preferences as a result of their experience and interaction" (Niemann 2006: 25). Thus, the evaluation of the different properties of solidarity results in a distinctive definition of solidarity and a conceptualisation, which allows me to make solidarity between Member States measurable (institutionalised/declarative).

Which features are part of solidarity?

There are many different definitions of solidarity. Most authors do not only take over a ‚standard' definition, which obviously does not exist, but create a definition which corresponds to their needs. This is both useful and understandable since solidarity changes its character depending on the level (e.g. micro or macro), on its exclusive or universalistic implications (group or humanity), on its form (common goal or support) and on the constraints (voluntary or sanctions). In order to identify the most important characteristics of solidarity I identified five categories which are regularly used in the definitions. All definitions mention at least three of the following five categories: „Actors", „Reasons", „Aim", „Form" and „Constraints and Compliance".

Actors: Actors are mentioned in each definition. Actors are the subjects pursuing solidarity, which can be the individual, a societal group, a nation state, a group of nation states and people(s) or mankind (Hayward 1959: 261f.). Even though these are many different levels, there is one main difference. Solidarity has either an exclusive character, if it refers to solidarity within a group or an inclusive (cosmopolitan) character, if it refers to all people(s) or humankind. This classification corresponds additionally to a continuum between self-interest and altruism. The category on the

---

2 See Tranow 2012 for a different approach of a wide version of rational choice theory concerning solidarity.

continuum determines the feeling of solidarity in a rather limited I-focus or rather general all-focus (Stjernø 2005: 16).

Reasons: This category reveals the reasons why actors exert solidarity. I have already provided further reflections in the chapter 2.1.2 (sources of solidarity). The reasons comprise „interdependence" (division of labour), „norms", „bonds" (values) and „interests" (rational choice). Not every author refers to reasons in the definition why actors exert solidarity. However, groups are very different depending on the bond which keeps the group together. This bond can consist of ‚identity', ‚empathy', ‚mutual trust', ‚mutual concern' and ‚responsibility for each other' (compare Taylor 2015; Miller 2017).

Aim: There are different goals of solidarity. Either solidarity aims at the provision of a collective good (or common weal) or group members want to provide help (or support) (Hechter 1988: 52f.). Both aims represent, in a more abstract way, any kinds of common goals or joint interests.

Form: This category contains all types of support, which are carried out by the individuals/within the group. Aims and form are partly overlapping since help can be the aim but also the form. Most authors refer to rights and obligations, which means that group members have access to solidarity but have also the duty to act in solidarity if needed (Hestermeyer 2012). The other forms include either very concrete support mechanisms (e.g. taxes), or the request not to harm others of the group, or mutual/reciprocal obligations (Engler 2016).

Constraints and Compliance: This category lists in how far authors imply mechanisms or other tools to put solidarity in place but also the limits to solidarity. Either authors refer particularly to sanctions or that solidarity must be „imposed". Norm based approaches state that a code of conduct ensures solidarity. Others argue that solidarity is voluntary (Baurmann 1999).

In the following, I will carry out an analysis of the single categories in order to have a more thorough understanding of each category and to determine which aspects are important in order to grasp solidarity between Member States.

Which actors are included? Aims of the actors/group

First, I start with some reflections on the question in which groups solidarity is demanded or applied. I connect the category actors with the categories aims and reason, since these categories are interwoven with each other. Solidarity is often used in the daily language. The term is used to express altruistic behaviour after natural catastrophes, but also as an emotional vehicle in political texts, such as government declarations or party programs. There is no common understanding of what solidarity means in practice, but there is apparently an understanding of what solidarity is about: Solidarity keeps people together, it is the cement of society (Kapeller and Wolkenstein 2013: 477). Solidarity is a very broad term comprising the Solidarność movement in Poland, but also the ‚occupy wall street‘ movement, which resulted from the financial crisis. As demonstrated in the chapter on the ideational development, solidarity can be found as reference to very different groups. This might be a neighbourhood, a certain community (e.g. LGBTQIA) or a group of people in a different country (e.g. development aid).

A difference exists between *solidarity ‚with‘* and *solidarity ‚among‘*. Miller's example of solidarity ‚with' is the Chilean Solidarity Group in Great Britain, which formed in the 1970ies in order to support Pinochet's victims. „It is a one-way relationship" (Miller 2017: 64). Solidarity ‚among‘ on the other side describes a group feeling. „First, there has to be a sufficiently precise, and shared, sense that they are a group. There must be some feature or set of features that binds them together" (Miller 2017: 64). Actors, which form the solidarity group, and underlying sources of their solidarity are therefore intertwined.

Miller claims that there must be *distinguishing features* that bind the group together, however, it is not of importance for solidarity that the group members know each other (e.g. national solidarity) (Miller 2017: 65f.). This observation goes hand in hand with Taylor's argument that solidarity is among other factors conditioned by *identification*. Identification with the group is bidirectional because the individual has to identify with the group but also the group must recognise the individual (Taylor 2015: 133f.).

Haversath states that group members are equals since they share a certain *emotional bond* as well as *common interests* (Haversath 2012). Bayertz underlines that identification with the group is one of the normative characteristics of solidarity which makes solidarity different from e.g. reciprocity (Bayertz 1998). According to Liebsch solidarity is demanded mostly in times of crises since only then interpersonal relations suffer from instability, unreliability and fragility. Solidarity is the treatment for this sickness. But it depends on the strength of solidarity, if solidarity can be successfully applied in crisis situations (Liebsch 2007: 147f.).

Empathy and mutual trust also ensure that groups are solid. Disposition of *empathy* means that group members are willing to understand the emotional configuration of the other group members as result from the social facts in relation to the joint interest. Either the empathy exists because the other group member can actually understand the feelings due to same experience or similar feelings resulting from a certain situation or the empathy exists because the other group members can understand the circumstances leading to a certain feeling (Taylor 2015: 135f.). *Mutual trust* is strongly dependent on three other conditions: „(…) trust involves: (1) that we be vulnerable to betrayal; (2) that we think well of others in certain domains; and (3) that we are optimistic that others are competent in certain respects" (Taylor 2015: 136). The bidirectional exposition to other's behaviour is the focal point of mutual trust. If group members do not trust each other, it is difficult to act in solidarity since there is no certitude that the other will act in favour of the group (Taylor 2015: 139).

Haversath follows the idea that it is 'interest' which determines a community of solidarity. A social bond might be working for a close and small-sized community, such as a family, but not when community members do not know each other. Nevertheless, Haversath postulates that trust is an important aspect of solidarity, since solidarity cannot be legally demanded (Haversath 2012). Miller goes in a similar direction by stating that solidarity needs *mutual concern* and that group members need to acknowledge collective responsibility. If a group is too heterogenous or the individual puts its self-interest above the common interest solidarity fails (Miller 2017: 62). Groups form around members which are relatively equal, because they share e.g. a similar social status (Hondrich and Koch-Arzberger 1992: 13). Engler underlines that a group's bond gets stronger if the *group distances it from others*, which creates or supports an emotional bond within the group (Engler 2016: 34).

Additionally, solidarity might express a spontaneous sympathy with an opposition against injustice, or it presents a form of mutual – often even legally bound – obligations, such as in a solidarity community (Soli-dargemeinschaft) (Loh and Skupien 2016: 581). Bayertz calls the former „Kampf-Solidarität" and the latter „Gemeinschafts-Solidarität". Hartwig and Nicolaides classify solidarity as sacrificing relationship between individuals and a group similar to Kampf-Solidarität (Hartwig and Nicolaides 2003: 21). Both versions of solidarity have in common that there is a willingness to act jointly to reach common goals or the goals of others, because these goals are threatened, valuable or legit.

Hechter argues that costs determine if a group member remains in the group. The dependence of the membership determines the extensiveness of obligations. If the actor is better off alone, the decision would always be against the group membership. If the actor has other options, an analysis takes place which costs occur in order to exit the group (Hechter 1988: 49). Jachtenfuchs and Kasack identify different forms of exit which are secession, exit from specific policies and autonomous application of collective policies (2017: 604ff.). Their analysis shows that exit options in the EU are much more diverse than in Hechter's approach.

From these aspects follow two theoretical implications: First, *normative solidarity approaches* underline the importance of the emotional bond, trust and concern since those approaches negate that solidarity can be legally claimed. Second, *rational choice solidarity approaches* emphasise the importance of the common interest and that group members joined the group because they can ensure that the benefits of following the common interest outweigh the costs of not fully endorsing the individual interest. Only if the costs exceed the benefits, members would abandon the group.

Box 4: Solidarity actors

To sum up, the category „actors" entails the following aspects:

A. There is a difference between solidarity „with" and solidarity „among". Only solidarity „among" describes solidarity within a group.

B. There are different reasons why a group forms to act in solidarity. Members join the group voluntarily. But the robustness of the group is dependent on its inner bond, I call this cohesion. The group's cohesion is influenced by the following conditions:
   – A common group interest exists;
   – The group distinguishes itself from ‚the others';
   – Group members identify themselves with the group and are recognised as group members;
   – The group is rather homogenous;

C. Normative approach:
   – There is an emotional bond;
   – Solidarity is voluntary and cannot be claimed legally;
   – Mutual trust and mutual concerns are features of the group.

D. RC approach:
   – Actors weigh the individual and collective interests;
   – Group members' solidarity increases with the group members' dependence on the group (cost-benefit calculation of the group members);
   – Group members exit the group if costs exceed its benefits.

Forms of solidarity: rights and obligations

One of the main claims of diverse solidarity concepts is that solidarity is *reciprocal*. Only if the group member can expect help in return, it is willing to help. However, reciprocity takes not necessarily place immediately. In this case, reciprocal action is understood as *long-term obligation*, which results in constant cooperation and trust (Engler 2016: 34). These long-term obligations ease cooperation between the members because they do not fear insecurity. The costs of interaction are also reduced, as group members do not have to calculate how to ensure mutual action. It is the group that determines the scope and content of obligations, but also the resulting privileges. The behaviour within the group is a life-long socialisation process that is stipulated by the solidarity norm (Engler 2016: 34).

Miller claims that reciprocity does not reflect sufficiently the *willingness to mutual aid* as understood by solidarity. While reciprocity demands – in Miller's view – the exact return of help, a person in a relation of solidarity with another has simply to *show the will to help*. The difference to altruism is that *help in return is expected*. The level of willingness to help each other can vary from group to group (Miller 2017: 64). Bayertz explains that the willingness to help reflects the normative dimension of solidarity, next to the identification with the group. Solidarity is legitimised by the conviction to serve the group's (or group members') interests (Bayertz 1998: 12). Hondrich and Koch-Arzberger claim however that solidarity is a *voluntary* act, and that individuals have the choice between spontaneous new and enduring solidarity (1992: 14). Also, Baurmann highlights the importance of reciprocity. Only if a good can be expected in return for giving (but not a payment!), an individual is willing to help. Therefore, even though reciprocity includes the obligation to provide mutual support, it does not automatically include a compensation mechanism. To the contrary, compensation is highly contested. Tranow (2012) explicitly excludes any form of compensation. The reciprocal behaviour is dependent on self-interest. Reciprocity mechanisms can either be carried out between two individuals (direct reciprocity) or within a group (indirect reciprocity). Reciprocity can only emerge if the relations between the individuals are long-term, so that investments in the future are reasonable, and the individuals must be informed about the behaviour of the others, which is most likely in small and closely linked groups (Baurmann 1999: 252).

In Roman law „obligatio in solidum" meant that a group member is *responsible* for the actions of another. If one group member is not capable of repaying a debt, the other group members would take over. Also, the distribution of negative and positive resources should be levelled out, e.g. to the effect that if one member benefits, the others should at least not suffer from this benefit (Miller 2017: 65). Haversath underlines that solidarity is only executed in cases, which occur through *no fault of one's own*, and that solidarity not only implies active support but also a *duty of omission* (Haversath 2012).

Taylor develops two different kinds of solidarities, which are ‚robust solidarity' and ‚expressional solidarity' (Taylor 2015: 129). While the former refers to solidarities which generate obligations due to group membership (solidarity with a group), the latter illuminates solidarities which are commitments since they result from a feeling of solidarity towards a group. Expressional solidarity is about motivation because actors are not obliged to act, they do something for someone else because of normative reasons.

Since expressional solidarity is not a duty, actors cannot be expected to carry out solidarity actions. Robust solidarity on the other hand is an *obligation* because group members „act in certain ways to *promote the groups' interest* or goals" (Taylor 2015: 130, emphasis added). If a group member acts against the common goal of the group, this behaviour might harm the group. Robust solidarity is either a result of obligations within the group or a result from opposition (Taylor 2015: 131).

Box 5: Forms of solidarity

To sum up, the following aspects are important regarding the category „forms of solidarity":
A. A solidarity group entails obligations but also privileges, which are determined by the group:
B. Normative approach:
 – Solidarity can be reciprocal.
 – Members have to show the will to help and are expected to help.
 – Reciprocal actions must not be short-term but long-term, which ensures trust.
 – There is direct reciprocity between two individuals or indirect reciprocity between a group member and the group.
 – The group's interest is of higher importance than the individual's interest.
 – Members of a solidarity group have the duty of omission. In case an action would hurt another member, members would refrain from doing so.
C. RC approach:
 – Solidarity is reciprocal.
 – The costs are determined by the group.

> - Reciprocity can also include direct compensation.
> - Members of a solidarity group must act responsibly and avert situation in which they would need to claim solidarity. Only if the situation is not self-inflicted, other members are willing to help.

Compliance and conditionality: How is solidarity ensured?

How do relations within a group change, if the individual's contributions are no longer necessary for additional benefits (e.g. such as a vote in a democratic election)? This is a typical case which might result in *freeriding*. Although the individual is interested in the provision of the public good, which is provided by the group, rational utility maximisation is no sufficient incentive for the individual to contribute to the public good, since there is the possibility to defect and to bear less costs. Eventually, all individuals will defect, and the public good is not provided at all. This course of events is the description of the prisoner's dilemma. Two argumentative strands explain how freeriding can be diminished to sustain solidarity relationships. One strand of arguments is based on the force of *norms*: Group members comply with their obligations due to the moral expectations and universal principles. The other strand of arguments is based on the *rational choice* assumption that only coercion can guarantee compliance. Both positions are united by the statement that group members have to exit the group if they do not comply and thus hurt the group.

Normative approach:

Baurmann follows a moral argumentation: „A principle of universalisation forbids placing the burdens of mutually desired goods only on the shoulders of others. Acting in solidarity to promote a public good under such conditions, therefore, is solidarity out of fairness" (Baurmann 1999: 245). Only the *principle of universalisation* can sustain solidarity if „there are not enough incentives for acting in solidarity out of self-interest" (Baurmann 1999: 251). The problem of lacking incentives cannot be resolved by putting in place institutions, since institutions are only implemented if the basic problem of the possibility to defect is resolved. Institutions are also public goods, which is why problems of „opportunistic exploitation" can occur (Baurmann 1999: 256). If a group member does not follow its solidarity obligations, it has to leave the community (Haversath 2012). In order to prevent the exiting of members, solidarity has also a *normative function*, which keeps members together. Therefore, it is the pre-existing bond, which determines the expectations towards solidarity. When expectations are met, the bond gets stronger. Haversath calls this interdependence „cycle of cooperation" (Haversath 2012). Also Hondrich and Koch-Arzberger argue that solidarity can be stabilised over time by institutionalisation or organisation. However, this is a voluntary act based on emotional bonds (1992: 22).

In order to differentiate between the daily connotation of solidarity, which is basically a normative understanding of solidarity as positive behaviour, it is important for the scientific understanding to distance the term from emotional ballast.

> „Solidarität ist nicht an sich gut oder schlecht, sondern bezeichnet lediglich die Fähigkeit einer Gruppe, ihre Mitglieder zur Kooperation oder zu Verzichtsleistungen zu bewegen. Diese kann stark oder schwach, stabil oder instabil sein. Solidarität kann dazu führen, dass sozial schwächere Mitglieder einer Gruppe unterstützt werden, aber ebenso dazu, dass Außenseiter oder ‚Fremde' marginalisiert, ausgeschlossen oder bekämpft werden" (Engler 2016: 32).

Solidarity measures are consequently enacted by *formal and informal rules*, which are determined by the solidarity norm enforced collectively by the group. This might result in a relinquishment or in an advantage to the benefit of the group. Over time, the solidarity norm is incorporated by the group, however, group members might also fail to accomplish the informal and formal rules. This behaviour might be acceptable to a certain degree and result in variations of costs and benefits. In the case that rules are overstretched, the group punishes the group member with *sanctions*, i.e. fines or exclusion (Engler 2016: 35). Beutler assumes that genuine solidarity means that solidarity is made explicit in real actions introduced by an *enforcing institutional system* (Beutler 2017: 27f.).

Rational choice approach:

Hechter's definition of group solidarity is based on rational choice perspective. The preliminary assumption is that individuals form a group in order to produce a joint product, which they could not produce on their own. However, once the agreement is established, the problem occurs on how to *avoid freeriding*. One of his major concerns focuses on the questions how to establish rules and how to guarantee the compliance with obligations. „An adequate theory of group solidarity must be able to explain variation in the extensiveness of corporate obligations and in a group's capacity to induce its members to honour these obligations" (Hechter 1988: 40). *Sanctions are necessary* „(b)ecause there is often a conflict of interest between the individual and the group" (Hechter 1988: 41). There are a number of situations, where conflict does not arise, because compliance is not costly, and non-compliance would even create costs (e.g. driving on the right side of the street).

Hechter develops the following framework: group members always choose their individual aim instead of the collective aim; furthermore, group obligations usually don't comply with the interests of the individual member. The dependence of each group member varies since the neediness of each group member to be part of the group to produce a joint product is different. But only if the consumption of the joint product exceeds the costs of its production, members will remain in the group.

Group members are obliged to produce the joint product; therefore, members face certain costs. The extensiveness of the obligation depends on the costs of production. A cost extensive good will also entail a high level of obligations. However, obligations alone are not sufficient to create solidarity. „What also matters is the probability that members will comply with these obligations" (Hechter 1988: 49). If members can access the good without contributing to its production, the group faces a *problem of compliance*. Therefore, a group – in order to work properly and to remain legitimate – needs *control capacity* in order to assure compliance and to punish free-riders. Additionally, a group needs to have sufficient resources in order to create a *system of possible rewards and penalties* that corresponds to members' performance. Hechter calls this a „group's sanctioning capacity" (Hechter 1988: 50).

Van Oorschot and Komter describe that according to Parsons „the essence of solidarity behaviour is that it derives from and conforms to institutionalised role obligations" (Van Oorschot and Komter 1998: 9). Furthermore „(s)olidarity behaviour means that one conforms to the solidarity obligations of one's role. The actual degree to which a collectivity can have its interests served by its members (i.e. the de facto internal level of solidarity) is thus a function of the degree to which *the collectivity succeeds in imposing solidarity obligations* on its members" (Van Oorschot and Komter 1998: 9, emphasis added). Group members only accept sanctions, if they are unlimited, adequate and expeditious. The exclusion of a member is the last option.

Also, the *monitoring capacity* is of importance as regards the interplay of control and compliance. The less efficient non-compliance can be monitored, the less possible is an adequate and expeditious sanction. Control mechanisms are not only costly, there are also situations which are difficult to control. Does the output of a member reflect its input? Is it possible to monitor all actions? The implementation of solidarity is therefore dependent on the compliance with concomitant obligations. Since freeriding is for each member the best strategy, no member would voluntarily take up the task to control others' behaviour. Therefore, the task is often carried out by *agents*.

Box 6: Ensuring Solidarity

To sum up, the following aspects are important regarding the category „compliance":

A. Compliance mechanisms are necessary in order to avoid freeriding.
B. Normative compliance:
   - Principles or norms make group members stick to their obligations;
   - Solidarity can be stabilised if group members trust each other due to successful solidarity action in the past;
   - Group members act out of fairness;
   - Group members act according to a solidarity norm.
C. Rational choice compliance:
   - Control capacity ensures compliance and punishes free-riders;
   - Group's sanctioning capacity is the capacity of a group's system to instruct rewards and penalties. Solidarity is dependent on the collectivity's ability to impose solidarity obligations;
   - The monitoring capacity tracks compliance with the obligations;
   - Agents are necessary to set up the compliance system since group members would fail to comply due to their own interests.

In this chapter, I identified the most important features of solidarity, which are the actors, the rules and obligations as well as compliance. Actors and forms are dependent on the research object. There is however a diverging line concerning compliance between two general strands of arguments, which are either normative-based or rational choice based assumptions. Taylor makes based on a normative argumentation a difference between expressional and robust solidarity. Expressional solidarity is not ensured since it is based on moral reasons only. Robust solidarity on the other hand is obliged by norms, which is why it is reliable. Hechter based his analysis on rational choice arguments highlighting the problem of compliance. He underlines that due to the problem of free riders a compliance system is essential. Engler takes up a position in between both camps by underlining the importance of sanctions. A solidarity norm ensures that group members act according to their obligations. A certain degree of non-accomplishment might even be tolerated, but if a certain threshold is reached, sanctions would be necessary.

In the following chapter, I carry out an analysis of definitions and discussions on EU solidarity in order to develop a more precise understanding of intergovernmental solidarity. I use the categories, which I identified in this chapter and adapt those accordingly to EU solidarity. Finally, I derive from the analysis of the different categories my definition of solidarity between Member States and define the features of this solidarity relationship.

2.1.5. Concept formation of solidarity between Member States

Solidarity can be found in a variety of places and at different levels. My concept of solidarity refers to actions which happen on the EU level, that is in this case between Member States. Solidarity has been evoked between Member States during the last years for different reasons, which are the Euro Crisis, the Refugee Crisis, the Gas Crises and in the face of emergencies such as floods and fires. In case of the Health Crisis (COVID-19 pandemic) Member States called for European solidarity since they could not anymore self-provide intubation machines, respiratory masks or other medical equipment. The treatment of patients in other Member States was declared as solidarity action. Also, foreign policy problems (e.g. Turkey's gas drilling at the shore of Cyprus) are regularly followed by a call for solidarity between the Member States. Additionally, the principle of solidarity is carried through in different policy fields even though this might not be spelled out: Member States receive special aids if they suffer from trade agreements, the cohesion policy aims at reducing major economic and social differences on the regional level and the overall budget. These actions are all representing acts of solidarity (Devuyst 2000: 22f.). There are thus different real-world phenomena where solidarity is voiced and eventually implemented.

Solidarity is a complex notion since it is interpreted very differently: „(…) there is very little analysis of what the nature of solidarity *is*, or why we should feel particularly moved by an appeal to it" (Sangiovanni 2013: 215, emphasis by author). This is particularly true for literature related to studies on the European Union.

> „Regardless of these theoretical premises, the questions of what lies behind solidarity, how it is generated in practice, and what its implications are all remain unclear (…). Most crucially, whether and to

what extent the complexities of solidarity practices and ideas can be transferred from a national to a European level is still highly contested in social scientific theoretical debates" (Greiner 2017: 841).

The research interests of the authors are manifold, which is why there is further groundwork on solidarity necessary. In the following, I uncover the different features of Member State solidarity.

Which aspects are important for EU Solidarity?

As already pointed out solidarity is part of the history of the EU. However, it remains as principle largely in the shadows even though it is a popular term. In the next step, I puzzle out the different approaches to EU solidarity in order to see which aspects are of importance for solidarity. As starting ground, I use the categories which I developed in the chapter before:

- Group cohesion: Which actors are included? Aims of the actors/group.
- Forms of solidarity: Solidarity rights and obligations (reciprocity).
- Compliance and conditionality: How is solidarity monitored and ensured?

The literature on EU solidarity comprises different studies on the development of EU law or the interpretation of solidarity as legal principle (Karagiannis 2007; Boutayeb and Laurent 2011; Calliess 2011; Domurath 2012; Härtel 2012). Political Sciences provide different studies on transnational solidarity which have been published in the recent years. Transnational studies worked on the conditions for and implications of transnational solidarity, i.e. solidarity between EU citizens (Federico and Lahusen 2018; Gerhards et al. 2020). Solidarity between Member States has been addressed by Saracino (2019) and Grimmel (2020). Andrea Sangiovanni contributed to the research area with different articles on the link between social justice and solidarity as well as understanding solidarity as political norm (Sangiovanni 2013 and 2015). In the following, I present reflections and results of the literature on solidarity between Member States.

Actors: different solidarity groups on the EU level

There are different forms of solidarity on the EU level. Kleger and Mehlhausen (2013) underline the importance to look at the different levels of solidarity, which might be *international, transnational, supranational* and *intergovernmental* (2013: 56). A similar approach is taken up by Knodt and Tews (2014).

Knodt and Tews underline that in the complex multi-level system there are different actors who can act in solidarity. Therefore, they refer to four different levels, on which solidarity between individual and collective actors can be found. These different categories of solidarity can be located on a horizontal and a vertical axis and depend on an individual or collective thinking: transnational, international, supranational and intergovernmental (Knodt and Tews 2014). This can be helpful as solidarity can thus be studied by taking into consideration different processes and responsible actors. Kadelbach identifies three different uses of solidarity in the treaties. 1) Solidarity expresses – similar to loyalty – fidelity with the aims of the union. 2) Solidarity is a value of the society proclaiming social rights, which is also reflected in the Union's citizenship. 3) Federal solidarity comprises actions to reduce large imbalances in prosperity among the member states, carrying jointly specific burdens and supporting each other in emergency situations (Kadelbach 2014: 16). Kadelbach differentiates thus 1) solidarity between the EU and its Member States, 2) solidarity between European citizens and 3) solidarity between the Member States.

Next to these level-related solidarities, Härtel claims that there is a time difference. Either we speak about „synchronic solidarity" which describes present solidarity actions or about „diachronic solidarity" which can be found between generations or in favour of the future generation (Härtel 2014: 228).

Transnational solidarity can be found between individuals of different nation states who are united by a common goal. Knodt and Tews cite as example the French Revolution but also today's movements such as Attac or the European Trade Union Conference (Knodt and Tews 2014). Lahusen and Federico argue that solidarity takes always place between individuals, but the level is different (micro, meso and macro) and groups can be formal or informal types (Federico and Lahusen 2018: 18). Härtel argues that both the constitutional state as well as the welfare state are based on the individual's solidarity comprehension (Härtel 2014: 231). Karagiannis (2007) underlines that solidarity functions as cement of society and is needed as such in Europe since societies are very heterogenous, but it could also be argued that „solidarity within Europe exists as the reflection of a relatively homogenous society" (Karagiannis 2007: 5).

Supranational solidarity also refers to individuals but can be found on the vertical scale. The source to act in solidarity is European identity. Examples are the European citizenship, which guarantees equal rights to other European citizens when they move within the EU.

International solidarity underlines the feeling of solidarity with societies and states beyond the Union. This is similar to the cosmopolitan approach to solidarity. International solidarity includes development policy but also aspects of climate policy.

Intergovernmental solidarity refers to solidarity between Member States. Membership solidarity is created due to challenges which could not be solved on the national level alone: „(l)a solidarité entre États est certainement d'une nature différente de celle qui peut exister entre des individus. Elle résulte de la coopération entre des gouvernements qui mettent en commun, pour des raisons d'intérêt partagé, des échanges de bons procédés" (Barbier 2012: 3). Ferreira-Pereira and Groom (2010: 596) argue that solidarity is associated with the inner cohesion of the EU. Solidarity is the cement which holds the Member States tightly together despite the different historical and emotional experiences and remembrances between them. It creates a ,we' perspective, which is a huge difference in comparison to other international organisations. Solidarity serves thus as integrative element, which has been historically part of the development of the EU and formed the relations between the Member States. Hartwig and Nicolaides claim, that solidarity is difficult to apply for the EU since the EU is lacking a we-feeling, which is a prerequisite for solidarity (Hartwig and Nicolaides 2003: 21). Dziedzic claims that solidarity is only possible if actions are based on an „us-modus". Groups, which function according to the „us-modus", act due to a common group ethos and because they are conscious that collective projects can only be jointly executed. This assumption leads the author to the statement, that solidarity between Member States is deficient (Dziedzic 2019). Even though there are different reasons why groups form in solidarity, cohesion is a necessary element for solidarity. „Cohesion is the degree to which group members stick together" (Willer et al. 2002: 67). The level of solidarity depends also on the trust developed in the past and the future expectations. Out of these experiences a shared norm or value arises (Ferreira-Pereira and Groom 2010: 596 f.).

The theoretical background of the sources of solidarity has been already depicted in the according chapter (ch. 2.1.3). The literature provides us with different reasons and aims why European actors implement solidarity. Authors refer to the community of interest (Boutayeb and Laurent 2011; Barbier 2012), interdependence and community of interests (Knodt and Tews 2017; Kleger and Mehlhausen 2013) as well as risk pools (Talus 2013).

> „Le dénominateur commun qui lie les différentes émanations de la solidarité dans le cadre de l'Union consiste en la reconnaissance de l'existence d'un « intérêt commun », séparé et séparable de la somme des intérêts individuels, et dont l'articulation autant que la défense est confiée à des institutions communes ainsi qu'aux Etats membres" (Bieber and Maiani 2012: 295).

Badanova (2019) and Bayertz (1998) underline that there must be a sense of community. The interdependence between the group members leads to the mutual understanding that every group member is important to reach the overall goals, which create the sense of community. This perception emphasises also the importance of the equality between the group members (Badanova 2019: 113). Grimmel believes that solidarity must be an act of selflessness excluding self-interest (Grimmel 2020: 8). Sangiovanni's approach is a reflection on how the EU should be designed. The principal aim of EU integration is to reach certain goals which would be unreachable without integration (Sangiovanni 2013). Others argue that solidarity is founded on the social bond between people (Talus 2013) or it serves as cement of a heterogenous society (Karagiannis 2007).

Box 7: Solidarity actors on the EU level

To sum up, the category „actors" entails the following aspects:

A. European solidarity exists on different levels, which can be outlined as follows:
   - Transnational solidarity (National citizens with other national citizens);
   - Supranational solidarity (EU citizens);
   - International solidarity (EU with the world);
   - Intergovernmental solidarity (between Member States).
B. Additionally, in the treaties we find solidarity:
   - Between generations (diachronic);
   - Between the EU and the Member States.
C. Features of intergovernmental solidarity:
   - Member States share interests, risks, burdens, challenges or goals;
   - Member States have a sense of community;
   - The common interest is favoured over the national interest;
   - Member States are interdependent;
   - Trust developed in the past due to successful cooperation;
     -> Member State solidarity is based on some form of cohesion.
D. Solidarity as norm:
   - Member States are aware of the cohesive bond and they identify with the Community;
   - Member States share the conviction that it is necessary to act in favour of the group's (or single group members) interest;
   - Serves as cement to hold them together, as integrative element;
   - Creates a ‚we'-perspective.

Forms of solidarity: rights and obligations between Member States

‚To help and support each other' (Boutayeb and Laurent 2011; Härtel 2012; Federico and Lahusen 2018) is one form how the implementation of solidarity can be understood.

> „Offenbar heißt ja Solidarität zuerst Hilfe und Unterstützung: Ein Mitgliedstaat hilft einem anderen (in Not geratenen) Mitgliedstaat, weil dieser der Hilfe bedarf. In diesem Sinn ist Solidarität eine Art aus freiwilliger Motivation entstandener Beistand und eine durch das Verständnis der Situation des anderen geprägte Unterstützungsleistung, die gleichwohl darauf vertraut, dass *auch im umgekehrten Falle Unterstützung und Beistand geleistet werden*. Diese Haltung hat dann im EUV ihren rechtlich bindenden Niederschlag gefunden: Moralisch-praktische und rechtliche Selbstbindungen der Mitgliedstaaten der föderalen Europäischen Union sind auch hier aufeinander bezogen" (Härtel 2014: 225, emphasis added).

In general, Member States share „(…) attitudes like solidarity or patriotism that imply a willingness (or a socially stabilized obligation) to accept personal sacrifices in the interest of (other members of) the political community" (Scharpf 2016: 22). Lais (2007) calls this „materielles Solidaritätsprinzip" (substantive solidarity principle). Substantive solidarity includes all arrangements, which aim at fair burden sharing, that states have to carry out due to EU membership (Lais 2007: 263). Härtel describes further that solidarity moves between two poles. One pole is „strong solidarity", which is the obligation to help each other and the other pole is „weak solidarity", which is the obligation not to harm each other (Härtel 2014: 228).

According to Boutayeb and Laurent solidarity is based on a relationship between different individuals forming a community of interest with the aim to support each other and to refrain from actions which could harm other partners (Boutayeb and Laurent 2011: 9). The authors depict two basic elements which can be found in community law: an active and a passive form of solidarity (ibid.). The passive form of solidarity refers to its constitutional character as value of the Union but also as regards the institutional system. Therefore, solidarity is rather static. But as result from the use of solidarity as fundamental value of solidarity, the aspiration has grown that also an active solidarity develops, therefore, putting in place *mechanisms of help and support* (Boutayeb and Laurent 2011: 10). Federico and Lahusen draw

„three general lessons from scholarly writing: First, solidarity is a relationship of support tied to (informal or formal) rights and obligations; second, solidarity might have universalist orientations but is most of the time conditional; and third, solidarity is institutionalised at several interdependent levels of aggregation" (Federico and Lahusen 2018: 15).

Group solidarity depends on the level of exchange relations among the members, these might be formalised rights and obligations or voluntary measures (Federico and Lahusen 2018: 18). To sum up, help might come voluntarily or linked to (informal or formal) rights and obligations, might be conditional and is connected with the expectation that similar support can be expected from the group member, which received help (reciprocity).

Collective action literature provides different approaches to reciprocity. Keohane analysed reciprocity in the framework of international relations. Reciprocity means not only the exchange of something good, but it might also mean that bad is returned for bad. There is no clarity, if reciprocity is mutually beneficial, if it is based on self-interest or on obligations. Also, the exchanged goods might not be comparable in value (Keohane 1986: 8). Keohane developed the concepts of specific and diffuse reciprocity. While specific reciprocity is clearly formulated, diffuse reciprocity is less predictable. According to the author, only countries which are linked by far-reaching joint interests would evolve towards diffuse reciprocity.

„Perhaps the closest approximations to diffuse reciprocity on a global level are found in international integration processes involving "upgrading the common interest," such as Haas discovered in the early years of European integration efforts. In such international regimes, actors recognize that a "veil of ignorance" separates them from the future but nevertheless offer benefits to others on the assumption that these will redound to their own advantage in the end" (Keohane 1986: 23).

Putnam's definition of reciprocity can be grouped together with diffuse reciprocity, since he interprets reciprocity as a „continuing relationship of exchange that is at any given time unrequited or imbalanced, but that involves mutual expectations that a benefit granted now should be repaid in the future" (Putnam et al. 1993: 172). Sangiovanni argues that European Integration leads to winners and losers, but it is unclear who will benefit and who will be burdened.

„By pooling these risks in a fair way, member states agree to constraints on the pursuit of the best overall outcome for their own citizens. The idea of insurance gives us a fruitful way to express the notion that *solidarity is best understood as a kind of reciprocity among states*" (Sangiovanni 2013: 230, emphasis added).

Boutayeb and Laurent underline that solidarity is carried out in relation to reciprocity and interdependence. The notion of reciprocity is repetitively seen in the treaties, described as mutual assistance („concours mutuel") (Boutayeb and Laurent 2011: 9). Talus states that solidarity has two different notions. One refers to the inherent idea of solidarity as social bond between the peoples of Europe. „The second type of solidarity notion is that of a risk pool: i.e. an agreement between states to intervene on a reciprocal basis if one encounters unforeseen difficulties – one for all and all for one" (Talus 2013: 278). Knodt and Tews argue that intergovernmental solidarity depends on a cost-benefit calculation. Member States benefit from e.g. the internal market but have also to calculate the possible costs resulting from free movement in the social system. Therefore, the Member States need to have a medium or even long-term perspective regarding their cost-benefit calculation because reciprocity might be delivered only belatedly. These preconditions lead the authors to the assumption that risk-seeking Member States are less willing to support solidarity than risk-averse Member States. Therefore, it is the group's risk perception which is decisive for the member's contribution to solidarity (Knodt and Tews 2017: 54). Crisis situations would also lead to less solidarity because decisions are taken on a short-time perspective. Another limit to solidarity would be the incapability of Member States to cross-issue calculate. By taking into account different policy fields, Member States are rather willing to accept solidarity (Knodt and Tews 2017: 53f.). Hence, reciprocity takes on various forms. Talus' understanding of a risk pool is similar to the precautionary principle. Member States act in solidarity because they are risk adverse. Solidarity works thus as insurance mechanism (Talus 2013). Domurath underlines that „in the absence of a prospect of reciprocal benefits, actors are reluctant to achieve consensus on solidary obligations" (Domurath 2012: 12). This would consequently mean that solidarity is connected to self-interest.

Fernandes and Rubio (2012) make reference to an insurance scheme as well. The authors discuss in their policy paper the features of (inter-state) solidarity within the Eurozone. They argue that there are two different rationales, which are

„a rationale based on direct reciprocity (I help the others so that they will help me in the future in case of need) and a rationale based on ‚enlightened self-interest' (I help the others because I know that acting in the interest of other EU members or in the interests of the EU as a whole ultimately serves my own self-interest)" (Fernandes and Rubio 2012: 4).

The authors refer to Durkheim's understanding of organic solidarity for their conceptualisation. Solidarity, which is understood as direct reciprocity, is similar to insurance-type schemes. The risk of e.g. being hit by a natural disaster is almost evenly dispersed in all Member States, which is why they support a risk-sharing pool, which they call solidarity. As examples serve Art. 222 regarding natural disasters but also responses to terrorism. The second type ‚enlightened self-interest solidarity' refers to actions by Member States, which support other Member States, which in return serve the Member States, which helped in the first place. As example serves the Cohesion Fund. Member States are willing to contribute financially, because the supported Member States develop thus economically faster, which has positive effects on the overall economic development in the EU (Fernandes and Rubio 2012: 4f.). If risk is rather equally spread, Member States can be easier convinced to act in ‚solidarity'. In the case of security, however, gains and risks are more difficult to measure, and the direct effect of an action is not always tangible. Trein develops the concept of negative solidarity and argues that this kind of solidarity is based on the calculation of repayment. Member States would only be interested in protecting their own property. Negative solidarity could even result in disintegration if those Member States evaluate that they are better off on their own (Trein 2020: 980).

Clearly, gains and risks are usually not equally spread between issues and Member States. Sangiovanni reflects about an insurance system, which determines the costs and benefits for each Member State. It is „a kind of solidarity, in which we share the burdens of each other's misfortune as it materializes within a mutually beneficial cooperative scheme" (Sangiovanni 2013: 19). Sangiovanni claims further, that

„the EU is best understood as a way for member states to enhance their problem-solving capacities in an era of globalization, while indemnifying each other against the risks and losses implicit in integration. By pooling these risks, we, as European citizens, agree to share one another's fates, to preserve our commitments to domestic solidarity, and to give each other the fair return expressed by the internationalist ideal" (Sangiovanni 2013: 29).

Consequently, there are two different forms of reciprocity. The risk pool refers to a joint organisation of an insurance-type scheme, i.e. Member States pay in a fund that all can access in case of urgency or funds are available to projects that meet different criteria. The other understanding of reciprocity (I call it direct reciprocity) occurs when a Member State supports another Member State immediately by providing e.g. equipment. Both forms have in common that solidarity is translated into a concrete mechanism.

Solidarity depends not only on the risk perception of one group member, but it is also subject to the will of the single group members to support others. There are different aspects which influence the willingness to act in solidarity.

- Solidarity can either be applied universally without any conditions or expectations, or it can be *limited depending on the group and depending rights*. When solidarity is *voluntary*, the readiness to support someone else is strongly dependent on the person's *neediness* (Federico and Lahusen 2018: 17); solidarity takes place in *situations of need* (e.g. *third-party responsibility*) (Boutayeb and Laurent 2011: 9).
- If a situation is self-conflicted, e.g. because a group member acted irresponsibly, the will to act in solidarity is reduced (Steinvorth 2017: 13). As consequence only conditional solidarity might be provided (Kneuer 2017: 22).
- Neediness is also coupled with fairness in that sense that the distribution of benefits and burdens must be considered as fair (Scharpf 1988: 263).

Box 8: Forms of solidarity between EU Member States

To sum up, the following features are important in the category „forms of solidarity":

A. Solidarity means to help and support each other:
   Normative approach:
   - Help comes voluntarily without direct payment and is unconditional;
   - Help and the willingness to help are expected by the group members;
   - Help might come in form of a sacrifice.

RC approach:
- Help is linked to (informal or formal) rights and obligations;
- Help is conditional and connected with the expectation that similar support can be expected from the group member, which received help (reciprocity).

B. Solidarity means also to refrain from actions which could harm the other(s).

C. Group members act reciprocally for two reasons:
- Group members are risk-averse and want to ensure to receive help in the future by taking part in a risk pool;
- Group members help since they know that support of others can contribute to the overall well-being of the group. Solidarity may pay off for themselves at a later point in time.

D. Solidarity is conditioned by:
- The group member might not be self-responsible for the difficult situation. Solidarity is applied in situations in need (when the situation is not self-inflicted). Therefore, solidarity is implemented on the basis of third-party responsibility, deservingness and neediness (the distribution of burdens and benefits must be fair);
- If the group member is to blame itself (deservingness is small), group members will take punitive measures (e.g. unattractive aid);
- The group member which receives help must show own efforts to resolve the situation.

Compliance and monitoring: How is solidarity ensured?

The „forms of solidarity" depicted under what conditions solidarity is implemented and the limits to it. But how is solidarity ensured? And what form of compliance system is implemented? Theoretical reflections have demonstrated that freeriding is a fundamental problem both for normative as for rational choice approaches to solidarity. Since there is an apparent lack of literature on the theoretical implications of solidarity compliance mechanisms on the EU level, I will in the following derive those mechanisms from secondary literature.

Härtel carries out that the fundament of the EU is the self-commitment of the Member States to adhere to the principles and values of the EU (Härtel 2012: 94).

„Member States are subject to an integrative pressure, meaning that they have to comply with Community/EU law. They need to apply European rules on the one hand, and on the other hand eliminate national rules -and refrain from adopting new measures- that are contrary to European law" (Saurugger and Terpan 2013: 7).

But is self-commitment sufficient to put solidarity in action? The credible commitment theory suggests that agents need as a precondition credible commitment in order to secure agreements and to avoid freeriding (Weale 2016: 189). Credible commitments include

> „a willingness to be monitored in one's behaviour; transparency in conduct and disposition; the existence of benefits conditional upon compliance with the rules; the existence of mechanisms of punishment conditional upon non-compliance; devices for self-binding; and vesting crucial decision-making powers in an authority distinct from the parties to the agreement" (ibid.).

Langford argues that trust between Member States is limited since Member States do not comply with „common standards with respect to asylum seekers" as regards human rights violations (Langford 2013: 218). But ‚true' solidarity can only be reached if compliance with secondary legislation is reached. This underlines the necessity of compliance in order to make solidarity work. Langford concludes that different compliance standards with the legislative framework cause „mistrust and resentment between member states" (Langford 2013: 264). This does not only entail that Member States themselves comply with the rules but also that they „(...) make honest assessments of other members' compliance with EU and international law and exert appropriate diplomatic pressure when needed to prevent violations" (Langford 2013: 264f.). Thus, trust between Member States is dependent on compliance. Only if Member States act reliably, trust is sufficiently established to put solidarity in action. It is, however, questionable if Member States are willing to assess the compliance of other EU Member States. Member States (also in the form of the European Council) are usually reluctant to denounce others (Pech and Scheppele 2017; Heinkelmann-Wild and Zangl 2019). Therefore, other agents (such as the Commission) need to ensure compliance in order to generate trust.

Keohane claims that trust (he calls it confidence) emerges also if members of a social system are mutually indebted. Staying indebted leads to further exchange in contrast to „simultaneous exchange, (when) obligations never exist, since the exchange is balanced at every moment" (Keohane 1986: 22). Tsourdi and De Bruycker claim that it is difficult to measure if Member States were assuming sufficient responsibility regarding their duties in the Common European Asylum System.

„Therefore, any claim by a Member State that it is ‚overburdened' cannot be objectively substantiated, and raises the suspicion among the others, who are also called on to carry part of the protection responsibility. This has led EU institutions to highlight that ‚it is fundamental to increase trust to strengthen solidarity'" (Tsourdi and De Bruycker 2015: 5).

But how would trust be ensured? The Commission states in the same document (COM(2011)835), that trust can be built by implementing better management systems as well as proper application and evaluation. Garlick, however, does not believe that full compliance is necessary.

„Full compliance with asylum obligations may not be realistic or meaningful as a precondition of solidarity. However, an approach is needed which incentivises Member States to invest in and use all available means to ensure their asylum systems function in an optimal way as far as possible" (Garlick 2014: 5).

Therefore, Garlick underlines the importance of responsibility in comparison to compliance, which eventually also generates trust. Habermas differs between different compliance mechanisms:

„*Moral commands* should be obeyed out of respect for the underlying norm itself without regard to the compliance of other persons, whereas the citizen's *obedience to the law* is conditional on the fact that the sanctioning power of the state ensures general compliance. Fulfilling an *ethical obligation*, by contrast, can neither be enforced nor is it categorically required. *It depends instead on the expectations of reciprocal favors — and on the confidence in this reciprocity over time*" (Habermas 2013: 8, emphasis by author).

Tsourdi and De Bruycker describe that there is a difference between the „inability to comply" and the „unwillingness to comply", which explains „current tensions between Member States in terms of distributing responsibilities" (Tsourdi and De Bruycker 2015: 6). Tsourdi and De Bruycker conclude that trust can only be built if there is an assessment of responsibility, which could also monitor if Member States are underperforming and thus do not live up to their national share of responsibility (Tsourdi and De Bruycker 2015: 8). Help – even in the context of solidarity – might come with conditions. *Conditionality* is thus the key for responsibility:

„(…) a constructive purpose (guaranteeing the most effective use of the aid deployed and inducing the country to undertake the necessary parallel reforms to get out from the situation of neediness) and a punitive purpose (making the aid provided as unattractive as possible to reduce the risk of moral hazard. I.e., the risk the recipient country behave irresponsibly in the future on the belief that it will be again helped in case of need)" (Fernandes and Rubio 2012: 7).

Domurath (2012) points out that the content of solidarity is determined by the Member States who either refrain from action, or send not the help, which is demanded. There is confusion about the obligations, and actions are often uncoordinated. Domurath observes a lack of competences on the EU level and proposes indirectly two mechanisms in order to enforce compliance. 1) Solidarity obligations need to be formulated in secondary law. Since obligations remain unclear, „the ECJ cannot operate as a solidarity-promoting authority" (Domurath 2012: 8). 2) If competences are shifted to the EU level, the Commission has automatically more possibilities to monitor policy implementation and to ensure compliance. But literature on the question how the Commission enforces compliance is scarce (Schmälter 2018: 1331).

Thielemann also underlines the importance of monitoring and enforcement mechanisms in order to reach convergence in implementation. Helpful tools in order to enhance convergence are the expansion of the CJEU's jurisdiction and an intensification of the Commission's infringement scrutiny. Additionally, reformed legislation might limit the discretion of Member States (Thielemann 2018: 74). In general, only "substantive co-operation and more credible commitments" (2018: 79) can control the free-rider problem. Compliance is a second-order problem since Member States need in a first step to jointly decide to implement obligations accompanied by self-responsibility and monitoring mechanisms.

Box 9: Ensuring solidarity between EU Member States

A. The ‚normative approach' claims that assurance of compliance is not necessary due to the confidence in reciprocity over time.

B. The ‚rational choice approach' claims that compliance is necessary in order to create trust and to generate stable solidarity.
   - The difference to the normative approach is that the latter includes already that group members are confident, while the RCA claims that trust will only build if group members can rely on each other (exclusion of freeriding).

C. Trust between Member States is endangered by:
   - Non-compliance of obligations by Member States;
   - Lack of assuming responsibility of Member States.

D. Member States would refrain from criticising or denouncing the other Member States. However, they are able to construct the legislative framework in such a way that a possible leeway remains narrow. Possible actions include:
   - Installation of credible commitments;
   - Harmonisation of legislation -> the less discretion the less differences between Member States (limiting discretion of Member States in new legislation);
   - Shifting competences to EU level in order to ensure proper application and evaluation;
   - Expanding the CJEU's jurisdiction;
   - Accepting joint responsibilities;
   - This is why agents, such as the Commission and the CJEU ensure compliance in order to sustain trust between Member States.
E. The EU has different instruments in order to ensure compliance:
   - Monitor policy implementation by e.g. the Commission;
   - Setting common standards;
   - Intensified infringement scrutiny;
   - The ECJ can rule on non-compliance, if solidarity is implemented in secondary law.

2.1.6. Definition and concept of solidarity

The conceptualisation process illustrated the complexity of the term solidarity. Solidarity is equipped with many characteristics both in daily language as well as in academic research, which is why solidarity is so difficult to grasp. Different real-world phenomena are covered by solidarity and – depending on the context – there are many features to interpret an action as solidarity act. These circumstances also explain why expectations arising from solidarity claims vary. I develop a definition and characteristics of solidarity, which determine my concept of solidarity. The concept of solidarity is based on the wide version of rational choice theory entailing the role of norms. The concept shall serve as analytical tool to examine if institutionalised solidarity is actually present in secondary law.

Box 10: Definition of solidarity between EU Member States
„Solidarity is expressed by mutually announced support within a certain group, that shares a sense of community. Group members consent to

joint goals, which can be achieved by collective efforts and assurance of compliance".

The definition is helpful since it covers the strong collective thought of solidarity as well as its normative dimension. At the same time, I underline the importance of the rational choice assumptions on solidarity. The conceptualisation process has illustrated that some characteristics are inherent to the concept of solidarity, while others are contested. But even if there is agreement on the characteristic, there might be differences in the interpretation. In order to make solidarity measurable (which is not quantifiable!), I provide a codebook of the qualitative assessment in annex 2. The following characteristics represent the conditional factors, which constitute solidarity between EU Member States. All three characteristics are intrinsically linked and mutually dependent:

Box 11: Features of solidarity

Group cohesion:
- Trust and responsibility for each other build the core of the group, which is characterised by a shared sense of community.
- A collective interest is formulated and backed by all group members. The collective interest takes precedence over the national interest.

Reciprocity and rules for implementation:
- All group members are obliged to fairly contribute to the production of a certain good.
- All group members have equal rights concerning the provided good dependent on the neediness and deservingness.

Monitoring and self-responsibility:
- The group possesses a control capacity (= monitoring system).
- Group members act self-responsible.

The *cohesion of the group* is an important aspect of solidarity for different reasons. First, solidarity refers to a certain group, which is composed of the Member States. The particular relationship under scrutiny is intergovernmental solidarity. Therefore, solidarity between EU Member States is not classed within cosmopolitan solidarity that follows universal rules. The group is exclusive since it has a shared sense of community. Second, a feeling of responsibility and interdependence within the group are two interwoven factors. Responsibility means in this case to be responsible for the aims of the group. This is not identical with identity but refers to the understanding of the EU as legal and political community. This aspect reflects the normative dimension of solidarity, since the group is the basis for trust-building in the collective entirety. Third, trust plays a crucial role as it ensures that Member States are confident that all group members will follow the common rules and that they will refrain from actions, which could hurt the other members. Trust and responsibility go hand in hand since both terms reflect the bond within a group. Fourth, it is important that the group's interest is collective and not only the sum of all individual interests. This means that there has to be an agreement on the joint goals, which have to be supported by all group members. This legitimises solidarity actions on the EU level. The collective interest takes precedence over the national interest. This might take the form of renouncing national solutions if they distort the collective interest, sacrifices for the Community and the willingness to contribute even though there is no direct benefit.

Reciprocity and rules of implementation is one characteristic of solidarity, which is generally less contested. Reciprocity entails that group members agree to support each other for different reasons. The central point is that all group members follow certain goals, which can only be reached if diffuse reciprocity is in place, i.e. the good in exchange is not absolutely equivalent. This means also that all group members are acknowledged by the other group members as necessary and thus as equal members in order to reach the joint goals. It is also important that all group members have access to the collective product even though there might be certain conditions for the access. The access to the good is dependent on the neediness and deservingness of the group members. Group members, who are or were acting irresponsible, might be deprived of the access. There might be different ways how group members can participate in the production of the collective good, but this contribution must be considered as fair. There are rights and obligations arising from the reciprocal relationship, which result in rules of implementation.

Monitoring and self-responsibility is an aspect owed to the rational choice approach. This feature of solidarity ensures that group members follow the reciprocal rules which goes beyond the norm of ‚sincere cooperation‘. The aim is to ensure compliance of Member States, which is strongly linked to trust and reciprocity. Freeriding is a problem of collective action, which is why compliance must be ensured. First, all group members are self-responsible, which means that they don't rest on the help of others. Self-responsibility is implemented before solidarity is demanded, thus contributing to prevent freeriding. Member States are not willing to engage in solidarity relations as long as there is not sufficient self-responsibility in place, i.e. the capability to resolve problems individually. Therefore, it is ensured that the situation is not self-conflicted. Second, the acceptance to engage in new solidarity relations, where doubts exist about the trustworthiness, also legitimises compliance and sanctioning mechanisms. The EU possesses a compliance mechanism, since the Commission is enabled to monitor the implementation of EU law and to start infringement procedures if necessary. But this refers to obligations arising from secondary law only. This is why the group members must agree to monitor the compliance with the agreed solidarity mechanisms. Therefore, this category covers monitoring systems implemented by secondary law as well as mechanisms which underline the self-responsibility of Member States.

2.1.7. Results

The conceptualisation of solidarity started with a historical and semantic account of the development of solidarity over time. The analysis showed that solidarity 1) is context-bound since it refers to many different situations, 2) changed the meaning over time without losing any former meaning and 3) changes according to the source (motivation factors). These observations led me to a more detailed evaluation of the different sources of solidarity, which revealed, that the form of solidarity depends on the underlying motivation. In order to clarify the characteristics of solidarity, I looked at various definitions. Based on the precedent reflections and the definitions I derived five aspects of solidarity, of which three aspects are of particular relevance to explain the motivation of Member States, which I further analysed. The last part of the conceptualisation process takes into account research results from reflections on EU solidarity. My concept of solidarity extracts the most promising parts of rational choice approaches to solidarity taking into account the role of norms. Norms are expectations, which are generated due to joint perceptions. Norms do not necessarily need compliance and sanctioning mechanisms, if the norm is useful and costless for all (e.g. driving on the right side of the street). As long as norms and interests converge, group members follow norms. Additionally, norms are complied with based on the logic of appropriateness (March and Olsen 1989), which applies according to the political allegiance source. This is where the willingness to show solidarity beyond the self-interest is based. However, although a solidarity community has formulated joint interests, the individual interests might not be in accordance with each other. If the single interest diverges from the norm or if following the norm becomes too costly, compliance and sanctioning mechanisms are necessary in order to institutionalise solidarity. The above-mentioned features of solidarity are not directly quantifiable, which is why a qualitative assessment of the features is necessary to evaluate in how far the features of solidarity are fulfilled. A detailed description on the process of the qualitative analysis is provided in the annex (Code Book – Concept of Solidarity). In the following, I will outline how my concept of solidarity and the chosen theoretical approach intersect and how this connection can contribute to an enhanced understanding of solidarity between Member States and its causes.

2.2. Theoretical framework

I understand solidarity as a particular phenomenon of European integration. European integration theories want to capture the phenomenon of European Integration by casting a particular net of theoretical assumptions. This point of departure requires as such a theory aiming to explain the European integration process. The manifoldness of theories to capture specific elements of European integration has increased over time to a large extent. One reason might be that the EU has undergone continuous transformation. Theories of European integration deal with a "moving target": a political phenomenon that is constantly changing and reshaping itself (Bieling and Lerch 2012: 9). The aim of European integration theories remains however equal: to comprehend and explain the process of integration and how Europe works.

2.2.1. Drivers for solidarity explained by neofunctionalism

European integration theories explain the drivers for (or against) integration. Integration is understood as the outcome of competitive and cooperative relations between different societal and governmental actors on different levels (Hooghe and Marks 2019: 1115). Neofunctionalism has been long time presented as outdated and defective, not least because its inventor himself – Ernst Haas – declared that neofunctionalism is dead. But the theory has proved its resistance and still enjoys application (Greer 2006; Niemann and Ioannou 2015) as well as variations (Sandholtz and Stone Sweet 2010; de Búrca 2005; Schmitter 2005; Greer and Löblová 2017; Haroche 2020). I consider the application of this theory as particularly useful since neofunctionalism „(…) is held up as a partial, wide-ranging theory that views integration as a dynamic and dialectical process, potentially helpful when analysing decision-making and policy development" (Stephenson 2010: 1042).

Neofunctionalism is based on the ontological assumption that the individualisation of society leads to more interdependence between the individuals (Wolf 2012: 56). Modern societies are coined by functional differentiation. Emile Durkheim argued that this evolution of society would lead consequently to solidarity, since no individual would be able to carry out all tasks. Haas did not further reflect on solidarity (at least not between Member States) but concluded that the core of analysis are thus the political constraints resulting from the increasing cross-border (transnational) societal interdependence for the political actors entrusted with decision making (Wolf 2012: 56). Neofunctionalism tries to identify the drivers for European Integration, and it provides us (at least the updated versions by Niemann 2006 and by Schmitter and Niemann in Wiener and Diez 2009) with a specific worldview including the nature of human beings, the relevance of actors in decision-making processes and certain expectations on how institutions are designed and how they develop a life of their own.

Haas defines political integration as follows:

> „*Political integration is the process whereby political actors in several distinct national settings are persuaded to shift their loyalties, expectations and political activities toward a new centre, whose institutions possess or demand jurisdiction over the pre-existing national ones*" (Haas 1958: 16, emphasis by author).

The process results in a „new political community, superimposed over the pre-existing ones" (Haas 1958: 16). This definition illuminates that integration is a process which leads to a political community (without any clarification on which kind of community) with new political institutions at its centre. *Actors* in the process are not only Member States, but also *institutions*, which have their own powers and goals, and, thus, slip through the control of Member States.

> „(…) (I)nstitutions can take on a life of their own and are difficult to control by those who created them. Concerned with increasing their own powers, supranational institutions become agents of integration, which can influence the perceptions of elites', and therefore governments' (national), interest" (Niemann 2006: 16).

Neo-functionalism defines *actors* as rational and self-interested, however, they have imperfect knowledge and must usually act under pressure arising from time or crisis (Schmitter 2005: 259). This leads to incremental decision-making and results in often unintended developments of political processes (Wolf 2012: 57). „(...) (M)ost political actors are incapable of long-range purposive behaviour since they 'stumble' from one decision into the next as a result of earlier decisions" (Niemann 2006: 16). Actors (e.g. member governments) perceive their *interests* not only in a national frame but are able to change their preferences and adapt to the European context (Niemann and Schmitter 2009: 48). Hence interests are *not static*.

Norms (understood as social learning and the impact of epistemic communities) have a crucial role in neofunctionalism since actors tend to incorporate new loyalties once the centre of policy making shifted to the supranational level. "(A)gents are more likely to enter into new relationships following an instrumental rationale, but tend to develop certain norms and identities and may change their preferences as a result of their experience and interaction" (Niemann 2006: 25). The theory explains the reasons for *collective action*, which is stipulated by the role of supranational actors and spill-over effects. The functional understanding of interdependence applies also to political elites who would change their preferences, that are per se based on self-interest and rationality, supporting co-operative solutions, since the actors see the benefits from integration. Therefore, games are positive-sum games and actors support the upgrading of the common interests by means of compromises (Niemann and Schmitter 2009: 48f.). Supranational institutions, first and foremost the Commission, are eager to find solutions which represent win-win situations. This also reflects the idea of ‚upgrading the common interest'. This approach is the contrary to liberal intergovernmentalist „lowest common denominator bargaining" (Niemann 2006: 19). Haas developed the idea of spillover effects which would automatically occur due to interdependence between single sectors as well as economies (Niemann 2006: 17).

The use of neofunctionalism promises to enlarge the understanding of solidarity on the European Union level. I assume that solidarity is one particular phenomenon of integration, which is why I postulate that neofunctionalism is able to explain why and under which conditions solidarity has been implemented. Solidarity is an expression of supranational integration since it implies that Member States pursue a joint solution, which might include the shifting of competences to the supranational level, but this is not all. Solidarity is enabled by specific features such as diffuse reciprocity and self-responsibility as outlined above. Due to these reasons, I assume that neofunctional assumptions are helpful to analyse the way towards solidarity but at the same time I want to investigate if there are particular conditions in place going beyond neofunctional explanations.

I examine if we can observe spillover effects concerning the application of solidarity as (unclear) political principle. In my research, I will concentrate on two forms of spillover which are functional and cultivated spillover. Political spillover provides the idea that national economic and political elites shift „their expectations, political activities and – according to Haas – even loyalties to a new European centre" (Niemann and Schmitter 2009: 49), because only further integration could resolve problems inherited by the functional-economic logic. Political spillover is not the focus of my research interest as it concentrates on non-governmental elites (Haas 1958) or on political elites (Lindberg 1963). I criticise that this form of spillover is very difficult to measure, since it would be difficult to isolate the effect of lobbying (economic elites) or to measure the shift of expectations from elites towards a new centre. Functional and cultivated spillover are more promising regarding their transformation in measurable variables.

The mentioned assumptions represent the key pillars of a neofunctional explanation of European integration. There are a number of critical voices since neofunctionalism entails a number of flaws and shortcomings. One critique concerns Haas' understanding of spillover as automatic process, which was also later insufficiently elaborated. Another major critical point relates to the limited theoretical implications. Neofunctionalism can only cope with a limited range of questions concerning the dynamics of the integration process (Niemann 2006: 21). Since Haas failed to develop explicit hypotheses (Schmitter 2005: 258), I follow the theoretical reflections by Niemann (2006; Niemann and Ioannou 2015) on how to hypothesise spillover effects.

Spillover effects

The evolvement of integration, which is the notion of change, is explained by the concept of spillover. Spillover effects result in integration outcomes which constitute „a form of integration characterised by increases of both autonomy and authority of supranational bodies on a given issue" (Nicoli 2019: 3). In the following, I will present functional and cultivated spillover as drivers for European integration. Based on these key concepts, I will develop my hypotheses to explain *the implementation of solidarity in secondary law*. In his original work, Haas assumed that integration starts with technical policy fields, which are the playgrounds of experts. Political problems usually do not arise in these areas, which would lead to integration.

> „Ein auf diese unpolitische, technische Art und Weise gestartetes supranationales Kooperationsvorhaben bleibt aber – so Haas' zentrales Diktum – aufgrund gegenstandsimmanenter Faktoren nicht auf den ursprünglichen Bereich der Zusammenarbeit begrenzt, sondern besitzt eine inhärent expansive Logik" (Wolf 2012: 60).

The logic of path-dependency explains why „integration develops in unintended ways, becomes inefficient or contradicts the preferences of major member states" (Schimmelfennig 2018: 974). This might even lead to the unintended integration of further political fields.

Functional spillover

Haas understood functional spillover as economic linkage between policy areas. Niemann argues that Lindberg's assumptions help to revise Haas' concept by stating that functional spillover happens as reaction to attain certain goals (Niemann 2006: 30). The underlying issue of functional spillover is that the original goal needs to be salient to produce functional pressure (Niemann and Ioannou 2015: 200). „Functional interdependencies between policy areas explain why the desire to achieve an original integrative objective may lead to further integration in a related area" (Niemann and Ioannou 2015: 201). The resonance of the interdependence between these sectors is so strong that isolation is impossible. The integration of one sector leads to the integration of another sector, since the problems which resulted from the integration of one sector can be only resolved by the integration of the other sector (Niemann 2006: 17). The wider concept of functional spillover allows to take into account not only economic pressure but „all types of endogenous-functional interdependencies" (Niemann 2006: 30). Based on this assumption, functional spillover applies not only to processes between policy fields, but also to processes within policy fields. However, the functional pressure might lead to different outcomes, which is dependent on the resulting controversies or tensions and their impact on the actors (Lindberg and Scheingold 1970: 117). Two aspects determine how functional pressures impact on further integration:

> „First, when functional dissonances are not balanced or offset through further integrative steps, this may foster shocks or crises that may in the process of their management/mastery generate amplified functional pressures, which are likely to prompt the 'necessary' integrational steps. Second, functional structures do not determine actors'

behaviour in a mechanical or predictable manner. Actors must regard functional logics as plausible or compelling in order for them to un-fold their potential. In other words, functional logics are only as strong as they are perceived by (relevant/important) actors" (Niemann and Ioannou 2015: 1989).

This means that crises might occur due to imperfect integration, which might be resolved by further integration. But further integration is depen-dent on the perception of the decision-makers and alternative solutions might be perceived as too costly. Niemann concludes that – in order to measure this variable – the political discourse serves as verification mechanism. If actors include the perception of functional pressures in the discourse, this will also be reflected in the political decisions (Niemann and Ioannou 2015: 204).

Cultivated spillover

Cultivated spillover is a consequence of the basic assumption of neofunc-tionalism that relevant actors include not only Member States but also oth-er supranational institutions. According to Haas there are three negotia-tion practices in international relations. Classical diplomatic negotiations hardly move beyond the ,lowest common denominator', which is deter-mined by the least cooperative partner (Tranholm-Mikkelsen 1991: 6). As second practice Haas illuminated the importance of a mediatory service, which is capable of „splitting the difference" (Haas 1961: 367). Instead of agreeing on the lowest common denominator, the parties agree to have a mediator who is capable of resolving the conflict between the parties „somewhere between the final bargaining positions" (Haas 1961: 367). Haas states that there is another way how to find common solutions: when parties dispose of an institutionalised but also autonomous mediator, such as the Commission, who is capable of upgrading the common interest, conflicts can be resolved. Involved parties redefine a conflict meaning by finding a solution on a higher level, which implies the extension of the mandate of the mediating institution (Haas 1961: 368). This means that Member States, due to interdependence and pressured by the Commission, change their original positions „(...) and end up resolving their conflicts by conceding a wider scope and devolving more authority to the regional organizations they have created" (Schmitter 2005: 257). Supranational in-stitutions have an inherent interest in more integration since their power and influence is growing accordingly. Thus, the agents might shirk from the control of the Member States and pursue their own interests. The supranational institutions have different possibilities to boost the integration process. Strategies include ‚policy entrepreneurship‘, ‚promotional brokerage‘ ‚strategic framing‘, ‚agenda-setting‘, ‚depolitization‘ and ‚leadership‘ (Niemann and Ioannou 2015: 199: Stephenson 2010: 1045; Rhinard 2010: 2; Schmitter 2005: 257).

2.2.2. Variables and Hypotheses

I situate my research between a positivist and an interpretive position since I follow Niemann's approach that positivism is not able to objectively observe and explain all kinds of social phenomena. At the same time, I support the positivist idea that observations can be made generalisable if the same units are applied (Niemann 2006: 52f.). The main objective of my research is to find out in a detailed process how the policy output (implementation of solidarity) was reached, which is an outcome-centred research design (Gschwend and Schimmelfennig 2007: 9). However, instead of comparing theoretical explanations by using many independent variables, I concentrate on one theory since I want to reveal if my chosen explaining variables have a specific influence on the outcome. Additionally, my research shows if the independent variables have a particular impact on the variance of the dependent variable. My study has an explorative character since I apply a concept of solidarity between Member States, a research area which is still in its infancy. This is another reason, why the exploration of the research area is of great interest. The thesis aims to contribute to reflections on the concept of solidarity between Member States and to the revelation of causes and political motives.

In the next step, I will translate the arguments and considerations of the theoretical approach into variables aiming to pursue my research question: *Why was solidarity implemented in secondary law in the highly securitised field of energy policy?*

The dependent variable (DV) of the research is 'implementation of solidarity'. It is necessary to see how solidarity can be understood and to clarify the features in order to make solidarity denotable. The dependent variable will be further clarified by the analysis in how far solidarity, which is introduced in secondary law, fulfils the characteristics based on my concept. I assume that there is a variance of the dependent variable. ‚Institutionalised solidarity‘ means that solidarity is implemented and ‚declarative solidarity‘ means that solidarity serves only as political notion.

„Die e*xperimentelle Varianz* bezieht sich auf die Varianz (beobachtete Differenzen zwischen den Fällen und/oder Wandel über Zeit) der abhängigen Variablen (Y) aus der Forschungsfrage, die systematisch mit der Varianz der unabhängigen Variable(n) (X) zusammenhängt" (Lauth et al. 2015: 28).

The presentation of neofunctionalism underlined that the interest of this theoretical approach is to explain European integration understood as a process developing towards a political community. Integration is dependent on interdependence between Member States:

„Policy interdependence is a condition-both physical and perceptual—under which governments are so sensitive and vulnerable to what their partners may or may not do that unilateral action becomes unwise and dangerous to their survival. (...) The notion of "integration," however, refers to institutionalized procedures devised by governments for coping with the condition of interdependence: coping, it must be stressed, may take the form of increasing, decreasing, or maintaining interdependence" (Haas 1976: 210).

I derive from this argument, that *solidarity is a particular coping strategy* to encounter interdependence and I assume that solidarity as such is a specific outcome of European integration as can be seen by its legal and political development in the EU over time.

The dependent variable ‚implementation of solidarity' covers references to solidarity, which can be found in secondary law. If the features, which I developed for the concept, are not fully or only partly fulfilled, I call this form ‚*declarative solidarity*'. If all features are present, I call it ‚*institutionalised solidarity*'. The difference between the two is that declarative solidarity is an announcement or an intention. Solidarity in this case is voluntary, uncertain and non-compliance is not sanctioned. Institutionalised solidarity entails rights and obligations. It is obligatory, reciprocal, sanctioned, rewarded or compensated and monitored. Solidarity is politically and legally ensured. To recall, institutionalised solidarity is present when the following characteristics apply:

Box 10: Features of solidarity

Group cohesion:
- Trust and responsibility for each other build the core of the group, which is characterised by a shared sense of community.
- A collective interest is formulated and backed by all group members. The collective interest takes precedence over the national interest.

Reciprocity and rules for implementation:
- All group members are obliged to fairly contribute to the production of a certain good.
- All group members have equal rights concerning the provided good dependent on the neediness and deservingness.

Monitoring and self-responsibility:
- The group possesses a control capacity (= monitoring system).
- Group members act self-responsible.

Therefore, each time solidarity is mentioned in secondary law, I examine whether the characteristics apply in order to see, if it is ‚institutionalised' or ‚declarative' solidarity. The difference is helpful, since it reveals which forms of solidarity are actually applied and the research clarifies the intentions of the policy makers. *Two independent variables* serve as explaining factors for the dependent variable. 1) Functional pressure and 2) influence of the supranational institutions. Based on the variables, I developed the following hypotheses:

Independent Variable 1: Functional spillover pressure

Functional spillover pressures occur when further integration is needed in order to reach an original objective. The basic assumption is that policy sectors are interdependent, which is why it is hardly possible to isolate them. In case that one policy sector leads to negative effects for another already integrated policy sector, the former must be integrated in order to resolve the problems.

> „Functional pressures may arise if/when there is a significant functional interdependence between issue A (Schengen/the abolition of internal frontiers) and issue B (external border control). To what extent does a lack of integration in issue area B create problems for issue area A (thus leading to dysfunctionalities)" (Niemann and Speyer 2018: 28)?

This is particularly true for cases if there is a lack of alternative solutions or if alternative solutions are blocked by „sunk costs, economic costs, as well as symbolic and political influence" (Niemann and Speyer 2018: 30). This argument is based on path-dependency, which makes a certain policy choice sticky (Niemann and Speyer 2018: 25). The final twist is the perception of policy-makers. „Functional spillover is a structural pressure and structures need agents to translate those pressures" (Niemann and

Schmitter 2009: 57). Only if agents perceive functional pressure as such, further integrative action will be taken.

H1 based on functional spill-over: solidarity emerges if policy-makers perceive functional pressure. Functional pressure rises if the interdependence between two interlinked policy areas is regarded as strong.

Independent Variable 2: Influence of supranational institutions

The implementation of solidarity promises a shift of competences to the supranational level, which is why the supranational institutions have a particular interest of fostering solidarity between Member States. They „become agents of integration" (Niemann and Speyer 2018: 26). The strategy of the Commission and the Parliament, who are eager to gain additional power, is to implement solidarity with help of agenda-setting (Kingdon 1995; Greer and Löblová 2017) and strategic framing (Rhinard 2010). The European Court of Justice understands its mission as promoter of European integration since it is responsible for the interpretation of the values mentioned in the treaties (Howarth and Roos 2017). Due to the explicit insertion of solidarity in the treaties and due to the increasing references to solidarity in secondary law, the CJEU asserts greater influence on solidarity.

H2 based on cultivated spill-over: The supranational actors push for solidarity since the implementation of solidarity promises a shift of competences to the EU level. Supranational actors use the constitutionalisation process (normative), the market interdependence (functional) and crises (security) to further the principle of solidarity to put solidarity successively on the agenda and to frame the insertion of solidarity as inevitable.

2.2.3. Operationalisation of variables

The presented variables need to be operationalised in order to interlink the theoretical assumptions with the empirical research. As already outlined, the research process comprises two steps, which I intertwine with each other. I will cover those steps in the empirical part in parallel by applying the developed concept of solidarity between the Member States and looking into the relationship of my variables. In the following, I present in detail how I operationalise the independent variables.

Independent Variable 1:

The first independent variable „*application of functional argumentation*" refers to functional pressures and how those pressures are perceived by the main policy actors. According to Niemann, there are several steps necessary in order to evaluate if functional spill-overs occur. First, the policy objective, which is in this case a functioning internal gas market, must be salient. Second, the issue A (functioning internal gas market) is interdependent with issue B (security of supply). Third, if other solutions than functional solutions are unavailable, the functional connection is persistent. Fourth, if the functional argument(s) are repeated within the political discourse by relevant decision makers the functional rationale is strengthened (Niemann 2006; Niemann and Speyer 2017). I fuse these steps described by Niemann by evaluating, first, the actual existing functional pressures, that call for further integration. To recall, functional pressures might arise from crisis or since an original policy objective is endangered (i.e. the functioning of the internal market). However, dysfunctionalities, which are expressed by e.g. a crisis, are not automatically leading to further integration. Perception of this functional necessity is key for further integration.

This is why I want to evaluate in a second step, if those *pressures are actually perceived as such by the decision-makers*. The crucial point to examine is the perception of the decision-makers, since the perception is decisive on the question of further integration. Therefore, I deviate from Niemann's approach by putting the main point of analysis on the perceptions of the decision-makers and their response to the ‚functional pressure'. The arguments pointing to functional pressures might refer to:
- Path dependency;
- Alternative solutions are risky / unavailable;
- Alternative solutions are employed but insufficient;
- National solutions are inadequate, which is why a shift to the supranational level is necessary.

The decision-makers are the Council and the Parliament, which produce secondary law. However, I will also take into account the European Council conclusions, since the EUCO gives not only political guidance but also deals with delicate issues (Puetter 2012: 162). Additionally, the European Council makes an impact on the ordinary policy-making process by issuing strategy programmes (Wessels and Wolters 2019: 14).

Functional pressure is about

> „the perceptions of decision-makers (how strong is the logic or pressure perceived as regards functional interdependencies, international competition/ threats, the consequences of uncoordinated/individual action or the manageability of increasingly broad problems?)" (Niemann 2006: 63).

The strategic communication of political elites is influencing change. It is thus of importance to look at the arguments brought forward by the main policy makers. Niemann acknowledges that „(m)anifestation in the policy discourse need not necessarily be a reflection of decision-makers' true perception, but when functional or exogenous arguments gain currency in the policy arena they nevertheless have an impact on outcomes" (Niemann 2006: 63). I evaluate thus frequent references to functional arguments in the main documents produced by the decision-making bodies during the legislative process as influential for the policy outcome. „(...) (F)unctional dynamics are much more likely to unfold, if they are openly discussed and considered during negotiation" (Niemann 2013: 639). This is why I look in detail at the policy formulation process. I evaluate the arguments, which are exchanged between the Parliament and the Council in different forms within the legislative process. The Parliament publishes reports and resolutions, which are mainly produced by the responsible Committee on Industry, Research and Energy (ITRE). The EP includes also explanations for the amendments. It is much more difficult to grasp the arguments put forward by the Council. The Transport, Telecommunications and Energy Council (TTE) is the key actor. The Council or the Council Presidency publishes results of discussion or open questions. As preparation for the Council meeting, the Presidency issues ‚background briefs' or ‚presidency briefings'. Public meetings are made available via video. Also, the outcome of the council meeting is published, which presents the main results of discussion. Additional sources comprise press statements and presidency programmes. Next to those documents, I evaluate the European Council conclusions.

Independent Variable 2:

In order to operationalise the IV2 *„Influence of the supranational institutions"* I apply the concept of policy entrepreneurs. Supranational actors (here the Commission and the Parliament) use different strategies in order to influence policy making, which are agenda-setting, as well as offering problem definitions and (a limited set of) policy solutions within the policy formulation process. The strategies are complemented by ‚strategic framing'. I analyse how the agenda developed, and focus on the policy design, which means on the development of the content of secondary law (problem definitions and solutions). Therefore, I look at the legislative process comprising the agenda-setting and the policy formulation process. Additionally, I evaluate the integrationist power of the CJEU and how the Court furthered the development of solidarity in order to ensure integration. The main focus of the analysis is on the three supranational actors European Commission, European Parliament and the European Court of Justice. Each institution follows different strategies and has different powers within the legislative process.

European Commission and European Parliament

The Parliament's and the Commission's role in decision-making in energy policy increased with the Treaty of Lisbon (Maltby 2013). I understand both the Parliament and the Commission as unitary actors. „In the one-dimensional, pro/anti-EU integration framework, the Parliament and the Commission are usually assumed to be more integrationist than the pivotal actors in the Council" (Hix and Høyland 2013: 174). While the Commission has greater influence in agenda-setting, the Parliament can exert its competences during the legislative process by amendments, adoption and veto power (Kreppel and Webb 2019: 2). The Commission has additionally the role of a mediator during trilogue negotiations.

European Court of Justice

The CJEU has a very different role compared to the Commission and the Parliament. The objective of the CJEU is to interpret law and to adhere to the objectives of the Treaties. This means that the power of the ECJ is dependent on case law. The CJEU has influence by establishing legal norms. „(…) (T)he ECJ will use its powers to promote integration (values that inhere in the treaties)" (Stone Sweet 2010: 24).

> „The necessity for the ECJ to remain credible as impartial interpreter of the law means that any attempts to implement an independent agenda must be consistent with maintaining legal legitimacy. For legal legitimacy to remain intact, the reasoning of the ECJ must be consistent with existing doctrine and the methodological requirements of legal deduction. But to the extent that it is, legal legitimacy may even be exploited to advance political goals (Burley and Mattli, 1993). This is why the ECJ, especially when it acts autonomously, goes to great lengths to anchor doctrinal advances in existing jurisprudence, and

often couples controversial steps with legitimizing objectives, such as securing individuals' rights. Open judicial activism, by contrast, could be highly detrimental, risking both the day-to-day erosion of respect and court-curbing initiatives from countervailing powers (Rasmussen, 1986)" (Tallberg 2000: 849).

The European Court of Justice incorporates a particular function since it takes not part in the legislative process itself but evaluates the implementation of secondary law according to the Treaties. The CJEU's opinions are precedent setting for the development of legal norms and the interpretation of the European values. The judicial activism makes the Court an important engine for integration (Bach 2018: 60).

Agenda-setting: The aim of agenda-setting is to arouse the interest of policymakers to pay attention to a certain issue (Kingdon 1995). This role can not only be taken by political actors but also private actors, such as lobbyists. However, this research concentrates on the formal legislative powers of the institutions, i.e. the shaping of legislation (Kreppel and Oztas 2017: 1120). Princen separates this process into two steps. 1) Sufficient supporters need to be found and 2) the EU must be acknowledged as suitable venue for this policy (Princen 2011: 928). This entails that there is a legal basis for joint action on EU level and that the EU is equipped with the necessary knowledge regarding the issue (Princen 2011: 930). Kreppel and Oztas underline the difference between political and technical agenda setters. The technical power concerns the procedural capacity to initiate a policy proposal. The political power reflects the capability of the actor to influence the „outcome of policy change" (Kreppel and Oztas 2017: 1121). The Commission possesses the formal power to propose legislative acts which is why it has agenda setting power as clarified in Art. 17(2) TEU (ibid.). The Commission cannot only propose new legislation but has also the possibility to start the discussion by publishing strategic papers. Strategies to make an issue viable and to find support include the combination of Green Papers and the opinion of policy experts as well as studies (Princen 2011: 934). To achieve agreement that the EU level is the right place to put a policy can be accomplished by issue linkage (in particular by establishing a link to the internal market) (Princen 2011: 937) or by underlining the added European value (Princen 2011: 938).

The power of the Parliament to influence the outcome of the policy change increased over time (Héritier 2017). The Parliament is empowered to adopt and amend legislation. Additionally, the Parliament can publish own-initiative reports (Art. 225 TFEU) by which the Parliament can request the Commission to propose legislation. EU energy law, which is based on Art. 194 TFEU, is passed through ordinary legislative procedure. The Council of Ministers and the Parliament possess equal weight within this process. Based on these considerations I analyse which actor introduced solidarity during the policy process including the time before the legislative proposal. These documents include among others own-initiative reports, European Council Conclusions, Green Papers and Presidency Programmes. This evaluation allows me to see which actor introduced solidarity to the political debate, reveals the underlying vision of solidarity and if and how this understanding of solidarity has been implemented in secondary law. This process will additionally illuminate if certain visions of solidarity prevail. The Parliament and the Council can adapt and veto policy change, which is why it is necessary to compare their individual input regarding solidarity within the policy process. The outcome of the legislative act (declarative or institutionalised solidarity) will shed light upon the question which institution has more influenced the outcome in comparison to the original proposal by the Commission.

Strategic Framing: This approach, which can be understood as a particular tool to influence the agenda, implies that actors offer problem definitions and (a limited set of) policy solutions within the policy formulation process. The Commission „is responsible for framing and projecting issues as problems (urgently) requiring solutions, and may do so by coupling issues with grand political visions or policies already deemed salient and high on the agenda, to make them more palatable" (Stephenson 2010: 1045). Strategic framing is understood as ‚soft power' strategy. A policy frame is provided by the actors in the policy process in order to define a certain problem and propose reactions. The Commission exerts further influence by providing preferred policy solutions. Since I also evaluate the Parliament as important supranational actor, I will additionally assess the frames used by the EP: The frames serve as argument, why solidarity should be implemented. I examine three different frames concerning the use of solidarity (functional, normative and security), which I screened during a first reading of the documents. I tagged the frames according to the following explanations:

– Normative: paradigms and belief systems (obligation to help; expression of values and principles; the situation is not self-inflicted, we against the other(s); unity; joint action and treaty references).
– Functional: Interdependence between Member States (market integration: solidarity needed due to market failures; rules are needed; market mechanisms).

– Security: solidarity as answer to security questions (emergency; crises; security of supply).

A frame is used in order to present an issue in a specific way aiming to achieve a certain policy result. The comparison of the frames will demonstrate which frames have been used by which actor and if there has been a dominant frame. Additionally, the comparison can provide an insight on the question if one frame is more successful than other frames. „When adopted by policymakers within a policy domain, a frame influences policymaking characteristics, such as which problem is being addressed, which actors are deemed relevant to participate, and which policy instruments are most appropriate" (Rhinard 2010: 2). Strategic communications encompass also that an actor chooses to provide certain information depending on the expected reaction of the audience. If the speakers communicate strategically, „(...) content and amount of available information can change" (Druckman and Lupia 2000: 17).

2.3. Methodological framework

„(...) (M)easurement as the link of between theory and empirical reality is the backbone of empirical research and therefore at the core of research design (...)" (Miller 2007: 83). In the following sub-chapters I will depict how I selected the cases for my study and explain my analytical framework (process-tracing). This is followed by a presentation of the data collection process and the tools used for the analysis which are both document and content analysis as well as the conduction of interviews.

2.3.1. Case Selection and Analysis

The thesis examines four different legislative processes and one Court case in the empirical part by applying a qualitative case study research design. I follow Gerring's definition of a case study, who defines

> „(...) the case study as an intensive study of a single unit for the purpose of understanding a larger class of (similar) units. A unit connotes a spatially bounded phenomenon – e.g., a nation-state, revolution, political party, election, or person – observed at a single point in time or over some delimited period of time" (Gerring 2004: 342).

Case studies contain sufficient material in order to reconstruct complex explanations. My dependent variable needs further investigation and a compatibility check with real world politics, which is why my research follows additionally an explorative character. One of the objectives of this study is to trace the intervening variables, which connect the explanatory variable (causal effect) with the outcome. The level of analysis is thus the within-case level, which is in comparison to the cross-case level, „concerned with causal mechanisms and processes" (Rohlfing 2012: 4).

The theory presumes that there is a causal effect between 1) supranational institutions and integration and between 2) functional pressures and integration. The operationalisation of the explanatory variables demonstrated that it is of importance to look at the strategies pursued by the supranational actors and how the decision-makers perceive functional pressures. These processes are reflected in the policy formulation and decision-making process in secondary law, which are manifestations of how European integration works in practice. To recall, I understand solidarity as particular outcome of integration, however, specific implications are yet to be discovered.

The depending variable was the driving force behind the case selection. There are 843 legal acts registered on eur-lex.europa.eu, which entail solidarity in the text (access in January 2019). 516 documents can be found by searching for ‚solidarity between Member States', of which 33 are legal acts. The main subjects, where solidarity is mentioned, are energy and environment, the area of freedom, security and justice, regional policy and budget. If the search keyword is ‚solidarity mechanism', I can identify three additional legal acts concerning migration flows (subject: area of freedom, security and justice). These 36 legal acts form thus the population of interest (Rohlfing 2012: 24).

I presume that there is a variance of the dependent variable, which is why I examine four cases which might include declarative or institutionalised solidarity and additionally, a variance regarding the dependent variable over time (declarative solidarity changes to institutionalised solidarity after revised legislation or vice versa). This is an exploratory undertaking since the outcome is unclear regarding the variance. If the outcome changes within cases, dominant explaining factors might vary over time or connect differently with other factors.

Box 12: Legislation on gas policy containing references to solidarity		
Legislative Act	Topic	Date of Publication
Directive 2004/67/EC	Security of gas supply	26.04.2004
Regulation (EU) 2010/994	Security of gas supply	20.10.2010
Regulation (EU) 2017/1938	Security of gas supply	25.10.2017
Directive 2009/73/EC	Common rules for internal gas market	13.07.2009
Directive (EU) 2019/692	Common rules for internal gas market	17.04.2019
Decision (EU) 2012/994	Information exchange mechanism	25.10.2012
Decision (EU) 2017/684	Information exchange mechanism	05.04.2017
Regulation (EU) 2013/347	Trans-European networks	17.04.2013

I chose a sub-set of four cases on solidarity in energy policy – concentrating on developments within the gas policy sector – since a selection of similar cases will provide more clarity about the influence of the independent variables of interest (Gerring 2006: 131ff.). The most recent legislative acts, which have been all put through after the Treaty of Lisbon came into force, have been carried through under the ‚ordinary legislative procedure'. Therefore, the formal rules how to influence these acts have been equal for all four cases, i.e. the Commission proposes a new legislative act (or to revise existing legislation) and the EP and the Council amend the proposal (Costello and Thomson 2013). Hence, the actors involved in the process have been the same (e.g. DG Energy for the Commission). All legislative acts have been based on Art. 194 TFEU. Only the regulation on guidelines for trans-European energy infrastructure ((EU) 347/2013) is based on Art. 172 TFEU (trans-European networks). *Additionally*, I present one case, which uncovers the legal dimension of the principle of solidarity. The CJEU presented in November 2019 its judgement on the principle of energy solidarity, which is in relation to the directive 2009/73/EC concerning common rules for the internal market in natural gas. In so far this case is *not comparable* to the other cases. However, since the judgement of the CJEU treats specifically the principle of solidarity, it is of particular interest to understand how solidarity is interpreted as legal principle. Furthermore, it can shed light on the role of the Court's intentions regarding the development of the principle.

My research „(...) is concerned with a specific empirical manifestation of the conceptualization of the outcome (...) that is specified at the outset of a case study" (Rohlfing 2012: 25). Energy policy has not only received additional political and legal impetus with the newly introduced energy article after the last treaty change but also because the treaty makes even two references to energy solidarity. Not only political communications and strategies or press texts refer to solidarity. In light of the gas crises in 2006 and 2009, solidarity was increasingly mentioned by the European Council. Solidarity can be found in secondary law of energy policy before and after the treaty change. Additionally, energy policy and in particular gas policy is a highly securitised policy sector where Member States and respectively the national leaders are driven by a sovereignty reflex (Øhrgaard 1997; Natorski and Herranz Surrallés 2008; Wessels 2016; Keukeleire and Delreux 2014: 225). I follow thus a ‚least-likely' case selection strategy since integration tends to fall short in highly securitised policy fields because Member States block further integration for the sake of their own national concerns.

Process-tracing

Since my research question focuses on the processes which led to the implementation of solidarity in secondary law, I am particularly interested in the policy formulation starting at an early stage of agenda-setting. The time span comprises 2002 until 2019 in order to grasp already early developments in the field of energy solidarity starting with the Commission's proposal of the first directive on security of gas supply. I evaluate each case as a process of several decisions, in order to carve out development trends. The application of case studies helps the researcher to understand why certain events happen (or not happen). „(...) (T)hick description that case study research produces provides the means to discover the causal mechanism" (Crasnow 2012: 658). Process-tracing, as developed by George and Bennett (2005), is a helpful instrument in order to reveal causal inferences. I use a theory-testing process-tracing (PT) research design as illustrated by Beach and Pedersen (2013). The aim is „to test whether a particular X was a cause of Y in case Z" (Mahoney 2015: 203). But the causal effect alone (if X is present or not) will not tell us if and in how far it influenced the outcome Y (Mahoney 2015: 202). „(...) (T)he goal is to evaluate whether evidence shows that the hypothesized causal mechanism linking X and Y was present and that it functioned as theorized" (Beach and Pedersen 2013: 11). The causal relation between both variables has to be examined. There is a correlation between supranational entrepreneurship (H1) / functional pressure (H2) and integration. To recall, I consider solidarity as particular outcome of integration. The aim of theory-testing PT is to identify the link between both variables with help of causal sequences. „Between the beginning (independent variables) and end (outcome of dependent variable), the researcher traces a number of theoretically predicted intermediate steps" (Checkel 2005: 15). Blatter and Haverland provide an instruction on how to observe causal processes, which are: „comprehensive storylines, smoking-gun observations and confessions" (2014: 67).

1) The researcher identifies with ‚comprehensive storylines' critical moments and the major events of the process.
2) Empirical evidence is provided by „smoking-gun observations embedded in a dense net of observations that show the temporal and spatial proximity of causes and effects" (Blatter and Haverland 2014: 67). This means in practice that cause and consequence (as empirical observations) are located close to each other.
3) ‚Confessions' may provide us with deeper insights about the perceptions and motivations of actors. Those confessions can be speeches and press statements but also interviews.

This method will contribute to answer the research question why solidarity was implemented in energy policy. I am aware that I cannot provide a full-fledged answer to my research question, however, I can contribute to reveal causes and conditions which might have instigated the process which led to the outcome. This is helpful for future research endeavours which can dig deeper on the question which factors cause solidarity.

Causal mechanisms

The outcome (dependent variable) under consideration is the ‚implementation of solidarity'. It is necessary to look only at cases where the outcome actually occurred (Blatter et al. 2018: 243), which is why I chose only legislative acts which include solidarity. However, the explicit outcome (declarative or institutionalised solidarity) is yet unknown. The process analysis helps to reveal step by step the causal factors, which led to the outcome. This analysis will provide further information why declarative or institutionalised solidarity has been implemented.

The first IV is „functional pressure": The original most far-reaching competence of the EU was the development of the single market. Energy policy has not been explicitly mentioned in the treaties and was nevertheless integrated (in particular the electricity and gas market). I argue that the interdependence, which developed due to the single market, led to a spillover within the policy field to find common solutions also in energy security. If I translate this rationale into energy policy, this leads, based on Niemann and Speyer (2018), to the following statement:

Figure 3: Causal mechanism – functional spillover

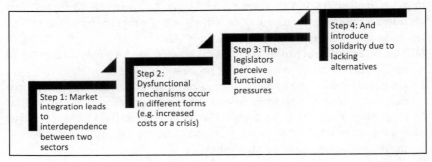

Functional pressures may arise if/when there is a significant functional interdependence between issue A (internal gas market) and issue B (security of gas supply). To what extent does a lack of integration in issue B create problems for issue area A (thus leading to dysfunctionalities)? Due to uneven benefits and burdens resulting from interdependence, the introduction of solidarity as political solution was perceived as necessary step by the decision-makers.

The second IV is *„influence of supranational actors"*: Supranational actors pursue a life of their own driven by the intention to gain more power. Power can be yielded by further integration which shifts the national competencies to the supranational level. This is why the supranational actors put new policy objectives on the agenda. The importance of the policy objective is underlined by different frames. The proposal entails policy solutions, which are preferred by the supranational actors. The legislators agree to further integration due to a lack of convincing alternative solutions. The influence by the supranational actors can be ascertained by looking in detail at the policy formulation process. Successful assertion can be determined by factors such as ,arguments are taken over', ,legislative proposal by Commission remains in final outcome' or ,legislative amendment by Parliament is accepted'.

Figure 4: Causal mechanism – cultivated spillover

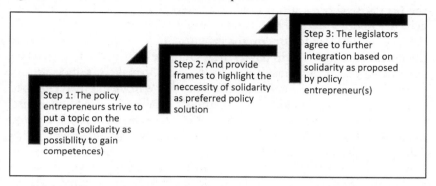

However, as Beach and Pedersen (2013: 15f.) argue, theory-testing PT tells us only if a mechanism was present or absent. It cannot be expected that these have been the only mechanisms in place. Therefore, the strength of the effect of each mechanism remains unclear. For my research this is nevertheless helpful since I aim to find out if and possibly how functional spillover and/or supranational entrepreneurship played a general role in the process of the implementation of solidarity. I can track how actors make use of solidarity within the process. „Moreover, tracing an explicitly theorized mechanism enables us to make stronger claims about a causal relationship between X and Y than we can with correlational-type data" (Reykers and Beach 2017: 256). If both mechanisms are not present, and we can nonetheless observe ,institutionalised' solidarity, they would be insignificant.

2.3.2. Data Collection and Analysis

Data collection is a necessary step in the research process in order to find reliable evidence. „Process tracers find it impossible to analyse processes without qualitative data, hence, they use primary sources such as documents and interviews, as well as secondary literature describing the specific outcome" (Trampusch and Palier 2016: 442). Document analysis is a helpful tool in order to systematically examine the research material (Bowen 2009). „As a research method, document analysis is particularly applicable to qualitative case studies—intensive studies producing rich descriptions of a single phenomenon, event, organisation, or program" (Bowen 2009: 29). In the following, I identify observable implications in order to evaluate if the causal mechanisms are working as described. A detailed account of the legislative process in relation with external events will provide a first evidence in order to trace the causal relations between my variables.

Since my research focuses on the evolution of secondary law, I collected the documents which were published within the legislation process. These are mainly the documents issued by the policy makers, which are the Commission, the Parliament and the Council. Within the policy proposes these documents include the Commission proposal including impact assessment and explanatory memorandum, the report by ITRE, changes by other MEPs and the subsequent amendments by the Parliament, policy debates within the Council, Presidency proposals and amendments by the Council. The so called four-column documents represent an important part of the legislative process. Those documents reveal in three different columns the positions of the single actors (Commission proposal, ITRE position, Council position) and the compromise proposal by the Presidency in column four. Additionally, I used the European Council Conclusions and presidency programmes in order to reveal the input by the European Council and the Member States within the process. The Commission and the Parliament also contribute with special reports (e.g. Green Papers, strategy papers and resolutions) and Commission officials deliver speeches or conference contributions. My data comprises also drafts and reports, which were published by the institutions. I chose only documents which mention solidarity or if the documents served as basis for further developments concerning solidarity. I exclude documents which only focus on ‚European cooperation‘ or similar expressions in order to make my take on solidarity more explicit. The main source to access official documents has been www.eur-lex.europa.eu since this is the official information platform about EU legislation and www.consilium.europa.eu for further access on documents of the legislative process. This has been complemented by sources such as speeches, conference contributions and press articles.

I use content analysis to discover the variance of the dependent variable ‚implementation of solidarity‘. The analysis follows Mayring's approach of a qualitative content analysis. For the coding I used a deductive approach which is based on my concept of solidarity. „Die Zuordnung der Kategorie zur Textstelle geschieht (…) nie automatisch, sondern gestaltet sich als regelgeleitete Interpretation" (Mayring 2010: 603). I classified the dependent variable ‚solidarity‘ into two forms (variance), which are ‚institutionalised solidarity' and ‚declarative solidarity'. According to my conceptualisation of solidarity, ‚institutionalised solidarity' needs to fulfil different characteristics. In comparison, ‚declarative solidarity' does not have these characteristics, or one or more characteristics are lacking. I tagged the codes according to the features of my developed concept (group cohesion, reciprocity and monitoring). The features are understood as the categories which subsume each two codes.

> „A code in qualitative inquiry is most often a word or short phrase that symbolically assigns a summative, salient, essence-capturing, and/or evocative attribute for a portion of language-based or visual data. The data can consist of interview transcripts, participant observation field notes, journals, documents, drawings, artifacts, photographs, video, Internet sites, e-mail correspondence, literature, and so on" (Saldaña 2012: 3)

The attached memos (descriptions of codes) show, how I identified the codes using a set of contextual propositions (see list of memos in the appendix). I read the legislative documents by looking 1) where is solidarity present/absent, 2) which characteristics of solidarity are present/absent and 3) what form take those characteristics. This has been an interpretative process instructed by a conceptual analysis aiming to provide information on the presence/absence of the conceptualised term. I investigated the documents in several cycles in order to achieve a coherent use of the codes and categories (Saldaña 2012: 8). Since the dependent variable refers to the policy outcome (= result in legislative act) I coded altogether 8 legislative acts (s. selection of case studies). I used MAXQDA as coding software in order to evaluate the single documents concerning the variance of my dependent variable.

Observable implications of causal mechanism H1:

ACER provides a definition of market integration: integration of gas markets can be measured by indicators such as mergers of „formerly separate hubs" and if „(end user) market relinquishes its own hub and 'co-uses' a neighbouring hub" (ACER 2015: 3). The direct effect of these market activities is that the wholesale price of gas would be uniform for the newly established market (ACER 2015: 3). Market Integration is here captured by economic indicators only. The European Energy Community captures market integration by a range of different activities such as security of supply, transmission system operator unbundling, market coupling and others (Energy Community 2018: 3). Additionally, the market can only be fully operational if sufficient pipelines connect the market. These different methods of measurement reveal that market integration is not a question of tools of analysis but also a question of the legislative framework which calls for market integration. The market and security of supply are interdependent since an event in one Member State can affect all Member States because of the market coupling and the connecting pipelines.

However, interdependence expresses not only vulnerability but also strength. More interconnections can absorb shocks of the energy system by transporting the gas to the spot where needed. But this interdependence has to be perceived as such. If decision-makers think only in national frames and how national systems could absorb shocks, European interdependence would not be decisive. This is why I analyse if the decision-makers referred to interdependence within the legislative process. Example: „The establishment of genuine solidarity between Member States in major emergency supply situations is essential, even more so as Member States become increasingly interdependent regarding security of supply" (Council 2004).

If a market is economically integrated but security of supply remains in national hands, dysfunctional consequences might arrive. Dysfunctionalities can take different forms within the internal gas market. Price peaks are signs of dysfunctional mechanisms. The most evident form is a gas supply crisis which can be a result of external supply difficulties. If gas is not sufficiently available, major security problems can arise since the gas sector is not only responsible for heating but also power generation. Dysfunctionalities occur in markets which are not sufficiently integrated, e.g. infrastructure is lacking, or national decisions stop gas deliveries. Therefore, I will also present how Member States acted during the gas crises of 2006 and 2009 and how the crises were managed.

However, only if decision-makers perceive the interdependence and dysfunctionalities as functional pressure they will implement solidarity mechanisms. In order to evaluate if the decision-makers perceived functional pressures, the arguments should entail a functional logic, i.e. the functioning of the internal gas market and resulting consequences for security of supply. Additionally, solidarity is presented as solution to these functional pressures. Example: „To allow the internal gas market to function even in the face of a shortage of supply, provision must be made for solidarity (…)" (Regulation(EU)2017/1938). I look at the arguments of the main policy makers, i.e. the policy proposals, impact assessments and reports by the Commission, the debate between and within Parliament (including opinions, resolutions and reports) and the Council (in form of presidency conclusions, policy debates, press releases and amendments). I include additionally the European Council conclusions, which demonstrate how the Heads of State and Government include solidarity in their argumentative framework.

Observable implications of causal mechanism H2:

The combined approach of document and content analysis reveals which characteristics are of particular importance for the single institutions and how the institutions envisioned solidarity (over time). With help of content analysis, it is possible to get an idea of the original (official) intention of a policy proposal and to track change within the legislation process (including the debate surrounding the process). The comparison of the initial proposal on solidarity, the amendments and final outcome show which institution influenced the insertion or exclusion of solidarity. This approach will help to structure and verify the causal mechanisms in particular in how far solidarity appears or disappears within the policy formulation process. This analysis will reveal the agenda-setting (here understood as agenda-shaping) powers of the Commission and the Parliament.

The approach is complemented by framing. Frames are either easy to grasp if there is an argumentative figure (e.g. solidarity develops with help of a functioning market), or more complex if the argument concerns the overall context of the text (e.g. general approval or disapproval of solidarity). The actors want to pursue solidarity, which is why they use different frames to underline its necessity as policy solution. This means that my focus is on the text itself and the explicit meaning of solidarity. I translate the frames into codes, which I then apply to the selected documents. This makes it possible to see which frames are present/absent and dominant/scarce. Subsequently, I control if the present frames have been present in the documents published by the legislators (Parliament/Council).

Example for functional frame: „Situations like the cold spell of 2012 and the stress test of 2014 showed that coordination of action and solidarity are of vital importance. An action in one country can provoke a shortage and risks of blackouts in neighbouring countries (…)" (Commission 2016f).

Normative frames on the other hand underline certain world views. Example for a normative frame: „While each Member State is responsible for its own security, solidarity between Member States is a basic feature of EU membership" (Commission 2008a).

Security frames are underlining specific perils. Example for a security frame during an EP debate by Tunne Kelam:

„This regulation is among the most crucial ones to ensuring the EU's resilience towards hostile policy from outside the EU. It is important to understand that the regulation is basically a legally-binding solidarity mechanism, aimed at protecting states and citizens against blackmail and political pressure" (Parliament 2017c).

In a third step I go back to document analysis and evaluate how the decision-makers discuss the possible policy options. But the Parliament tries also to influence the agenda before the legislative procedure is carried through, which is by publishing e.g. own-initiative reports. Due to my case selection I know that solidarity is present, why there should be a clear statement of the decision-makers (Council and Parliament) within the legislative process that takes up the arguments of the Commission to prove the influence of the Commission's role.

Expert Interviews

In addition to the document analysis I conducted semi-structured expert interviews in order to reflect on the outcomes and to get a more coherent insight on the influence of the institutions and the arguments put forward in the documents. The methodological triangulation intends to build up deep knowledge of the cases and to provide by means of thick description the narrative context to improve the credibility of the research analysis (Crasnow 2017: 10). The interviews are used to collect further evidence on how the insertion of solidarity was carried through. Experts are people, who are in any kind involved in the policy process and have proven expertise of the topic. The focus of the interview is on the content, the opinion and information (Pickel and Pickel 2018: 120).

I carried out the interviews in order to evaluate the role of the respective institution within the process, to uncover the institution's perspective on solidarity and individual perceptions of the policy making process. The particular use of interviews is to gain a deeper insight into the process and to get stronger validity of identified causes. The number of interviews is dependent on the additional knowledge acquired. In advance of the semi-structured interviews core questions are identified and prepared. However, during the interview the respondent is free to express openly without pre-defined answers. The order of question can be changed and adapted to the situation and also the interviewee can add topics.

Box 13: Examples of interview questions

- Which events would you describe as milestones of energy solidarity?
- How do you perceive the development of energy solidarity over time?
- How do you evaluate the influence of your institution / department on the insertion of solidarity?

This flexibility is helpful in order to uncover new or less clear processes and might reveal other causes or unknown events. Additionally, the interviews were conducted unanimously in order to receive more detailed information and to have an open and confiding atmosphere. The list of conducted transcribed interviews can be found in the annex disclosing names and positions. The interviews were conducted in 2017 and 2020. Due to the Covid-19 health crisis in 2020, I conducted the interviews by using different contact channels such as telephone, WhatsApp video, skype and zoom. I have translated the interviews, which were conducted in German, into English.

3. The principle of solidarity as political commitment and legal norm

The following chapter aims to capture the European dimension and the specific meaning of solidarity in EU law. The main focus is on the development of solidarity in EU primary law (i.e. treaties) and the interpretation of solidarity by the Court of Justice. I present three different stages of EU solidarity as legal principle in the making: 1) Solidarity is running through the EU's bloodlines, 2) From Maastricht to Nice: inclusion of solidarity as legal principle and 3) The new impetus by the Treaty of Lisbon.

In the second part, I unpack how solidarity has developed in energy policy concentrating on major political trends and decisions which influence the emergence of an EU energy policy and secondary law (s. annex 4 for timeline).

3.1. Solidarity is running through the EU's bloodlines

„Although the 1950 Schuman Declaration and the founding Treaties presume solidarity to be one of the central values underlying European integration, the concept of solidarity remains undefined and undertheorised as a principle of EU primary law" (Van Cleynenbreugel 2018: 13). As stated in this quote, solidarity is also a highly debated and controversial research topic in legal studies, which involves two different aspects: On the one hand, it can be perceived as an abstract value, which informs the design of legal norms. On the other hand, it can be understood as a legal principle, which defines societal relationships (Van Cleynenbreugel 2014: 294).

Solidarity has always been the glue for the community-building process of the EU (Ferreira-Pereira and Groom 2010). „European integration is often narrated as the history of European solidarity in practice" (Schmale 2017: 854). General Advocate Sharpston even declared that „(s)olidarity is the lifeblood of the European project" (Sharpston 2019). This was not only highlighted by the *de facto solidarity* announcement by Schuman but also by Winston Churchill, who underlined the necessity of a Franco-German reconciliation in 1946. Even if solidarity was not invoked explicitly in the Treaty of Rome, the treaty refers indirectly to the value by postulating an ‚ever closer union' (Ferreira-Pereira and Groom 2010: 599). It was only with the Single European Act (SEA) in 1987 that solidarity was included in the treaties for the first (and only) time. The SEA preamble mentions solidarity by pointing to the necessity to speak internationally with one voice. Solidarity is listed together with other important principles such as democracy and the rule of law, which shows its relevance for the community-building process (Ferreira-Pereira and Groom 2010: 599).

> „AWARE of the responsibility incumbent upon Europe to aim at speaking ever increasingly with one voice *and to act with consistency and solidarity in order more effectively to protect its common interests and independence*, in particular to display the principles of democracy and compliance with the law and with human rights to which they are attached, so that together they may make their own contribution to the preservation of international peace and security in accordance with the undertaking entered into by them within the framework of the United Nations Charter" (Single European Act 1987, emphasis added).

The foundation of the European Communities is itself understood as an act of solidarity: „the whole EU legal order, from its very beginnings, has been based on the solidarity principle" (Hilpold 2015: 8). Therefore, the duty of Union allegiance is an obligation of solidarity as is the acceptance of political compromise and the compliance with legal acts (Kadelbach 2014: 12).

Solidarity has been a cornerstone in the EU treaties and has a particular prominence in EU law. However, the CJEU has never given a fully-fledged definition of solidarity within its judgements, which is why it remains a nebulous concept (Schiek 2020: 13). There are several reasons for the Court's position on solidarity. First, the CJEU can only provide a definition of solidarity if it is also implemented in secondary law. In the past, the Court interpreted solidarity only as instrument in order to achieve the communal interest of the single market (Art. 3, ECSC). Second, solidarity is a politically inflated term and as such the Court avoids its concretisation if possible. Third, solidarity is used in such an expansive fashion that a coherent definition proves as difficult (Küçük 2016: 980ff.). In order to investigate the concept's legal meaning, it is necessary to look at its normative function in law, its application in the treaties and the arguments by the CJEU (Küçük 2016: 967).

The first Court ruling on solidarity was issued by the CJEU in 1969, but the most important statement on solidarity was made in a case against Italy in 1973.

„For a state unilaterally to break, according to its own conception of national interest, the equilibrium between advantages and obligations flowing from its adherence to the Community brings into question the equality of Member States before Community, brings into question the discriminations at the expense of their nationals, and above all of the nationals of the state itself which places itself outside the Community rules. This failure in the duty of solidarity accepted by Member States by the fact of their adherence to the community strikes at the fundamental basis of the Community legal order" (CJEU 1973).

The Court held that regulations are valid in all Member States without exceptions. The content of solidarity was shaped already at an early stage. The principle of solidarity is the product of the principle of equality between Member States. According to this, Member States have to comply with EU legislation in order to impede the Member States to deviate from equality (Terhechte 2014). Bieber and Maiani (2012) argue similarly that the CJEU discussed the solidarity-loyalty dimension, which the treaty calls the principle of loyal cooperation. Individual measures would distort the Union's function violating the obligation to act in solidarity. They also reiterate the necessity that all Member States comply with EU legislation even though the legislation might contradict national interests, since non-compliance would have detrimental effects on the other Member States. „La Cour a également constaté un ‚manquement aux devoirs de solidarité' lorsqu'un Etat membre a refusé délibérément d'appliquer certaines prescriptions du droit de l'Union en invoquant la défense de ‚certains intérêts nationaux'" (Bieber and Maiani 2012: 296).

The CJEU further clarified the content of the principle of solidarity in Spain v. Council in 1988 (CJEU 1988). Spain argued that the milk quota scheme should not be applied to Spain since Spain was not to blame for the milk surplus in the Community. The Council argued that the implementation of particular rules for Spain would contradict the solidarity principle: „(…) the contested measure intended to deal with the supply and demand balance in the sector, and this required the solidaristic effort of all participants in an equal manner" (Küçük 2016: 979). The Court highlighted that the principle of solidarity reflects a balance of gains and sacrifices as part of the Union (Küçük 2016: 980). Solidarity was in the early days understood as a legal norm to discourage Member States from opting out of the internal market, so that there would be no preferential treatment concerning community rules. Despite these early rulings by the CJEU, solidarity became only increasingly important in primary as well as secondary law in the 1990ies.

3.1.1. From Maastricht to Nice: inclusion of solidarity as a legal principle

Although solidarity was considered as a somehow significant principle, it was only marginally reflected in the treaties. In 1992, solidarity was added a as legal principle in the Maastricht treaty: „(T)he Treaty endorsed the principle of solidarity (Note 5) in the European Union's policy fields (e.g. external action on the international scene [Art 21 TEU], common foreign and security policy [Art 24.2, 31 TEU]) and introduced provisions related to solidarity and coordination within the EMU (Note 6)" (Kontochristou and Mascha 2014: 52). There are six references to solidarity. Solidarity can be found in the preamble of the Maastricht Treaty and in Title I, Art. A, both referring to solidarity between peoples of the Union. In Title II, Art. 2 develops the underlying principles of the common market of the Communities where solidarity was inserted as a responsibility between the Member States. Declaration on Art. 4(2) stipulates "the economic and social cohesion and solidarity between Member States" as a goal of the treaty. The intention was, that a political union would not be possible without solidarity, which is more than only the prospect of a common economic development. This is also mirrored in the TEU, where solidarity is part of external policy, thus expressing the unity to the outside world (Wydra 2010: 107).

Devuyst presents how solidarity was interpreted in the legal context in the post-Maastricht era. First, solidarity entails that Member States and the Community are connected by cooperation and mutual loyalty. Additionally, it can be derived from the treaties that solidarity means that

> „the Member States must take all necessary measures to ensure fulfillment of the obligations arising out of the Treaty; they must facilitate the achievement of the Community's tasks; and they must abstain from any measure which could jeopardize the attainment of the objectives of the Treaty" (Devuyst 2000: 19).

In the presidency conclusions of the European Council in Laeken in 2001, the heads of states and governments confirmed the principal values of the European Union. Solidarity was, just like democracy and liberty, underlined as one of the guiding principles. Europe is even called the „continent of (...) solidarity" (Conclusions 2001). Furthermore, solidarity is referred to as the reason why „(t)he European Union is a success story (...) (and) Europe has been at peace" (ibid.). This development is „(the) result of mutual solidarity and fair distribution of the benefits of economic development" (ibid.).

Nevertheless, up to this point, it was not very clear from the treaties what solidarity actually meant. „This silence on solidarity was supposed to come to an end with the Convention on the future of Europe which intended to spell out its meaning" (Hartwig and Nicolaides 2003: 20). However, solidarity was not discussed as a stand-alone topic in the working groups of the convention because no group had any specific responsibility to debate on solidarity. Solidarity was mentioned in three different dimensions: First, as a strong reference to the integration process, in which solidarity was praised as overarching value; Second, as a reference to crisis situations of whatever kind (reciprocity thought) and third, as a reference to a stable and fair economy (solidarity between individuals) (Hartwig and Nicolaides 2003: 20). Solidarity received a new impetus with the Constitutional Treaty. Kimmo Kiljunen, Member of the European Convention, assessed that solidarity was one of the „new union values" (Kiljunen 2004: 55). But why did the drafters of the Treaty not provide a full-fledged definition of the concept? Wouldn't it be simpler to have a clear definition than to leave the definition open to the context (Koeck 2019)?

> „(...) (T)his invokes the proverbial chicken and egg: clearly the drafters of the Treaty found it optimal or convenient not to fully define solidarity, even if some suggested and continue to suggest that a definition could theoretically facilitate the achievement of the principle. Or perhaps they rather surmised that defining solidarity too precisely might impede its actual development. (...) (A)mendments to include a definition or exclude certain aspects of solidarity were not adopted" (Vanheule et al. 2011: 99).

3.1.2. The new impetus by the Treaty of Lisbon

In the following, I provide a detailed overview of solidarity in the Treaty of Lisbon, in which solidarity made a prominent appearance and became upgraded on different levels: The Lisbon Treaty literally ignites a "firework of solidarity" (Calliess 2011: 14). The term is used a total of 22 times in the treaties (including the Charter of Fundamental Rights and Protocols). „(W)hich overall expectations, moral obligations, political assumptions and normative force can be attributed to what the Union's primary law calls ‚solidarity'" (Kotzur 2017: 38)? Solidarity can be used programmatically but also as a principle on different levels (domestic, national or transnational). Solidarity is „the animating force that informs all types of dynamics, not only among member states and central institutions, or between the Union and the international community, but also among and between its member states" (Arban 2017: 254). It can serve as a moral obligation being of pre-legal nature or as a legal duty. However, norms and values are always contested because there is never one general understanding, but rather a landscape of values (Sedmak 2010: 15). „Solidarity can draw a real-world picture or call for a better world. Going even further, it can programmatically and purposefully be used as a means of policy making, constitution building and social engineering" (Kotzur 2017: 39).

The TEU contains 10 references to solidarity, starting with the preamble, where the Member States express their desire to deepen solidarity between their peoples. This is followed by Art. 2, which included the vague formulation of solidarity as a value within the society, however, solidarity is not interpreted as a value like democracy or rule of law. Solidarity is not mentioned as a value, but as a characteristic of European society (Jacqué 2015). Therefore, the sanctioning mechanism in case of violation of values of Art. 2 does not refer to those characteristics (Hilf and Schorkopf 2019).

In Art. 3 TEU, solidarity is mentioned three times. First, solidarity between generations is declared as a social aim. Second, solidarity among Member States is invoked concerning economic, social and territorial cohesion. Third, solidarity refers to the wider world by underlining the need that the Union should contribute to solidarity among peoples. Therefore, solidarity is a principle which manifests itself as a value between Member States, between individuals and Member States as well as between generations (Art. 3(3) TEU). „Sämtliche horizontalen und vertikalen Formen von Solidarität scheinen abgedeckt zu sein, wobei die soziale Solidarität eingehender in der Charta der Grundrechte der Mitgliedsstaaten behandelt wird" (Jacqué 2015). But it is also argued that the modification of the TEU from ‚members' of the EU to ‚Member States' of the EU diminishes the extension of the term, i.e. instead of including the citizens, now it refers only to Member States. However, consequences of this change might not be intended (Terhechte 2014).

Chapter 1, which covers the General Provisions on the Union's External Action, refers to solidarity as one of the principles which inspired the Union's creation, why the Union wants to advance these principles also in the wider world. Chapter 2 on the specific provisions on the common foreign and security policy mentions solidarity five times. Art. 24(2) elaborates that the CFSP shall be based on the development of mutual *political solidarity* among Member States. Art. 24(3) states further that the Union's external and security policy shall be supported by the Member States in a spirit of loyalty and mutual solidarity. Additionally, „The Member

States shall work together to enhance and develop their mutual *political* solidarity. They shall refrain from any action which is contrary to the interests of the Union or likely to impair its effectiveness as a cohesive force in international relations" (Art. 24(3) TEU, emphasis added). The second phrase is a specification of mutual political solidarity and contains a particular feature of solidarity, which is to refrain from action which hurts other group members. This is further expanded on in Art. 31 on the voting procedure in this area. Usually, decisions are taken by the European Council and Council acting unanimously, however, Art. 31 offers the possibility to abstain. The Member State would then not have to apply the decision, but in a spirit of mutual solidarity, the Member State shall refrain from action harming the Union's decision and the other Member States shall equally accept its decision. The common approach of the Union in external action is also ensured by the principle of solidarity. Member States shall develop a common approach concerning matters of general interest and consult within the Union if they intend to undertake external action which could affect the Union's interest.

In the preamble of the Treaty on the Functioning of the EU (TFEU), solidarity refers to the relation between Europe and the overseas countries. Art. 67(2) and Art. 80 TFEU implement solidarity as principle in the area of freedom, security and justice.

> „It shall ensure the absence of internal border controls for persons and shall frame a common policy on asylum, immigration and external border control, *based on solidarity between Member States*, which is fair towards third-country nationals. For the purpose of this Title, stateless persons shall be treated as third-country nationals" (Art. 67(2) TFEU, emphasis added).

Solidarity is here directed towards Member States and excludes third-country nationals. Additionally, Art. 67(2) points out two dimensions, which are the internal and external border system. Solidarity is, therefore, inwards-directed by ensuring that borders remain open, while it is outwards-directed underlining the common policy on external border control. Art. 80 reads differently with regards to the legal component:

> „The policies of the Union set out in this Chapter and their implementation shall be *governed by the principle of solidarity* and fair sharing of responsibility, including its financial implications, between the Member States. Whenever necessary, the Union acts adopted pursuant to this Chapter shall contain appropriate measures to give effect to this principle" (Art. 80 TFEU, emphasis added).

Solidarity – again only referring to Member States – is the bonding feature for all policies and their implementation set out in this chapter. Additionally, the term comes with two clarifications. Art. 80 underlines the fair sharing of responsibilities and emphasises that this issue is particularly demanded as regards the financial implications. „Dogmatisch wirkt das so konkretisierte Solidaritätsprinzip als Orientierungs- und Kontrollmaßstab für die Unionsorgane und für die vollziehenden mitgliedsstaatlichen Stellen" (Bast 2014: 4). The second phrase of Art. 80 highlights the obligation of the Union to put the principle into action. Furthermore, this sentence allows the legislator(s) to take measures to share the effort, financially or otherwise. Bast claims that Art. 80 thus also clarifies the range of possible measures stipulated by Art. 77–79, which set out the common policies on borders, asylum and immigration. All measures must be implemented under the umbrella of solidarity and balance of (financial) efforts (Bast 2014: 4f.).

Art. 122 TFEU addresses severe difficulties in the supply of certain products, notably in the area of energy. The Council shall decide, in a spirit of solidarity between Member States, upon the appropriate measures to the economic situation. Also, article 194 TFEU refers to a spirit of solidarity regarding the Union policy on energy (the implications of this article are further outlined in ch. 3.1.4). Art. 222 TFEU is called *Solidarity Clause*. Member States shall jointly act in a spirit of solidarity in case of a terrorist attack or natural or man-made disasters. While terrorism was on the mind due to September 11, it was Michel Barnier, chair of the Working Group, who introduced the idea to expand solidarity to natural and man-made disasters. The need to respond to threats at community level was also expressed in the final report of Working Group VIII – Defence (Convention 2002). Barnier's intention was to form a stronger EU (Myrdal and Rhinard 2010: 3f.). Barnier explained that „we thought it necessary to make provision in the constitutional Treaty for a solidarity clause enabling all the Member States to present a united front against any new threats" (Barnier 2002). Furthermore, solidarity is mentioned in the protocols and declarations. Protocol NO. 28 reiterates the „objective of promoting economic, social and territorial cohesion and solidarity between Member States" and its application as shared competence in Art. 4(2)c TFEU. Declaration 37 refers to Art. 222 TFEU and states that the solidarity commitments between the Union and the Member States are not intended to affect the solidarity obligations between single Member States. The EU Charter of Fundamental Rights of the European Union came into force with the Treaty of Lisbon in 2009. The Charter entails the fundamental rights, which are shared by the EU Member States. The EU is founded on solidarity, which is one of the indivisible universal values of the EU. The title of chapter IV is *solidarity*. Here, solidarity refers to different social rights including rights of workers (e.g. fair working conditions) but also underlines the importance of family and environment.

3.1.3. Solidarity as legal norm and binding commitment

Solidarity does not appear in a coherent form, nor is it defined in the treaties, which leaves sufficient room for interpretation. The excessive use of the term, which can be found not only in primary law but also in secondary law as well as the public discourse can stipulate follow-up actions – at least gradually (Nettesheim 2020: 264). The idea of solidarity is much more often in practical use, but not always explicitly stated (Müller 2010: 77). Solidarity is acknowledged as a legal principle that has a positive integrative function. The legal understanding of solidarity includes that „EU membership implies ‚reciprocal intrusiveness'" (Kotzur 2017: 42). Solidarity creates rights and obligations which take different shapes (Kotzur 2017: 40). „Being a constitutional paradigm, solidarity displays a reasonably selfish motivation of how to build a politically stable integrated order" (Kotzur 2017: 44). Nettesheim as well as Bieber and Maiani understand solidarity as a legal norm. The intention of adding a value to the treaties is that behaviour changes accordingly (Nettesheim 2020: 266f.).

> „En droit de l'Union, il existe ainsi une étroite proximité entre l'affirmation de l'existence d'une solidarité, de l'exigence de son approfondissement aussi, et le dépassement progressif des intérêts nationaux en faveur d'un intérêt commun au sein d'une 'union sans cesse plus étroite'" (Bieber and Maiani 2012: 295).

However, solidarity is a value which cannot result in direct regulatory action, it serves as orientation or benchmark instead. „Solidarität als Grund ist (...) keine Rechtspflicht; sie strukturiert aber den teleologischen Entscheidungshorizont und die Abwägung kollidierender Werte, Interessen und Belange" (Nettesheim 2020: 267). Nettesheim argues that the reasons for an upgrade of solidarity as a legal norm are clear: European integration is no longer only about cooperation between states but shall be pursued as a solidarity project – a union of values. This has become necessary since the Union is not only a union aiming to integrate economically but also cooperates in areas such as the area of freedom, security and justice. This results in new rights and obligations, which can only be accepted, if the common nominator is solidarity (Nettesheim 2020: 266).

Klamert contends that the principle of solidarity can neither be directly applied in concrete cases nor be used for the development of EU law. However, solidarity is a systemic principle and therefore of importance for the shape and form of the EU. „Solidarität (...) ist ein systemisches Prinzip mit eingeschränkter Maßstabsfunktion ohne Leitfunktion und ohne Regelcharakter" (Klamert 2014: 25, see also Obradovic 2017). But even though the concept of solidarity might be programmatic, this does not mean that it lacks legal meaning (Jacqué 2015).

> „Solidarität ist zugleich ein 'systemtragender Leitwert' im Staaten-, Verfassungs- und Werteverbund der Europäischen Union. (...) Die Mitgliedstaaten erkennen mit den europäischen Verträgen an, daß ihnen die EU die Verfolgung ihrer mit den anderen Mitgliedstaaten gemeinsamen Ziele ermöglicht und damit nicht dazu dient, sich ein-seitig und nur auf die nationalen Interessen bedacht Vorteile zu ver-schaffen" (Calliess and Ruffert 2016).

Jacqué supports the argument that principles can only be justifiable if they are operationalized. As a consequence, solidarity can only be litigable if it is transposed into secondary law. The main function of the solidarity principle is to provide, as a leading norm, arguments on how to shape secondary law (Kadelbach 2014: 17). Solidarity can only be an operative legal principle, if its content is sufficiently precise in order to become legally examined. However,

> „(t)he CJEU does not provide precise and mutually consistent guide-lines on the matter. It seems that the exact effect of the solidarity prin-ciple among Member States depends on the concrete circumstances existing in the sector in which the principle will apply" (Obradovic 2017).

The legal weight of solidarity must be determined on a case by case basis by the acting organs (Nettesheim 2020: 268). Nevertheless, a trend can be observed towards an accumulation and condensation of references to the concept of solidarity in European law. This is relevant for both primary and secondary law (Müller 2010: 78f.).

The legal interpretation of solidarity is manifold and remains unclear regarding the possible influence and function of solidarity. The history of solidarity in EU law shows that the meaning of solidarity changed. The principle of solidarity no longer only refers to the obligation of the

Member States to follow EU rules (Jacqué calls this form „institutional solidarity" (Jacqué 2015)). Solidarity became a specific provision for different policy areas. „(…) (L)a notion de solidarité est devenue, contre toute attente, non seulement un ressort essentiel dans l'action de l'Union mais aussi un principe immanent au droit de l'Union" (Boutayeb and Laurent 2011: 5).

3.1.4. European energy policy and the effects of solidarity as a legal principle

Even though energy policy has been an essential feature of European integration since its early days, the policy field remained bolted and barred for further integration. This only changed with the liberalisation of the electricity and gas market from the 1990s onwards. Legislative bases for energy policy were e.g. Euratom, but also the titles on trans-European networks, environment and the responsibility for harmonisation.

> „(L)'énergie dans l'Europe communautaire est toujours restée une affaire d'Etat(s), éloignée des solidarités de fait a nouer que proclamaient Jean Monnet et Robert Schuman dans la Déclaration du 9 mai 1950. Même les crises pétrolières des années 1973 et 1979 n'ont pas convaincu les Etats membres d'adopter et de mettre en avant une position commune solide dans le domaine énergétique" (Boudant 2010: 174).

The energy article 194 TFEU was introduced as a shared principle with the Treaty of Lisbon in 2009 entailing the solidarity principle as a historical novelty. Solidarity had a prominent place in energy policy ever since, as it is mentioned twice with reference to energy policy (Art. 122 and Art. 194 TFEU). Streinz and Bings explain that the solidarity aspect goes hand in hand with the introduction of the energy article, since the introduction was a necessity due to an increased scarcity of energy resources which demanded EU-wide legislation and external action (Streinz and Bings 2012: 1–16).

TITLE XXI
ENERGY
Article 194
1. In the context of the establishment and functioning of the internal market and with regard for the need to preserve and improve the envi-

---

ronment, Union policy on energy shall aim, *in a spirit of solidarity between Member States*, to:

(a) ensure the functioning of the energy market;

(b) ensure security of energy supply in the Union;

(c) promote energy efficiency and energy saving and the development of new and renewable forms of energy; and

(d) promote the interconnection of energy networks.

2. Without prejudice to the application of other provisions of the Treaties, the European Parliament and the Council, acting in accordance with the ordinary legislative procedure, shall establish the measures necessary to achieve the objectives in paragraph 1. Such measures shall be adopted after consultation of the Economic and Social Committee and the Committee of the Regions.

Such measures shall not affect a Member State's right to determine the conditions for exploiting its energy resources, its choice between different energy sources and the general structure of its energy supply, without prejudice to Article 192(2)(c).

3. By way of derogation from paragraph 2, the Council, acting in accordance with a special legislative procedure, shall unanimously and after consulting the European Parliament, establish the measures referred to therein when they are primarily of a fiscal nature.

And Art. 122 TFEU refers to particular problems, which could occur regarding security of supply:

TITLE VIII

ECONOMIC AND MONETARY POLICY

Article 122

I. Without prejudice to any other procedures provided for in the Treaties, the Council, on a proposal from the Commission, may decide, *in a spirit of solidarity between Member States*, upon the measures appropriate to the economic situation, in particular if severe difficulties arise in the supply of certain products, notably in the area of energy.

Solidarity serves as overarching principle of all aims mentioned in Art. 194, namely the single energy market, security of energy supply, energy efficiency, energy saving, the development of new and renewable forms of energy and the interconnection of energy networks. Therefore, solidarity is introduced in Art. 194 as foundation for further integration of energy policy.

> „Energiepolitische *Solidarität bedeutet*, dass die Mitgliedstaaten aufgrund ihrer Zugehörigkeit zur EU in den Grenzen von Art. 194 AEUV *gemeinsam energiepolitisch handeln* und nicht einzeln vorgehen. Das schließt ein, die Verwirklichung der vier Ziele nicht zu behindern und sich in Notlagen gegenseitig zu helfen" (Hamer 2015, emphasis added).

At the same time there is no clarification on its application (Andoura 2013: 31). The Lisbon Treaty foresees in Art. 122 that, especially when it comes to energy questions, Member States shall support each other 'in the spirit of solidarity' in case of severe supply difficulties. Hence, solidarity is seen as a mechanism for securing energy supply. Nevertheless, solidarity is no direct obligation resulting from the Treaty, but only decisive for measures which are introduced for solidarity reasons based on Art. 194 TFEU (Küçük 2016: 972). Hermes also argues that energy solidarity is more than a proclamation for good conduct. The particular reference to energy in comparison to the general solidarity principle entails that energy solidarity implies a specific content (Hermes 2014: 62f.). The reference to the internal market in the beginning of Art. 194 TFEU seems to be a limitation to the energy competence as is the reference to the environment. Solidarity on the other hand could be understood as the aim of energy policy. It would also be possible to interpret solidarity as a corrective to the internal market (Ehricke and Hackländer 2008: 592). The energy article provides that Member States remain sovereign with regard to their internal energy sources structure (194(2) TFEU), i.e. each Member State can decide which sources it uses to what extent. Looking at the struggle to insert the energy article, this additional provision is hardly surprising. According to the literature, this provision has been demanded by Germany: „Il a été ajouté à la demande de l'Allemagne, en raison de la sensibilité particulière du débat sur l'énergie nucléaire dans ce pays, et probablement de sa volonté de préserver l'utilisation du charbon" (Stoffaës 2010: 100). Hermes illustrates that there are two interpretations of energy solidarity in 194 TFEU. On the one hand, Art. 194(2) underlines the national right to determine the use and choice of its energy sources. Consequently, Member States would not have to share resources with other Member States. On the other hand, solidarity refers to the responsibility of each Member State to adhere to European objectives and to take into account the national interests of other Member States (Hermes 2014: 62). This argument is a strong reminder that energy policy as shared competence is situated between the poles of solidarity and subsidiarity. „Without any definition of the principle of solidarity (…), it remains unclear whether it will receive any application in practice, or whether any concrete obligations will be derived from it for the EU and the member states" (Andoura 2010: 4). Calliess and Ruffert argue however, that solidarity became the focal point in European energy policy with the Treaty of Lisbon:

> „In Übereinstimmung mit einer generellen Stärkung des europäischen Solidaritätsprinzips im Vertrag von Lissabon ist die *mitgliedstaatliche Solidarität der prominent platzierte Zentralbegriff des Energierechts der EU.* (…) (I)mmer mehr bisher nationale Anliegen werden zu gemeinsamen Anliegen einer Solidargemeinschaft. Die Solidarität fungiert in dieser Entwicklung als Katalysator zwischen einem wachsenden tatsächlichen Bedürfnis nach gemeinsamem Vorgehen und (noch) unzureichenden positiv-rechtlichen Beistandspflichten" (Calliess and Ruffert 2016, emphasis added).

The authors explain that solidarity is above all of significance for security of supply. Member States could not act alone anymore e.g. in times of crisis and diversification of energy supplies is no longer sufficient. Member States need to ground their action on cooperation and trust due to the integration of the gas market, which is also a prerequisite of the Energy Union (ibid.). Solidarity is the „oil in the machinery", a guiding principle (Interview 10, Commission Official). According to Talus, solidarity refers primarily to security of supply, and can be understood as „corrective mechanism to the failure of the markets to achieve security of supply" (Talus 2013: 281). Instead of following only the market-based scheme of the 1980s and 1990s, supply disruptions demonstrated that an additional public-sector based solidarity scheme was necessary (ibid.). This, however, does not reflect the even earlier (Treaty of Maastricht) promotion of trans-border interconnections in both the gas and electricity sector, which was not only established to enhance social and economic cohesion but also to make the single energy market work in the long run. Calliess and Ruffert also point out that procedural solidarity obligations would in addition be needed regarding the transformation of national energy policies, such as the German Energiewende. With procedural solidarity obligations, they mean information, coordination and harmonisation (Calliess and Ruffert 2016). Solidarity unfolds as an instrument to implement policy measures which focus on the legal obligation of mutual assistance. Therefore, the CJEU can only verify if the legislator took into account the solidarity principle.

However, it is difficult to judge the implementation of solidarity. „Danach handelt es sich also um einen begrenzten verfassungsrechtlichen Maßstab für bestimmte Arten von Unionsgesetzgebung" (Hermes 2014: 64). The literature review demonstrated that there is no clear idea on how to transfer the legal interpretation of energy solidarity on practical solidarity. In addition, „the ‚solidarity principle' does not provide for a mere code of conduct, but rather carries with it special duties" (Tramountana 2019: 7). The consequences of this for political decision-making are still unclear.

3.2. The different stages of European energy policy

In this sub-chapter, I show how solidarity in European energy policy developed and present energy solidarity milestones (a list of the milestones can be found in annex 4). The chapter aims further to uncover the visions of solidarity of the EU institutions. Even if solidarity and energy policy integration go hand in hand as corner stones of the EU, they were hardly used in conjunction with each other until the Treaty of Lisbon came into force. This is demonstrated by the oil crises in 1973 and 1979, which did not lead to a joint reaction by the Member States. To the contrary, the Member States chose to pursue national strategies to secure the oil supply by concluding bilateral contracts (Petit 2010: 771), although the Council declared already in 1977 that „(...) the establishment of genuine solidarity between the Member States in the event of supply difficulties is one of the basic requirements for a Community energy policy" (Council 1977).

In the following, I depict the development of European energy policy with a particular focus on solidarity in order to demonstrate how the different actors applied solidarity and how the discussion on solidarity emerged over time. The story of energy solidarity starts officially in light of the gas crises in the 2000s (Petit 2010: 771), when „European institutions increasingly mention energy solidarity in their Strategies and Communications" (Andoura 2014). Solidarity was summoned in major policies and papers, such as the European Council Conclusions of 2006 and 2007, the Second Strategic Energy Review – An EU Energy Security and Solidarity Action Plan (2008) by the Commission, the Treaty of Lisbon (2009) as well as the Energy Union (as of 2014).

3.2.1. Phase I: Energy policy under pressure to reform (2005 – 2008)

Although energy represents a corner stone of the EU since its beginning, it was only during the Convention on the Constitutional Treaty that a new treaty article on energy policy was discussed. At first, the energy article was not supported but, in the end, introduced successfully due to the pressure of the Commission (Maichel 2005: 63). An informal EUCO meeting took place at Hampton Court on 27 September 2005, where Member States agreed to implement a European energy policy – a policy approach put forward by Tony Blair (Blair 2005). In the past, the British government was rather sceptic towards further integration in energy policy, which changed due to the fact that the UK became a net importer of gas in 2005 and that Blair's governments was interested in developing a joint climate change strategy.

> „(…) (T)he focus on energy at the Hampton Court summit in October 2005 was the result of intensive cooperation between the British Prime Minister and the President of the European Commission and a lot of work was done behind the scenes beforehand to ensure by-in by other member states. The Conclusions of the Hampton Court European Council have been the authority for, and driver of, subsequent Commission proposals" (House of Commons 2008: 29).

After the first gas crisis, which hit EU Member States in January 2006, a shift in the perception of security of gas supplies can be observed (Andoura 2013: 30). The gas crisis developed due to dissent between Ukraine and Russia in March 2005. Ukraine was the main transit zone for Russian gas in 2004, about 80 % of the total exported gas volumes to Europe transited the country (Stern 2006: 2). Ukraine had huge debts against Russia and did not pay for the imported gas, which resulted in shortcuts in gas by Russia. That is the reason why Ukraine took gas of the volumes which were provisioned for Europe. This conflictive situation resulted in disruptions of European gas supplies. The Member States were affected as of January 1 and the crisis was resolved three days later.

Box 14: Gas crisis 2006	
Country affected	Russian gas volumes not delivered
Hungary	40 %
Poland, Austria, Romania	34 %
France	25 – 30 %
Italy	25 %
Based on data of Stern 2006: 8f; own compilation	

However, Member States were capable of resolving the crisis individually due to the short amount of time of supply interruption. The IEA report states that „(i)n OECD Europe, drawdown of storage and voluntary fuel switching were able to make up for the shortfall relatively easily, because the duration of the interruption was short" (IEA 2006: 25). The crisis led policy makers to discuss additional measures, such as supply diversification and energy efficiency measures in order to decrease import dependency (IEA 2006: 25). Poland, a Member State which was already deeply concerned by Russia's behaviour towards Ukraine, felt increasing pressure. Additionally, Germany has announced to start building the Nord Stream pipeline in 2005, which would directly connect Russia and Germany therefore circumventing the traditional transit states Ukraine, Belarus and Poland. Poland announced the need to create a treaty on energy security, the Energy NATO, taking on board EU and NATO members. The Prime Minister of Poland, Kazimierz Marcinkiewicz, called upon Europe's energy musketeers:

> „It is the right time, in my view, to suggest a common effort to face not only current but also future challenges. That is why I want to propose to our partners from the EU and the Nato alliance *a treaty on energy security. It would be an expression of solidarity for all parties*, uniting them in the face of any energy threat provoked by either a cut or a diminution of supply sources that may occur because of natural disasters, disruption of wide distribution and supply systems or political decisions by suppliers" (Marcinkiewicz 2006, emphasis added).

In 2006, the European Council announced the implementation of an ‚Energy Policy for Europe'. A number of reasons have been identified in the literature for this step by the European Council, such as the reaction to the gas crisis, the resulting pressure from new Member States, the different perceptions of security of energy supply as well as the changing preference of the UK (Pointvogl 2009; Maltby 2013; Benson and Russel 2015).

The discussion on energy policy with a focus on the principle of solidarity started with the Green Paper ,A European Strategy for Sustainable, Competitive and Secure Energy' published by the Commission in March 2006 (Commission 2006a; see also Bundestag 2006: 2). The Commission raised four concerns under the heading of solidarity: First, terrorism is a threat to the physical infrastructure. Hence, the answer to these risks must be solidarity. Second, infrastructure is the precondition for solidarity. Third, a functioning internal market is the solution for supply risks. And fourth, information-sharing and collaboration impede market failures (Commission 2006a: 8).

The EP held a debate on security of energy supply on 22 March 2006 (Parliament 2006g). The debate demonstrated that there had not been a clear vision of solidarity in the EP or European energy policy in general at this time. Nearly all contributions to the debate concerning solidarity came from MEPs from the new central, Eastern and Baltic Member States. Andris Piebalgs (Latvia), Commissioner for Energy, supported solidarity as one important tool to create a European energy policy. „The Union is strong when there is solidarity. Solidarity means, firstly, being ready for extreme situations; secondly, it involves the solidarity mechanism and, thirdly, it involves a lot of information on what is happening on the energy markets" (Parliament 2006g). Piebalgs understood solidarity not only as tool to be used in extreme situations, but also as prerequisite for the energy market. Also, the creation of a European energy policy based on solidarity („une politique énergique plus solidaire") was debated as an answer to the Russian-Ukrainian gas conflict. It was feared that Russia would use energy as geopolitical weapon, which is why projects like the Northern Pipeline (now Nord Stream) were not needed. The build-up of infrastructure and the finalisation of the internal market were seen as crucial elements to make solidarity work. The founding Member States were perceived as self-interested building an 'anti-solidarity movement'.

The EP's debate demonstrated that there was a dividing line between old and new Member States. While new Member States feared the political pressure and power by Russia during and after the Russia-Ukraine gas crisis, the old Member States did not fully support solidarity measures as reaction to crisis situations. However, there was an agreement that energy networks are the basis to make 1) the internal energy market work and 2) to make solidarity operational. Another aspect of solidarity, which was under discussion, was the wish of some MEPs to put national preferences aside in favour of European solutions.

The European Council conclusions from March 2006 announced the implementation of an *Energy Policy for Europe* (Conclusions 2006b). The European Council acknowledged that there are several challenges concerning the development of an energy policy within the EU. The Member States tried to create a common vision on energy policy by ensuring 'coherence between Member States' and by building a „shared perspective on long term supply and demand". Solidarity was only mentioned in relation to the supply crises as counter-principle to subsidiarity (Conclusions 2006b: 29).

Just shortly after, in June 2006, the Commission and the High Representative presented a paper to the European Council on „An external policy to serve Europe's energy interests". The paper indicated that there are two „building blocks of energy security: functioning markets and diversification" (Commission 2006c: 2) not mentioning solidarity once. In June 2006, the EUCO reconfirmed its call for an *Energy Policy for Europe* focusing on energy security. The EUCO underlined that external policy shall be implemented in a spirit of solidarity as proposed in the June paper of the Commission and the High Representative (although solidarity was not mentioned in the paper). Overall, solidarity only seemed to be a buzzword used as a response to Eastern concerns. The European Council promoted two forms of solidarity. First, solidarity refers to the conduct of foreign policy, which means that Member States refrain from action, which would hurt other Member States. Second, solidarity refers to the will to balance the financial burdens concerning infrastructure projects (Conclusions 2006a).

In November 2006, the Commission compiled different answers and reactions in the summary report on the analysis of the debate on the green paper "A European Strategy for Sustainable, Competitive and Secure Energy" (Commission 2006b). The Commission identified „closer political collaboration and full implementation of legislation" as the most critical aspects of solidarity. In order to increase security of supply, solidarity mechanisms were said to be most useful next to further investments in the electricty sector and smart electricity networks. Under the bullet point of ‚solidarity' the Commission listed different points, without clarifying their direct connection to solidarity (Commission 2006b: 26). A fully integrated market was supported by most of the contributors, however, without any further EU intervention. The Commission asked „which measures need to be taken at Community level to manage energy supply crises if they do occur?". 40,7 % of respondents supported the idea of a solidarity mechanism in case of supply disruptions in order to assist a Member State. The assessment of the Commission demonstrated that even though Member States agreed to put forward an Energy Policy for Europe there was no agreement on the goals and the level of cooperation. Member States were reluctant to promote further integration. Nevertheless, the EP became a strong supporter of solidarity.

The need for solidarity was also repeated during an EP plenary debate in December 2006. Solidarity was said to have two tasks: Inner EU solidarity towards external suppliers and solidarity to achieve a fully integrated market (Parliament 2006f). In February 2007, the TTE Council emphasised that different measures were needed to ameliorate security of supply in a spirit of solidarity. The list of possible measures included diversification of energy supplies, development of crisis response mechanisms, improving oil transparency, gas storage facilities, an impact assessment of imports and network security of each Member State and the establishment of an Energy Observatory by the Commission (Council 2007: 12f.). In the Presidency Conclusions of March 2007, the European Council agreed to the following statement as regards the implementation of the EPE:

> „Given that energy production and use are the main sources for greenhouse gas emissions, an integrated approach to climate and energy policy is needed to realise this objective. Integration should be achieved in a mutually supportive way. With this in mind, the Energy Policy for Europe (EPE) will pursue the following three objectives, fully respecting Member States' choice of energy mix and sovereignty over primary energy sources and *underpinned by a spirit of solidarity amongst Member States*:
> – Increasing security of supply;
> – Ensuring the competitiveness of European economies and the availability of affordable energy;
> – Promoting environmental sustainability and combating climate change" (Conclusions 2007, emphasis added).

The three points security of supply, competitiveness and sustainability have been known as the energy triangle, which informs the making of a secure energy policy. This triangle has already been formulated in the Green Paper of 2006 (Tagliapietra 2017). It was for the first time that energy policy took over such a prominent place at a European Council meeting. Solidarity became a foundation for all policy objectives: the EPE was „underpinned by a spirit of solidarity amongst Member States" (Conclusions 2007). However, the mentioning of solidarity in the European Council Conclusions of March 2007 was only a small concession to the Central and Eastern Member States to calm them down (Fischer 2017a: 137). Therefore, even though the conclusions acknowledged that solidarity was part of the overall framework, the notion of solidarity remained shallow.

The point on solidarity was taken up again in the discussion on the treaty change during the European Council meeting on 21/22 June 2007 and in the Presidency Conclusion. The reference to solidarity in the Treaty Art. 194 TFEU was only made in 2007, when Poland pushed for the mentioning of solidarity in the new treaty article since the Member State was threatened by the gas crisis of 2006 (Fischer 2009: 52; Andoura 2010: 6; Jegen 2014). „Poland succeeded at placing the issue of 'energy solidarity' onto the EU agenda and successfully exploited the opportunity of the reform treaty negotiations to secure the inclusion of scaled-down references on 'energy solidarity' into the Lisbon treaty" (Roth 2011: 604). Member States agreed to refer to solidarity as regards energy supply in Art. 100 and Art. 194 TFEU (see chapter 3.1.2 on legal developments for more details).

> „m) In Article 100 (measures in case of severe difficulties in the supply of certain products), a reference to the spirit of solidarity between Member States and to the particular case of energy as regards difficulties in the supply of certain products will be inserted (see point 3) of Annex 2).
> Q) In the Article on energy, agreed in the 2004 IGC, a reference to the spirit of solidarity between Member States will be inserted (see point 5) of Annex 2), as well as a new point (d) on the promotion of interconnection of energy networks".

The agreement of the European Council to insert solidarity in the energy article had direct consequences. In September 2007, Jacek Saryusz-Wolski, the rapporteur of the Committee on Foreign Affairs (AFET) published an own-initiative report on „towards a common European foreign policy on energy" (Parliament 2007b) as reaction to the Commission's Green Paper of December 2006. The Green Paper „External energy relations – from principles to action" (Commission 2006d) did not make any reference to solidarity. AFET, however, considered solidarity as one of the critical elements to build up a robust European energy policy. In addition to that, „a basis for solidarity in the area of energy policy can become a precedent for future solidarity in other areas and thus help to strengthen the role of the EU in its external relations" (Parliament 2007b). The implementation of solidarity in energy policy can work as a catalyst for similar arrangements in other policy fields (point 26). Under point C on „Solidarity in crisis situation", the report strongly urges the implementation of solidarity mechanisms, which would be justified by the Treaty:

> „30. (…) calls on the Council and the Member States to create a solidarity mechanism, in accordance with the spirit of solidarity between Members States referred to in the new Reform Treaty agreed upon by the European Council in June 2007, which would allow the EU to act efficiently, swiftly and coherently in crisis situations caused by disruption of supply, damage to critical infrastructure or any other event" (ibid.).

Based on this reflection, Saryusz-Wolski's report called for a common European foreign policy on energy based on solidarity and diversification: „The EU's 27 Member States need to replace their current preference for energy unilateralism with a new common policy of energy solidarity. It is only by acting collectively that Europe can hope to deal with main suppliers on even terms". The Parliament adopted the resolution based on the report on 26 September 2007 (Parliament 2007a) repeating the main points of the report. During the debate on the topic, MEP Ana Maria Gomes (PSE, Portugal) stated how the approach of *strategic autonomy* entailed solidarity:

> „This resolution reveals the glaring inadequacies of European policies in the field of energy. In fact, the European Union is not a global actor here. Those who, like me, believe that the European Union should guarantee itself a minimum *strategic autonomy*, can only view with consternation our vulnerability in this matter. It is not a question of aiming for a Utopian self-sufficiency, *but rather of recognising the need for greater coordination of national policies, ensuring there is solidarity between Member States and developing relationships with global partners which are less asymmetrical but predictable and based on a truly European approach*. For example, it is up to us Europeans to work against the 'divide and rule' attitude which has marked relations with Russia in this area" (Parliament 2007c, emphasis added).

Gomes interprets solidarity here as a sub-strategy to reach ‚strategic autonomy'. The pursuit of ‚strategic autonomy'[3] in the energy sector started at

---

3 Other authors refer to ‚strategic sovereignty' or ‚European sovereignty' instead (see Leonard, Mark and Shapiro, Jeremy (2019) 'Strategic sovereignty: How Europe

the Commission at this particular time and solidarity was part of this strategy. The Commission intended to implement ‚strategic autonomy' which means that a government "should never be in the position to make a decision about any policy whilst thinking about the impact on the energy sector" (Interview 2, DG Energy). Strategic autonomy is

> „most developed in gas, (…) we (the Commission) have developed that. And it's the major driver for our infrastructure policies, particularly in gas, and for our policy aims and legislation and for all the political organisation of energy in Central and Eastern Europe and in particular the Energy Community. (…) So the 2006 and 2009 gas cuts showed that if one state acted in its own narrow interests or in the interests of a third state, such as Russia, it could drain the gas network of all gas or it could disrupt the electricity system in such a way that the whole EU would suffer. So the decision was taken that we shouldn't allow this to happen and that all MS have strategic autonomy so they didn't have to choose between their relationship with Russia, in this case, and their relationship with Brussels" (Interview 2, DG Energy).

Strategic autonomy became, however, not officially part of the EU vocabulary since the general messages implied ‚multilateralism' and ‚peace' at that time. Only the geopolitical developments made the expression acceptable in the recent years (Interview 5, EP). „You take, so to speak, the European security interest, European solidarity and when you bring that together, you have European sovereignty" (Interview 10, Commission Official). However, the expression ‚strategic autonomy' is disputed. Other Commission Officials neglected the existence of such a strategy (Interview 3 and 8, DG Energy), or understood it as the general security of supply strategy (Interview 4, DG Energy).

The Commission agreed with most of the content of the EP's resolution (Commission 2007a): A means to ensure solidarity is to take into account the interests of other Member States and the EU as a whole. The other point referred to solidarity in crisis repeating the points raised by the European Council of March 2007. Commissioner Piebalgs gave a speech at the

---

can regain the capacity to act', European Council on Foreign Relations. Strategic autonomy is rooted in the beginning of the European Communities but has appeared more frequently in EU documents only in the last years (Lippert, Barbara, Ondarza, Nicolai von and Perthes, Volker (2019) 'European Strategic Autonomy – Actors, Issues, Conflicts of Interests', SWP Research Paper, 4(March 2019): 6).

Vilnius Energy Security Conference in October 2007, where he underlined the solidarity aspect:

> „(...) I should emphasize the EU's commitment to energy solidarity. This is essential within the EU energy market. National borders no longer delineate energy interests. The energy security of one Member State is linked to the energy security of the whole EU. The new Reform Treaty will enshrine the principle of energy solidarity, and we are developing the mechanisms to ensure that it works in practice" (Piebalgs 2007a).

Thus, Piebalgs highlighted the interdependence of the single Member States and supported his argument by the reference to the Treaty. He also promised that solidarity would be translated into practice. The EUCO met for a special meeting on 1 September 2008 due to the military intervention from Russia in Georgia. The EUCO expressed its deep concern about the possible consequences for the stability in the region. „Recent events illustrate the need for Europe to intensify its efforts with regard to the security of energy supplies (...) in particular as regards diversification of energy sources and supply routes" (Conclusions 2008b). It is evident that there was a growing unease towards Russia's behaviour, which was spurred by the insecurity of Eastern Member States. In October 2008, the EUCO included a chapter on security of energy supply in its conclusions: „Security of energy supply is a priority for the European Union. It involves the responsibility and solidarity of all the Member States" (Conclusions 2008a). Even though this is not the first reference of the European Council to solidarity, there is a novelty, which is *responsibility*. However, it remains unclear what kind of responsibility the European Council had in mind. Looking at the listed proposals and initiatives, the EUCO probably meant both the responsibility of each Member State to ensure its security of supply (stronger market, more transparency) and the responsibility to enhance the system for the profit of all Member States (adding critical infrastructures, such as LNG terminals) (Conclusions 2008a: 7).

In November 2008, the Commission presented ‚An EU Energy Security and Solidarity Action Plan' (Commission 2008d). The Commission emphasised that „solidarity between Member States is a basic feature of EU membership" (ibid.). The Commission argued also that every „state is responsible for its own security (...), (but that) national solutions are often insufficient" (ibid.). The Commission repeated similar arguments regarding solidarity by pointing out that some states rely on one supplier only, which is why diversification of supplies is needed. Furthermore,

„(i)nterconnection and solidarity within the internal market is not only a natural feature of an integrated market-based system but is equally
essential to spread and reduce individual risk. The EU therefore needs
to take concrete measures to ensure that these markets increase the
diversity of their gas supply" (ibid.).

Additionally, the Commission urged for the implementation of liquefied
natural gas and adequate gas storage. „Sufficient LNG capacity (…) should
be available to all Member States (…) on the basis of a solidarity arrangement. This is particularly important for Member States currently overwhelmingly dependent on a single gas supplier" (ibid.).

The Commission found that there is general support for the Commission's initiatives, which it proposed in the Second Strategic Energy Review,
but „there are nuances in the support, with greatest appreciation from
those Member States (mainly new MS and peripheral areas) who feel
more vulnerable energy-wise and want to see more concrete solidarity
mechanisms" (Council 2008a). The Council held a public debate on the
topic in December 2008 in order to prepare the input for the European
Council meeting of March 2009. One point concerned the improvement
of solidarity: „which priority measures should be developed to improve
Member States' responsibility and solidarity when faced with the risks
of a crisis?" (Council 2008c). This question shows that the reflections on
solidarity were only about to begin.

The first phase demonstrated that solidarity was increasingly on the
agenda for different reasons. The accession of the new Member States,
which were much more vulnerable towards supply disruptions, changed
the debate within the EP in favour of solidarity. The Parliament rushed
forward showing fierce determination to put energy policy on the agenda with solidarity at its centre. Solidarity was urged to be the leading
principle for the policy development (also due to its inclusion in the
Treaty of Lisbon). Solidarity was, however, at this point in time used as
a buzzword only in order to make a political statement. Member States
remained very sceptic towards further integration, although a functioning
single energy market would resolve major security problems (Geden 2009:
15). „(…) (E)nergy markets remained highly concentrated and national
in scope" (Maltby 2013: 439). I call the phase until 2009 ‚identification
phase‘, since both the Member States as well as the EU institutions tried
to develop a vision of a European energy policy. Part of this undertaking
was the building up of a „we-perspective". The European Council added
responsibility as a counterpart to solidarity. However, Member States had
severe differences concerning energy sources (e.g. Energiewende in Ger-

many vs. intensified lignite production in Poland) and external supplies, which is why a common perspective was only developing at the pace of the integration of the internal market. In view of Russia's foreign policy and the gas crisis in 2006, the Commission strived for the implementation of an integrated security of supply policy with solidarity at its core (strategic autonomy). Altogether, the Commission was eager to promote solidarity as feature of an EU energy policy and actively pursued its insertion in strategy papers.

3.2.2. Phase II: Changing old patterns (2009 – 2013)

2009 presented a year of major changes for EU energy policy. The year started with the gas crisis, which demonstrated not only the dependence from Russian gas but also the insufficient responses on the European level. In September 2009, the Lisbon Treaty came into force. The newly introduced energy Art. 194 TFEU as well as Art. 122 TFEU on energy supply crises included solidarity as a basis for community action. It was also as of 2009 that solidarity was increasingly inserted in secondary law. During phase II, four different legislative acts which included solidarity, were implemented or revised. However, as the analysis of the case studies will show, only declarative solidarity was achieved.

The gas crisis in 2009 took place between 6 and 20 January. The gas flow was interrupted between Russia and the EU via Ukraine, through which still 80 % of Russian imports were transited to the EU. The reason for the interruption was a commercial disagreement between the energy companies Naftogaz (Ukraine) and Gazprom (Russia). European Member States were affected as of January 2nd, however, in the early morning of January 6, there were vast shortfalls of gas (e.g. Slovakia received only 10 % of gas, which further effected EU Member relying on Slovakian gas flows). The EU, headed by the Czech presidency and the Commission, facilitated an agreement between Russia and Ukraine, which included 10-year agreements on gas purchase by Ukraine and gas transits via Ukraine to the EU. Due to the crisis in 2006, the EU had installed an early warning mechanism between the Russian government and the Commission. The Commission received a warning from Russia on 18 December 2008 but was not further notified about when the supply would be disrupted and that the disruption would be 100 %, which happened on 6 and 7 January 2009. A concrete contingency plan did not exist and sufficient information about each state's gas systems was missing, which is why it was challenging to respond to the crisis at the EU level (Commission 2009d).

„The January 2009 gas disruptions resulted in the most serious gas supply crisis to hit the EU in its history, depriving EU Member States of 20 % of their gas supplies. Coinciding with a cold spell in many parts of Europe, it demonstrated the vulnerability of the EU and some of its Member States to gas disruptions" (Vanhoorn and Faas 2009: 19).

The Member States' reactions depended on their possibilities to carry out supply and demand side measures. The biggest challenges for the Member States were the lack of coherent infrastructure (in particular inter-connectors) and insufficient diversification of external suppliers (Vanhoorn and Faas 2009). The solutions at hand for the supply cut were 1) to release gas from storage, 2) additional LNG imports, 3) fuel switch and 4) extra purchase from neighbouring countries. Another vital measure was the diversification as regards both routes and suppliers. Alternative suppliers were Norway and Libya, alternative routes were via Belarus and Turkey. The gas industry concluded new agreements between individual companies to facilitate gas trade. However, as the Commission stated, there were also major difficulties for the suppliers: „the lack of alternative suppliers, limited or non-existent connections to alternative supplies, slowness of accessing gas from storage, few options for fuel-switching and high levels of demand as a result of cold weather" (Commission 2009d: 10). Solidarity failed because the necessary precondition in form of the necessary infrastructure was unfulfilled (Crisan and Kuhn 2017: 168). Therefore, the Commission called for regulatory intervention. Additionally, the Commission criticised lacking infrastructure as well as the national concentration of Transmission System Operators (TSOs) which led to difficulties in the neighbourhood (Crisan and Kuhn 2017: 168). A major problem concerned the lack of inter-connectors:

„(...) when Russians cut the gas supply via Ukraine, Slovakia was definitely in the cold. And not because there was no gas in the EU. There was just not the ability to deliver the gas by any mechanism, neither by solidarity neither by market mechanisms, because there have been no interconnections, no bi-directional flows (...)" (Interview 4, DG Energy).

As a lesson learnt, the Commission underlined the importance of a political framework in case of crisis: „Companies are willing to cooperate in a crisis, but to do so they need a clearly defined and consistent political framework. This needs to set out clearly what constitutes a crisis, how to respond, and the respective role of markets and public authorities" (Commission 2009d: 11). This crisis illustrated to what extent Member States are interdependent and that their efforts up until then were not sufficient in order to resolve interruptions of gas supply. „Solidarity is still just words, due to a lack of political will in some countries" (Mandil 2009). The problem of free-riding was paramount:

> „We have seen this also in the crisis of 2009, the Italians have called all the gas to come to Italy (…) and then created depression in Slovenia. So these countries were not able to tackle the problem, because you had some free-rider in the system. And this is a lack of solidarity. Pure selfish behaviour. And that is where you need to have obligations" (Interview 3, DG Energy).

But solidarity was up to this point hardly included in energy policy legislation. During the crisis of 2009, it depended on the willingness of the Member States if and up to what extent they wanted to help each other and share information. The Lisbon Treaty changed this voluntariness in so far that there was a legal basis in place, which could impact the further development of a European energy policy (Rocco 2019: 4).

> „At least on a symbolic level, Polish security concerns met with a positive response. The Lisbon Treaty adopted in 2009 includes a reference to the spirit of solidarity between Member States to ensure security of energy supply in the Union as well as to the promotion of the interconnection of energy networks" (Jegen 2014: 15).

However, „the Treaty is silent on the duties or obligations which derive from such a clause. (…) „(N)o common concepts or generally accepted working definitions of solidarity have been developed which might form a basis for action" (Andoura 2010: 12; see chapter on solidarity as legal norm). This means that there is uncertainty if and how the principle will be applied in practice in energy policy (Andoura 2010: 4). Up to that point, there was only Directive 2004/67/EC, which contained a reference to solidarity. Nevertheless, the gas crises were the decisive factor for Member States to agree on the introduction of solidarity (personal communication 2, Council).

The Parliament held a debate on „Gas supplies by Russia to Ukraine and the EU" on 14 January 2009. Main issues were the unreliability of both partners Ukraine and Russia, the lacking infrastructure and the need to develop a long-term energy policy including solidarity mechanisms

(Parliament 2009b). The solidarity claims came almost exclusively from MEPs from Central and Eastern Europe. On 3 February 2009, the EP published a resolution on the Second Strategic Energy Review (Parliament 2009d). The Parliament underlined several times the importance of solidarity regarding security of supply: „(...) energy solidarity must become a major European concern at European, regional and bilateral level and that damaging energy supply in a Member State afflicts the European Union as a whole" (Recital 9). The EP highlighted that Member States agreed to practice solidarity with the Lisbon Treaty (Recital 14) and connected the functioning of the internal market with the promotion of solidarity to guarantee security of supply (Recital 40).

In May 2010, the Commission published a discussion paper called „Stock taking document: Towards a new Energy Strategy for Europe 2011–2020" (Commission 2010d) in preparation for the Europe 2020 strategy. Solidarity has a prominent place in the document encompassing all different aspects of EU energy policy. The aim of the Commission was to underline the need for joint action and the development of a coherent policy: First, the Treaty of Lisbon provides now a legal basis for energy policy based on solidarity. Second, „(e)nergy solidarity and security concerns have become more prominent in recent years". Third, interconnected markets and the operationalisation of solidarity are intertwined. Fourth, the EU's external energy policy would be strengthened if the principle of solidarity is applied. In the conclusion, solidarity is mentioned as a basic principle of energy policy.

On 25 November 2010, the EP published a resolution „on towards a new Energy Strategy for Europe 2011–2020" (Parliament 2010b) as reply to the Commission's stock taking document (Commission 2010d). There are three references to solidarity. First, the EP recognised solidarity as a basis for energy policy underlining that the new legal basis in the Lisbon Treaty entails solidarity. In the next step, the EP created a vision of solidarity:

> „Emphasises that the proposed strategy should be carried out, above all, in a spirit of solidarity and responsibility, on the basis that no Member State can be left behind or isolated and all Member States take measures to ensure the Union's mutual security; stresses the significance of the inclusion in the Treaty of a specific chapter on energy (Article 194 TFEU), providing a firm legal basis for Union action based on the Community method" (Parliament 2010b).

Solidarity and responsibility are two sides of the same coin, which aim to balance an energy policy that is now a shared competence. Responsibility means to avoid freeriding and also to act in fairness towards the others. Third, the EP emphasises the significance of compliance in the spirit of energy solidarity and „not give in to the vested interests of individual European countries, especially not exporters of gas to the European market". The resolution reveals that the Parliament eventually agreed to the caveats of the Member States that responsibility was a necessary counterpart to solidarity.

In November 2010, the Commission published a document entitled „Energy 2020: A strategy for competitive, sustainable and secure energy" (Commission 2010a). This communication was the output of the consultation process, which was started by the stock taking document of May 2010. The Commission repeats that „the obligation of solidarity among Member States will be null and void without a sufficient internal infrastructure and interconnectors across external borders and maritime areas". Solidarity is mentioned also as criterion for the funding of infrastructure. Finally, the Commission points out that „the EU's external energy policy must ensure effective solidarity, responsibility and transparency among all Member States" (Commission 2010a). Solidarity is again the keyword to design European energy policy. However, it remains unclear how such solidarity could look like in practice.

In September 2013, Marc Tarabella (S&D), MEP, submitted a question for written answer to the Commission on the subject ‚Definition of energy solidarity'.

> „The solidarity between Member States called for by the EU Treaty should apply to both the daily working and the crisis management of the internal and external energy policy. Should the Commission not provide a clear definition of 'energy solidarity' in order to ensure that it is respected by all Member States?" (Tarabella 2013).

Oettinger, who was then Energy Commissioner, answered the following on behalf of the Commission:

> „Achieving tangible solidarity between Member States in the field of energy is one of the main underlying themes of EU energy policy. It is pursued through provisions in many pieces of EU legislation (e.g. Regulation (EU) 994/2010 on measures to safeguard security of gas supplies; Directive 2005/89/EC concerning measures to safeguard security of electricity supply and infrastructure investment; and the TEN-E Regulation (347/2013) on guidelines for trans-European energy infrastructure). The main prerequisite for solidarity to work well in the area of energy is the existence of a well-functioning internal ener-

gy market, the completion of which is a key priority of the Commission" (Oettinger 2013).

Oettinger's answer is far from a definition, as demanded by the MEP. This statement demonstrates that the Commission could not provide a clear vision of solidarity, but that solidarity was permeating different aspects of energy policy. The answer also reveals that the Commissioner did not understand solidarity purely in terms of security of supply, since Oettinger also mentioned the TEN-E regulation.

Phase II was coined by an increasing trend of discussing the implications of solidarity, which was coming up as a reference point in Parliament debates, at (European) Council meetings and in strategic papers by the Commission. The Treaty, which ensured that energy was a shared competence, supported the further development of a European energy policy beyond the functioning of the internal market. The EP had already illustrated concrete ideas of how solidarity should be applied in practice. Responsibility, fairness and the condition not to hurt other Member States were part of this vision. The term responsibility gained equal importance as a counterpart of solidarity, which was demanded by the Member States and was eventually also inserted in the resolutions by the Parliament. The Commission remained vague about the impact of solidarity, although the term received a lot of attention. At the same time, the Commission was very active in introducing new legislation on energy policy. The four pieces of legislation, which will be analysed in more detail later, were either reformed or newly introduced during this phase.

3.2.3. Phase III: The Energy Union (as of 2014)

The European Council Conclusions from March 2014 expressed the increasing interest in diversification (Conclusions 2014a). EUCO asked the Commission to undertake a study on how to reduce energy dependence, in particular concerning the most dependent Member States. Solidarity is only mentioned once in the study: „Member States will show solidarity in case of sudden disruptions of energy supply in one or several Member States" (Conclusions 2014a: 10). This seems to be a firm commitment. However, since there is no clear guideline it remained a political promise without substance. The EUCO Conclusions reacted to the annexation of Crimea by Russia in March 2014. In April 2014, Putin declared that EU countries would be confronted with an increased risk of gas supply disruptions if Ukraine would not pay prepayments to Russia (Umbach 2014).

In this context, Donald Tusk, who was then Prime Minister of Poland, proposed his ideas of an Energy Union. He outlined that „an energy union (...) would be based on solidarity and common economic interests" (Tusk 2014). Six pillars would form the Energy Union. Solidarity was mentioned in the second dimension:

> „Second, mechanisms guaranteeing solidarity among member states should be strengthened in case energy supplies are again cut off, as they were in the cold winter of 2009 when Russia's previous dispute with Ukraine stopped gas flowing to a number of EU nations" (Tusk 2014).

In May 2014, the Commission published the European Energy Security Strategy (Commission 2014b) arguing that a such a strategy is needed due to the crises in 2006 and 2009 which had severe consequences for Eastern Member States. Above all, interdependence between Member States increased since the EU created the internal market. However, the internal market is not yet finalised, and additionally, security of supply is carried out on the national and not on the community level. Due to these reasons, the Commission urged for a „more collective approach through a functioning internal market and greater cooperation at regional and European levels" (Commission 2014b: 3). In addition to this internal approach, a „more coherent external approach" was also urged for (ibid.). The Commission described the key pillars of the strategy, „that together promote closer cooperation beneficial for all Member States while respecting national energy choices, and are underpinned by the principle of solidarity" (Commission 2014b: 3). The first key pillar concentrates on immediate action by referring to „the EU's capacity to overcome a major disruption during the winter 2014/2015". The second pillar concerns „strengthening emergency/solidarity mechanisms including coordination of risk assessments and contingency plans; and protecting strategic infrastructure" (Commission 2014b: 3). The other pillars include

> „moderating energy demand; building a well-functioning internal market; increasing energy production in the EU; developing of energy technology; diversifying external supplies and related infrastructure; Improving coordination of national energy policies and speaking with one voice in external energy policy" (Commission 2014b: 3).

The headline of point 2.4 is „solidarity mechanisms among Member States". The paragraph starts with a normative frame: „The solidarity that is the hallmark of the EU requires practical assistance for those Member

States most vulnerable to severe energy supply disruptions". This solidarity mechanism entails an evaluation of the energy system and collection of information "with the aim of guaranteeing minimum levels of intra-EU deliveries of alternative fuel supplies to complement emergency stocks". The Commission prioritises the more vulnerable Eastern Member States. There is no clear vision on how a solidarity mechanism could practically look like, the Commission only reaffirms its willingness to implement a mechanism which should „deliver energy to countries in times of need, based on risk assessments (energy security stress tests)". Infrastructure projects (27 gas projects), which have a crucial impact on security of supply, have been identified. Their „implementation is expected to enhance diversification of supply possibilities and solidarity in the most vulnerable parts of Europe". In the conclusions, the Commission underlined again the necessity to reinforce existing solidarity mechanisms.

Based on the Commission's energy security strategy, the EUCO agreed that „in the light of the assessments of the risk of short-term supply disruption, existing emergency and solidarity mechanisms (…) will be reinforced in order to address this risk primarily in the most vulnerable Member States" (Conclusions 2014b). The European Council

> „endorsed on 27 June 2014 the Commission's proposal to launch a so-called stress test exercise with the purpose of assessing the resilience of the European gas system to cope with a severe disruption of gas supply to the EU this winter" (Commission 2014a) (see details in chapter 4.1.2).

In 2014, the Ukraine crisis led to tremendous security concerns in the EU. The EU faced again the threat of a supply crisis (Pirani et al. 2014). The EU successfully implemented a deal with Russia and Ukraine securing sufficient gas supply during the winter period. However, due to solidarity with Ukraine, Poland was undersupplied stating a drop of supplies of 45 % in September 2014. This shortfall was resolved thanks to the reverse flow installation at the Yamal Pipeline, which made it possible for Poland to purchase additional gas from Germany and the Czech Republic (Łoskot-Strachota 2014). The Policy Department of DG EXPO of the EP published a study on the quest for natural gas pipelines in 2014. The study underlined the need for „joint action based on the solidarity principle" since all energy actions are interconnected, which is why an external shock cannot be absorbed on the national level only. „In a situation of international tension, common security interests should prevail over national interests or short-term economic considerations (such as the fact that Russian gas may be cheaper than other options)" (De Micco 2014: 28).

In February 2015, the Commission sent out a communication on the ,Energy Union Package – A Framework Strategy for a Resilient Energy Union with a Forward-Looking Climate Change Policy' (Commission 2015b). The Commission described how this Energy Union should look like in a comprehensive way: „Our vision is of an Energy Union where Member States see that they depend on each other to deliver secure energy to their citizens, based on true solidarity and trust, and of an Energy Union that speaks with one voice in global affairs" (Commission 2015b: 2). The Commission argued that Member States have to see that they are inter-dependent. The Commission wanted thus to underline that a European solution is unavoidable. Solidarity is also part of the title of the first dimension of the Energy Union, which is called „Energy Security, Solidarity and Trust". „The spirit of solidarity in energy matters is explicitly mentioned in the Treaty and is at the heart of the Energy Union" (Commission 2015b: 4). The pillar „security, solidarity and trust" covers the topics of diversification, security of supply (where solidarity is again explicitly mentioned), the EU's role in global energy markets and transparency on gas supply. According to one interview, solidarity became part of the Energy Union „(...) to please a bit the Poles. I think Juncker, when he came with the Energy Union, he put solidarity in it" (Interview 3, DG Energy). Western European States were also against Tusk's original proposal of a joint gas purchase and the Greens demanded a more comprehensive approach (Interview 11, Official, Government of Luxembourg). At the end of 2015, the Commission published a report entitled ,State of the Energy Union 2015' (Commission 2015c). This report was published on an annual basis as of 2015 in order to evaluate the progress of the different dimensions of the Energy Union. The Energy Union „gives hope for solving the major paradox of EU energy policy – the tension between national sovereignty over the energy sector and a community perspective based on solidarity, cooperation and scale" (Szulecki et al. 2016: 548).

In June 2016, the European External Action Service (EEAS) published "A Global Strategy for the European Union's Foreign and Security Policy" (EEAS 2016). (Energy) solidarity was part of the priorities of external action:

> „An appropriate level of ambition and strategic autonomy is important for Europe's ability to promote peace and security within and beyond its borders. We will therefore enhance our efforts on defence, cyber, counterterrorism, energy and strategic communications. Mem-

ber States must translate their commitments to mutual assistance and solidarity enshrined in the Treaties into action" (EEAS 2016: 9).

However, the text also reveals that solidarity is a sub-strategy in order to reach strategic autonomy, which is a reply to perceived and real threats such as energy insecurity, terrorism and climate change.

3.2.4. Results and discussion

Analysing the general developments over time (2005 – 2016) different observations can be drawn upon. The strategy of the Commission included the creation of closer ties with Russia in the early 2000s. Additionally, the internal market was suspected to be a sufficiently reliable solution for any problems in gas supply (Roth 2011: 607). Even the EP did not support further integration until 2004. The evaluation from the internal debates of the EP demonstrates that above all Central and Eastern European Member States supported the further integration of energy security policy and demanded European solidarity. In 2005, the EUCO decided to introduce an Energy Policy for Europe. This decision picked up pace when the crisis hit Eastern Member States in 2006. The Commission hardly used security frames to push its argument for further energy solidarity. None of the actors had a full-fledged idea how to understand solidarity or how to apply it, and solidarity was not sincerely pursued until the second gas crisis happened. Until this point in time, the EU did not fear possible consequences of gas dependence. „So for West Europeans, Russians at least until 2009 have been the best suppliers – never trouble – for East experience definitely for other reasons has been different. So if you go just by saying it's security of supply, it would never get majority" (Interview 4, DG Energy). The crises have been a game changer for all actors, since security concerns increased. The Commission used these concerns for advancing the integration of the gas sector and to develop a European perspective based on the functioning of the internal market.

The introduction of an energy article was already decided on before the Constitutional Treaty failed. However, Poland lobbied successfully for the insertion of solidarity in both energy Art. 194 TFEU as well as Art. 122 TFEU on supply disruptions. In 2009, the European Council agreed to reshuffle competences in order to carry out energy security policy on the community level. The European Council conclusions (2004 and 2019) referred to energy solidarity the last time in 2014 underlining three main aspects of energy solidarity, which are the conduct of external energy policy, solidarity as a crisis response mechanism and solidarity as a reason for the implementation of infrastructure. Since 2015, the Commission tries to put life in the Energy Union with different legislative packages, which will be further discussed in the following chapter.

4. Solidarity in secondary law: only cosmetic improvements?

In the following chapter, I will elaborate on the question which kind of solidarity (declarative or institutionalised) has been introduced in secondary law. This is accompanied by a comprehensive analysis of why and how solidarity was introduced in four different legislative acts taking into consideration policy entrepreneurship and policy formulation. Additionally, I provide a detailed analysis of the Court case on the OPAL pipeline, which stipulated energy solidarity. I will examine if functional pressure occurred and in how far this pressure was perceived by the decision-makers (Hypothesis 1). In addition, I will analyse the strategies which were used by the different actors to introduce solidarity in secondary legislation and the role of the CJEU as promotor of integration (Hypothesis 2).

I reconstruct the process of policy formulation by conducting an in-depth analysis of the case studies evaluating if and how the supranational institutions influenced the decision-making process and in how far functional pressures were perceived as pressing by the policy makers. The application of my concept of solidarity in each case study provides an answer if declarative or institutionalised solidarity has been inserted in the legal act. The results show in detail in which form declarative and institutionalised solidarity are present in the different legal documents. In the following, I present the legislative acts, which include solidarity.

The *directive on security of gas supply*, which first came into effect in 2004, has been reformed twice in 2010 and in 2017. Additionally, its legal basis changed due to the treaty changes. The negotiations about the first revision started after the second gas crisis in 2009. Due to the new legal basis – Art. 194 TFEU – the form changed from a directive to a regulation. *Directive 2009/73/EC* concerning common rules for the internal market on gas has included the measure of regional solidarity as particular response to ensure gas security of supply. It was revised in 2019, and since then disparaged as Lex Nord Stream 2. In addition, I will analyse the *decision (EU) 2017/684* establishing an information exchange mechanism with regard to intergovernmental agreements (IGAs) and non-binding instruments between Member States and third countries in the field of energy and its predecessor decision No 994/2012/EU. The decision was coming into existence due to mismatches between IGAs and the third energy package. Solidarity is included in the evaluation process of IGAs. Finally, I examine the *regulation (EU) 347/2013* on trans-European networks where solidarity was inserted as selection criterion for projects of common interests (PCIs). Another relevant research object is the legal dispute about the OPAL pipeline. In 2019, the CJEU ruled in favour of the applicant Poland, which demanded the annulment of the Commission decision to exempt the pipeline from capacity rules (Case T-883/16).

I will justify in detail what makes the difference between declarative and institutionalised solidarity. The assessment of the documents has been carried through with the assistance of the qualitative data analysis tool MAXQDA as explained in the chapter on methodology. The process analysis concentrates on the evaluation of the hypotheses i.e. the functional pressures and the discourse within the Council, the European Council and the supranational actors as well as the role of the Court.

Box 15:	Presentation of variance of solidarity			
Case	Legislative Act	Topic	Declarative Solidarity	Institutionalised Solidarity
1.	Council Directive 2004/67/EC	Security of gas supply	Solidarity only reference.	
	Regulation (EU) 2010/994	Security of gas supply	There are no clear rules for solidarity in place. It is not obliged.	
	Regulation (EU) 2017/1938	Security of gas supply		Obligation to provide solidarity.
2.	Directive 2009/73/EC	Common rules for internal gas market	Mechanism is a voluntary tool between MS.	
	Directive (EU) 2019/692	Application of 3rd energy package to import pipelines	No change on solidarity.	
3.	Decision (EU) 994/2012	Information exchange mechanism / IGAs	Obligations are limited and only voluntarily monitored. Strong trust-building dimension.	
	Decision (EU) 2017/684	Information exchange mechanism / IGAs	Role of Commission extended (ex-ante control), solidarity thwarted.	
4.	Regulation (EU) 347/2013	Trans-European networks	No clarification of solidarity. Represents goal.	
5.	Case T-883/16	OPAL gas pipeline		Definition of principle of solidarity.

4.1. Case 1: SoS – solidarity in case of emergency

The following chapter maps out how the directive towards security of gas supply developed between 2002 and 2019. In 2004, the first directive on security of gas supply was adopted. In 2010, the directive was substituted by the regulation 994/2010, which was again revised in 2017. It was only then when solidarity was institutionalised even though solidarity was called for already in the directive of 2004 and made more explicit in 2010.

In 2002, the Commission issued a communication (Commission 2002b), in which it announced to propose a directive concerning measures to safeguard security of gas supply for the first time. The strategic papers (e.g. Green Papers of 2000 or 1995), which have been published before 2002 did not mention solidarity. The communication focused on oil and gas frequently underlining solidarity in the gas sector. The Commission declared that the internal market cannot fully guarantee security of supply. Therefore, new policies should clarify the responsibilities of all market players concerning security of supply. „The internal market is also based on the need for solidarity between the Member States of the European Union (...)" (Commission 2002b: 3). At that time, gas imports were still expected to rise and ever more Member States became entirely dependent on one supplier only. Therefore, distortions in one Member State might have severe effects on another Member State. The internal market makes Member States more interdependent (Commission 2002b: 12), which is why it is necessary to introduce measures on security of supply. „Common rules will help to ensure the solidarity and unity of action needed for the proper functioning of the internal market in the event of a crisis" (Commission 2002b: 15).

Gas import and thus dependence were also expected to rise due to the EU enlargement to Central and Eastern Europe, which augments overall gas „imports to 35–40 % by 2010" (Commission 2002b: 43). The Commission recommended a harmonised approach in order to avoid any market distortions during a supply crisis. „Measures taken shall be notified to other Member States and the Commission, which may decide that the Member State concerned must amend or abolish such measures if they distort competition or trade in a manner which is not in the common interest" (Commission 2002b: 45). The second concern of the Commission was the different storage capacities in the Union. Storage is seen as an essential tool, for example, to combat price volatility and to ensure security of supply in winter. Therefore, the Commission has promoted the idea of developing storage facilities in remote areas to strengthen solidarity between Member States (Commission 2002b: 19).

As a third point, the Commission underlined the importance of long-term contracts and liquid gas supplies, which are both necessary for a functioning gas market. Member States, which e.g. share the same supplier, have common risks. The integration of the internal gas market and the resulting interdependence demand to work on joint solutions to respond to any security of supply threats. The Commission proposed as a solution in case of a gas crisis „solidarity at EU level to minimise any negative impact" (Commission 2002b: 51).

In the concluding remarks, the Commission underlined that due to all aforementioned reasons measures to safeguard security of supply are necessary. „In the event of a crisis, they will ensure the solidarity and the joint Community action necessary in order to respond effectively to uncertainties in the energy market and to promote in this context the proper functioning of the internal market" (Commission 2002b: 32). The Commission chose Article 95 EC (harmonisation article used for completion of the internal market) as legal basis. The main argument by the Commission was that an internal market requires also a joint approach towards security of supply. The evaluation of the frames in use show, that more than half of the references to solidarity were referring to interdependence or the functioning of the market (functional frame), 35 % to security of supply (partly overlapping with the functional frame) and only one normative reference underlines the need of a new energy solidarity between the EU and Russia.

Figure 5: Frames in Commission Communication on Security of Supply 2002

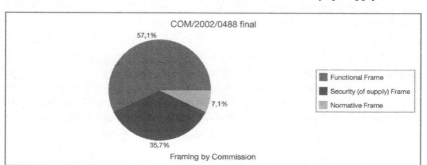

In the proposal of the directive itself, which was published on 11 September 2002, *solidarity* is only mentioned once with regards to emergencies. „For the well functioning of the internal market for gas and the security of supply, solidarity between Member States in emergency supply situations is essential" (Commission 2002b, recital 14). How solidarity mechanisms should work in the case of emergency is spelt out in Art. 8 of the directive. The Commission intended to submit recommendations to Member States how to assist troubled Member States. The proposed measures include the release of gas stocks, provision of pipeline capacities and disconnection of interruptible demand (Commission 2002b, Art. 8). In case that those measures are not sufficient, the Commission can, by decision, demand specific measures of the Member States. The same day press release of the Commission on the proposal referred to the fact that current legislation is inadequate: „These mechanisms do not provide any solidarity between Member States in the event of a crisis. In the gas sector, there is at present no Community framework aimed at guaranteeing a minimum level of security of supply" (Commission 2002a).

At the Council meeting in May 2003, the Council did not make any reference to solidarity. To the contrary, the Council underlined the necessity that the use of market mechanisms is sufficient to guarantee security of supply.

> „(As) regards gas, harmonised rules should not go beyond the absolute minimum necessary for supply measures and standards for ensuring security of supply. Market forces are in general considered to be sufficient to ensure both security of gas supply and a level playing field regarding security of supply obligations" (Council 2003a: 4).

The European Parliament's Committee on Industry, External Trade, Research and Energy (ITRE) issued a report on the proposed directive in October 2003. The rapporteur Peter Mombaur (EPP, Germany) expressed the Committee's concern about unnecessary harmonisation and required to underline responsibility of the single Member States regarding security of supply as well as the subsidiarity principle. ITRE listed different measures to ensure security of supply, which have to be taken by each Member State individually (Parliament 2003). The rapporteur's final assessment entails a discussion on the legal basis of the proposal. The proposal

> „(...) contains the possibility of reacting to supply restrictions by third countries (lack of competence), regulates more than is necessary (proportionality principle) and fails to take account of the existence of adequate Member State measures (subsidiarity principle). According-

ly we may state that the rules proposed here are by no means 'an integral part of the internal market' (Commission's explanatory memorandum) *but create entirely new competences at Community level. This is questionable in legal terms (…)*" (Parliament 2003, emphasis added).

Additionally, the Committee members highly doubted that gas supply disruptions could occur thanks to stable import relations. These statements prove that the Parliament did also not support any shift of competences and thus did not support the Commission's proposal towards solidarity. The EP and the Council did not perceive functional pressures but underlined national responsibility.

In December 2003, the Council presented its agreement on a more general approach to security of supply (Council 2003b). Responsibility for security of supply should be mainly in the hands of Member States. However, solidarity was confirmed:

> „In the event of a gas supply crisis, the text provides for a solidarity mechanism based on a three step approach comprising reactions of the industry, measures by Member States and, if appropriate, action at Community level whereby the Commission, in consultation with the Gas Coordination Group established by the text, may provide guidance to Member States or, if necessary, submit appropriate proposals to the Council" (Council 2003b).

Even though this statement reflects a certain agreement to solidarity, the text expresses the hesitance of the Member States to act on the Union level. Also in December 2003, the Commission issued its report on ,Better Lawmaking 2003'. The Commission displayed the arguments exchanged with the EP concerning the proposed security of supply measures. While the Parliament found the action too intrusive and underlined the prerogative of subsidiarity, the Commission referred to the Treaty objectives (Commission 2003d).

ITRE presented a report on the security of supply directive on 22 March 2004, which indicates that subsidiarity was of primary concern (Parliament 2004). The report repeats the arguments from October 2003, that Member States' security of supply situations are not comparable due to the use of different sources of supply. Therefore, it is the responsibility of the Member States to organise their individual security of supply. ITRE stressed the fact that the Commission was interested in filing an unnecessary harmonisation directive. This point was also crucial for the choice of the legal basis. Instead of choosing Art. 95 EC as proposed by the Commission, which would entail the co-decision procedure, the Council and the Parliament supported the change of the legal basis to Art. 100 EC (severe difficulties in supply of certain products) (Parliament 2004).

On 1 April 2004, the Council presented the final directive, which was adopted on 26 April 2004. The Gas Coordination Group (GCG) was implemented consisting of Member States' representatives and part of the industry and chaired by the Commission. The group is responsible to „facilitate the coordination of security of supply measure" (Art. 7). The GCG came into life in 2006 and meets at least four times a year. Its primary aim is to exchange information in order to secure the gas supply (see for background on GCG: Commission 2009f).

The final wording on solidarity reads as following: „(13) The establishment of genuine solidarity between Member States in major emergency supply situations is essential, even more so as Member States become increasingly interdependent regarding security of supply" (Directive 2004/67/EC). Instead of referring to the functioning of the internal market as in the original proposal, the Council underlined that increasing independence calls for solidarity. The emergency procedure is explained in Art. 8 and 9 of the directive. Art. 8 explains that Member States should draw up emergency plans and notify them to the Commission. However, the responsibility for emergency measures lies with the industry. Art. 9 defines the Community mechanism by sketching out reporting lines in case of emergency. Only if industry entities and Member States fail to ensure security of supply, the Commission may give guidance to the Member States, as agreed upon with the GCG. If there are further measures needed, the Commission may make proposals to the Council. Finally, the directive states „(a)ny measures at Community level referred to in this Article shall contain provisions aimed at ensuring fair and equitable compensation of the undertakings concerned by the measures to be taken" (Directive 2004/67/EC). But there are no further specifications regarding compensation.

How solidarity would exactly work in a case of emergency is not clarified, and there are no monitoring competencies, which is why this directive constitutes *declarative solidarity* only. The Commission raised the issue in order to get more power by integrating security of supply. Nevertheless, the Commission was successful by amending ‚solidarity' as part of the directive. However, neither did the Member States agree to define a genuine solidarity mechanism (even if they call it this way in the final directive) nor did the Parliament see any reason to act on the community level.

Solidarity did only play a marginal role in the final directive. Looking at the developed concept this also becomes clear by investigating what solidarity means at that time. First, the common interest in organising security of supply jointly – as defined by the Commission – stems from the possibility of supply interruptions which could affect several Member States at once. This common interest is neglected by the Parliament since supply interruptions seem unlikely. Second, the common understanding is, that the industry and Member States are responsible for their individual security of supply. Subsidiarity is the dominating principle which underlines the sovereignty of Member States. Joint action is not necessary as the Community level is not considered to be the more appropriate level for introducing security of supply measures. Member States emphasise that the industry is responsible for security of supply. Only if the industry is not able to solve a crisis, each Member State has to decide what measures to take. Member States fear interference in internal security matters and corresponding consequences for the choice of energy sources.

4.1.1. Times of crisis – solidarity in crisis

The Green Paper 'A European Strategy for Sustainable, Competitive and Secure Energy' (Commission 2006e), which was published in March 2006, announced the necessity of a solidarity mechanism as an instrument of mutual assistance in case of a gas crisis. The paper was published just after the gas crisis happened in January 2006. The Commission initiated a reflection process in order to deliberate how a new European energy policy could look like. One of the questions concerned the design of possible preventive mechanisms and reactions to supply crises with the help of solidarity. Solidarity plays also a crucial role as regards the planning, financing and protection of interconnections. The fear that physical interconnectors could be damaged led the Commission to propose the establishment of a solidarity mechanism in response to a crisis situation due to infrastructure problems. Furthermore, the Commission stressed the fact that the current directive on gas supply security is not sufficient for guaranteeing security of gas supply. Gas stocks would enable Member States to assist each other in crisis situations ensuring thus solidarity between Member States. Under the heading *security of supply and solidarity*, the Commission proposed a set of measures, which have partly been already under discussion for the first security of gas supply directive:

   – „A review of the existing Community legislation on oil and gas stocks, to focus them on today's challenges.

- A European energy supply observatory, enhancing transparency on security of energy supply issues within the EU.
- Improved network security through increased cooperation between network operators and possibly a formal European grouping of network operators.
- Greater physical security of infrastructure, possibly through common standards.
- Improved transparency on energy stocks at the European level" (Commission 2006e).

Additionally, the Commission proposed to carry out regularly a Strategic Energy Review, which would consider all aspects of energy policy. Energy Commissioner Piebalgs stated in a speech on 9 March 2006 that the second priority of the latest Green Paper on energy concerned security of supply, which is „often referred to in terms of solidarity between Member States in the event of a crisis" (Piebalgs 2006). One of the proposals under this priority entails a „new crisis mechanism to prepare for and ensure rapid solidarity" needed in case of severe problems with essential infrastructure. The second reference concerned the idea to ensure solidarity between Member States by developing a new legislation on gas stocks. Hence, the existing security of gas supply directive needed to be re-examined (Piebalgs 2006).

On 23 March, the European Parliament reacted to the Green Paper and the crisis from January by publishing a 'resolution on the security of energy supply in the European Union' (Parliament 2006e). The general disagreement on European security of supply solutions, and in particular solidarity, completely vanished. The Parliament no longer underlined the principle of subsidiarity but argued that solidarity is needed as „essential element of a common energy policy" to ensure security of supply and to guarantee the „physical security of infrastructure" (Parliament 2006e). Additionally, solidarity would help to have more weight at the international level. The Parliament also underlined the principles of fairness and shared responsibility, which should restrain Member States to take actions on the national level which might (negatively) affect other member states. The reasons for this changed behaviour are manifold. In the resolution itself, the Parliament underlined the following points: the gas dispute with Russia, the not yet fully integrated market and the resulting vulnerability regarding security of supply. The resolution describes a changing moment in the behaviour of the Parliament, and it reveals a new conflict. There is a dividing line between old and new Member States regarding energy solidarity. MEPs from new Member States which were also primarily hit by the gas crisis, support much stronger energy solidarity than MEPs from old Member States.

Only two days later, the European Council presented its conclusions, which dealt among other topics with energy security and solidarity (Conclusions 2006b). Even though the EUCO addressed solidarity as a way of action in a supply crisis, this reference remained a rather vague instruction. The European Council underlined the responsibility of each Member State for energy security and referred as many times to subsidiarity as to solidarity in this context.

In October 2006, the Committee on Economic and Monetary Affairs (ECON) called on ITRE to include several suggestions in its motion for a resolution on the Commission's Green Paper. The Committee observed that due to problems in gas supply during winter, enterprises of energy intensive industry decided to move to other countries. Therefore, the committee called for solidarity between Member States in case of supply disruptions underlining that not only interconnections play an important role for an integrated market, but also the question how to design mutual assistance during supply disruptions (ECON 2006). The question how to resolve supply crises is also put forward in the opinion by the Committee on Foreign Affairs. The Committee highlighted the importance that solidarity should be implemented „with concrete targets, obligations and steps" namely as regards both the functioning of the internal market as well as external energy relations (AFET 2006). In the debate on the report, the Spanish MEP Joan Calabuig Rull (PSE) made a link between the market, confidence and solidarity:

> „I believe that we must ask ourselves why the market is not progressing and why there is not sufficient confidence and that the answer lies in the need for a common energy policy, and not just in the external field. We need cooperation and solidarity amongst the Member States because, otherwise, it will be very difficult to achieve our objectives and meet the challenges facing us" (Parliament 2006a).

The result from these considerations was the „European Parliament resolution on a European strategy for sustainable, competitive and secure energy – Green paper" (Parliament 2006c), which was published in December 2006. The Parliament observed that security of supply is under serious risk due to the limited number of suppliers and supply routes. Therefore, the EP supported „the introduction of a mechanism able to ensure solidarity and rapid assistance to Member States facing difficulties following damage to their infrastructure" (Parliament 2006d: 30). Additionally, the EP took up the point made by ECON as regards the effects of winter on the supply of energy intensive industries, which is why it wants to sound out opportunities to promote solidarity. The MEPs used mainly references to security of supply to underline the necessity of solidarity.

In January 2007, the European Commission published the Communication „An Energy Policy for Europe" (Commission 2007c). The Commission emphasised the risks of supply failures and that „the mechanisms to ensure solidarity between Member States in the event of an energy crisis are not yet in place and several Member States are largely or completely dependent on one single gas supplier" (Commission 2007c: 4).

Commissioner Piebalgs stated during a speech at the EU Energy Law and Policy conference in January 2007, that „the second key area of the new European Energy Policy concerns solidarity between Member States and security of supply for oil, gas and electricity" (Piebalgs 2007b). He illustrated that the Commission already proposed different mechanisms to ensure solidarity between Member States. Piebalgs referred to the increased risk of security since some Member States have only one or few suppliers. The Commissioner repeated that the current SoS directive from 2004 must be assessed and that it was necessary to explore and strengthen crisis solidarity mechanisms. There are two aspects to his vision of solidarity: First, he referred to the changed situation that Member States rely only on one or few suppliers. This means that the group is heterogenous, comprising both strong members (several suppliers -> less risk) and weak members (one or few suppliers -> higher risk). Second, he underlined that solidarity mechanisms must benefit all Member States (Piebalgs 2007b).

In September 2007, the Commission published a proposal to reform the internal market directive on gas, which included in the accompanying impact assessment the demand that also directive 2004/67/EC needs to be reviewed, since the directive does not „foresee any binding solidarity agreement, nor (...) a framework for such agreements" (Commission 2007b). France took over the Presidency in July 2008. The work programme called upon the implementation of a „unified energy area" by

> „working together to anticipate and forestall energy supply crises by means of greater transparency, particularly in relation to stocks of oil and gas, by establishing emergency plans in each Member State and defining the necessary crisis management arrangements at the Community level" (France 2008).

This objective is also reflected in a presidency briefing from October 2008 (Presidency 2008). The draft report to the European Council on energy security highlights the importance of solidarity for energy security. The presidency briefing states that „(…) improving energy security, which is a key issue for the protection of Europe's citizens, requires a dual effort in the European Union and its Member States in terms of responsibility and solidarity". Every Member State needs to be self-responsible in order to do everything possible at the national level to avert a crisis. The other side of the coin is to

> „be prepared to contribute to any solidarity measures. Solidarity, insofar as any Member State which is confronted with a sudden and temporary disruption in its energy supply must be able to rely on the support of the other Member States and the Union. It is only on this condition that solidarity mechanisms can be put in place at European level" (Presidency 2008: 4).

The Presidency proposed among other measures solidarity instruments based on trust. The aim was that the Commission inserts these measures in the legislative proposals in November 2008 as well as in the second Strategic Energy Review. Most notably, the Presidency supported a mechanism, with which it is possible to free up resources in the case of a gas crisis in order to liquify the market. This approach is called ‚default supply standard' and can be carried out by „drawing on stocks, increasing production or imports, or reducing consumption" (Presidency 2008). The French Presidency leaves further details up to the Commission:

> „The Commission is invited to make practical suggestions in November for the establishment of a solidarity mechanism based on each Member State's capacity to free up security margins, in the framework of the review of the gas supply security directive which it will be proposing in 2009" (Presidency 2008).

The main features of solidarity as envisioned by the Council were responsibility (be prepared to ward off crises and to contribute to security), but also trust (to rely on support of other Member States). Hence, the solidarity mechanism was no longer blocked at the Council. A policy proposal which the Commission already called for in 2002.

In November 2008, the Commission published a communication stating that a revision of the directive on security of gas supply was needed (Commission 2008b). The Commission argued that „(s)hort-term supply security and solidarity between Member States are high on today's agendas relating to the gas markets" (Commission 2008b: 4). Since market failures may still occur it is necessary to implement an EU emergency plan to supplement national emergency plans. In the following, the Commission described the lengthy reaction process in case of a crisis. For this reason Member States demand „a wider (regional or EU-level) emergency plan and/or solidarity mechanism" (Commission 2008b: 6). The implementation of an EU Emergency Plan should provide the actors with a framework on prevention mechanisms as well as different emergency levels. The Commission called this approach „a de facto solidarity action" (Commission 2008b: 10). However, the Commission emphasised as well that solidarity is not charity and that solidarity actions must entail compensation mechanisms. Additionally, each Member State must make the necessary arrangements to meet the defined security of supply standards. The first responsibility remains with the Member States. The Commission spells out different strategies on the demand and supply side in order to free up gas. On the supply side this could entail higher import or production and on the demand side interruptible contracts. Member States could also agree to a contractual transfer of gas if the necessary infrastructure for backflows is not existing. During the policy process Member States are urged to reflect on these questions and also how to compensate solidarity.

In comparison to the policy proposal leading to the directive of 2004, the Commission was aware of the concerns of the Member States as regards freeriding. Therefore, the Commission underlined the importance of each state's own responsibility for security of supply and that solidarity is by no means charity.

It has to be underlined that the Commission proposed a revision of the 2004 directive already in November 2008. In the literature it is common sense to declare that „EU institutions assessed that new measures were needed and that habits need to be changed" (Fleming 2019: 102) and that „Regulation 994/2010 was born out of unprecedented events of January 2009 when for almost two weeks Russian gas transit through Ukraine was halted, leaving the EU without the critical supply source" (Badanova 2019: 123). There has been certainly an effect of the crisis on the revision process of the directive since the necessity to stipulate joint action became clear in face of the crisis (Vinois 2017: 34). „(A)t that time when we are looking at the crisis with Russia and Ukraine, we looked at the instruments we had and we discovered that we had only one directive of 2004 on security of gas supply and this directive was not organising anything" (Interview 3, DG Energy). However, it was not due to the crisis from 2009 that the Commission urged for its revision, but the Commission successively underlined the need for European solidarity until the European Council, the Council and the Parliament demonstrated willingness.

Commission President Barroso gave a speech in Brussels on the last day of the gas crisis on 20 January 2009 in which he already noted how well solidarity worked: „First, solidarity worked inside the EU and with our near neighbours. Mitigation measures taken by EU companies and the Member States allowed most countries to manage the situation successfully" (Barroso 2009b). However, he emphasised that although Member States were capable of warding off a major crisis, a situation like this should not recur. Therefore, he proposed three different actions in order to prevent future crisis situations. One of the suggestions was the revision of the security of gas supply directive in order to be prepared for both the next crisis and the next winter. Barroso's evaluation that solidarity worked during the crisis is challenged by an assessment of the Commission on the 2009 gas crisis: „There were no solidarity actions between Member State governments". On the contrary, some countries' actions even resulted in harming others. „Slovakia introduced an emergency regulation prohibiting exports from storage facilities in Slovakia. Italy introduced an emergency regulation optimising use of import pipelines. Such regulations may have prevented some gas flows which would have been useful" (Commission 2009a: 12). However, the work of the Gas Coordination Group (GCG) was evaluated as useful tool „(...) as it was the only venue where Member State officials, the gas industry and other market stakeholders could meet and find out exactly what was happening. It was also useful for discussing the options for finding a solution to the crisis" (Commission 2009e). The Commission enforced the European dimension by repurposing the GCG in a crisis management group, which was legally not provided for.

> „Then we convened this group, didn't really know what we were supposed to do, and then we ordered the press and so on, so that you get the feeling that Europe was active. And the people from the ministries came together. And that was the beginning of an ad-hoc managed crisis mechanism (...) And then we adapted the legislation" (Interview 10, Commission Official).

The mindset within the GCG has become more European because it provides the venue for the MS to exchange information and to relieve tension (Personal Communication 1, DG Energy). The gas crisis revealed the different levels of preparedness between Eastern and Western Member States. Even though the GCG underlined its success, it is doubtful if the success was not based on coincidence. Some Member States had gas sufficiently in stock due to the economic recession, which allowed the industry to sell gas to high prices (Pirani et al. 2009: 56).

In the Parliament's resolution on the Second Strategic Energy Review (Parliament 2009d) of 3 February 2009, the Parliament:

> „notes the *failure of the Member States to demonstrate solidarity*, with regard to increasing the amount of gas available to the affected Member States during the recent gas crisis between Ukraine and Russia; *urges the Council and the Commission to create a solidarity mechanism, in accordance with the Treaty of Lisbon*, which would allow the EU to act efficiently, swiftly and coherently in crisis situations caused by disruption of supply, damage to critical infrastructure or any other such event" (Parliament 2009d, recital 65, emphasis added).

Since the principle of energy solidarity came into force with the Treaty of Lisbon, the development of a common European energy policy received new impetus (Westphal 2009: 27). The Parliament intended to remind the Member States of the importance of solidarity, and if this was not voluntarily possible, solidarity mechanisms should be legally implemented. The demonstration of solidarity was interpreted differently by the Commissioner Piebalgs, who „noted the solidarity displayed during the crisis by all actors, public and private, as well as the EU's ability to speak with one voice, that of the Presidency and the Commission, and recalled that the core elements of the EU energy policy are security and solidarity" (Council 2009c: 6). On 19 February 2009, the Council (TTE) conclusions included the following reference to solidarity: „Solidarity between Member States that has to be strengthened and balanced with Member States' responsibility over their energy security, fully respecting Member States' choice of energy mix and sovereignty over energy sources" (Council 2009c: 7). This can be evaluated as agreement to the proposal of the Commission to revise the current directive on security of gas supply. However, the text emphasised also very clearly that Member States remained mainly responsible and that any solidarity mechanism would have no influence on each state's energy mix. Even though the Council admitted that solidarity must be strengthened, it diminished the statement again by highlighting the responsibility of each Member State for its security, choice of energy mix and energy sources. In the following, the Council agreed on a set of priorities to reach these aims, where solidarity is not mentioned once (Council 2009c: 7ff.). The Council accepted to „deliver consistent messages (‚speaking with one voice')" towards third states and to „develop a common approach to external energy policy" (Council 2009c: 9). The Council further demanded to revise the gas SoS directive 2004/67 in order to enhance crisis response mechanisms (Council 2009c: 8), and the „Council also outlined that the framework of the revised proposal should be *responsibility and solidarity*" (Council 2009c: 13, emphasis added). Interviews confirmed that the gas crisis led to a change of views:

> „the French who were usually quite opposed to – well – it was a sovereignty issue and they were considering that in this case, they said, well we now realise that the gas is coming from Russia to Ukraine and is passing Slovakia, Czechia and Germany before it reaches France. And of course, what is happening in all these countries before it is coming to us, it is a common issue. And then they have accepted to work on a regulation on security of gas supply" (Interview 3, DG Energy).

The Council and the Parliament agreed on the revision of the gas security of supply directive 2004/67 directly after the 2009 gas crisis, but the impulse of the Commission to revise the directive was already put forward in November 2008, and it was the French Presidency who demanded the Commission to develop solidarity mechanisms in October 2008. The Commission was informed by Russia on upcoming supply problems only in December. Therefore, the crisis can be evaluated as amplifier for the development of the gas security of supply directive, however, the arguments by the Commission up to this point were framed primarily functionally. The crisis presented the opportunity for the Commission to push for common rules concerning security of supply.

In the Presidency Conclusions of the European Council on 19/20 March 2009, the European Council highlighted the role of solidarity for energy security. "In order to deliver on energy security, the EU collectively, as well as each Member State, must be prepared to *combine solidarity with responsibility*" (Conclusions 2009: 8, emphasis added). The EUCO supported the initiatives put forward by the Commission and the Council (TTE). The January gas crisis is mentioned as reason for urgent action in the area of energy security. On the one hand the EUCO called for supply guarantees by partners and on the other hand it supported the Commission's proposal to revise the security of gas supply directive by including „solidarity among Member States through the development of regional plans" (Conclusions 2009: 9). Furthermore, the European Council asked for an „improved assessment and coordination through the redefinition of the threshold for deciding actions at Community level" (Conclusions 2009: 9). This means that energy security was no longer of national concern only (even though the responsibility of each Member State for its security is not denied), but the need for concerted community action was acknowledged. At this summit the EUCO also stressed the importance to finalise the internal market, which is a prerequisite to energy security, and to diversify supply routes and sources. „Speaking with one voice" is repeated like a mantra as internal and external message (Conclusions 2009: 10). Pursuing only national interests in external energy policy can have negative consequences for the energy security situation of other Member States.

Both the Council and the European Council highlighted that responsibility and solidarity are intertwined. Responsibility means that every Member State is self-responsible for its security of supply in order to avoid freeriding. Responsibility creates trust since comparable and harmonised standards guarantee that a certain amount of action has been implemented. At the same time the Member States wanted to demonstrate unity by underlining the importance of a common foreign energy policy. A functioning internal market played for both institutions a crucial role in order to guarantee security of supply. However, the institutions followed the security frame (solidarity is necessary due to crisis).

In July 2009, the Commission published its proposal for a regulation on security of gas supply revising the directive from 2004 (Commission 2009g). As legal basis the Commission chose Art. 95 TEC on approximation of laws. The Commission explained that a revision is necessary due to a myriad of reasons: on the one hand there are security concerns such as growing import dependencies and increasing risks regarding supply and transit and on the other hand there is a functional need due to the development of the internal market. Additionally, the gas crisis put pressure on the EU to act. For this reason, both the European Council and the European Parliament called for a revision of the directive. The Commission argued further that the crisis proved that the reaction could be more efficient which is why action on the Community level is requested.

The Commission imagined different actions to realise solidarity. These included „measures such as commercial agreements between natural gas undertakings, compensation mechanisms, increased gas exports or increased releases from storages" (23). Reasons for such solidarity measures were the occurrence „of a Community Emergency and in particular to support Member States which are exposed to less favourable geographical or geological conditions" (23). The term ‚Community Emergency' uploads national security of supply problems to the Community. It supports the argument that due to interdependence supply disruptions in one Member State can lead to supply difficulties in other member states. Additionally, the Commission's reference to Member States which have less favourable circumstances is a call for more solidarity (helping the weak). For these reasons, the Commission recommends the implementation of "joint preventive actions plans or emergency plans at regional level" (23). Again, none of these measures shall affect the choice of energy mix of each Member State. There is no further reference to solidarity in the draft regulation. The Emergency Plan should entail measures how Member States can cooperate and lists the agreements in case of emergency as well as compensation mechanisms. The Commission also wished to introduce a Community emergency response, where the Commission is mainly responsible for surveillance and declaring the emergency status as well as steering and monitoring the response. Even though solidarity was not explicitly mentioned, some mechanisms can be considered as solidarity actions, e.g. Member States shall refrain from restricting the gas flows and ensure the cross-border access to storage facilities. The Commission took a great leap by demanding the shift of competences to the Commission to coordinate the community emergency response. In total, solidarity measures are under discussion, but the details remained in the proposal very unspecific. However, it is clear that the solidarity measure is rather envisioned as insurance tool (regarding security of supply) and not as redistributive tool (which would be e.g. a common fund to help individual member states in an emergency situation). An important feature of the regulation is the definition of ‚protected customers' (18). Those are the customers, which need to be supplied with gas at any time. In the proposal of the Commission these customers include households, schools and hospitals, but can also extended to small and medium enterprises. The issue of protected customers and solidarity is a sensible issue, since it determines for how many ‚national' customers the gas supply must be ensured. The more protected customers are included (flexibility of Member States with small and medium enterprises), the less solidarity a Member State can eventually show in the case of emergency.

In the accompanying Impact Assessment, the Commission reiterated the instructions of the European Council, which called in particular for „solidarity among Member States through the development of regional plans" (Commission 2009a: 4). The summary on the public consultation on security of gas supply underlined that solidarity actions can only be developed on the basis of a shared responsibility for security of supply. There was general agreement that market mechanisms should work as long as possible and that other measures, such as solidarity mechanisms, should be used as a last resort. The organisation of regional cooperation was generally supported, but there were two different opinions on scope and actions. One group was reflecting on solidarity mechanisms and regional emergency mechanisms and the other group on infrastructure and regional trading. The question on how to compensate solidarity got only few replies. It remained a marginal option, some did not support its use at all. „If it is used, it should be based on pre-agreements between the operators with market-based compensation (concerning for example, reservation of capacity rights or purchase of gas for solidarity reasons)" (Commission 2009a: 8). While solidarity measures are seen as a last resort, national security of supply measures should also not be introduced if they have a negative impact on the functioning of the internal market. One of the main difficulties is that there is great uncertainty when a state of emergency actually occurs. If Member States act unilaterally this could distort the market even when market mechanisms still function. It must be also clarified what an emergency implies and how long it is in place. All actors needed clarity since the internal market developed and supply disruptions were still possible in the future. Although the text remains altogether very unclear on the issue of solidarity, it was noted that solidarity is one of the main features of energy policy:

> „A driver of both issues – adequacy of investments and organization of emergency arrangements – is the objective of solidarity in the EU. In the energy field, reflecting interdependence of Member States, the ideas of responsibility and solidarity have been linked. Thus there may be greater readiness to agree in advance on solidarity measures which would come into play in an emergency when there is trust that all Member States have acted to reduce the risks of an unmanageable gas supply disruption spilling over into other Member States. Several Member States repeated this in the public consultation on the revision of the 2004 Directive" (Commission 2009a: 15).

Member States feared that solidarity would not be realised (in the context of the 2009 gas crisis, the Commission noted that no solidarity mechanisms had been established between Member States) because other Member States would not do everything in their power to prevent and mitigate disruptions in gas supply. Solidarity and responsibility go hand in hand which is why the security of supply standards should also be clear and common for all Member States. The concern of freeriding could be dissolved if all followed the same security of supply standards. The Commission made again a functional argument by underlining the interdependence of Member States, which would be mirrored in solidarity and responsibility. Responsibility for the own supply would lead to sufficient trust to be sure that solidarity mechanisms can be put in place in case of crisis. The underlying drivers are external constraints (dependency, transit, crisis) that reveal the vulnerability of the system and thus indicate the need for action (security frame).

In addition, in July 2009, the Commission published an assessment of the January 2009 gas supply disruption as an accompanying document to the proposal (SEC(2009) 977 final). It highlighted the importance of the Gas Coordination Group which could deliver solutions for the supply problems and its function as a platform to bring together all actors involved. The Commission supposed that the GCG „could also have the potential (...) to coordinate emergency and solidarity measures" (Commission 2009b: 13). Solidarity is evaluated as important principle of EU energy policy: „Political solidarity in the EU is vital both in domestic responses, to ensure that the market can work properly, and in dealing with external partners" (Commission 2009b: 17). In the same document the Commission listed different factors which mirrored the lack of cooperation and coherence between the Member States. The Commission criticised the national view of Transmission System Operators, „which brought local relief placed neighbours under additional strain" (p. 10), but the main problem was the „the inadequacies in gas transport which constrained flows (capacities, reverse flow capabilities, unusual routes, insufficient integration of gas networks in Central and South Eastern Europe), not an aggregate shortage of gas" (p. 14). Altogether, the document entailed two features of solidarity: 1) solidarity means to act according to market rules and 2) not to harm others by supporting a common external energy approach.

President Barroso stressed the importance of solidarity for the EU in his political guidelines (3 September 2009) for the mandate of the next European Commission (Barroso 2009a). He stated that solidarity and subsidiarity are the two principles which, enshrined in the Treaty of Lisbon, determine the level of action (p. 1). Furthermore, he outlined that solidarity must be expressed in practical terms, such as the political solidarity shown in the Russia-Ukraine crisis (p. 12). Solidarity closed his speech: Barroso called for creating „a Europe based on the values of freedom and solidarity" (p. 41). Similar to his speech in 2004, the focus of the speech was on solidarity, which was now also emphasised in the Lisbon Treaty (in 2004 he referred to solidarity concerning the Eastern enlargement).

In the Council progress report from November 2009, the Council Secretariat underlined that „few delegations proposed reflecting the solidarity aspect in the objective of the proposal, while some others wished to see a reference to the principles of proportionality and subsidiarity" (Council 2009d). In the subsequent policy debate, Greece was concerned about solidarity: „As a general principle we feel that the Member States should be encouraged to deliver on investments instead of relying on the existence of solidarity mechanisms" (Council 2009f). A contrary argument was brought forward by Hungary: „Regional cooperation and the solidarity among Member States is a key prerequisite, EU needs an overall crisis management strategy because with common, coordinated measures we can ensure the energy supply in the Union" (Council 2009g). Denmark underlined the necessity of solidarity and responsibility: „We have to strengthen solidarity while at the same time ensuring that all member states take responsibility for their own energy security" (Council 2009e). In a press release from December 2009, the Council stated that it had concerns regarding solidarity emphasising again the responsibility aspect.

> „Many ministers stressed, in particular, the need to clarify further the roles and responsibilities of the market actors, the member states and the Commission, in line with the subsidiarity principle. For ensuring gas supply, the hierarchy going from gas undertakings, Member States, to the regional and the EU level was underlined. *Crisis management should be based on an in-depth risk analysis, and there must be a balance between solidarity, the market's responsibilities and Member States' responsibility for their own gas supply*" (Council 2009a, emphasis added).

The Council was worried that the reorganisation of security of supply would not only entail a power shift to the supranational level but could also lead to a less responsible behaviour concerning security of supply. There has been a continuous dividing line between new and old Member States, who have been differently prepared for crisis events (Westphal 2009: 27). Member States, such as Germany, had put different tools in place to reduce the impact of the crises and were at the same time „(...)" capable of aiding other EU Member States. Thus, they furnished examples that crisis mechanisms and the principle of solidarity can work. Some of the other countries do not see it that way, which raises the question of free riders versus and burden sharing" (Westphal 2009: 28).

In January 2010, the Council Secretariat published a text on regional cooperation that should be part of the annex of the new regulation, which stated that „regional cooperation is a major expression of solidarity" (Council 2010g: 2). This is also the concept in the internal gas market directive (2009/73/EC) and the regulation (2009/715/EC) on the access to gas transmission networks. Since regional cooperation served as underlying concept of the regulation, it should be inserted:

> „In the spirit of solidarity, regional cooperation, involving public authorities and gas undertakings, will be widely established to implement this Regulation in order to optimise the benefits in terms of coordination of measures to mitigate the risks identified and to implement the most cost effective measures for the parties concerned" (Council 2010g: 3).

In March 2010, ITRE published its report on the proposal (Parliament 2010c). The opinion of the EP changed in comparison to the 2004 directive. Further integration of security of supply was accepted. „The European Parliament urged to put the major responsibilities in the Commission's hands, especially when it comes to handling emergency situations" (Brutschin 2017: 74). The report received opinions from the Committee on Foreign Affairs, the Committee on Economic and Monetary Affairs (ECON), the Committee on the Environment, Public Health and Food Safety (ENVI) and the Committee on the Internal Market and Consumer Protection (IMCO). Solidarity was added to the proposal several times. Justifying these changes, ECON stated that solidarity was now part of the energy article in the Lisbon Treaty (p. 89).

This reference to Art. 194 TFEU but also Art. 122 TFEU (s. amendment 10) occured several times in the report. The rapporteur of the Committee of Foreign Affairs, Saryusz-Wolski, explained this more detailed in the justifications on the report:

> „The Proposal shall be considered in light of the new legal environment provided by the Lisbon Treaty which in its article 176 A stipulates "Union policy on energy shall aim, in the spirit of solidarity between Member States, to ensure security of energy supply in the Union". The Rapporteur considers this solidarity to be vital for the building of a common EU policy on energy and believes that it should be developed both internally and externally at political level in dialogue with third countries during and outside supply crisis situations" (Parliament 2010c :70).

However, ENVI had the opinion that „No binding rules should be laid down concerning possible solidarity measures or compensation arrangements" (p. 110). There is no further explanation on this point. ENVI also underlined the importance of solidarity as actual policy designing stimulus because it is necessary to be able to react to threats of disruption (p. 111). IMCO criticised that

> „(…) the concept of costumer protection and solidarity is not fully integrated in this proposal. As this regulation concerns security of gas supply, taking into consideration customer protection and solidarity between Member States is essential for the preparation of the response to disruptions of supply" (p. 126).

Altogether, the report underlined two points: On the one hand, the importance of the treaty amendment and its particular meaning for solidarity was highlighted. On the other hand, the Parliament envisioned solidarity to be implemented for the general conduct of energy policy and not security of supply only.

On 19 May, the Council Secretariat published a progress report (Council 2010e), where it underlined that EUCO prioritised this dossier. For this reason, both the Council and the Parliament aimed at a first reading agreement. The progress report summarises the results of the informal contacts and technical meeting with the EP. The rapporteur – the chair of the Energy Working Party – was concerned that a minimum supply standard and an extended definition of protected customers „might entail a risk of lack of capacity to implement the solidarity principle in case of an emergency" (Council 2010e: 2). Additionally, he underlined that solidarity is reflected in the cooperation between the different actors regarding risk assessment, preventive action and emergency plans (p. 3).

In May 2010, the Council published its second press release on the issue. This time, its reluctance to introduce a true solidarity mechanism was spelled out:

> „Ministers also underlined the importance of regional cooperation as a valuable element of the solidarity among member states which is acknowledged and encouraged in the regulation although its modalities will remain voluntary and will have to be implemented in a flexible way" (Council 2010a).

The statement that modalities will remain voluntary and implementation will be flexible is a clear rejection of institutionalised solidarity. The preparation of the informal trilogue started on 4 June (Council 2010f):

1) The Council inserted in recital 6 that a wide definition of protected customers should not conflict with European solidarity mechanisms. 2) Recital 23 was clarified in agreement with the Parliament and the Council to the effect that natural gas companies should take measures, such as

trade agreements, e.g. providing for increased gas exports in the event of an emergency in the Union, in order to show solidarity. The Emergency Plans should ensure fair compensation. 3) Solidarity was added by the EP and Council in Art. 1 as basis for the emergency mechanisms. 4) The Parliament requested that natural gas undertakings should be able to supply protected customers for 45 days in Art. 7. The Council reduced to 30 days and added solidarity as prerogative for the decision of the competent authority to reduce the supply standard in case of emergency. 5) The EP tried to insert solidarity as aim in Art. 11 by creating sub-groups of the GCG, which was deleted.

On 23 June 2010, the Presidency briefing included the outcome of the informal trilogue and an analysis of the final compromise text with a view to agreement (Council 2010h). One of the main elements of the final compromise text is about solidarity under the headline „Plans at Union level": *„Union solidarity and consistency* aspects of the plans are highlighted by requesting in *Article 14* the Commission to report on the consistency and contribution Member States' PAP and Emergency Plans to solidarity and preparedness from a Union perspective" (Council 2010h: 2, emphasis by author). The most important point in this brief explanation is the Union's perspective. If security of supply is viewed from the Union's perspective, Member States would certainly react differently in emergencies.

Not only the Council remained vague on the solidarity mechanism, but also the Parliament. This is reflected in the position by the Parliament, which was published on 21 September 2010 (Parliament 2010a). The Parliament added the term solidarity several times, and it mentioned again that energy solidarity was implemented in the new treaty. This is mainly expressed by the change of the legal basis of the regulation. Instead of using Art. 95 on approximation of laws, the European Parliament used Art. 194(2) TFEU, which is the newly introduced energy article. The Commission could not yet use this article as basis, since its proposal was made before the Treaty of Lisbon entered into force. Additionally, solidarity is expressed by regional cooperation, which is also the underlying concept of this regulation. The reason for the need of solidarity is mainly seen in the different security of supply structures, which the Member States implemented nationally. There are, however, no clarifications on how solidarity mechanisms could look like in detail. Natural gas undertakings are supposed to carry out voluntary agreements, comprising e.g. increased releases from storage or increased gas exports. Based on these arrangements, the emergency plans should also entail compensation mechanisms. Solidarity should play a certain role in national and joint Preventive Action Plans and the national and joint Emergency Plans. Member States shall ensure not only their own level of security of supply, but also that their actions do not harm other's security of supply. Additionally, The Parliament took up the topic of protected customers and solidarity. The supply standard, which each Member State has to guarantee, is calculated based on the number of protected customers, peaks in temperature, exceptionally high-gas demand and particularly severe gas disruptions. If an increased supply standard is implemented, the Competent Authority must prepare a plan to lower this standard in an emergency situation. The supply standard should not be increased during an emergency situation as this would hamper the supply of gas to a neighbouring country that might be in a more severe supply situation. The EP text shows that most of the solidarity references have been already agreed upon in the trilogue process.

Figure 6: European Parliament Debate on Security of Gas Supply 2010

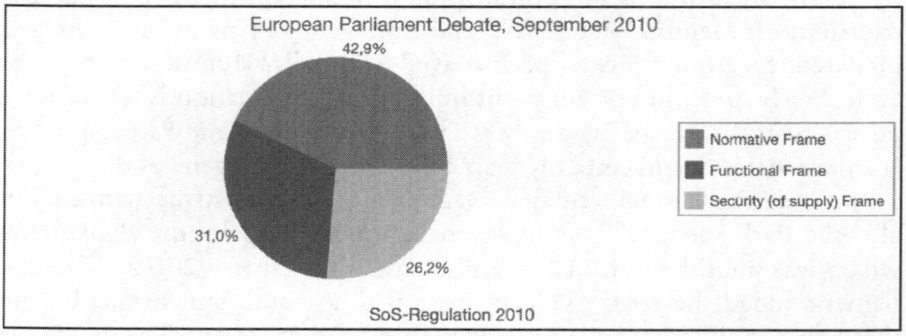

own compilation; based on frame analysis of EP debate on security of gas supply 2010 (Parliament 2010d)

The general support of the Parliament towards solidarity is also reflected in the debate that took place on 21 September 2010 (Parliament 2010d). Solidarity was mentioned in the debate 29 times, which illustrates the importance of the principle for most discussants. Even though most references on solidarity were made by Eastern European and Baltic MEPs, some MEPs from Italy, Spain, Luxembourg and Portugal also underlined the importance of solidarity. Most references implied a normative frame mentioning the new energy article 194 TFEU. The Spanish rapporteur Vidal-Quadras highlighted that solidarity is extended by the regulation: „However, the legitimate eagerness of a Member State when it comes to protecting consumers in its national market must be balanced by an undertaking of solidarity with citizens of other Union Member States" (Parliament 2010d).

The solidarity mechanism implies that solidarity is not only for the citizens of the national state but also towards other European citizens. There are seven references which link solidarity with the Treaty of Lisbon. The MEPs underline mainly that solidarity is demanded in case of an energy crisis. In order to avoid a second reading, the EP and the Council met informally in order to resolve remaining differences (Council 2010d: 2).

On 11 October 2010, the Council voted unanimously in favour of the new regulation (Council 2010i). The regulation 994/2010 concerning measures to safeguard security of gas supply and repealing Council directive 2004/67/EC was put into force in October 2010. There have been no additional changes regarding solidarity. There are nine references to solidarity in the introductory part, three in the articles and one in the annex. There were only four references to solidarity in the original proposal by the Commission, and those have been in the introductory part only. Solidarity has been added these many times *at the instigation of the Parliament and the Council*. The Parliament's focus was on changing the national perspective to a European perspective. The Council wanted to clarify the conditions for solidarity.

One driving force has been definitely the entry into force of the Treaty of Lisbon, which gave a new normative impetus on the role of solidarity and which officially underlined that energy policy is a shared competence. Of course, the supply crisis from January 2009 played a major role, which is why Member States felt the pressure to act on the European level. But it is necessary to mention again that the Commission published already in November 2008 a document, which proposed to review the directive from 2004. The gas crisis changed the view of the European Council in particular, which not only advocated the revision of the Directive, but also that it was necessary to reassess which measures should be implemented at Community level. This can be understood as an invitation to the Commission to develop a European policy on security of supply. „(...) (T)he security of supply Regulation recognises explicitly the inter-linkages between various Member States actions. It emphasis that the measures of one Member State in case of an emergency will impact the other Member States" (Talus 2013: 46). In comparison to the directive from 2004, solidarity made its appearance, even though responsibility plays a decisive role for the Member States. The Commission's role was advanced by the regulation (Brutschin 2017: 74). The regulation of 2010 permitted the Commission to declare a Union emergency or regional emergency at the request of the competent authority.

Nevertheless, the regulation of 2010 puts forward *declarative solidarity*. Based on my concept there are several conditions not fulfilled even though the assessment via MAXQDA shows that all criteria are met in general. The analysis of the document shows, however, that solidarity remains purely voluntarily, i.e. there is neither the obligation to supply gas in emergencies nor is it made clear under which conditions Member States can have access. „(…) Member States have committed to mutual solidarity in case of energy security threats without having agreed on enforcement mechanisms, EU-level policymaking easily flounders in such a system of large grey areas“ (Aalto and Korkmaz Temel 2014: 765).

Group Cohesion: The regulation can be interpreted as trust-building measure and as preparatory tool to investigate further cooperation. The regulation underlines that a common approach is necessary since security of supply is a joint endeavour, and that security of gas supply is a *shared responsibility*. A trust-building measure is that competent authorities and natural gas undertakings (regional cooperation) shall work together.

Reciprocity: The solidarity mechanisms, e.g. increased gas exports in case of emergency are not specified. However, there are no rules of implementation. The definition of ‚protected customers‘ was not sufficiently clear, so that Member States with a wide definition might not contribute in case of an emergency.

Monitoring and self-responsibility: The extension of the tasks of the Gas Coordination Group entails that more information about the individual gas situations, the preventive action, the emergency plans and other measures are provided to all Member States and that coordination can take place within that body. The Commission can monitor what agreements are made, but it has no say in the implementation of these agreements.

On 10 October 2010, the Council published a press release about the adoption of the new SoS regulation. Solidarity is not mentioned once. The regulation is summarised as follows:

> „The aim of the regulation is to establish measures for safeguarding the security of gas supply by ensuring the proper and continuous functioning of the internal gas market and by providing a clear definition and allocation of responsibilities, as well as efficient coordination of the response at member state and Union level regarding both preventive action and the response to specific disruptions of supply“ (Council 2010b).

Regulation 994/2010 is a trust-building measure which ameliorates further cooperation with the help of information exchange and the institutionalisation of transnational cooperation. It follows that the gas crises have not sufficiently pressured the Member States to agree to full solidarity. Solidarity was increasingly incorporated since the Commission and the Parliament repetitively pushed for the principle, which was now also officially enshrined in the Treaty of Lisbon. Member States still refused to institutionalise solidarity, however, the general agreement to insert solidarity increased since self-responsibility was emphasised. Regulation (EU) No 994/2010 has been interpreted as „solid basis for the management of unforeseen supply interruptions" (de Jong et al. 2012: 10) and „is considered to have been instrumental in establishing the basic building blocks of gas supply security across the EU" (Aoun and Rutten 2016: 2). The regulation represents a major change for EU energy policy, since security of supply was in the past only a matter of national responsibility (de Jong et al. 2012: 5).

4.1.2. The stony way to Regulation 2017/1938

The Lithuanian president Grybauskaitė called for more solidarity in energy policy in mid-September 2013:

> „Europe needs a decisive step forward towards greater solidarity in the energy field, just as foreseen by the Lisbon Treaty. (…) I believe that energy can help drive a vision of a better European future, based on our real solidarity inside the EU and in our dealings with the EU's energy partners. I am certain that greater solidarity in the energy field would bring clear benefits for all Europeans" (Grybauskaitė 2013).

The Energy Security Strategy, which was published in 2014, reflected on how to prevent and mitigate gas supply disruption risks. The Commission stated that necessary back-up infrastructure is obliged so that every Member State can meet peak demand in case of „disruption of the single largest infrastructure asset" (Commission 2014b: 5). Also, other rules, such as the protected customers, the implementation of the Emergency Preparedness Plans and Emergency Response Plans as well as the GCG have ameliorated the EU's resilience towards supply shocks. „These rules provide a European framework that creates trust and ensures solidarity as it guarantees that Member States act on their national responsibilities and collectively enhance security of supply" (Commission 2014b: 5). The Commission underlined the need that every Member State is sufficiently prepared in case of a supply disruption. This precondition creates trust, as the Member States know that support would only be demanded under very strict conditions.

Energy Commissioner Oettinger held a speech on the internal market at the Conference of the Council of European Energy Regulators (CEER) in June 2014 (Oettinger 2014). He stated that solidarity mechanisms on the EU level but also with international partners are necessary in order to guarantee stable supplies in the upcoming winter. Energy security stress tests would assess the current state of the system. However, these points were immediately followed by the announcement that energy security can only be achieved by a better functioning internal energy market. Oettinger argued that the market is not sufficiently reliable, which is why solidarity mechanisms need to straighten out this deficit.

In October 2014, the Commission published a „report on the implementation of Regulation (EU) 994/2010 and its contribution to solidarity and preparedness for gas disruptions in the EU" (Commission 2014e). The Commission illustrated that the „lessons learnt from the implementation of Directive 2004/67/EC had shown that it was necessary to harmonise national measures in order to ensure that all Member States are prepared at least on a common minimum level" (Commission 2014e: 1). A common level would lead to more solidarity, since freeriding would be excluded. Additionally, increased supply standards in one Member State could limit the market liquidity. Some Member States feared negative effects in case that their supply standard was higher than the one defined in the regulation. This was taken into account by the regulation, accepting increased supply standards under the conditions that they are

> „clearly defined and based on well-identified risks. However, Member States which have an increased supply standard are required to identify in their Preventive Action Plans and Emergency Plans how the national standard may be temporarily reduced to the default standard of Regulation 994/2010 in the event of a regional or Union emergency, in order to provide solidarity and help at regional and EU level. In other words, higher national standards should not stand in the way of regional solidarity" (Commission 2014e: 3).

The Commission further explained that harmonisation is not sufficient, since diverging supply standards may put solidarity at risk. Therefore, the Commission demanded a revision of the current legislation. The concern of the Commission was that in case of an emergency situation, responsibilities would be unclear, since the actors involved – the Commission, the

Member States, the competent authorities and the natural gas undertak-ings – have different roles and tasks. „It remains to be decided whether a regional or Union emergency would automatically make it possible to introduce non-market based measures – or EU solidarity mechanisms in case such are created – in those Member States where the market is still working" (Commission 2014e: 23). The Commission argued that the „hierarchy and priority of national vs. Union interest would need to be better defined in order to ensure smooth decision making" (Commission 2014e: 23). Hence, the Commission wanted to explore the conditions for solidarity by asking a series of questions, concerning e.g. the possible cur-tailment of own non-protected customers to supply protected customers from other Member States, but also how such action could be financially compensated. The Commission argued that it is necessary to revise the regulation, since the competences are not clearly allocated between the national and the Union level. However, the regulation from 2010 included also too many uncertainties on how to act. The Commission stated, that the problems concerned not only the question of authority, but also the allocation of resources. Regarding the concept of solidarity, there were two main concerns: 1) solidarity can only work if the problem of free riders is excluded. Member States must therefore introduce sufficient security of supply standards at national level to obtain guaranteed aid at Community level. 2) Solidarity is not charity and must be financially compensated.

This report was accompanied by a communication from the Commis-sion „on the short term resilience of the European gas system Preparedness for a possible disruption of supplies from the East during the fall and winter of 2014/2015" (Commission 2014a). The Commission referred to the study by ENTSOG which examined two scenarios of supply disrup-tions. The cooperative scenario included an equal burden sharing between neighbouring Member States and the non-cooperative scenario included a stop of gas flows. The simulation was based on two different scenarios either having one month or six months of supply disruptions (50 % cut of Russian imports and disruption of the Ukraine transit route) (Commission 2014d). One of the main findings was that if Member States perfectly cooperated by also allowing gas transit to a neighbouring country in a crisis situation, the affected countries would suffer less from the supply disruption. Sub-optimal crisis management would mean that „Member States export gas only if own demand (is) completely satisfied" (ENTSOG 2014: 31). The Commission further explained that

„(...) the "cooperative" scenarios of ENTSOG presuppose the crucial element of *equal (relative) burden sharing* by which solidarity between

Member States is applied to such an extent that shortfalls in gas are spread equally between neighbouring Member States" (Commission 2014a: 5, emphasis by author).

The Commission clarified that solidarity measures would not be charity but that the Member State concerned would need to contribute. This also means that each state would need to prepare (i.e. take up responsibility) in such a way that there is no fear of freeriding. "Approaches based on isolation and suspicions go against the solidarity that is needed to create a true Energy Union" (Commission 2014a: 19). Therefore, the Commission brings forward a clearer vision of what solidarity means for the first time:

Box 16: Solidarity features named by the Commission

Solidarity is no one-way street, it is reciprocal.
- The solidarity taker needs to compensate for the loss of the giver.
- Solidarity is not altruistic; it is no gift.
- Solidarity is not a business.

Solidarity includes responsibility and exclusion of freeriding.
- Solidarity cannot work if there are different standards of consumer protection.
- Each Member State has to act responsibly in order to avoid mistrust.
- Solidarity must exclude incentives for freeriding.

The last point underlines that the Member States should not take advantage of crises situations. These points have also been repeated by the Commission in the Press Release and the Stress Test Communication. The Commission used in particular the study by ENTSOG – although ENTSOG never explicitly talked about solidarity but cooperation – as expert input to strengthen the argument that solidarity would be needed based on objective calculations.

In May 2015, the EP published a motion for an own-initiative report (ITRE rapporteur: Algirdas Saudargas, EPP, Lithuania) as a reaction to the Commission's European Energy Security Strategy (Parliament 2015a). Solidarity was mentioned regarding the implementation of a fully functioning cross-border solidarity mechanism as a reaction to supply shocks and as overarching principle between all Member States. The debate in the Parliament was heated over the point if Russia was a reliable partner, which led to the rejection of the procedure.

In a communication on the "State of the Energy Union 2015" (Commission 2015c) in November 2015, the Commission announced how security of gas supply should be managed in the future. The Commission chose a security frame by stating that „geopolitical challenges will not go away in 2016" (p. 11). The Commission repeated its mantra that the EU needs to speak with one voice and that a new energy diplomacy should be pursued, implemented by energy diplomacy action plans and diversification. One vital instrument to create more resilience concerning security of gas supply would be the revision of the SoS regulation. „It will be particularly important to strengthen regional cooperation between Member States, both to prevent and to mitigate supply shocks, as well as to ensure solidarity in the event of an emergency" (p. 12). The Commission insisted on the point to revise the SoS regulation in order to strengthen solidarity.

> „In the gas sector, I can say that it was the Commission. I'm not just saying that because I work here, it was done quite deliberately. Because we also thought that the area of security of supply was the predestined area." (Interview 1, DG Energy).

The Parliament published the own-initiative report ‚Towards a European Energy Union' (Parliament 2015b) on 15 December 2015. The main argument was that solidarity mechanisms are necessary to ensure security of supply in case of supply disruptions in addition to internal market mechanisms. In this context, the EP demanded that (among other issues) solidarity must be reflected in energy legislation, in particular the SoS regulation must be revised. The Parliament underlined thus again the importance of solidarity concerning SoS but also manifested solidarity in this document as general principle.

The revision of the security of gas supply regulation 994/2010 started in February 2016. The Council and its preparatory body met over 30 times in order to resolve conflictive points. There have been three points on the agenda, which have been of particular difficulty, which were ‚regional cooperation', ‚solidarity' and ‚transparency'. The main concern was the compensation of solidarity and the exact definition of solidarity since Member States feared the consequences of solidarity concerning the distribution of financial resources (Interview 1, DG Energy). The Explanatory Memorandum (COM(2016) 52 final) of the proposal for a regulation of the European Parliament and of the Council concerning measures to safeguard the security of gas supply and repealing Regulation (EU) No 994/2010 starts with a short explanation on the reasons and objectives of the proposal. The primary purpose of the regulation is „to ensure that all Member States put in place appropriate tools to prepare for and manage the effects of a gas shortage due to a disruption in supply or exceptionally high demand" (Commission 2016f: 2). By introducing, among other items, more robust regional cooperation, the Commission wanted to diminish the risk of supply crises which cannot be resolved on the national level only. The ongoing tensions between Russia and Ukraine serve as the geopolitical context (Commission 2016g: 2). The interviews revealed that the Council was a particularly hard nut to crack mostly due to the issue of compensation for solidarity. The EP acted very supportingly (Interview 1, DG Energy; Personal Communication 1,DG Energy; Interview 7, EP).

As already for regulation 994/2010, Art. 194 TFEU was chosen as the legal basis. The Commission remarked that more concerted action on the EU level was needed since the energy market was increasingly inter-connected. Coordinated action and solidarity are indispensable as demon-strated by the cold spell of 2012 and the 2014 stress test. „(N)ational approaches both result in sub-optimal measures and aggravate the impact of a crisis" (Commission 2016f: 3). Furthermore, „(c)ooperation should also be extended to specific measures to foster solidarity between Member States in security of supply matters" (Commission 2016f: 4).

The proposal – which made in total 13 references to solidarity – entailed that ‚protected customers' continue to include small and medium-sized businesses, but the solidarity principle might not cover them.

> „It is worth recalling, however, that the point of this principle is to ensure a continued supply to households and essential social services in emergencies. This mechanism is a last resort, intended only for use in situations of extreme gas shortage. While the revised Regulation is designed to avoid such situations, we must nonetheless be prepared for them" (Commission 2016f: 7).

The Commission illustrated that the revised regulation „explicitly incorpo-rates the new solidarity principle" (Commission 2016f: 12). This explicit solidarity principle entails that:
- Member States must reduce their supply standard to the EU default level, if the higher supply standard deteriorates the security of supply situation in a neighbouring state in a case of emergency.
- The implementation of the solidarity principle should be mandatory. If one Member State suffers from an emergency situation (which is that protected customers are not supplied with gas), the non-protected customers from the Member State „are not being supplied in another Member State in emergency to which the first country's transmission network is connected" (ibid.).

– Member States need to put in place technical devices to ensure that protected customers receive gas and to „avoid non-eligible customers consuming gas" (ibid.).

The Commission's proposal towards regional solidarity was interpreted as conflictive with the right of each Member State to freely chose its external energy supply sources. „(...) (I)f one member state's external supply choice (...) could put its neighbours' gas security at risk, it will have to take collective security obligations in case of major disruptions. This is especially relevant in light of the Nord Stream 2 dispute" (Giuli 2016: 1).

In the preamble of the proposal (COM(2016) 52) the Commission highlights in recital 6

> „that the Energy Union rests on solidarity and trust, which are necessary features of energy security. *This regulation should aim to boost solidarity and trust between the Member States* and should put in place the measures needed to achieve these aims, thus paving the way for implementing the Energy Union" (emphasis added).

Whereas in recital 7 the Commission underlines that the internal gas market is the best mechanism in order to guarantee security of supply. However, to „allow the internal gas market to function even in the face of a shortage of supply, provision must be made for solidarity and coordination in the response to supply crises, as regards both preventive action and the reaction to actual disruptions of supply". Recital 9 states that regional cooperation, in a spirit of solidarity, should be the guiding principle of this regulation. This is an interesting approach, as regional cooperation is understood as a principle and solidarity only as a kind of esprit. Another reference to solidarity is made in recital 10. „A definition of (...) protected customers should not conflict with the Union solidarity mechanisms". A spirit of solidarity is also called for in recital 10 referring to bi-directional capacity, which „(...) can be used to supply gas both to the neighbouring Member State and to others along the gas supply corridor". In recital 36 the Commission underlines the value of solidarity regarding security of supply and refers to the results of the October 2014 stress test, which proved that solidarity is necessary both for security of supply and to reduce costs.

> „If an emergency is declared in any Member State, a two-step approach should be applied to strengthen solidarity. Firstly, all Member States which have introduced a higher supply standard should reduce it to default values to make the gas market more liquid. Secondly, if the first step fails to provide the necessary supply, further measures by

neighbouring Member States, even if not in an emergency situation, should be triggered to ensure the supply to households, essential social services and district heating installations in the Member State experiencing the emergency. Member States should identify and describe the details of these solidarity measures in their emergency plans, ensuring fair and equitable compensation of the natural gas undertakings" (Commission 2016f: Recital 36).

The introductory part demonstrates that solidarity can have many forms and shapes. It is simultaneously objective, esprit, mechanism and principle. In the central part of the regulation, this changes in so far, as solidarity sets the tone for the design of policy actions. This is stipulated both in article 1 on the subject matter and article 12, which is headed ‚solidarity'.

The regulation aims to guarantee the functioning of the internal market in order to safeguard security of gas supply in case that the market is unable to deliver this security. Hence, both the Member States and the Union need to clarify the responsibilities and to define preventive as well as post-crisis actions. In case of an emergency at Member State, regional or Union level, this „Regulation also provides transparent mechanisms, in a spirit of solidarity (…)" (Art. 1). Article 12 defines which solidarity measures should be taken in case of emergency. First, other Member States need to reduce their supply standard to the default level. Secondly, Member States directly connected to the Member State that has declared a state of emergency and whose protected customers are undersupplied must also reduce their supplies to the level of the protected customers in order to release gas supplies to supply the protected customers of the Member State that has declared a state of emergency. The form of technical, legal and financial agreements for the application of this solidarity mechanism lies in the hand of the Member States. All Member States, which are directly connected, should agree on those forms and describe their arrangement in the emergency plans of their respective regions. If Member States fail to agree on an arrangement, the Commission may propose the next steps.

The Impact Assessment (Commission 2016b) starts in the introduction with a quote from the Energy Union strategy that „(…) *Member States see that they depend on each other to deliver secure energy to their citizens, based on true solidarity and trust (…)*" (p.3, emphasis by Commission). The regulation 994/2010 needs to be revised to make the EU more resilient towards supply disruptions. The revision „is one of the actions identified and framed in the dimension of ‚energy security, solidarity and trust'" (ibid.). The Commission argued that Member States have the problem of behavioural biases, which means, that they only consider national solutions to ensure security of supply. The consequences of the behavioural biases are manifold according to the Commission. Self-protective measures lead to limits in the availability of gas, national approaches do (naturally) not consider their effects on other states, and synergies are often overlooked (e.g. cross border use of storages). Another problem is the existing mistrust between Member States, because they fear the negative consequences of other Member States' actions. There is also the fear of free riders as Member States take different measures to ensure security of supply.

> „Then you come to the issue, that is the trust. It Is exactly what you see in all the European debates today. The frugal countries they say ok you get the money, but there are conditions to use the money. And they don't trust the beneficiaries to use the money properly, there is corruption in the system and the money would not reach the projects and thinks like that. This is a key issue in the EU and when you come to anything which is monetizable, which is an expression in money, you have always the suspicion that you have free riders in the system. And it is true free-riding – If you will not invest enough in your infrastructure, you will pay the price and don't ask the others to pay the price for you. That is why of course, e.g. the SoS: if you don't implement infrastructure, the N-1 infrastructure, if there is an accident one day, don't ask the others to come in. If you have been the imprudence" (Interview 3, DG Energy).

Therefore, the Commission argued, Member States would be less willing to corporate with more vulnerable Member States in a spirit of solidarity. However, solidarity is the only solution when it comes to security of supply. These arguments illustrate various concerns of the Member States that have already arisen previously. Freeriding is one problem, which might exist if rules are different for each Member State and/or not obligatory. Vulnerability describes here a situation, where a Member State does not sufficiently guarantee security of supply. The Commission argued finally that more integration is absolutely necessary to avert security of supply problems. Thinking about security of supply only on a national level is not only insufficient, but even dangerous for the overall situation of security of supply. This clearly demonstrates the Commission's attempt to gain more competences in the area. The explanation, why national approaches still prevail, however, is linked to solidarity. Mistrust is the result of fears of freeriding and unfair burden sharing, which is why solidarity cannot be implemented, even though only solidarity can resolve the problem. As further reason why solidarity is not working, the Commission detects that

Member States follow different approaches regarding protected customers (p.13). A high standard of protected customers would lead to a lower availability of gas in case of emergency.

The increasing interconnection of the EU gas market is not convergent with national security of supply approaches. The weakness of national solutions has been demonstrated during the Cold Spell in 2012 and the stress test of 2014 (p. 16/17). Additionally, the Commission underlined that the general objective of the regulation, which is security of supply, is reflected by the Treaty, in particular Art. 3(3) TEU and Art. 194(1) TFEU. While Art. 3(3) TEU refers to the implementation of a functioning internal market, Art. 194(1) TFEU refers to security of supply as particular goal of energy policy in a spirit of solidarity. In the following, the Commission proposed five different policy options ranging from ,no further action on EU level' (Option 0) to ,Full harmonisation of EU level' (Option 4). In option 0 and option 1 ,Enhanced implementation and soft law measures' solidarity does not play any role. The Commission describes how solidarity could be implemented under option 2 (p. 22). When a Member State declares emergency, because it cannot supply its protected customers with sufficient amounts of gas, the connected Member States would need to send their excess gas to the affected Member State. Member States would need to explain how this solidarity action works in their respective emergency plan. Option 3 ,Enhanced coordination with some principles/standards set at EU level' goes a step further by a) making the principle of solidarity „mandatory and not only a best efforts obligation" and b) Member States would need to disrupt gas supply to customers other than protected customers in order to ensure security of supply in the affected Member State. As regards option 4, there would be a full harmonisation on the definition of protected customers and the solidarity mechanism would work as such, that „missing volume of gas for protected customers in Country A can only be acquired via a market-based mechanism (e.g. tender or auction) among non-protected customers in Country B" (p. 28). Solidarity under option 2 is evaluated as follows:

> „Solidarity would also be improved under this option, on the one hand, as a result of the measures on protected customers and to en-hance coordination; on the other hand, via the obligation to consider a solidarity principle. As a best efforts obligation, this option has the benefit of flexibility both in terms of implementation and form. More-over, the regional approach provided by the joint Risk Assessment ensures a comprehensive outlook" (p. 34).

The financial burden of introducing solidarity is expected to be limited (p. 35). Option 3 would entail the replacement of national plans by regional plans. The Commission argues that national plans do not consider regional consequences, consequently they are not fully reflecting the spirit of solidarity. The Commission evaluates that solidarity under this option would be „a substantially better defined obligation, (which) ensures the application of a minimum solidarity in case of extreme circumstances" (p. 37). The Commission argued similarly for option 4 regarding the definition of protected customers. The stricter the definition of protected customers, the more solidarity can be expected. The application of the solidarity mechanism would be more precise, but there might be shortcomings due to rigidity preventing flexibility (p. 44).

By comparing all options considering effectiveness, efficiency and consistency with other policies, the Commission declared that option 2 (but also option 1) would not contribute sufficiently to solidarity as the rules are neither clear nor strict enough. „Where clear rules are absent, Member States would be less well-prepared and disruptions can have more serious consequences. This lack could result in *freeriding* and, as such, hampers efforts for regional solidarity" (p. 50, emphasis by author). However, there is one major difference between options 1 and 2:

> „The current Regulation does not contain specific provisions regarding solidarity and therefore, it is highly unlikely that an enhanced implementation, as proposed in option 1, would result in more solidarity. In this regard, *option 2, as well as options 3 and 4, represents the first time that this principle would be reflected in secondary legislation under Article 194 TFUE"* (p. 50, emphasis added).

Option 3 would be the best solution according to the Commission, since it applies the principle of solidarity exclusively to households and essential social services, which would not be the case under option 4 (p. 51).

The Commission's analysis shows that strict rules and commitments are necessary to successfully implement solidarity. The absence of commitments would not only lead to a loss of confidence, as Member States would fear free riders. It would also hinder the willingness to implement solidarity measures, which would have a negative impact on the overall security of supply. Therefore, the Commission has identified that solidarity requires strict common rules, mutual trust and the exclusion of free riders.

In a press release (Commission 2016d), which the Commission published the same day, the Commission explained that the gas system is fragile due to external dependence. The Commission argued that it is necessary to shift from a national to a regional approach to „reap full benefits of liquid and competitive market". However, the principle of solidarity, which should ensure the continuing supply to protected customers, is needed „in case their supply was affected due to a severe crisis" (Commission 2016d).

The frame analysis shows that the Commission used in preparation of the revision of regulation 994/2010 primarily functionally framed arguments in relation to the functioning of the internal market to demonstrate why solidarity was needed. Main arguments referred to 1) the interdependence of Member States due to the internal market, 2) the effects of national decision-making on the internal market and 3) the need to carry out security of supply on the Union level in order to not distort the internal market.

Figure 7: Framing of solidarity by Commission

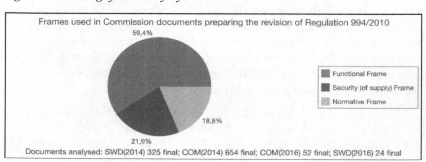

In mid-May 2016, the Presidency initiated a policy debate on the content of the Commission's proposal. Two groups of Member States had opposing opinions on the solidarity issue. Scandinavian countries, the UK and Germany were in favour of market enforcing mechanisms, while Eastern European Member States and France supported regulatory ‚solidarity' mechanisms (interview 9, WP on Energy).

> „The Commission's proposal has first put the wording and the clause on the table anyway. (...) No Member State says we reject European energy solidarity. That is just before we reject the EU. (...) Once it's on the table, no Member State will say that European solidarity is a bad point, that it has to come out completely" (Interview 9, WP on Energy).

The Dutch presidency chaired the Council in the first half of 2016. The text revealed that „the EU's preparedness and capacity to respond effectively to a gas supply crisis would be limited" (Council 2016h: 2). It was underlined that solidarity „is one of the main novelties in this legislation", and that it can be a „significant tool (…) in case of extreme emergencies" (p. 3). The principle of solidarity, which would be an obligation to assist, „has been welcomed by the Member States" (ibid.), however, its form and function are still under discussion. Therefore, the presidency asked the Member States which modalities of the application of solidarity should be envisaged and under which terms and conditions it could be implemented. The Dutch presidency prepared a background note for the next Council meeting in June. It was again announced that the new SoS regulation would entail a mandatory solidarity mechanism. The Presidency asked about the necessary terms and conditions to implement solidarity (Council 2016k). The Council met on 6 and 7 June to discuss further details of the SoS proposal. It was repeated that the new solidarity principle would be mandatory, which was in general supported by all ministers. Details such as technical, administrative and financial arrangements as well as the definition of protected customers were still too unclear (Council 2016b). On 9 June 2016, the Presidency presented its first compromise, however, without significant changes to the solidarity principle. But there was one clarification on the definition of protected customers: essential social services exclude educational or public administration service (Council 2016f: 45).

The second half of 2016 was chaired by the Slovakian Presidency, which stated in its presidency programme: „the Presidency will support efforts to improve the security of gas supply by tapping the potential of cross-border and regional cooperation and applying the principle of solidarity". Furthermore, the programme mentions that the „aim of the revision of the Security of Gas Supply Regulation is to enhance the principle of solidarity (…)" (Presidency 2016: 28). Jerzy Buzek (ITRE Rapporteur) also expressed in his explanatory statement on the report on the SoS proposal, that solidarity has been introduced as mechanism with the regulation of 2010, however, he supported its revision in order to strengthen the solidarity mechanism (Parliament 2016b). His concept of solidarity entails that it is a mechanism of last resorts, not replacing any market mechanisms, and that every state is primarily responsible for its security of supply by ensuring its resilience.

During the following discussions at the Council different adjustments have been made to article 12 on solidarity, however, there have been no conceptual changes. The debate was concentrating on making the article fully operational, how to prevent freeriding and how to organise compensation. It was underlined several times that the Working Party, Coreper, the Member States as well as the Parliament supported solidarity as action of last resort. It was also mentioned that such a solidarity principle was proposed for the first time by the Commission in EU energy legislation. Full harmonisation was not approved since the differences across the EU could only be approached by taking into account a certain amount of flexibility (e.g. option to limit or suspend solidarity mechanism by mutual agreement).

In a policy debate in November 2016, this optional flexibility was discussed. „Some Member States pointed out that the possibility to limit or suspend solidarity is in contradiction to the principle itself; others have welcomed this flexibility" (Council 2016i: 8). However, the „general principle of solidarity was overwhelmingly supported at the Working Party and in Coreper" (ibid.). Also the

> „European Parliament welcomed the introduction of the solidarity clause as a legally-binding principle of last resort. Solidarity should not be regarded as an alternative to market-based preventive action available in the EU internal gas market, nor should it substitute any country's own efforts to improve its resilience to supply disruptions by diversifying its suppliers, routes of supply and sources of energy and increasing its energy efficiency" (Council 2016i: 8).

The Presidency followed from the discussion that as next steps, the Member States would need to decide which options they would finally support, and proposed A) either a full harmonisation of the solidarity mechanism or B) that the solidarity mechanism would be defined in the regulation but leaving compensation to the Member States.

On 5 December 2016, there was a discussion within the Council (TTE) on these proposals (Council 2016l, webcast). The session started with an introduction by Commissioner Cañete. He argued that the energy union is based on solidarity, as is Art. 194 TFEU. As a consequence burdens and benefits must be shared. He reiterated that all Member States support solidarity in gas supply, but that a balance between flexibility and harmonisation is needed. Solidarity must be operational. But it would be necessary to ensure that market mechanisms are used first, followed by all emergency measures, and solidarity only as last resort. Solidarity must be used for the sake of all citizens. However, it is not for free, there has to be compensation (Minutes 05.00 – 08.00). Member States argued that the reasons for introducing solidarity were the dependence on third states and the 2009 gas crisis. Additionally, solidarity was said to be a symbolic act.

In order to implement solidarity, trust and responsibility were identified as necessary elements. Commissioner Cañete concluded the session by claiming that option B was the preferred option (no harmonisation).

The presidency continuously confirmed the „broad agreement on the need for solidarity between Member States" (Council 2016j). It also remained unchanged that solidarity is a last resort mechanism. The Presidency conclusions indicate that while solidarity and compensation need to be defined in the regulation, the definitions will allow „Member States to take into account their national situation", which is a reference to the demanded flexibility (Council 2016j). This meeting was evaluated as essential „to break the stalemate and pave the way for the Maltese Presidency to finalise Council's mandate on 1 February, 2017" (Council 2017b). The Slovak Presidency could present conclusions, which were all accepted by the Ministers. The point on solidarity was summarised as follows: „The Council agreed that solidarity should be a last resort mechanism after all the emergency measures have been exhausted. New rules for compensations and burden sharing were established" (ibid.). In the presidency's revised compromise of December 2016, solidarity remained somewhat flexible per se. Even though some Member States expressed their concern about the possibility to limit or suspend solidarity (see the debate of November), the text on this limitation of solidarity was still in the document (see recital 36) (Council 2016g).

Malta took over the Council's presidency in January 2017. The presidency's programme included the revision of the SoS regulation: „The Presidency believes that this Regulation is a key element in ensuring a strengthened security of energy supply for all EU citizens particularly in times of crisis" (Presidency 2017: 32). The presidency's revised compromise of 6 January 2017 demonstrated a significant change regarding the flexibility of solidarity. Recital 36 was rewritten entirely (Council 2017c). Solidarity was strengthened on the one hand, because the sentence on the possibility to limit or suspend solidarity was erased. However, it was added several times that solidarity is a mechanism of last resort, which could be only used if all other measures have been exhausted. Instead of a two-step approach (1. Reducing supply standard to default level, 2. Putting in place solidarity measures) the compromise entailed a gradual approach: 1. Reducing supply standard to a normal level, 2. The concerned Member State needs to implement all emergency mechanisms, 3. Solidarity measures will be introduced as measures of last resort. This change of recital 36 proves that Member States ensured that no freeriding is possible by the insertion of the ‚gradual approach'. Every Member State is at first self-responsible in case of a crisis, which is why solidarity is a mechanism of last resort. Only if freeriding can be excluded, Member States are willing to provide solidarity. The mistrust, which was reflected by the possibility to limit or suspend solidarity, was thus resolved.

On 16 February 2017, the preparation for the second informal trilogue started between the Commission, ITRE and the Council (Council 2017d). ITRE inserted in recital 6 that solidarity is a principle enshrined in Article 194 TFEU. This was later deleted by the Presidency, since solidarity is not called a principle in Art. 194 TFEU. Furthermore, ITRE demanded a harmonised approach of protected customers in recital 10. At the same time, it called for flexibility concerning the insertion of small- and medium-sized enterprises as protected customers. In contrast to the Council, ITRE shortened recital 36 and did not specify when the solidarity measures should take place. In the original Commission's proposal, it was also foreseen to involve the European Energy Community Contracting Parties. ITRE tried to pursue the inclusion of those parties in the solidarity mechanism. This has not been supported by the Council, which only declared further cooperation. This point underlines the *exclusive aspect of solidarity*, which is only applicable to the pre-defined solidarity group. The Council provided a very detailed approach on how to implement solidarity in Art. 12, but the Parliament remained very vague. It was the Council which inserted solidarity this many times in the regulation.

In April 2017, Konrad Mizzi, Minister within the Office of the Prime Minister of Malta was quoted for a press release of the Council:

> „This legislation will make a major contribution to our energy security. It will reduce our dependency on others for our energy supplies and enable us to deal more quickly and efficiently with any gas supply crises. It will also contribute to build greater trust and solidarity both within the EU and with our partners from the Energy Community" (Council 2017a).

Additionally, the Press Release repeated the most important aspects of solidarity: solidarity as mechanism of last resort, compensation and ‚solidarity protected customers'. A compromise on solidarity was reached on 5 May 2017: „The 40 % derogation within the burden sharing mechanism was deleted and a safeguard regarding Union liability was added in Article 12(9). Further clarifications were added in recitals and throughout Article 12 regarding functioning of the mechanism" (Council 2017e: 1).

During the revision of the regulation 994/2010, the General Court worked on a case (Case C-226/16) between the ENI spa and others v Premier Ministre and Ministre de l'Environnement, de l'Énergie et de la Mer. The topic concerned the question of who can be entitled as ‚protected customers' since the French law included more entities as protected customers than provisioned by the SoS regulation. The Advocate General Mengozzi delivered his opinion on 26 July 2017. Advocate General Mengozzi made several references to solidarity in his opinion. First, he acknowledged that Union energy policy must be pursued in a spirit of solidarity between Member States. He stated that the principle of solidarity „has taken on a character that could be defined as a 'constitutional principle'" due to its expression in the Treaties, both the TFEU and TEU. Concerning security of energy supply, it is even referred to twice in the TFEU. Not only is the regulation 994/2010 based on this principle but it „permeates the whole regulation", it is mentioned both in recitals and provisions. In addition to that, strengthening solidarity between Member States is an explicit aim of the regulation, which proves the fundamental role of solidarity in designing this regulation. As the last argument, GA Mengozzi points out that the principle of solidarity has been introduced in the revised regulation of 994/2010: „the principle of solidarity plays an even more important role and is expressly incorporated into the text of the regulation with an article devoted specifically to solidarity". Even though the GA's opinion included multiple references to solidarity and underlined its importance, solidarity did not play any role in the final judgment of the case. This case showed that the legal interpretation of solidarity was necessary, but a final interpretation of the Court was still missing.

Several MEPs expressed how important it was to insert solidarity as a concrete mechanism during the EP debate on 12 September 2017 (Parliament 2017c). MEP Buzek illustrated that geopolitical circumstances make it necessary to act together. Solidarity is one mechanism to ensure security of supply. Energy Commissioner Cañete underlined that solidarity is a novelty:

> „The spirit of solidarity is a cornerstone of the new Regulation, ensuring that all households will receive gas supplies even during a crisis. With the new processes laid down in the Regulation, for the first time, solidarity is not only a political declaration but an obligation and a concrete way to help" (Parliament 2017c).

Pavel Teličkа (Czech Republic), on behalf of the ALDE Group, stated how difficult the negotiations have been on the one hand because the issues at stake are very sensitive (such as solidarity) and on the other hand because some Member States were still thinking that they would be better off on their own which is contrary to the aims of the Energy Union. Claude Turmes (Luxembourg), on behalf of the Verts/ALE Group, referred again to the geopolitical importance of solidarity, which is now a tangible instrument:

> „We now have a solution for one of the biggest divides in Europe, which was that Gazprom and Russia could abuse not only markets, but also gas, to put political pressure on eastern Europe. With this legislation I think we have a real weapon against this and it is important that we got it. It was a bit shameful that we had an uphill fight against Germany, France, Austria, the Netherlands, a bit of Belgium; western European governments not understanding why it is so important for eastern Europe to have this solidarity" (Parliament 2017c).

Krzysztof Hetman (PPE, Poland) explained that solidarity makes the EU stronger towards external partners. And Tunne Kelam (PPE, Estonia) also underlined the geopolitical importance of the regulation:

> „This regulation is among the most crucial ones to ensuring the EU's resilience towards hostile policy from outside the EU. It is important to understand that the regulation is basically a legally-binding solidarity mechanism, aimed at protecting states and citizens against blackmail and political pressure. The EU needs to complete its own instruments to make sure that gas supplies cannot be used against any Member State as a political weapon" (Parliament 2017c).

Again, most of the speakers are coming from Central and Eastern European Member States. At the same time, the MEPs underlined the unity of the Parliament, and stressed that the Parliament acted as one undivided house as Claude Turmes, for example, emphasised. Overall, the Parliament aimed for a much more idealistic solution, while the Council dealt with the technical details (personal communication 1, DG Energy). Following the Parliament debate, the Commission issued a press release on the same day, in which it welcomed the strong report by the Parliament to the revised regulation, which „applies the solidarity principle for the first time" (Commission 2017c). The Commission argued that thanks to the new regulation the EU will be better prepared in case of a gas crises, that Member States will help each other „so that European households do not stay in the cold" (ibid.). This Press release did not at all speak about responsibility or compensation but underlined the ‚will to help'. The Commission sought to define solidarity by law:

„(We have) quite deliberately juridified this principle, and in the end the legal service - although it grumbled - did not manage to get its view accepted, even via the Presidential Cabinet. Because we argued that if we do not legalise the principle in the core area of security of supply, then it makes little sense only as a political declaration of intent" (Interview 1, DG Energy).

On 9 October 2017, the Council voted with 27 Member States in favour of the Regulation. Hungary was the only Member State to reject the regulation. Regulation (EU)2017/1938 of the European Parliament and of the Council of 25 October 2017 concerning measures to safeguard the security of gas supply and repealing regulation (EU) No 994/2010 was published in the Official Journal on 25 October 2017. Solidarity occurs 104 times in the text.

„The agreed text introduces considerably more detail about the operation of the solidarity mechanism (Article 12), which should be activated only when all market-based measures have been exhausted; on the basis of an explicit and justified request to the Commission and national competent authorities; and must include a commitment to pay fair and prompt compensation" (Parliament 2017a).

One crucial point is that the energy article 194 (TFEU) was added in the new regulation to underline the importance of solidarity as legal principle (s. recital 6). Additionally, protected customers are now called ‚solidarity protected customers‘.

„(…) (T)he definition of solidarity protected customers should be limited to households while still being able to include, under specific conditions, certain essential social services and district heating installations. It is therefore possible for Member States to treat, in accordance with this framework, healthcare, essential social care, emergency and security services as solidarity protected customers, including where these services are performed by a public administration" (recital 24).

In recital 38, the regulation sets the framework for solidarity by stating that solidarity „ensures cooperation with most vulnerable Member States", that it spreads effects of crises more evenly and that it remains a mechanism of last resort. The process of freeing up gas volumes starts with voluntary measures (demand-side regulated) up to non-market-based measures, such as the curtailment of certain groups of customers (recital 41). Compensation must be prompt and fair. Member States need to adopt technical, legal and financial agreements in order to make solidarity work in practice (recital 42). As already mentioned above there was no longer the 40 % derogation within the burden sharing mechanism. Instead the Member State concerned should just take the most advantageous offer based on costs in case several Member States can provide solidarity (recital 44)

4.1.3. Results and discussion

The SoS regulation represents a case of *‚institutionalised solidarity'*, since all three features of solidarity are implemented. "This is the first time you see really a provision which is devoted to the concrete mechanism of solidarity which is coming to an issue of contract. The contract of solidarity" (Interview 3, DG Energy). The solidarity mechanism is a tool, which divides clearly the responsibilities between all actors. The tool represents as ‚mechanism of last resort', which represents a compromise between self-responsibility and solidarity.

Group Cohesion: In recital 6, solidarity is mentioned both as a pillar of the European Union, but also as legally enshrined in Art. 194 (TFEU). Solidarity also defines the goal of the regulation: „This Regulation is intended to boost solidarity and trust between the Member States and put in place the measures needed to achieve those aims". And again in recital 10 solidarity is underlined as „guiding principle of this Regulation". Responsibility for the group is expressed by underlining the obligation to protect the vulnerable Member States and to avoid unilateral action. Several references highlight the interdependence of the group, that national solutions are insufficient, and a cooperative approach needed. Gas has to be exported to protected customers, which might (in the worst case) lead to lower supply to the own non-protected customers (sacrifice for community).

Reciprocity: Recital 7 explains that to „allow the internal gas market to function even in the face of a shortage of supply, provision must be made for solidarity and coordination in the response to the supply crises, as regards both preventive action and the reaction to actual disruptions of gas supply". Recitals 38 – 49 explain the conditions of and for solidarity (e.g. compensation). Article 13 is headed ‚Solidarity' and explains in detail how solidarity is implemented. Solidarity is a mechanism of last resort, designed for solidarity protected customers. Solidarity must be compensated, and the form of compensation must be fixed in agreements before solidarity is requested. However, if member states fail to reach the necessary agreement, ad hoc solidarity measures should be taken in case of emergency.

Monitoring: The Commission shall lay down the guidelines for the agreements and if Member States fail to conclude an agreement, the Commission may propose a framework. The Commission shall also be requested in case of emergency and the Commission can declare the end of an emergency. Additionally, Member States are obliged to act self-responsibly since solidarity is a mechanism of last resort and national preventive measures, e.g. national storage, must be implemented. Thus, solidarity can only be demanded if the Member State concerned exhausted all national measures (self-responsibility).

The implementation of the SoS regulation was acknowledged in the third report on the state of the Energy Union as a successful delivery of the legislative framework (COM(2017) 688 final). The Commission published the recommendation (EU) 2018/177 at the beginning of February 2018 „on the elements to be included in the technical, legal and financial arrangements between Member States for the application of the solidarity mechanism under Article 13 of Regulation (EU) 2017/1938". The recommendation repeats that solidarity is part of Art. 194 TFEU and that the regulation's aim is „to enhance solidarity and trust between the Member States and to allow the internal gas market to function for as long as possible, even when there is a shortage of supply".

A solidarity mechanism was implemented for the first time, and as consequence Member States need to agree on different terms in the bilateral agreements. The solidarity mechanism is the obligation „to prioritise supply to solidarity-protected customers in the requesting Member State over domestic customers with no solidarity protection". Possible restrictions to deliver gas are among others lacking infrastructure and the stability of a Member State's gas network. Even though conditions to receive solidarity are strict, solidarity protected customers are ensured of an uninterrupted gas supply. Also, the rules of compensation are essential to make solidarity work. The bilateral agreements cover necessary aspects for compensation, and these arrangements must be, at least partly, described in the emergency plans.

Regulation 2017/1938 is evaluated as a first step to turning „an often soft political claim to hard law" (Buschle and Talus 2019: 12). Fleming also assessed solidarity as „big theme" of the new regulation, however, he is more hesitant on the actual impact of solidarity. Member States still have „exit gateways" in case they do not want to participate and Member States have above all demonstrated their unwillingness to contribute to solidarity in crisis.

> „Against this backdrop the new provisions constitute a big step and could be deemed as a considerable ˋwin´ for the Commission. But as previous gas crises have shown, the words on paper are not worth much if there is no willingness to comply when push comes to shove" (Fleming 2019: 110).

Even though it needs to be seen whether Member States will meet their responsibility in case of emergency, the legislative framework has been evaluated as a big success by most of the actors involved. Interviews also revealed that it was only possible to insert solidarity since it was no longer needed to be activated due to the development of the internal market and the infrastructure (personal communication 2, Council, and interview 2, DG Energy). Additionally, Member States needed to ensure that solidarity would be hardly demanded, since all had to act in a self-responsible manner (personal communication 1, DG Energy, Interview 9, WP on Energy).

Although functional pressure played a role in the general introduction of the concept of solidarity, it was not sufficient to institutionalise solidarity. The Council only recognised the need to establish a solidarity mechanism after the first gas crisis. The European Council concluded that emergency responses must be coordinated, as national decisions would have a significant impact on the other Member States. The second gas crisis put additional pressure on the decision-makers, who – as described in an interview – begged the Commission for a European response.

Solidarity was needed in order to act cooperatively with two functions: 1) National decisions should be based on the consideration of the situation of other Member States, i.e. not to carry out measures which could harm others and 2) Solidarity as a mechanism (insurance) to help each other in case of emergency. Member States were willing to further insert solidarity in the regulation from 2010 since functional pressures resulted in a changed perception of decision-makers with regards to solidarity. However, Member States remained sceptical towards solidarity since self-responsibility was not sufficiently in place. Pressure increased again in light of the cold spell 2012 and the Russia-Ukraine crisis, which started in 2014.

Decisive for the institutionalisation of solidarity was the successful framing of the Commission. It was only after the last revision of the SoS regulation that institutionalised solidarity was implemented. However, the concept of the solidarity mechanism was developed over time. It goes back to the promotion of the Commission in 2002. But at that time security of supply legislation was hardly supported by the Council and the Parliament. The Commission continued to express the need for solidarity and coordination on the EU level. The Commission prepared the revision of the regulation very well in advance. The 2014 Gas Stress Test brought forward solid arguments why solidarity would be needed in case of crisis. The Commission used a mix of functional and security of supply frames, which targeted the interdependence of Member States. Functional argumentation was strengthened by the study of ENTSOG on the advantages of cooperation. This study was taken up by the Commission, which reframed cooperation as solidarity. Interdependence would lead to greater vulnerability in a market which has functional deficits. Therefore, solidarity would be needed to encounter the flaws of the market.

The aim of the Commission was the juridification of the solidarity principle: „Just writing it (solidarity) in the preambles or reasons was not enough for us. (...) We wanted to juridify it (the principle) and we managed to do so" (Interview 1, DG Energy). The Parliament strongly supported further implementation of the solidarity mechanism, which was requested insistently by Baltic and East European Member States over time. The Parliament strengthened normative claims by repeating the impact of solidarity as European value, which is enshrined in the Treaty. The Council, which could not dismiss solidarity due to the normative pressure, could agree to this tool under the conditions that every Member State needed to do its homework first.

For some the regulation is a first step only:

> „(...) nobody is against solidarity as a principle, and everybody would say again we want solidarity, we want solidarity, but what does it mean concretely? It means nothing. And here at least it is a real attempt to make it concrete. And I think as such it is a step forward" (Interview 11, Official, Government of Luxembourg).

However, the Council was clearly struggling over the purpose and scope of a solidarity mechanism. Solidarity would only be a mechanism of last resort and thus exclude freeriding. The interviews revealed that the exclusion of freeriding and strengthening of self-responsibility were the necessary features, which needed to be implemented, in order to make the Council agree to an institutionalised solidarity mechanism. Nevertheless, the Commission was the main driver for ‚institutionalised solidarity'.

4.2. Case 2: The integration of the gas market: the pursuit of solidarity

This chapter is dedicated to the development of the directive 2009/73/EC concerning common rules for the internal market in natural gas (2009) and its successor directive (EU) 2019/692. The predecessor of the directive (2003/55/EC) did not make any reference to solidarity. The directive 2009/72/EC was adopted after second reading.

4.2.1. Regional solidarity as answer to the gas crisis

In September 2007, the European Commission issued a proposal for a directive of the European Parliament and of the Council amending directive 2003/55/EC concerning common rules for the internal market in natural gas (Commission 2007d). In the explanatory memorandum the Commission made several references to solidarity. First, it legitimised its proposal with reference to the European Council conclusions from 2007, which „underlined the need to strengthen security of supply in a spirit of solidarity between Member States". Based on this, the Commission reflected on how to implement solidarity:

> „It is proposed that Member States cooperate in order to promote regional and bilateral solidarity. This cooperation is intended to cover situations which would be likely to result in severe disruptions of gas supply affecting a Member State. Examples of this coordination are the streamlining of national measures to deal with emergencies and the elaboration of practical modalities for mutual assistance. The Commission will adopt guidelines for regional solidarity cooperation, if needed" (p. 8).

The Commission proposed „to provide a framework for regional solidarity cooperation" (recital 24), which would contribute to security of supply (e.g. in the event of a supply crisis). Solidarity should take the form of coordination of national emergency measures, identification and development of necessary gas interconnections and a framework (conditions and mutual modalities) for mutual assistance. The Commission's competences would be extended, since a) it has to be informed about this cooperation and b) it can set guidelines for regional solidarity cooperation (Article 24.4).

In the accompanying Impact Assessment (Commission 2007b), the Commission first set out the political context that triggered a revision of the directive. The Commission underlined that the EUCO and the EP support the idea of strengthening European energy policy. The second strand of arguments concerned the functional deficits and showed that the internal market still has considerable shortcomings. The Commission referred also to the supply of gas situation, which was under severe stress during the gas crises in 2006 and 2007. The crises „showed the dangers of relying on a single supplier. (…) The Commission intends to propose a solidarity mechanism between the Member States in order to mitigate the effects of such future possible disruptions" (p. 28). The Commission wanted to carry out a study on possible costs and benefits of such a mechanism and argued further that the mechanisms, which are in place by directives 2003/55/EC and 2004/67/EC, need to be reviewed. The directives do not „foresee any binding solidarity agreement, nor do they establish a framework for such agreements" (p. 56). Possible options to reinforce those mechanisms are:

> „Option 1: impose mandatory strategic stocks on the companies as required by the existing oil directive; Option 2: improve the existing mechanism by imposing more transparency and reporting obligation on the levels of commercial stocks; Option 3: create a solidarity mechanism at regional level between Member States" (Commission 2007b: 29).

The Commission provided no further information on how such a solidarity mechanism could look like. Even though the Commission used normative and functional frames for proposing more EU action, the security frame was used to justify the implementation of solidarity mechanisms. But the Commission identified market failures as the problems at hand and offered a number of solutions to address these poor developments. At that time, solidarity was only understood as 'call for help' but responsibility was missing (Interview 10, Commission Official).

> „I was always very suspicious of the term because I didn't know exactly what it meant. (…) I never wanted to operate with big empty words when we proposed legislation, so I was always very reluctant to use the term solidarity. In my mind it was always the case that solidarity can be prescribed less by a legal text, but you have to make it concrete. And I was also suspicious because depending on who you talked to, people always understood it differently. There were those who always used solidarity when it was a matter of helping them, directly, interventionist, dirigiste, somehow directly helping in an emergency. Very often they concealed the fact that they themselves had not made sufficient provisions. And when the difficulties arose, they turned to

others for help and shouted solidarity, solidarity" (Interview 8, DG Energy).

At a dinner speech at the European Energy Forum in February 2008, Jean-Arnold Vinois, the Head of Unit for Energy Policy and Security of Supply at the DG for Energy and Transport, gave a presentation on security of gas supply. He explained that gas demand would be growing over the years and listed the possible instruments. The second instrument on his list to conquer fears of energy disruptions was solidarity. Vinois outlined that solidarity cooperation is part of the proposed internal gas market directive. Member States needed to cooperate to overcome supply difficulties. Cooperation can take the form of „streamlining of national measures to deal with emergencies" and „elaboration of practical modalities for mutual assistance". At the same time he underlined the importance that each Member State has its own responsibilities, solidarity „shall not serve as excuse not to invest in security of supply infrastructure e.g. storage" (Vinois 2008: 6).

In June 2008, the Council Presidency (Slovenia) presented in its conclusions to the Delegations its thought on regional solidarity as follows (point 3k):

> „Regarding the related provisions on regional solidarity (art. 5a, Gas D.) they build, to a large extent, upon existing mechanisms (e.g. directive on security of gas supply) and remain fairly flexible as to the manner in which to contribute to this solidarity, e.g. relying on market-based mechanisms or not" (Council 2008b).

There is no further evaluation of the Commission's proposal included. Also in June 2008, ITRE Rapporteur Romano La Russa (UEN, Italy) issued the report on the proposal (Parliament 2008c). The following amendments were suggested: In recital 24, IMCO inserted that the framework for regional solidarity cooperation should be *transparent and effective.* This was justified by the argument that public scrutiny should be possible, since „(e)ffective provision of solutions for eventual energy supply crisis is essential for the well-being of EU citizens" (p. 150). Additionally, ITRE added that "(d)irective 2004/67 EG covers comprehensively aspects of security of supply" (p. 19). Apparently, ITRE did not pursue the same aims as expressed in the report by Jacek Saryusz-Wolski from 2007 (Parliament 2007b). Saryusz-Wolski urged for the implementation of solidarity mechanisms, which has not been supported during the revision of the internal gas market directive. Further amendments on solidarity underlined that ITRE was not convinced by the solidarity mechanisms. The amendment of

Art. 1 included that „member states shall, *without imposing a disproportionate burden on market participants,* cooperate in order to promote regional
and bilateral solidarity" (emphasis added). This was justified by the argument that solidarity measures should not distort the market so that pricing
signals can work properly. Furthermore, ITRE deleted the Commission's
proposed new competence to adopt guidelines for regional solidarity cooperation (Art. 5a, paragraph 4). ITRE argued that this measure exceeds
the scope of comitology and the Commission's role to develop a framework under the adequate decision-making procedure. The final position
of the European Parliament reflected the report's position (Parliament
2008b). Therefore, solidarity remained weak but the proposed cooperation
mechanisms by the Commission were accepted, such as coordination of
national emergency measures, development of gas interconnections and
framework for mutual assistance.

On 22 September 2008, the Council published a consolidated text based
on the outcome of the TTE Council and further adjustments. Recital 24
was amended (change is in italics) as following:

> „In order to contribute to security of supply whilst maintaining a
> spirit of solidarity between Member States, notably in the event of
> a supply crisis, it is important to provide a framework for regional
> solidarity cooperation. *This solidarity cooperation may rely, if Member
> States so decide, first and foremost on marked-based mechanisms*" (Council
> 13169/08, emphasis by author).

This is a first hint that solidarity was interpreted as a mechanism of
last resort. On 6 October, the presidency compromise added again the
phrase that the „Commission may adopt guidelines for regional solidarity
cooperation", which was deleted before by ITRE in June 2008 (Council
13393/08). The Presidency briefing on the draft report to the European
Council on energy security (Presidency 2008), which was published in
October 2008, is a clear call on the European Council to take some steps
forward regarding energy security of supply and solidarity (see for details
chapter on SoS regulation). The Council declared in his common position
on the directive on 9 January 2009, that one of the objectives of the
proposal was to insert „provisions aiming at improving regional solidarity
and cooperation" (Council 2009b). Member States were willing to shift
security of supply to the EU level due to the dependence from external
suppliers which act beyond the internal market (Personal Communication
2, Council). The objective of solidarity was also reflected in the Commission Communication of January 2009. One of the main measures of the

decision is „increased solidarity and regional cooperation between Member States to ensure greater security of supply" (Commission 2009c: 2).

In the report by ITRE of 3 April 2009 (rapporteur: Antonio Mussa, UNE, Italy), there were only two changes regarding the insertion of solidarity. In recital 19, the change refers to transmission system unbundling by third persons:

> „To ensure, in addition, respect for the international obligations of the Community *and solidarity and energy security within the European Union*, the Commission should have the right to give an opinion on certification in relation to a transmission system owner or a transmission system operator which is controlled by a person or persons from a third country or third countries" (Parliament 2009e: 9, emphasis by author).

Even if solidarity is included, it does not thereby unfold effect as a principle. The second change regards solidarity in case of a supply crisis:

> „In order to contribute to security of supply whilst maintaining a spirit of solidarity between Member States, notably in the event of an energy supply crisis, it is important to provide a framework for regional cooperation in a spirit of solidarity. This cooperation in a spirit of solidarity may rely, if Member States so decide, first and foremost on market-based mechanisms. Cooperation for the promotion of regional and bilateral solidarity should not impose a disproportionate burden on or discriminate between market participants" (Parliament 2009e: 16).

This is a similar phrase to the one which was deleted by the Council. Instead of putting the reference of disproportionate burden in the Article on regional solidarity, this time ITRE tried to insert it in the introductory part of the directive.

Different considerations on solidarity were taken up during the EP debate on the new gas directive in April 2009 (Parliament 2009c). The Bulgarian MEP Atanas Paparizov argued that 2009 started with disruption to gas supplies. But that „thanks to more material resources and greater solidarity", which is both reflected in the new gas directive, the EU will be well equipped to encounter upcoming difficulties. Jerzy Buzek claimed that „a common market for energy is becoming a fact, and the principle of solidarity is today in evidence". Paparizov added that this energy package is sufficient to reach all goals, but

„the solution is exact implementation and solidarity among Member States in creating the market, especially by developing new initiatives for regional cooperation, especially for countries most vulnerable to energy supplies and to countries that, for the moment, are part of energy islands" (Parliament 2009c).

Paparizov is referring to two solidarity mechanisms: the first one concerns solidarity with the most vulnerable countries to ensure security of supply, and the second one concerns redistributive solidarity, which means making funds available to break up energy islands. The Council accepted the changes by the EP on solidarity and other topics. On 13 July 2009, the directive 2009/73/EC of the European Parliament and of the Council concerning common rules for the internal market in natural gas and repealing directive 2003/55/EC was published.

4.2.2. Results and discussion

Even though the directive devotes even an explicit article to „regional solidarity", it is only *declarative solidarity* since the single categories of solidarity are hardly present.

Group Cohesion: Art. 6 on ‚Regional Solidarity' reads as follows: „In order to safeguard a secure supply on the internal market in natural gas, Member States shall cooperate in order to promote regional and bilateral solidarity". This underlines the interdependence between cooperation, solidarity and the functioning of the internal market. However, it is the only point, that points out that cooperation is needed to safeguard security of supply. The regulation is needed to establish an effective internal gas market.

Reciprocity: The cooperation shall (as mentioned above) be based on three pillars, which are coordination of national emergency measures (with reference to the SoS directive of 2004), identification and development of infrastructure and the development of a framework of mutual assistance. It is up to the Member States to decide to what extent these forms of cooperation will be implemented. There are no concrete indications of how to implement and control solidarity, which is why also the category ‚reciprocity' is very weak.

Monitoring is not firmly inserted since the Commission cannot sufficiently ensure solidarity. The Commission gained only access to information on any forms of cooperation, which come into being under Art. 6, and she „may adopt Guidelines for regional cooperation in a spirit of solidarity". Additionally, the Commission may give an opinion regarding certification in relation to a transmission system owner or a transmission system operator under third country ownership.

The crisis had a significant impact on the legislation, which was the first direct legislative response to the 2009 crisis. It was evident that there were two major problems. 1) Member States reacted not in a spirit of solidarity by blocking further gas export (interview 3, DG Energy). 2) Even if there was willingness to help, the necessary infrastructure was lacking (Interview 4, DG Energy). Hence, Member States called for a European solution after the second gas crisis (Interview 3, DG Energy). The strategy included the diversification of supply routes and sources in gas but also the increase in renewable energy sources and the further unbundling of the market (Interview 4 and 8, both DG Energy).

The Commission initiated the need to introduce a solidarity mechanism as a response to the gas crises which illustrates that the Commission was the promoter of solidarity. The Commission realised that there was not sufficient EU action, which is why further cooperation was needed. However, solidarity was only introduced as a possible strategy and the Commission remained very vague on its meaning. The intention of the Commission was to activate regional cooperation (Interview 8, DG Energy). Therefore, even though the Commission was successful by inserting solidarity in the directive, solidarity did not have a substantive impact on the design of security of supply.

> „In 2007, it (solidarity) was not yet something that primarily concerned us. It was more about the internal market and security of supply. We were all aware that solidarity played a subliminal role somewhere, but we didn't carry it forward as a flag" (Interview 8, DG Energy).

The reactions of the Council and the Parliament show that neither institution paid particular attention to solidarity. Solidarity was acknowledged as a political value but not understood as a principle since it was implemented flexibly and voluntarily. Solidarity was neglected as an important principle by all three institutions, which explains why no institution anticipated how the principle would unfold over time. However, solidarity is identified as a solution for the regional level in relation to short-term security of supply. Long-term measures are both carried out on the national level (e.g. safeguarding measures Art. 46) and the EU-level (implementation of the Agency for the Cooperation of Energy Regulators (ACER) responsible for reporting and supervision) (Talus 2013: 46).

4.2.3. Lex Nord Stream 2

The subject of the application of the internal gas market regime on pipelines entering the EU became delicate after the annexation of the Crimea by Russia. In November 2015, EU leaders from Estonia, Latvia, Lithuania, Poland, Slovakia, Hungary and Romania explained that Nord Stream 2 „contravenes the spirit of European energy policy and in particular violates the idea of energy solidarity" (Lang and Westphal 2017: 29).

Energy Commissioner Šefčovič underlined in a speech on "Nord Stream II – Energy Union at the crossroads" that NS2 is problematic as there is a legal void because Germany and Russia have not concluded an intergovernmental agreement. But the Commissioner feared not only that the pipeline would not apply with EU law but also that it would have detrimental effects on the EU's energy landscape.

> „As regards security of supply, Nord Stream 2 could lead to decreasing gas transportation corridors from three to at least two – abandoning the route through Ukraine. Also, the Yamal route via Poland could be endangered. Such a reduction of routes would not improve security of supply" (Šefčovič 2016).

Neither the Commission did support NS2 nor did several Member States who feared a decrease of energy security and that NS2 would be a breach of energy solidarity. But there was no possibility to enforce solidarity (Interview 11, Official, Government of Luxembourg). The Commission tried to get a mandate in order to negotiate an agreement on NS2 with Russia, but the Council's legal service rejected the Commission's arguments (Fischer 2017b: 3).

As consequence, the Commission proposed a revision of the internal gas market directive in 2017. „President Juncker announced (…) that following up to the solidarity aspect of the Energy Union, the Commission will propose common rules for gas pipelines entering the European internal gas market" (Commission 2017b). Solidarity was in this case used as an argument for further integration. The goal of the amendment was to include not only pipelines running on the EU's territory but also pipelines which enter the European internal gas market. MEP Claude Turmes explained that the revision is

> „(…) a step towards greater energy solidarity in the EU. The derogations afforded to any pipeline project need to be placed under much stricter scrutiny by the Commission. The Nord Stream II project is particularly unacceptable. It undermines the principle of solidarity in

the energy union by exposing Central and Eastern European Member States to Putin's gas blackmail (…)" (Turmes 2018).

A press release from the Commission from 12 February 2019 (Commission 2019d) underlines that these new rules would strengthen solidarity between Member States and reflect the solidarity dimension of the Energy Union. Commissioner Arias Cañete emphasised the importance of the agreement:

„This is a major step forward in the creation of a truly integrated internal gas market which is based on solidarity and trust with full involvement of the European Commission. Today, Europe is closing a loophole in the EU legal framework. The new rules ensure that EU law will be applied to pipelines bringing gas to Europe and that everyone interested in selling gas to Europe must respect European energy law" (Commission 2019d).

Cañete highlighted energy solidarity again during the EP's debate on the directive:

"Today's debate has shown again that, as the European Commission, we can count on this Parliament as a strong ally when it comes to defending the principle of solidarity in our energy policy. This has been a major strength in our cooperation over this entire mandate. It has been our longstanding objective that when it comes to our external energy relations, the European Union should speak with one voice. With the legislation we have passed during this mandate – the IGAs Decision, the Security of Gas Supply Directive, and the amended Gas Directive discussed today – we now have the tools in place to do just that" (Parliament 2019).

The directive has been amended in 2019 (directive (EU) 2019/692). Although there has been no direct effect as to the wording on solidarity, the Commission stated that changes are made due to solidarity. The discussion on solidarity has demonstrated that there is no toolbox for ensuring solidarity in case of disparate interests. This revision is of particular importance because the process of unbundling must also be applied to pipelines coming from third countries. The policy provides exemptions for connections implemented by 23 May 2019. This is why the directive is also called the „Lex Nord Stream 2" by the Nord Stream 2 pipeline company since it concerns, according to the company's understanding, exclusively the NS2 pipeline which is in its completion phase. The company demanded the annulment of the directive by the General Court, arguing that the directive breaches EU law, in particular the principles of equal treatment and proportionality (Gotev 2019a). But the Court declared that the actions are inadmissible (Court 2020).

The Commission's proposal can be evaluated as an attempt to shift competences to the EU level. Applying EU law to pipelines entering the internal market might have consequences on the free choice of the energy mix, a national sovereignty which is underlined in energy article 194(2) TFEU (Bochkarev 2018). The debate on solidarity shifted away from regional solidarity as emphasised by the directive's predecessor but referred now to geopolitical developments and how the internal gas market could be used to react to those challenges. However, this was not further clarified in the directive (EU) 2019/692 but implicitly understood by extending European energy law outside of EU soil. There is a dividing line between Member States in favour and Member States opposing Nord Stream 2 which „as such touches on the political question of solidarity within the EU" (Lang and Westphal 2017: 25). Nord Stream 2 would be like Nord Stream 1 directly connected to the OPAL and NEL gas pipelines. This division between old and new Member States on the role of solidarity in general and on the consequences of the OPAL pipeline for Poland's energy security in particular was brought before the CJEU in 2017. The resulting consequences of the application of solidarity as legal principle is further discussed in the chapter on the Court's ruling on the OPAL pipeline (ch. 4.5).

4.3. Case 3: Intergovernmental agreements under European scrutiny

This chapter focuses on the decision on establishing an information exchange mechanism with regard to intergovernmental agreements and non-binding instruments between Member States and third countries in the field of energy, which was first published in 2012 (Decision (EU) 994/2012) and revised in 2017 (Decision (EU) 2017/684). The Commission already stated in a communication on „External energy relations – from principles to action" in 2006 that the EU needed to speak with one voice: „The Union should use all its weight in current and future bilateral negotiations and agreements, offering balanced, market-based solutions, first of all with its traditional suppliers, but also with other main producing and consuming countries" (Commission 2006d: 3). However, it should take six years until the Commission gained limited additional weight in the negotiation process of intergovernmental agreements with third countries.

4.3.1. Decision (EU)2012/994: solidarity should guide our actions

Commissioner Oettinger stated at his confirmation hearing with the European Parliament in January 2010 that he plans to enforce the principle of solidarity and that he „was prepared to work with lawmakers on how binding solidarity measures could 'work in practice'" (Euractiv.com 2010). This statement was referring to the Nord Stream 2 pipeline, which would circumvent Poland and the idea that the *Commission should negotiate energy supply contracts*. „Oettinger pledged to enforce the principle of solidarity on energy policy contained in the EU's Lisbon Treaty so that no member state could be left disadvantaged" (ibid.).

His words were followed by action in September 2011, when the Commission presented a proposal for a new decision of the Parliament and the Council on „setting up an information exchange mechanism with regard to intergovernmental agreements between Member States and third countries in the field of energy" (Commission 2011a).

> „Ultimately, the prerequisite to solidarity is transparency. In this respect the increased efforts in the area of foreign energy relations with supplier countries play an important role. Following the long awaited Communication of the EC in September 2011 here especially the proposal for a Decision setting up an information exchange mechanism with regard to intergovernmental agreements between Member States and third countries in the field of energy is a promising step in the right direction" (de Jong et al. 2012: 40).

The proposal aimed at political agreements, which are supportingly concluded before commercial contracts are signed. In February 2011, the European Council called upon the Member States to inform the Commission „of all their new and existing bilateral energy agreements with third countries" as of 1 January 2012 (Conclusions 2011). The Commission intended to transform the demand by the EUCO into a concrete policy mechanism on exchange information concerning intergovernmental agreements. The Commission argued under ‚Policy Objectives' that the need for those agreements is functional. If Member States sign contracts with third states unilaterally, it is possible that the contracts entail provisions, which could infringe the internal market rules. This means, that „intergovernmental agreements that contain unlawful provisions put Member States into a situation of conflicting legal obligations and threaten the operation and proper functioning of the Union internal market for energy" (Commission 2011a: 2).

The second argument referred to the endangered security of supply situation caused by an improperly functioning internal market. The gas crisis of 2009 illustrated the link between market failures and the increased vulnerability concerning security of supply. These circumstances make it necessary „to improve the exchange of information between Member States and between Member States and the Commission on existing, provisionally applied and future intergovernmental agreements" (Commission 2011a: 2). This mechanism will

> „ultimately increase consistency and coherence, in a spirit of solidarity, in the Union's external energy relations and allow Member States to better benefit from the political and economic weight of the Union and the expertise of the Commission with respect to Union law" (ibid.).

Solidarity is here understood as the underlying principle for coherence in EU external policy. This is of importance since solidarity thus implies that other Member States are not to be harmed and that their interests must be considered. Solidarity is one of the guiding principles of the proposed decision, even though it is mentioned only twice. Compliance with Union law is the ultimate aim of the decision, which means that transparency regarding IGAs is important to „allow the Union to take coordinated action, in a spirit of solidarity, in order to ensure that such agreements are in accordance with Union legislation and effectively secure the supply of energy" (Commission 2011a, recital 3). Coordinated action, based on a spirit of solidarity, refers thus to both EU law compliance and security of supply. The Commission wanted to gain more competences: Member States shall not only inform the Commission and other Member States about existing agreements but also about its intentions. The Commission should participate as observer and have an ex-ante compatibility control function to examine the agreement.

On 16 March 2012, the Secretariat of the Council published the document ,preparation for informal trilogue'. Solidarity was inserted in recital 9, which is about the Commission's role during the negotiation process, although this was not demanded by neither the EP nor the Council. If Member States request the Commission's assistance, „(...) the Commission should have the possibility to provide advice on how to avoid incompatibilities with Union law, and to draw attention to the Union's long-term policy objectives and the principle of solidarity between Member States" (Council 2012b: 10).

In the trilogue preparation document from 3 May 2012, solidarity remained included in recital 3 and recital 9 (Council 2012a). Additionally, ITRE proposed to insert solidarity in Art. 3.2 concerning the Commission's role during negotiations.

> „The Commission may, on its own initiative, and shall, at the request of the Member State, participate as an observer in the negotiations and provide the negotiating Member State with non-binding standard clauses (…), taking account of the Union's long-term policy objectives and the principle of solidarity between Member States" (Council 2012a: 23).

This amendment was however blocked by the Council, which underlined that the solidarity aspect was already part of recital 9 (ibid.). ITRE additionally proposed that the Commission should encourage coordination among Member States with a view to solidarity (among others) in Art. 6. This proposal was rejected (Council 2012a: 32).

On 11 May 2012, the Council Secretariat published the ‚provisional text of the Council compromise offer'. No further amendments of solidarity have occurred (Council 2012c). Solidarity was inserted – as consequence of the trilogue – in recital 9 on the Commission's role as assistant during the negotiations: „the Commission should have the possibility to provide advice on how to avoid incompatibility with Union law, and to draw attention to the Union's energy policy objectives and the principle of solidarity between Member States" (Council 2012c). The insertion of solidarity highlights the importance of solidarity as principle, which is important regarding its possible consequences. This entails that Member States need to take into account the interests of other Member States when negotiating new intergovernmental agreements, which could impact on gas sources and routes. On 16 May 2012, ITRE published an own-initiative report by Edit Herczog (S&D Group Hungary) „on engaging in energy policy cooperation with partners beyond our borders: A strategic approach to secure, sustainable and competitive energy supply" (Parliament 2012b). Under point 1, ITRE underlined „(…) the need for strong coordination between Member States' policies and for joint action and solidarity in the field of external energy policy and energy security, recognising the importance of transparency and full implementation of the internal energy market (…)" (Parliament 2012b: 5). Under point 35 ITRE demanded the Commission to clarify the principle of solidarity:

> „(…) the EU Treaty calls for solidarity between Member States, which should be part of both the daily work and crisis management of inter-

nal and external energy policy; calls on the Commission to provide a clear definition of 'energy solidarity' in order to ensure that it can be respected by all Member States" (Parliament 2012b: 9).

Additionally, it points out under point 43 „(...) that further instruments based on solidarity between EU Member States are needed in order to provide the EU with the ability to protect its energy security interests and in negotiating with its external partners, in particular in crisis situations" (Parliament 2012b: 10). These points are repeated in the European Parliament resolution of 12 June 2012 (P7_TA(2012)0238). The EP thus underlined its awareness of the lack of clarity regarding the principle of solidarity and that solidarity should play a general role in both internal and external energy policy.

In the opinion of the Committee on International Trade, which was published in July 2012 as part of the ITRE report on the proposal, rapporteur Yannick Jadot (France; Greens/EFA) described in the justification that the proposed decision „supports the realisation of the solidarity mechanisms provided for in the security of gas supply regulation by informing on the amount and sources of energy imported, in order to make security of supply a reality for all EU Member States" (Parliament 2012c). The report also included the amendments of the Parliament (Parliament 2012c), which entailed no further changes on solidarity.

The Parliament debated the proposal on 12 September 2012. Solidarity was mentioned twice during the debate. While the Romanian MEP (Silvia-Adriana Țicău) only referred to solidarity as objective, Lena Kolarska-Bobińska (PPE) from Poland underlined that the Council is not hard enough on Russia's guidelines on Gazprom and that the „Council allowed national interests to prevail over European energy solidarity" (Parliament 2012a). Therefore, Kolarska-Bobińska also stressed the understanding that solidarity is to be taken into account when a Member State (resp. its industry) decides on its import strategies. The conflict between the right of each Member State to choose its energy sources and determine its energy mix on the one hand and the principle of solidarity on the other hand (taking into account the interests of other Member States) is thus predestined. The Commission underlined that the decision regarding intergovernmental agreements „represents a first step towards more transparency, solidarity and consistency with internal market rules" (Council 2012d).

On 4 October 2012, the Council voted unanimously in favour of the decision and the decision No 994/2012/EU „establishing an information exchange mechanism with regard to intergovernmental agreements between Member States and third countries in the field of energy" came officially into force on 25 October 2012. Main changes included that the Commission's competence to participate was limited in so far, that the Member State needed to invite the Commission to negotiations and ex-ante examination of the agreement. There was no change concerning the point of coordinated action and solidarity. The additional insertion by the Council of the principle of solidarity remained in the final text. The Parliament failed to insert solidarity more prominently. Instead solidarity was only part of the recitals as proposed by the Commission and the Council. The evaluation of the features of solidarity shows the following:

Group Cohesion: The decision is a trust-strengthening mechanism, since it encourages Member States to provide and share sensitive information in order to achieve a more coherent external energy policy. „That legislation could not have passed if member countries would not have trusted each other or the Commission" (Interview 4, DG Energy). The decision underlines the interdependence between a functioning single market and security of supply. More transparency contributes to consistency between Member States (recital 9). There is a strong collective interest since „improved coordination should enable Member States to benefit fully from the political and economic weight of the Union" (recital 17), which is, however, not fully tapped due to ex-post assessment only.

Reciprocity: Member States are obliged to deliver information and the information is accessible to all Member States. However, since the information is only provided ex-post, Member States refuse to provide information, which could be helpful for the aims of the whole group. In case that a Member State does not wish to share all information, it has to provide at least a summary of the content. The Commission can check if the IGAs comply with solidarity between Member States.

Monitoring: The Commission has no robust monitoring and control function, but it serves as a facilitator between the Member States since it can defend the Union's interests. The Member States must inform the Commission about all existing and newly concluded intergovernmental agreements. If there are any doubts as regards the compatibility with Union law, the Commission shall inform the Member States concerned (Art. 3). However, the same article underlines that before or during negotiating new intergovernmental agreements (or amendments) the Commission may be informed. This is not an obligation, which is why the Commission has only a minimal control capacity. Member States might also request assistance by the Commission during negotiations and invite the Commission as an observer and get advice concerning the consistency of the agreement with Union law. The Member States shall also inform the

Commission (self-responsibility) if they have doubts about the consistency of the agreement with Union law before the closure of the agreement. The Commission can give hints if the IGA does not comply with solidarity between Member States but there is no further clarification what this means.

This decision itself represents a case of *‚declarative solidarity‘*, since the single features of solidarity are not entirely fulfilled. The Commission has only limited control capacity (ex-post) regarding the implemented intergovernmental agreements. Therefore, the single national interest is more important than the overall European (group) interest to develop a more coherent external energy policy and to avoid contracts which are not in line with EU law. The decision nevertheless contributes to trust-building between Member States since information is crucial to building confidence in each other. The Commission stated that this decision was the first step towards more transparency, solidarity and coherence with the internal market rules but still wishes for a more ambitious approach. This expresses that the Commission was not yet fully satisfied with the level of coherence and that she wanted to implement further measures, which were also part of the initial approach (Council 2013: 4).

4.3.2. Solidarity? We are not so sure about it: Decision (EU) 2017/684

Developments from 2014 onwards must be seen against the backdrop of the Russian-Ukrainian conflict and the resulting security concerns for the EU (cf. Phase III). In the Energy Security Strategy from 2014, point 8 of the key pillars, which were all underpinned by the principle of solidarity, focused on „improving coordination of national energy policies and speaking with one voice in external energy policy" (Commission 2014b). This point referred in particular to information sharing between Member States and the Commission about energy agreements with third states. Even though „decisions on energy mix are a national prerogative, (...) fundamental political decisions on energy should be discussed with neighbouring countries" (Commission 2014b: 17). This means, however, that national decisions on the energy mix should be reconsidered if they influence the energy mix of other Member States. The Commission wanted to implemented „a mechanism that would enable Member States to inform each other of important decisions related to their energy mix prior to their adoption and detailed deliberation, so as to take on board relevant comments in the national decision process" (ibid.).

This is a far-reaching demand, since the energy article 194(2) TFEU explicitly states that the choice of the national energy mix remains in the hands of the Member States. Taking into account other members' concerns about a change in the national energy mix can be interpreted as interference in national security concerns and is at odds with the energy article. The Commission declared that Member States should

> „(e)nsure early information of the Commission before initiating negotiations on intergovernmental agreements having a potential impact on security of energy supplies and engage the Commission into the negotiations. This would ensure that agreements are concluded in full compliance with Union law" (Commission 2014b: 19).

Oettinger stated: „We want strong and stable partnerships with important suppliers, but must avoid falling victim to political and commercial blackmail. The EU and its Member States have a long list of homework in front of them: *Collectively, we need to reinforce our solidarity with more vulnerable Member States*" (Commission 2014c, emphasis added). The Commission carried out a „consultation on the revision of the intergovernmental agreements decision" in 2015 (Commission 2015a). The objective of the consultation was to improve the 2012 decision. „In the new context of the Energy Union strategy and in an international situation where energy security is at the centre of the political debate, the Commission is therefore considering reviewing the IGA Decision" (Commission 2015a). The public consultation was answered by ten public bodies (including governments and competent authorities) and 11 respondents from industry and business federations. Lithuania, Estonia and Germany all underlined the need for solidarity. Germany made a very unspecific reference to solidarity (solidarity is increased by cooperation) but Lithuania demanded that during the assessment of IGAs „(...) *solidarity* among the Member States should always be kept in mind" (Lithuania 2015: 3, emphasis by author). This was similarly expressed by Estonia.

In February 2016, the Commission issued a new proposal for a decision „on establishing an information exchange mechanism with regard to intergovernmental agreements and non-binding instruments between Member States and third countries in the field of energy" (Commission 2016e). The proposal was together with the proposal for a new Security of Gas Supply regulation part of the „winter package" on energy security (Commission 2016c). The aim of the winter package was to „re-write practically all of EU energy legislation" (van Renssen 2016). Also the Dutch Presidency, which took over on 1 January 2016, intended to put life into the Energy Union (compare presidency programme discussed in ch. 4.1 on SoS regulation). The Commission declared in the explanatory memorandum that one of the objectives of the decision was to enhance the transparency of the inter-governmental agreements „in order to increase the (...) solidarity between Member States" (Commission 2016a: 21).

The Commission explained the EU-added value as follows:

> „The progressive integration of energy infrastructure and markets, the common reliance on external suppliers, the need to ensure solidarity in times of crisis, all imply that fundamental political decisions on energy should not be taken exclusively at national level without involvement of neighbouring countries and the EU" (Commission 2016e).

Thus, the Commission underlined that national solo strategies are counter-efficient to the policy goals. The Commission claimed that non-compliant IGAs might have negative impacts, which could be avoided if IGAs were assessed before completion. The most prominent example is the South Stream pipeline, which was discontinued. „The fact that the Commission was able to address the non-compatibility of the South Stream related IGAs only ex-post created a complex and difficult legal, political and economic situation for the parties involved" (Commission 2016a: 10).

In the accompanying impact assessment (SWD(2016) 27 final), the Commission explained that transparency on energy supply is a translation of the vision of an Energy Union, based on true solidarity and trust, into concrete policy proposals. The provisions of the decision enable „the EU to speak with one voice and apply the best available negotiation techniques, as this contributes to greater solidarity and a deeper and fairer economic union" (Commission 2016a: 20). Solidarity is a political goal (ibid.). The general objectives of the proposal are in line with the EU Treaties, in particular with the objective „to establish a functioning internal energy market, in the spirit of solidarity between the Member States (Article 3(3) TEU; Article 194(1) TFEU)" (Commission 2016a: 21). The Commission underlined the importance of solidarity as legal principle as written in the respective Treaty articles and proposed different options how to reform the decision. Two main factors influence the IGA decision: „the increased level of compliance of IGAs with EU law and the increased level of transparency / solidarity between Member States" (Commission 2016a: 33). An increased level of solidarity reflects the need for trust and information sharing. The references to solidarity were normatively (treaty) and functionally (internal market) framed.

The proposal itself included solidarity only once in the preamble: „The Commission should have the possibility to draw attention to the Union's energy policy objectives and the principle of solidarity between Member States and Union policy positions adopted in Council or European Council conclusions" (recital 6). The phrase is slightly different from the predecessor from 2012. The focus of the Commission was to highlight the importance to speak externally with one voice, which would be much more efficient, if the Commission could be part of ex-ante assessments in order to clarify any legal uncertainties. Additionally, decisions should not be carried out unilaterally but by assessing the impact on neighbouring Member States. This point was underlined by the Energy Security Strategy of 2014.

Notwithstanding the Commission's efforts, the reference to solidarity was detracted at the first meeting of the Energy Working Party in March 2016. Recital 6 about the Commission's possibility to point out the principle of solidarity between Member States was changed. This advice by the Commission should not be part of the Commission's legal assessment of the draft agreement. This limitation of solidarity is a clear rejection of the principle of solidarity (Council 2016d). The legislative proposal was regarded generally with great cautiousness in the Council. Seven Member States (Austria, France, Malta, Portugal, Romania, Italy, Spain) raised the point that the decision would exceed the competences of the EU for several reasons. Above all they argued that the decision would perturb national affairs. The Austrian Bundesrat argued that the Commission should limit its advice to compliance with Union law and not refer to other non-obligatory instruments in the energy sector (Austria 2016).

On 6 April 2016, Vice-President Maroš Šefčovič gave a speech on "Nord Stream II – Energy Union at the crossroads" at the European Parliament. Šefčovič was concerned about the impact of Nord Stream 2 on the landscape of the EU's gas market since it would increase the dependence from Russia. He underlined that „(e)nergy security, solidarity and trust constitute a key dimension of our framework strategy of 25 February 2015. (...) More *transparency and solidarity* between the Member States are equally important" (Šefčovič 2016, emphasis added).

ITRE published a report on the proposal in October 2016, which was written by the ITRE Rapporteur Zdzisław Krasnodębski. In the explanatory statement, Krasnodębski argued that Member States need to „show solidarity (...) with less privileged members of the bloc" (Parliament 2016a: 30) in order to put pressure on third parties to play by the market rules. „Equal scrutiny of intergovernmental contracts and non-binding instruments will also prevent temptation by the parties to play ‚regulatory jugglery' and pursue negotiations based on a less rigorous cooperation model" (ibid.). Krasnodębski concluded that energy policy is at a crossroads:

> „The EU is in desperate need of a success. Torn apart between migratory and eurozone crises, it needs a new integration narrative that will prove Europe can successfully move forward. Energy is one of the fields where the EU's potential has remained largely untapped. *This can be changed by applying the basic principles on which the integration project was founded, i.e. solidarity and trust among member states*, to future European energy endeavours" (Parliament 2016a: 31, emphasis added).

Therefore, Krasnodębski underlined that solidarity is a founding principle of the EU and that its application can secure future EU endeavours (normative frame). Both the Commission and the Parliament argued that the goal of the decision would be to increase solidarity between Member States. However, solidarity is only mentioned once in the preamble of the proposal, which leads to the conclusion that the transparency process itself was understood as an expression of solidarity (this interpretation was shared in interview 3, DG Energy).

The opinion that solidarity should be stronger reflected in the IGA decision was also put forward in the amendments by the Parliament. The Parliament wanted to insert under point 4(a): „A high degree of transparency with regard to agreements between Member States and third countries in the field of energy allows the Union to take coordinated action, in the spirit of solidarity (…)" (Council 2016c). After discussions between the EP and the Council solidarity was excluded:

> „A high degree of transparency with regard to agreements between Member States and third countries in the field of energy [] will be of benefit in achieving both closer intra-Union cooperation in the field of external energy relations and the Union's long-term policy objectives relating to energy, climate and security of energy supply" (Council 2016e).

Here, once again, the scepticism of the Council to insert solidarity further into the text becomes apparent. To reach an agreement in the Council was a delicate process. Similar to the SoS regulation the Council had to go a long way (29 discussions within the Council or its preparatory bodies) in order to find consensus. There was much divergence between the Member States on the issue of a mandatory ex-ante assessment of IGAs by the Commission, which is why the final decision was not very ambitious in comparison to the original proposal of the Commission. One of the reasons was the opposition by Germany:

> „The German-Polish controversy (on North Stream 2) is mirrored in the attempt to provide the European Commission with stronger powers to veto Member States' bilateral intergovernmental agreements with third countries, a move allegedly supported by Poland and opposed by Germany" (Kocak and De Micco 2016: 15).

The Commission, but also the Parliament, wanted to reach much more unity. Solidarity was repelled by the Council. In December 2016, the reference to „principle" of solidarity was deleted (Council 2016a). The explanation for the deletion was that „the principle of" is also not part of Art. 194 TFEU. Nevertheless, Commissioner Cañete promised in his speech at the EP debate in March 2017 that this directive would increase solidarity:

> „The review therefore has two main objectives: to ensure full compliance of IGAs with European Union law (...). And to increase the transparency of IGAs in order to increase the cost-effectiveness of European Union energy supply and increase solidarity between Member States" (Parliament 2017b).

The Council voted unanimously in favour of the decision on 21 March 2017.

4.3.3. Results and discussion

The final text of the decision (EU) 2017/684 entails references to the Energy Union Strategy from 2015, which is thus an indirect reference to solidarity. Information exchange regarding external energy relations (more information on gas supply) belongs to the first dimension of the Energy Union, which is called „Energy security, solidarity and trust". The Energy Union Strategy makes an explicit reference to compliance checks for intergovernmental agreements. The main leap forward of the decision is that the Commission has obtained the right to be informed about upcoming negotiations or changes of intergovernmental agreements and that the Commission should be regularly informed about the negotiations (Art. 3). The Commission shall assess the agreement before the closure on its compatibility with Union law and the Member States are obliged to take into account the Commission's opinion (ex-ante assessment).

Consequently, „the right of judicial interpretation, which normally rests with the CJEU, de facto shifts to the Commission. The result is a significant strengthening of executive powers with a prerogative of the judiciary" (Thaler and Pakalkaite 2020: 3). The further intention of the ex-post assessment was to avoid infringement procedures, which would less likely occur under the Commission's scrutiny. Art. 9 states that the Commission shall strive for „consistency and coherence in the Union's external energy relations with producer, transit, and consumer countries" (Decision (EU) 2017/684). The pressure to shift power to the supranational level is functional, since the functioning of the internal market was endangered by non-compliant IGAs.

Overall, the decision reads completely differently from its predecessor. The text follows a technical approach, emphasising the need to put Union law into effect. Solidarity plays only a marginal role, as it is hardly mentioned, although the mechanism envisaged is much more in line with solidarity than the mechanism of the 2012 decision. Transparency is the translation of solidarity into practice. Therefore, procedural solidarity obligations are introduced. But only the Commission can refer to solidarity between Member States by giving advice to the Member States on the political consequences of intergovernmental agreements (recital 9). The decision's solidarity features can be evaluated as ‚declarative solidarity' although the decision represents a power shift to the EU level, since the Commission gained additional competences. But institutionalised solidarity, as a particular outcome of integration, has not been implemented.

Group Cohesion: By accepting the ex-ante assessment, Member States agree that the EU interest (adherence to EU law; coherence of external energy policy) is of greater importance than national interests. This is a crucial difference to the 2012 decision since Member States thus underline their affiliation to the Union. Renouncing national solutions gained additional importance with the ex-ante assessment.

Reciprocity: Solidarity is only marginally reflected since there is no clarification on how solidarity could be considered nor to what extent.

Monitoring: The Commission has not only greater power to influence the negotiations during the ex-ante assessment, but also the monitoring competences increased. The Commission must be informed as early as negotiations start and be regularly informed. Finally, the Commission makes an ex-ante assessment of the agreement and can thus judge which parts might breach EU law. The Commission gained thus real power in the negotiation process. Nevertheless, a breakpoint for solidarity was created: during the ex-ante assessment of IGAs the Commission may only indicate if the IGA hampers solidarity between Member States but this advice (on solidarity) is excluded from the legal assessment.

Even though the decision represents only ‚declarative solidarity', it manifests a further step in the implication of the ‚principle' of solidarity. Based on the regulation, the Commission can evaluate if an IGA is conflictive with solidarity. In the absence of an overall definition of solidarity, it is now up to the Commission to decide under which conditions an IGA breaches solidarity between Member States. This decision also proves that there is an increasing awareness of the possible impact of solidarity.

4.4. Case 4: Making solidarity work: investments in infrastructure

The chapter on the infrastructure legislation presents a significant aspect of the implementation of solidarity, as it reveals how the European interest in solidarity has been pursued over time in contrast to the national interest. The focus of this chapter is on the Trans-European Networks for Energy (TEN-E) legislative framework. The Trans-European Networks date back to the Treaty of Maastricht with the aim to create cohesion. The first decision with the purpose of „laying down a series of measures aimed at creating a more favourable context for the development of trans-European networks in the energy sector" was implemented in 1996 (Council Decision 96/391/ EC). The decision was intended to contribute to the integration of the internal energy market by creating the necessary infrastructure. Security of supply and solidarity did not play a role at that time. In 2003, the Commission issued a proposal to reform the decision, which contained no reference to solidarity. The Commission's arguments followed a purely functional logic: Only if the necessary infrastructure is in place, the market can work effectively and ensure security of supply (Commission 2003c: 2). However, in the Extended Impact Assessment, which was published by the Commission in December 2003, the Commission explained the following:

> „Within the TEN-E Guidelines the main beliefs of solidarity between Member States and hence of cohesion are stated. In the context of the guidelines a project can be considered of common interest, if it corresponds to the objectives and priorities and displays potential economic viability" (Commission 2003a: 26).

Similar to the first directive on Security of Gas Supply, the Commission was the first actor to put forward the term ‚solidarity'. Solidarity (the common interest) is positioned as the counterpart to subsidiarity. Infrastructure is implemented according to the principle of subsidiarity, expressing the responsibility of the Member States (ibid.).

The Commission's proposal entailed a list of projects, which should be financed according to the TEN-E guidelines. These projects include ‚projects of common interest' (‚priority projects' are part of these projects and fulfil additional criteria) and ‚projects of European interest' (cross-border projects). This means that projects are funded that have a specific impact on security of supply and/or the functioning of the internal market (efficient market, reducing costs). The European Parliament discussed the proposal in July 2005, but did not mention solidarity. However, it was underlined that the Baltic states did not support an offshore pipeline in the Baltic Sea, thus opposing Nord Stream 1, but preferred a pipeline crossing the Baltic States in order to increase their security of supply (Parliament 2005).

On 3 April 2006, the European Parliament debated the new guidelines for trans-European energy networks (Parliament 2006b). Only few MEPs raised their concern about the projects, which have been selected. As already in the debate from 2005, the North European Pipeline, as an exclusive Russian-German project, was seen as problematic. The French MEP Anne Laperrouze (ALDE) regretted not only the low level of funding which is far from sufficient to move some projects forward. Her most urgent concern was the funding of projects, which, in her view, did not sufficiently represent the European dimension. MEP Laperrouze argued that the „Russian-German gas pipeline" (i.e. Nord Stream 1) was prioritised instead of much more urging projects in the Baltic region. The Italian MEP Vittorio Prodi (ALDE) pointed to the need to interconnect European states:

> „The recent reduction in supplies (…) highlighted how both the interconnection between originally national systems and the effective introduction of storage facilities (…) are absolutely crucial in terms of implementing solidarity among countries. Such solidarity is inalienable, as has already been highlighted effectively in the Green Paper" (Parliament 2006b).

The Lithuanian MEP Šarūnas Birutis (ALDE) supported together with the Lithuanian MEP Danutė Budreikaitė (ALDE) the argument that the

Baltic region remained isolated and that the North European Pipeline even worsened the situation.

> „In 2006, the European Commission must prepare a plan of priority connections, which would determine concrete measures for the integration of isolated energy markets. *Member States must show solidarity, taking common interests into account.* This is the only way to guarantee a secure supply of energy resources across the European Union" (Parliament 2006b, emphasis added).

The debate shows that there was disagreement on the selected projects (in particular the projects of European interest). The Commission argued that e.g. Nord Stream is of European interest since it connects main supply points and it can serve as an additional line to bring gas to the Baltic region. This point was not shared by some MEPs who feared further isolation of the Baltic market and growing dependence from Russia. The Baltic states thus interconnected the isolation of their markets and the necessity to act in solidarity on the European level. The Baltic perception created a different consciousness of security of gas supply and its implications for the EU.

The Decision 1364/2006/EC of 6 September 2006 laying down guidelines for trans-European energy networks included three main arguments: First, the accession of new Member States makes it necessary to integrate the respective areas. Second, the overall aim is that the internal market works without deficits which cannot be reached without sufficient interconnections. And third, only a fully integrated market can deliver a high level of security of supply. The arguments are based on a functional logic. Even though security of supply plays a role, the arguments on this topic were not expressed in a pressing way but underlined functional dynamics, e.g.:

> „Indeed, the Community's neighbouring countries play a vital role in its energy policy. They supply a major part of the Community's natural gas requirements, are key partners for the transit of primary energy to the Community and will progressively become more important players in its internal gas and electricity markets" (Decision No 1364/2006/EC, recital 7).

The objectives of the decision included the improvement of the effectiveness of the internal market and the necessity to connect energy islands, „thereby helping to strengthen economic and social cohesion" (Art. 3), ameliorating security of supply and advancing environmental concerns.

The guidelines lay down rules on the selection of projects, which can receive financial aid. There are three different kinds of projects, which are ‚projects of common interest‘, ‚priority projects‘, and ‚projects of European interest‘. Projects of European interest, which have first priority for funding, have to meet the same criteria as ‚priority projects‘ (they shall have a significant impact on the competitive operation of the internal market; and/or they shall strengthen security of supply in the Community; and/or they shall result in an increase in the use of renewable energies.). In addition, they are of cross-border nature or have „significant impact on cross-border transmission capacity" (Art. 10).

The North European gas pipeline (later known as Nord Stream) was also part of those projects of European interest (the pipeline was already introduced in 2000 as project of common interest by Commission Decision 2000/761/EC). It can be seen from the criteria that the selection process of the projects followed market criteria. The security of supply criterion refers only to the stability of the internal market and not to any possible disruptions caused by a third party. The decision thus shows that in 2006 the conviction prevailed that security of supply was first and foremost a concern of the Member States. The internal market was declared to be the solution to security of supply problems without any consideration of how pipelines from third countries might affect security of supply of Member States. The underlying rationale was that within an internal market external supply must only be economically viable.

4.4.1. The TEN-E Regulation: Did pipe dreams come true?

The Commission called for an update of the TEN-E guidelines in its Green Paper – Towards a secure, sustainable and competitive european energy network of November 2008 (Commission 2008c). The Commission referred to the European Council Conclusions from October 2008, where the European Council stated the following: „Security of energy supply is a priority for the European Union. It involves the responsibility and solidarity of all the Member States" (Conclusions 2008a: 7). This statement was followed by a list of actions, which should be propelled forward.

Point (f) concerned the strengthening and addition of critical infrastructure (ibid.). The Commission's Green Paper mentioned solidarity 16 times. Under the title "Putting TEN-E at the service of security and solidarity", the Commission stated that the „TEN-E objectives should be driven by the European energy policy (the 20–20–20 objectives, and the complementary goals of security of supply and solidarity, sustainability and competitiveness)" (Commission 2008c: 11). This is already very close to the final proposal by the Commission for a new regulation from October 2011. Additionally, the Commission claimed that the „(...) regional (cross-border and multi-country) networks are important for security of supply and solidarity and are a first step towards a fully interconnected internal energy market" (Commission 2008c: 10).

The Commission explained the necessary steps in order to ensure solidarity between Member States. Even though these steps are not interlinked, they give hints on the understanding of solidarity by the Commission. The Commission proposed e.g. that EU groupings, such as the GCG, would discuss „international energy projects at an early stage. This will help build up solidarity among Member States and anticipate political sensitivities" (Commission 2008c: 9). This underlines the need for trust between group members in order to establish solidarity. The Commission designated six priority infrastructure projects, which have already been explained in detail in the EU Energy Security and Solidarity Action Plan (Commission 2008d). All in all, the Commission highlighted with the Green Paper the significance of solidarity. Solidarity has a bridging function between the implementation of the necessary infrastructure and security of supply. The Commission used functional frames (fully interconnected internal energy market) to illustrate the need for solidarity, but solidarity was again strongly interlinked with security of supply. Solidarity was demanded in order to end the energy isolation of specific regions (e.g. the Baltics) which would increase security of supply and unify the internal gas market.

The Council presented the six priority infrastructure actions in February 2009 (Council 2009c). Although solidarity is not directly mentioned in relation to infrastructures, the spirit of solidarity is reflected in the priority to establish critical infrastructures in the TEN-E framework. Infrastructure selection criteria should be revised according to the European energy policy goals, which have been defined as security of supply and solidarity, sustainability and competitiveness. Even though the energy policy goals have not been named explicitly, these actions can also be understood as solidarity mechanisms, since for TEN-E projects not only economic efficiency is decisive, but also the energy policy objectives (Council 2009c: 8).

In May 2010, the Commission issued a report on the implementation of the trans-European energy networks in the period 2007–2009 (Commission 2010c). The quintessence of the report was that TEN-E is no longer the appropriate tool to meet the new goals and to master the diverse challenges. The change of European energy policy is reflected by the ‚Energy Policy for Europe' which has been implemented in 2007, but also the gas crisis in 2009 and the revision of the security of gas supply regulation, which included – next to a strong market-based approach – common standards for security of supply and supply standards for protected customers (p. 9). Under point 5 on „Strengthening Coordination and Cooperation", the Commission underlined that the European Coordinators „were able to bring Member States together at the highest level to iron out political or administrative problems" (p. 6). The Commission also included the implementation of a forum to bring together stakeholders „with the aim to build consensus on the way ahead of politically sensitive and complex regional projects" (p. 7).

These points illuminate that there was not yet sufficient trust and comprehension between Member States. Additionally, the Commission intended to change definitions of what is meant by ‚projects of common interest' and that the „external dimension of infrastructure and the diversification of supply routes and sources" needed to be considered (p. 10). „There is a need to narrow the focus of TEN- E on a limited number of strategic projects demonstrating European priorities" (p. 4). The Commission proposed a new approach pursuing regional initiatives such as the Southern Corridor or the Baltic Interconnection Plan (p. 10). This reflects the strategic interest of the Commission to diversify transit routes and sources (Interview 8, DG Energy).

DG Energy published in 2010 its „priorities for 2020 and beyond – a blueprint for an integrated European energy network" (COM(2010) 677 final). The proposal mentioned solidarity once.

> „A fully interconnected European market will also improve security of supply and help stabilise consumer prices by ensuring that electricity and gas goes to where it is needed. European networks including, as appropriate, neighbouring countries, will also facilitate competition in the EU's single energy market and build up solidarity among Member States" (Commission 2010b: 8).

This statement underlined again the interpretation of the Commission that solidarity can only be build up if the market is fully interconnected. The Council reacted to the 2020 strategy by publishing a "General overview of reactions by Member States" in December 2010. The document underlined that appropriate infrastructure was needed for the „practical application of solidarity" and that solidarity should be an eligibility criterion for projects (Council 2010c).

In February 2011, the European Council again referred to energy solidarity. Solidarity is the aim, that can only be achieved if the necessary infrastructure is put in place. The European Council stressed that the economic viability of a project should not be decisive for whether it receives funding. Therefore, „some projects that would be justified from a security of supply/solidarity perspective, but are unable to attract enough market-based finance, may require some limited public finance to leverage private funding" (Conclusions 2011: 3). However, national competences and procedures should be respected in the process of new infrastructure building (ibid.).

The need to create infrastructures to connect the member states was justified by the common interest to increase energy security for each member state. The agreement to invest in interconnectors was justified by the need to connect the Baltic States with continental Europe in order to end the Baltic States' total dependence on Russia. This was a genuine strategic interest in the European Council. Money from the cohesion fund was therefore earmarked for trans-European interconnectors (interview 10, Commission Official). Therefore, this is an expression of the dual meaning of solidarity concerning infrastructure, which intends, on the one hand, to protect weaker Member States which are more susceptible to supply risks and, on the other hand, to take into account political sensibilities when choosing infrastructure projects.

On 14 June 2011, ITRE reacted to the priorities set by the Commission by delivering a „motion for a European Parliament resolution on energy infrastructure priorities for 2020 and beyond". Solidarity was mentioned several times referring to both energy crises and EU solidarity objectives (Parliament 2011c). During the discussion at the Parliament several MEPs from Eastern Europe and the Baltics referred to solidarity as necessary feature of energy policy. Polish MEP Zbigniew Ziobro (ECR) explained that „(t)he Treaty of Lisbon has only recently indicated a need for building energy solidarity in Europe in this field. (...) In particular, we need to increase the capacity of energy links between EU Member States and to build alternative, strategic routes" (Parliament 2011a). Ziobro talks not only about interconnecting the internal gas market but also about pipelines entering the EU gas market, which should be built under the auspices of solidarity. Similar arguments were made in the final resolution by the Parliament. The resolution stated that

„the Lisbon Treaty provides a specific legal basis for developing an EU energy policy promoting the successful interconnection of energy networks between Member States across national and regional borders, which is necessary to achieve the other EU energy policy and solidarity objectives (functioning of the energy market, energy efficiency and renewable energy, security of supply and diversification of energy sources and forms of supply)" (Parliament 2011b).

The Parliament thus underlined that solidarity objectives comprise EU energy policy in general and not only particular dimensions. Additionally, solidarity would only become operational if the necessary infrastructure was built. The *enhancement of solidarity between Member States is included as eligibility criterion* in order to decide on the prioritisation of projects (Parliament 2011b, recital 79).

In October 2011, the Commission presented its proposal for a regulation „on guidelines for trans-European infrastructure and repealing Decision No 1364/2006/EC" (COM(2011) 658 final). The Commission referred to its 2020 priorities of November 2010, where it explained the need to establish „a new EU energy infrastructure policy to coordinate and optimise network development on a continental scale" (Commission 2011b: 2). A new policy would be necessary to make solidarity operational, to complete the internal market, to end energy isolation, to open up alternative routes and energy sources and to make renewables compatible with traditional sources. The regulation, as part of the 20–20–20 framework, shall ensure „security of supply and solidarity among Member States" (ibid.). However, solidarity as a criterion for project selection played only a marginal role in the Commission's proposal. Solidarity – next to security of supply and innovation (all described as positive externalities) – is an eligibility criterion for projects of common interest (Commission 2011b: 30). But one interviewee mentioned, that solidarity was simply inserted since it fits everywhere (Interview 8, DG Energy). The Commission published together with the proposal an impact assessment and an executive summary of the impact assessment, in which solidarity was not mentioned with a single word.

The Council debate on the Commission's proposal started in February 2012. Greece declared the following: „Greece welcomes the significant role attached to Regional Groups by the Commission's infrastructure proposal and expresses confidence that their functioning will serve to reinforce the spirit of solidarity between Member States" (Council 2012e). On 21 September 2012, the Council Secretariat published a 4-column text, which included the unofficial result of the ITRE vote of 18 September. The amendments by ITRE included three additional references to solidarity: a balanced development of all European regions to comply with the solidarity principle (recital 13a), solidarity between Member States in case of energy shortage (Art. 4) and a similar reference to energy shortage in Annex IV (Council 2012f). The amendments on solidarity were not accepted by the Council.

In February 2013, ITRE published a report on the proposal. Solidarity was welcomed as guiding principle of the new regulation (Parliament 2013b). MEP Correia de Campos, the rapporteur of ITRE, explained that the growing interdependence of the European gas market would generate solidarity and security of supply. Solidarity was thus recognised as principle and aim of infrastructure policy, however, there was no further clarification on the implications. In March 2013, Energy Commissioner Oettinger also underlined in the parliamentary debate the importance of infrastructure to make solidarity operational (Parliament 2013a).

The regulation on guidelines for trans-European energy infrastructure ((EU) No 347/2013) was published on 17 April 2013. It was again underlined that solidarity would only become operational with help of infrastructure. The second point referred to the PCIs, with solidarity being one of the criteria at the eligibility process. „The project specific cost-benefit analysis (…) provides evidence concerning the existence of significant positive externalities, such as security of supply, solidarity or innovation" (Art. 14).

Solidarity is taken into account during the decision process on the projects of common interest as part of the cost-benefit analysis. However, a detailed description of the assessment of solidarity is not provided. The identification of PCIs

> „is really a solidarity process because you ensure that infrastructure that somebody wants to promote at the national level is also understood of your neighbours – if it's an interconnection of course – and then you have the same level of information and the region also is aware of what is happening. (…) It is solidarity because as soon as you are going beyond your national interest and you are considering the other side, for me this is solidarity" (Interview 3, DG Energy).

The regulation has been based on Art. 172 TFEU (Trans-European Networks) and not on the energy article 194 TFEU since Art. 172 TFEU covers explicitly trans-European networks. The implementation of infrastructure has been partly successful since energy islands were integrated over time. Both the Baltic region as well as the Southern Gas Corridor are examples of further integration and diversification of internal and external gas sup-

ply routes (Commission 2019b, Commission 2019a). However, a definition is missing how the solidarity criterion could be reached. Solidarity
might include projects, which build „alternative supply and transit routes
and new interconnections between Member States" (Parliament 2011b),
but this point lacks further clarification. Additionally, there is no obligation that infrastructure projects need to fulfil solidarity.

In the first half of 2015, Latvia held the Council Presidency. Latvia
underlined the necessity to create „an energy policy built on solidarity,
trust and security". Additionally, the „EU would benefit from a better integrated energy infrastructure grid and improved governance, in particular,
better exploiting regional governance across the European Union" (Presidency 2015). In 2018, the Commission published a study entitled "Evaluation of the TEN-E Regulation and assessing the impacts of alternative
policy scenarios". Solidarity was mentioned 14 times. In general, the report
concluded that „interconnections enable the solidarity between (neighbouring) countries to ensure cross-border supplies" (Commission 2018: 7).
Additionally, PCIs can usually only receive up to 50 % funding, but if
they e.g. strengthen the solidarity of the Union, the financial rate can be
increased up to 75 %. The contributions of the stakeholder consultation
were also evaluated. One critique towards the coherence of the implementation of the principle of solidarity was put forward:

> „Another respondent to the targeted survey pointed to a lack of co-
> herence between the TEN-E and security of gas supply Regulations.
> The new security of supply rules focus on the solidarity principle. It
> would be essential, for the evaluation of possible PCI projects, to also
> consider specific parameters related to the application of this solidarity
> principle, such as increasing reverse flow capacity, enhancing new
> transit routes and acquiring new supply sources" (Commission 2018:
> 49).

The critique demonstrates that there is no coherent definition of what
solidarity means regarding TEN-E. The analysis of the documents revealed
that solidarity is mainly seen in connection with a functioning market,
which can enable solidarity provided that the necessary infrastructure is
created. The revision of the TEN-E started in 2020 in the framework of the
Green Deal, which was developed by the Commission in 2019.

4.4.2. Results and discussion

The chapter on energy networks has shown that in this case solidarity is mainly understood as a goal and has therefore a declarative function. Even if the construction of infrastructure beyond the criterion of economic feasibility can be interpreted as an act of solidarity, solidarity actually served as an objective of the infrastructure policy to ensure security of supply. Only if all Member States are connected with sufficient infrastructure, solidarity (as condition for security of supply) can emerge. The different perspectives on solidarity reveal the difficulty to grasp solidarity as a policy objective. Additionally, solidarity is a selection criterion for projects of common interest, but a definition on the concrete meaning is not provided.

It is difficult to assess in how far functional pressure worked as theorised but functional arguments were important in the overall debate. On the one hand, the Council did not make any references to solidarity. But on the other hand, the European Council supported the infrastructure development based on solidarity. Solidarity was put on the agenda due to the enlargement in 2004 as well as the gas crises. Hence, functional pressure provides some explanation why in this case solidarity was promoted by the Commission as well as certain Member States. The infrastructure needed to be fully integrated in order to make solidarity operational. In 2011, the European Council agreed to further invest in energy infrastructure due to the pressure resulting from the lack of infrastructure. Interviews revealed that the crises had a major impact on the necessity of implementing infrastructure. The internal gas market was not fully operational without inter-connectors. The Parliament acted due to normative and security of supply reasons, which is why it consequently requested solidarity. But the Parliament was not successful in inserting further references to solidarity.

Although the supranational institutions worked towards more solidarity, the final implementation of solidarity lacks consistency. In the newly developed guidelines from 2008, solidarity played a significant role in the Green Paper. The Commission used predominantly a functional frame linked to security of supply by arguing that it is necessary to implement infrastructure in order to make the market work (ameliorating competition) and thus security of supply. However, in the final proposal solidarity was hardly referred to. The Parliament framed solidarity mostly in a normative way, since it discussed the obligations arising from the Treaty of Lisbon and criticised, using a security of supply frame, the impact of Nord Stream 1 on the security of supply situation of the Baltic region. Only the

Parliament raised points on solidarity underlining the importance of European vs. national interests. A particular concern was the support of Nord Stream 1. There was a dividing line between old and new Member States concerning the support of infrastructure, in particular NS1, which was illustrated in the debates at the Parliament. This conflictual point raised the issue of considering the impact of infrastructure on other Member States. Altogether, solidarity entails three different implications regarding infrastructure:

– The internal market and security of supply: making solidarity operational;
– The PCIs: taking into account the interests of the neighbours;
– Gas pipelines to the EU: not endanger other Member States' security of supply.

The Parliament tried also to add more references to solidarity in the regulation. Both the Commission and the Parliament can thus be evaluated as drivers of solidarity within the legislation process but with limited success (H2): „Solidarity as a principle is quite clear to grasp, even across institutional or parliamentary divisions. What really differs is the willingness to adhere to solidarity in the daily policymaking and apply it into concrete decisions" (Interview 6, MEP). However, the final result of the TEN-E regulation demonstrates that solidarity did not play a major role in the debate.

Since the case of Nord Stream 1 permeates different policies, I will illuminate in the following section the development of Nord Stream 1 and the OPAL gas pipeline. This case is of particular interest since solidarity played a crucial role in the court cases T-883/16 and Case T-130/17 on the OPAL gas pipeline (Poland vs. Commission).

4.5. The Court Case: Speaking with one voice? Nord Stream 1 as solidarity quest

The assessment of the legislative framework has demonstrated that solidarity is not yet fully integrated into EU energy policy making. However, there was a boost with the implementation of the SoS regulation in 2017 and the first proper ,solidarity mechanism'. The general development of energy policy also showed that solidarity became more important over time. Member States, which were in the beginning very hesitant towards a European energy policy, included solidarity in primary law and the European Council underlined several times that solidarity is a cornerstone of energy policy. In the following, I present the OPAL pipeline case, which was brought before the General Court in 2016. The judgement proves that solidarity is not only a political watchword but has developed to be a legal norm in the making. „(T)he General Court examined, for the first time, the principle of energy solidarity laid down in Article 194(1) (…)" (Case T-883/16). The General Court presented its judgement on the case of Poland vs. the Commission in September 2019. It held that solidarity is a principle, which is not only to be considered in crisis situations but determines the whole implementation of European energy policy (Case T-883/16). The judgement was welcomed by Poland since, as a consequence, the Commission had to withdraw a decision that guaranteed Gazprom extensive use of the OPAL pipeline. It was expected that the principle of solidarity would need to be clarified in case secondary legislation was to be contested.

> „Value-laden concepts, such as the principle of solidarity between EU Member States, are unlikely to produce legally binding commitments on their own. They can be enforceable in courts only when they are transformed into concrete hard law provisions adopted in accordance with a legislative procedure" (Obradovic 2017).

Even though the annulment of the OPAL exemption rules prove that the Court could only act since there has been a concrete question arising from secondary law, the judgement comprises not only an evaluation of the case but an interpretation of the principle of energy solidarity in general. The legal assessment of the Court refers explicitly to obligations arising from primary law.

On 16 December 2016, Poland brought action before the General Court „concerning amendments to the conditions of the exemption of the Opal gas pipeline from the requirements on third-party access (TPA) and tariff regulation granted under Directive 2003/55/EC". This case T-883/16 is significant for the understanding of the interpretation of the energy solidarity article 194 TFEU by the General Court.

4.5.1. The development of Nord Stream 1

In order to understand the overall process, I start with a review of the development of the OPAL and respectively the Nord Stream 1 (NS1) pipeline, to which the OPAL pipeline is connected. The Nord Stream project already goes back to 1995. The political and economic circumstances within the EU as well as Russia have changed tremendously since then. Originally, gas for the Nord Stream pipeline was to come from the Shtokman field, which lies in the Barents Sea in the Arctic. However, the Shtokman field was not developed for a long time for technical reasons, which is why gas was finally taken from the Yuzhno-Russkoye field. Already in 2000, the project had the official status of a ,project of common interest' (Commission 2000). Initially, there was no political opposition to the project, as it allowed for diversification of supply routes and was considered necessary in response to increasing gas demand (Interview 4, DG Energy). The EU-Russia energy dialogue was launched in 2001 (Commission 2003e). In November 2002, as result of the EU-Russia Summit, projects of common interest between Russia and the EU were defined. The actors agreed to give „special attention to the implementation" of those projects. One of those projects was the „northern trans-European gas pipeline" (Summit 2002).

Russia wanted to apply its new strategy to diversify transit routes, since Gazprom was unable to resolve its conflicts with Ukraine, Belarus and Moldova regarding transit fees and gas prices (Götz 2005: 2f.; Yafimava 2017: 1). The general European interest on the other hand was originally to secure gas supply since the own production of gas would decrease and the diversification of supply routes was deemed necessary (Götz 2005: 3f.; Parliament 2009a: 7). Germany pursued a particular strategic interest since the pipeline symbolised a flagship project between both countries (Götz 2005: 4).

The gas pipeline was to be approximately 1,295 kilometres long and was supposed to transport Russian gas from the Russian coast north of St. Petersburg underneath the Baltic Sea to Northern Germany and then onwards via the Netherlands to the United Kingdom. The capacity was to be between 20 and 30 billion cubic metres of gas a year (in comparison: Nord Stream 1 and 2 would have a joint capacity of 55 billion cubic meters of gas a year (Gazprom n.d.)). The Commission published a communication in 2003 {Commission 2003b} on energy infrastructure and security of supply. The pre-crisis argumentation declared deeper cooperation with Russia as valid strategy to enhance security of supply. Alternatives to Russian gas supply were not considered. The main argument was that, given that the EU imported more than 40 % of its gas from Russia, it would be helpful to further integrate the markets on the basis of joint regulatory principles and long-term contracts. This strategy would eventually increase security of supply (Commission 2003b: 17).

Germany and Russia agreed on the terms of the pipeline in 2004 and signed an agreement in 2005 in presence of Gerhard Schröder and Russian President Vladimir Putin (Cameron 2007: 1). The consortium of enterprises involved included Gazprom, E.ON Ruhrgas and BASF/Wintershall. The „Nordstream AG" was founded in 2005 with headquarters in Zug, Switzerland (Cameron 2007: 8). In 2007, the Dutch company Gasunie joined the consortium. The largest shareholder remained Gazprom with 51 % (Whist 2008: 6).

> „In 2004, Poland and the Baltic States saw the Nord Stream project as a Russian Trojan Horse put in place to circumvent their countries, causing uncertainty about gas delivery and/or a substantial loss of transit revenues, as well as challenging the nascent solidarity between 'old' and 'new' EU Member States. On some occasions, the project was referred to as a 'new Ribbentrop-Molotov Pact', even by moderate politicians in Central Europe. Instead of Nord Stream, Poland and the Baltics favoured onshore projects on their soil (e.g. Amber Pipeline and Yamal 2)" (Commission 2017a: 4).

Although there were some objections to the project, the opposition was rather moderate. Major concerns concentrated on the environmental aspects of an undersea pipeline (Interview 4, DG Energy). The final decision (1364/2006/EC) to include the Northern trans-European gas pipeline was taken on 6 September 2006 despite the concerns of Eastern Europe following the first gas crisis. Poland, with the support from Latvia and Lithuania, pushed for the Amber pipeline, which would alternatively connect Russia with Germany via Lithuania, Latvia and Poland. Amber might have brought Germany and the affected Eastern European Member States closer together as partners. The project was, however, not developed although it was also included in the TEN-E guidelines as project of common interest (Thompson 2015: 184).

The European perception changed on the pipeline project over time. In July 2008, the EP held a debate on „Conditions for access to the natural gas transmission networks" (Parliament 2008a). The British MEP Derek Roland Clark questioned Nord Stream 1: „This is tantamount to approving a project to bring Russian natural gas direct to Germany, bypassing Poland, thus preserving their supplies and never mind the rest of us. Is that what they call solidarity?". Šarūnas Birutis, MEP from Lithuania, assessed the dependence on a few suppliers as a negative consequence:

> „There is no doubt that the Kremlin is prepared to maintain and increase its authority in the EU gas supply sector. No financial resources

are being spared. Everyone has witnessed the level of lobbying with regard to the Nord Stream and other projects. This is not economics, it is politics, and quite aggressive at that. The only way we can resist this dictatorship is through solidarity in our actions and the creation of a common EU energy system (...)" (Parliament 2008a).

Overall, there were four major debates accompanying the implementation. Germany and Russia underlined the importance of additional gas supply coming via Nord Stream. Different arguments served as explanations for the need of additional supply, e.g. the German Energiewende or general increase of consumption. European partners on the other side feared that Russia tried to implement the strategy „dividae et impera" in order to divide Europe over the battle of supply routes and respective fears of being cut off. The third line of argumentation was based on military concerns since the construction of the pipeline would lead to more naval presence in the Baltic Sea. This threat was majorly perceived by Sweden, Finland and Estonia. The fourth debate concentrated on the environmental concerns regarding the difficult construction of an offshore pipeline of 1200km (Whist 2008).

In 2009, the European Commission granted OPAL – the connecting pipeline of Nord Stream – an exemption from the internal gas market directive 2003/55/EC concerning third party access. However, the capacity that Gazprom could use was capped at 50 %, „(s)ince Gazprom has not implemented the gas release programme referred to in the original decision" (CJEU 2019). In 2011, Nord Stream 1 delivered gas to Germany for the first time. OPAL is connected with the Nord Stream pipeline in Lubmin (Mecklenburg-Vorpommern) and has its ending point in Brandov (Czech Republic). The construction of the OPAL pipeline was also finished in 2011. The other connecting pipeline from Lubmin is the „Nordeuropäische Erdgasleitung" (NEL), which transports gas through Northern Germany to Rehden (Lower Saxony).

Since NS1 is operational, two main discussions evolved around the German-Russian gas project. First, in 2011, the Nord Stream AG started to evaluate the possibility of a parallel pipeline to Nord Stream 1, called Nord Stream 2. Germany's behaviour with regard to Nord Stream 2 has been criticised ever since:

„But from a European perspective, such a project is not simply an economic project that can be left to industry. That's exactly where we fall into the trap where - as I said before - we leave solidarity purely to industry, purely to the market. NS is a pipeline that, unlike all the other pipelines I have come across, is not embedded in an intergovernmental agreement. There is no agreement, no governmental agreement between Russia and Germany on this pipeline. The German government never wanted to get its feet wet. At the inauguration of NS1, Schröder and Putin still appeared together. (...) No government representative was present at NS2, they all wanted to stay out of it, also - I suspect - because they knew that if we raised it to the state level, we would have to talk to our partner countries in the Eastern part of the EU. They didn't want that. I don't really think that is in the spirit of Article 6 of the Directive, not in the spirit of the Gas Supply Regulation. That was not solidarity in action. Not so much in the matter, but in the way the problem was approached and the way the government level behaved towards it" (Interview 8, DG Energy).

Second, in 2016, the Commission altered its exemption decision allowing third parties (thus also Gazprom) to bid for the remaining 50 % of transport capacity. The Parliament published an own-initiative report ‚Towards a European Energy Union' in 2015, where it

„(e)xpresses concern at the proposed doubling of capacity of the Nordstream pipeline and the effects this would have on energy security and diversification of supply and the principle of solidarity between Member States; highlights, in the context of the ongoing trilateral talks between the EU, Ukraine and Russia, the need to ensure long-term energy supplies to and through the Ukraine" (Parliament 2015b, recital 21).

The EP also declared its opposition to Nord Stream 2, which it considered to be incompatible with the aims of the Energy Union (Kocak and De Micco 2016: 15). The additional concern that NS2 would make other pipeline routes redundant is not only of concern for Ukraine, but also for transit states like Slovakia and Poland (Goldthau 2016: 7; ENTSOG 2017). Additionally, the US-Congress issued the Protecting Europe's Energy Security Act (PEES Act) in December 2019, which imposed sanctions on Nord Stream 2 (and Turkstream) in order to stop NS2. This action put additional political pressure on the issue (Interview 11, Official, Government of Luxembourg).

4.5.2. The OPAL Case T-883/16 and Case C-848/19 P

The exemption decision of 2016 led to a judgement by the General Court on European energy solidarity, which is why it represents an important case for the implementation of European energy solidarity. Following the exemption decision of 2016, Poland brought a case based on this decision against the Commission, which was supported by Germany, to the Court in January 2017. Poland was supported by Lithuania and Latvia as interveners. In the application, Poland made six pleas in law alleging infringements of European law provisions and lack of competence.

> „The first plea in law alleges infringement of Article 36(1)(a) of Directive 2009/73/EC, in conjunction with Article 194(1)(b) TFEU, and of the principle of solidarity through the granting of a new regulatory exemption for the Opal gas pipeline, even though that exemption undermines the security of gas supplies" (CJEU 2016).

At first, the Court analysed the interrelation of energy security and solidarity. The Court recalled that according to the Bundesnetzagentur (BNetzA) and the Commission security of supply was enhanced by the OPAL pipeline. The Commission argued that additional gas via Nord Stream 1 would not „replace entirely the quantities of gas flowing hitherto through the Braterstwo and Yamal pipelines" (CJEU 2019, recital 50). Poland, supported by Lithuania, argued on the other hand that „the reduction of the transport of gas through the Yamal and Braterstwo pipelines could lead to a weakening of the energy security of Poland and considerably undermine the diversification of sources of supply of gas" (recital 51). The legal argument was that „the contested decision infringes the principle of energy security and the principle of energy solidarity, and hence contravenes Article 36(1)(a) of Directive 2009/73, read in conjunction with Article 194(1)(b) TFEU". Art. 36(1) refers to the question under which conditions new and existing infrastructure can be exempted from the general rules. While Art. 36(1)(a) refers in particular to the amelioration of security of supply, Art. 194(1)(b) TFEU refers to the implementation of a European energy policy in a spirit of solidarity.

Poland noted that, as underlined by Art. 194 TFEU, the principle of solidarity is a priority for the field of energy policy. It argued that Member States and EU institutions need to implement EU energy policy in a spirit of solidarity. „In particular, measures adopted by EU institutions that compromise the energy security of certain regions or in certain Member States, including their security of gas supply, would be contrary to the principle of energy solidarity" (recital 60). In particular, Poland feared that due to the increase of capacity of Nord Stream 1, the gas pipelines bringing gas directly to Poland via Ukraine and Belarus would no longer be supplied with gas, since the contracts regarding these routes end in 2020 and 2022. This would endanger security of supply, diminish the diversification of the sources of gas supply in Poland and most likely lead to an increase in the cost of obtaining gas (recitals 62–64).

The Commission „submits that *energy solidarity is a political notion that appears in its communications and documents*, whereas the contested decision must satisfy the legal criteria laid down in Article 36(1) of Directive 2009/73" (recital 65, emphasis added). Furthermore, the Commission argued that the principle of solidarity must be applied by the legislator but not to the „administration applying the legislation" and solidarity refers to crisis situations only and not to the overall functioning of the internal market. „In any event, the criterion of enhancement of security of supply, set out in Article 36(1) of that directive, which it examined in the contested decision, may be regarded as taking into account the notion of energy solidarity" (ibid.). The final argument of the Commission was that NS1 is a priority project of European interest: „the contested decision could enable the increased use of such an infrastructure (which) is consistent with the common and European interests" (ibid.).

Following these divergent interpretations of the meaning of the principle of solidarity and the arising obligations, the General Court determined its scope of application. First, the Court quoted the language of Art. 194 TFEU, which is the new legal basis for the European energy article since the Treaty of Lisbon. Furthermore, it explained that solidarity is a general principle between Member States

> „mentioned, inter alia, in Article 2 TEU, in Article 3(3) TEU, Article 24(2) and (3) TEU, Article 122(1) TFEU and Article 222 TFEU. *That principle is at the basis of the whole Union system* in accordance with the undertaking provided for in Article 4(3) TEU (see, to that effect, judgment of 10 December 1969, Commission v France, 6/69 and 11/69, not published, EU:C:1969:68, paragraph 16)" (recital 69, emphasis added).

The principle of solidarity entails rights and obligations which are expressed between the EU and the Member States, and „the Member States are bound by an obligation of solidarity between themselves and with regard to the common interest of the European Union and the policies pursued by it" (recital 70). The Court did not agree with the Commission that the principle of solidarity refers only to crises situations, such as consequences of natural disasters or terrorist attacks. This kind of ‚crisis solidarity‘ is expressed in secondary law by regulation (EU) 2017/1938 (SoS regulation) (recital 71). „On the contrary, the principle of solidarity also entails a general obligation on the part of the European Union and the Member States, in the exercise of their respective competences, to take into account the interests of the other stakeholders" (recital 72). Recital 72 underlines herewith that the principle of solidarity is *a general legal principle not only applicable to energy policy*. This means that the principle of solidarity obliges Member States to refrain from any action

> „liable to affect the interests of the European Union and the other Member States, as regards security of supply, its economic and political viability, the diversification of supply or of sources of supply, and to do so in order to *take account of their interdependence and de facto solidarity*" (recital 73, emphasis added).

The interdependence is also considered in Article 36(1)(e) of directive 2009/73 by the concept of the effective functioning of the internal market. The Court stated that solidarity does not refer only to exemptional circumstances as described in regulation (EU) 2017/1938. Solidarity is additionally an aim of the TEN-E guidelines (Regulation (EU) No 347/2013), which provide that infrastructure must be built in order make solidarity operational (recital 75). In this regard, the Court also rejected the argument of the Commission that the principle of solidarity was sufficiently taken into account by examining the criteria listed in Art. 36(1) of directive 2009/73 (recital 76). However, this does not mean that the principle of solidarity cannot „have negative impacts for the particular interests of a Member State in the field of energy". However, these interests must be taken into account and also balanced in the event of a conflict (recital 77). It would therefore have been the Commission's task to examine how the amendment of the legal framework for the OPAL pipeline would affect the interests of other Member States (recital 78).

This assessment of the principle of solidarity is followed by the „(c)onsideration of whether the contested decision infringes the principle of energy solidarity". First, the Court stated that the principle of solidarity was not considered in the contested decision and that the Commission did not examine possible implications of the principle (recital 79). The Commission carried out, however, an examination „of the criterion of the enhancement of security of supply" (recital 80), which according to the Commission was still satisfied with the contested decision.

> „Like the principle of proportionality, and to lesser extent, the princi-
> ple of subsidiarity, the principle of energy solidarity does not create
> an obligation for a certain result, but calls for the performance of
> a balancing test of which the features are still largely unknown and
> subject to future clarification" (Buschle and Talus 2019: 8).

Additionally, the Court criticised that the Commission only reflected upon the security of supply situation of the whole EU and did not consider
single Member States. „One aspect of solidarity which is often overlooked
in the EU is to take into consideration others' vulnerabilities and EU's
common good while making decisions and pursing certain policy" (Interview 6, MEP). The principle of solidarity would also entail that the
Commission should consider that volumes would be diminished via the
Broterstwo and Yamal pipelines and the respective consequences for security of supply (recital 81/82). These arguments led to the judgement of the
Court „that the contested decision was adopted in breach of the principle
of energy solidarity, as provided for in Article 194(1) TFEU" (recital 83).

The Commission published in its Quarterly Report on European Gas
Markets (2019/3) that „(t)he decision resulted in a short-lived wholesale
price spike on most of the European gas hubs, especially in Central and
Eastern Europe" (Commission 2019e). Poland, Lithuania and Latvia were
nevertheless pleased with the judgement. The Commission refrained from
an appeal of the judgement. It would also be difficult for the Commission
to appeal a judgement through which the principle of solidarity gained
strength and the Commission itself too (Łoskot-Strachota and Kardaś
2019: 3). Germany appealed the judgement on 20 November 2019 (Case
C-848/19 P). The underlying reason for Germany's appeal is its comparative economic advantage ensured by a low gas price:

> „Of course, Germany has these economic interests in maintaining the
> competitiveness of its energy-intensive industry. And thus, of course,
> not to enshrine too strong a principle in law, which would lead to
> giving up this competitive advantage, but at the same time to drive
> the issue of European solidarity in sum as an important political prin-
> ciple" (Interview 9, WP on Energy).

The first ground of appeal states that the principle of solidarity is not a
legal criterion and thus „cannot give rise to specific rights and obligations
for the European Union and/or for the Member States". Therefore, the
Commission does not need to consider the principle in its general decision-making. The second ground of appeal states that solidarity is only
applicable in the context of the contingency mechanism, which is not the

case regarding the OPAL decision. The third and fourth grounds of appeal underlined that, on the one hand, solidarity was sufficiently covered by considering the security of supply impacts and, on the other hand, there is no obligation for the Commission to refer to solidarity in general in such a decision. The German government expressed its opinion on the principle of solidarity as follows:

> „Die Bundesregierung teilt nicht die Einschätzung des EuG, dass aus diesem Grundsatz (Solidaritätsprinzip) ein unmittelbar anwendbarer Prüfmaßstab für die Kommission erwächst, der hier anzuwenden gewesen wäre. Vielmehr werden die Ziele des Art. 194 AEUV in vielfältiger Weise durch das Sekundärrecht konkretisiert, das die Kommission, aber auch die Regulierungsbehörde zuvor angewandt hatte" (Bundestag 2019).

This statement underlines again that the German government believed that only concrete secondary law can institutionalise solidarity – a common opinion among lawyers. General-Advocate Campos Sánchez-Bordona agreed with the General Court in its opinion from March 2021: the principle of energy solidarity „entails rights and obligations both for the European Union and for the Member States" and the „principle of energy solidarity under Article 194 TFEU produces effects that are legal, and not merely political" (Sánchez-Bordona 2021).

On 15 July 2021, the European Court of Justice provided its judgement on Germany's appeal (Case C-848/19 P). "The *legality of any act* of the EU institutions falling within the European Union's energy policy must be assessed in the light of the principle of energy solidarity" (Press Release No 129/21, emphasis added). The principle "forms the basis of all of the objectives of the European Union's energy policy, serving as the thread that brings them together and gives them coherence" (Case C-848/19 P). The Court thus contradicts Germany's arguments that first, solidarity is only a political notion. To the contrary, it entails rights and obligations both for the Member States and the EU; second, solidarity must always be taken into account "even if there is no express reference to that principle in the secondary legislation applicable" (Press Release No 129/21); third, solidarity is not only applicable to crisis situations but concerns any action taken under Art. 194(1) TFEU. The principle of energy solidarity therefore means that the interests of other actors need to be taken into account and balanced and "the adoption of measures that might affect the interests of stakeholders liable to be affected" must be avoided (ibid.). However, "the principle of energy solidarity does not mean that EU energy policy must never, under any circumstances, have negative impacts for the particular interests of a Member State in that field" (Case C-848/19 P). Based on this statement, the Court underlines that the principle of solidarity is not equal to 'unconditional loyalty' as argued by Germany.

4.5.3. Results and discussion

The judgement by the Court changed the impetus of solidarity: „Seitdem ist es nicht mehr nur politisches Leitbild, sondern als Kriterium für administrativ-regulatorische Entscheidungen etabliert" (Westphal 2020: 3). Looking at the arguments put forward by the Commission, the question arises why the Commission claimed that solidarity is only a political notion. This argument seems to be in contradiction to former statements by the Commission. Interviews with Commission officials revealed that the Commission's legal service interpreted solidarity only as political notion, as the consequences of implementing solidarity as a legal principle would be incalculable. The political opinion of the Commission, however, is different. The juridification of the principle was even the declared aim of the Commission. The introduction of solidarity as legal principle could have many positive aspects on the development of joint solutions, not only in the energy sector but also concerning migration. Nevertheless, possible consequences could entail further interference in national energy systems, such as the German Energiewende (and its negative effects on the stability of the electricity sector) or the coal phase-out (reaching the energy and climate objectives 2050 in solidarity) (Interview 1, DG Energy). The hidden impact on the decision to support solidarity was also emphasised in another interview:

> „we were going to change the mentality of how people would approach the questions. You might say that this fed also in the decision of the Court. It's a way about how people approach the issue. When we first started it in 2001, nobody thought solidarity is an issue. But in 2015, solidarity was the reflex" (Interview 2, DG Energy).

The most impressive outcome of the judgement is, however, its impact on the interrelation between solidarity and national sovereignty. Art. 194(2) TFEU spells out that „EU level measures shall not affect a Member State's right to determine the conditions for exploiting its energy resources, its choice between different energy sources and the general structure of its energy supply, without prejudice to Article 192(2)". Member States lose their leeway in the free choice of energy sources if they have to take into account the interests of other Member States (Buschle and Talus 2019: 6). There are two possible interpretations of the judgement: Either the judgement effects the implementation of all energy decisions by the Member States, e.g. the exit from nuclear power, since these decisions have an effect on other (neighbouring) Member States (Interview 10, Commission Official). Or the judgement has an effect on decisions only in case they are taken in the framework of EU decision making. This second interpretation is true for the case of the OPAL pipeline. The judgement referred to a project which was decided under EU law. Both interpretations provide the Commission with additional room of manoeuvre and the obligation to examine national decisions that might impact European interests (Buschle and Talus 2019: 8f.). The judgement states that "it is necessary to assess whether there are risks for the energy interests of the Member States and the European Union, and in particular to security of energy supply" (recital 69). Riley argues that all national decisions with a cross-border impact need to take into account the interests of other Member States in a spirit of solidarity. Consequently, it will be possible „to bring legal challenges against those member states who infringe the principle of solidarity" (Riley 2019). It remains difficult to determine to what degree solidarity must be taken into account. The Court's ruling underlines that negative impacts can occur, but that they must be assessed and balanced (recitals 77 and 78).

The decision of the General Court can thus have further implications for the future of Nord Stream 2 and its onshore connection Eugal. It is questionable if Nord Stream 2 can be fully utilised if solidarity must be considered in all capacity allocation decisions (Stein 2019; Interview 1, DG Energy). Another controversial issue is the consequence for Ukraine due to the OPAL decision. It was argued that the decision could have a positive impact for Ukraine's negotiation position (Kellermann 2019). However, the negotiations between Russia, Ukraine and the EU on the new gas treaty between Russia and Ukraine were very difficult. The parties reached only an agreement two days after the US passed the law on Europe's energy security, which consequently put a halt on the completion of Nord Stream 2 (Gotev 2019b). Another question is how the judgement will affect the implementation of other pipelines, such as the European leg of Turkstream (Interview 6, former MEP). Bulgaria fears a decrease in transit via the trans-Balkan pipeline, as soon as Turkstream becomes operational, which is why the opposition to the pipeline received additional arguments with the judgement (Łoskot-Strachota and Kardaś 2019). However, Turkstream, respectively the connecting pipelines to the EU internal market, might not fall under the same legal regime so that problems are less probable (Interview 1, DG Energy).

With this ruling, the Court proved its function as catalyst of European integration, since it upgraded the principle of solidarity as genuine principle of EU law although this step was not seen as necessary (Interview 1, DG Energy).

> „The European Union is based on solidarity and on the assumption that acting together is making it stronger. As the 10 September 2019 General Court decision shows, there are not many areas like energy where this principle could be applied as efficiently and for the benefit of all the Member States" (Vinois and Bros 2019: 15).

However, the Court still needs to provide further reflections on the solidarity principle as the current state of the art leaves too much insecurity (Buschle and Talus 2019: 11). Nevertheless, with this judgement, the Court has shown that the principle of solidarity is not just a political buzzword, but that it has become a legal principle in the making since its introduction in primary law and permeation of secondary law.

5. Conclusions

Solidarity has been a buzzword in the EU in the last two decades undergoing a metamorphosis to become a legal principle in the making. The EU, which has gone through a myriad of different crises in the last 15 years, conjured solidarity to bring salvation in light of those challenges. However, at first, solidarity remained shallow without clarity on its political or legal meaning. The lack of a clear concept to accurately grasp solidarity was my initial motivation for this study. This book aimed to answer two research questions: The first question concerned the conceptualisation of solidarity, a chameleonic term, which superseded EU discourse in the last 10 years. The second question focused on the explanatory power of spill-over effects regarding the insertion of solidarity into secondary law. Additionally, the second question implied a critical research endeavour aiming to further develop my concept of solidarity through its application and to explore, which factors might make the difference between ,institutionalised' and ,declarative' solidarity.

One main objective of the study was to shed light on the principle of solidarity, „which is *per se* a quite fuzzy notion" (Lang and Westphal 2020: 89, emphasis by authors). The process of conceptualisation and its application have shown that many different expectations arise from the call for solidarity. This made it all the more important to clarify the features of solidarity and what they imply. I had to undertake several steps to conceptualise solidarity, to reveal the interpretation of solidarity by European actors, to examine why and how solidarity was inserted and to deplore if institutionalised solidarity – built on my concept – was actually applied in secondary law. This was a delicate process since solidarity is morally and emotionally charged, and at the same time a legal principle under discussion and used in politics in a nebulous and conflictive fashion. This study has carefully investigated how solidarity is transposed on the European level and how it was envisioned over time.

The study used the updated version of neofunctionalism (Niemann 2006) in order to shed light on the causal mechanisms. Based on the neofunctional presuppositions, I assumed that the dependent variable – the implementation of solidarity in EU secondary law as particular form of integration – is influenced by functional and cultivated spill-over effects. I developed two hypotheses to capture these potential causal mechanisms.

Solidarity is applied in different policy fields in secondary law. Based on the population of cases, I decided to choose four legislative acts concerning the gas sector and one legal case as case studies. The comparison of those cases would contribute to understand the variance of the dependent variable. Using process analysis to reveal inch by inch the mechanisms leading to solidarity, I examined the policy formulation process and its results with help of document analysis and semi-structured expert interviews. For the evaluation of the concept's features I used different codes reflecting the features. I described in the memos (s. annex) the screening and analytical processes. The process was an interpretative task since I adapted the memos during the analytical process which led to a reassessment of all acts. This step has been necessary in order to get a clear picture of the features' components.

In this last chapter, I will summarise the main empirical findings. I will present in a first part a discussion on my concept of solidarity. This is followed by an evaluation of the empirical part where I will resume the research results. I conclude the study with an outlook on future research avenues.

5.1. Theoretical reflections on solidarity

The conceptualisation process, which aimed to build a concept of solidarity between Member States, was influenced by Sartori, Gerring and Goertz. Several steps were needed in order to develop the features of solidarity. The conceptualisation of solidarity underlined one critical point on the understanding of solidarity: Either we interpret solidarity as voluntary normative obligation or as phenomenon based on rational choice assumptions. Both understandings are valid, but it is necessary to illuminate which features correspond to these two forms.

The normative interpretation emphasises that solidarity is something voluntary: a selfless act, which is either based on a strong identification with the group (e.g. based on identity) or a moral understanding of solidarity as human value, leading to cosmopolitan solidarity, which does not necessarily include reciprocity. Due to these pre-conditions, I was not convinced that this form of solidarity could be fully applied to the solidarity relationship between EU Member States. I based my concept of solidarity between Member States on a wide version of rational choice theory. Solidarity is in this regard sourced by interdependence, self-interest and political allegiance. These theoretical reflections result in particular characteristics of solidarity, which are 1) group cohesion, 2) reciprocity as well as 3) monitoring and self-responsibility.

Box 10: Features of solidarity

Group cohesion:
- Trust and responsibility for each other build the core of the group, which is characterised by a shared sense of community.
- A collective interest is formulated and backed by all group members. The collective interest takes precedence over the national interest.

Reciprocity and rules for implementation:
- All group members are obliged to fairly contribute to the production of a certain good.
- All group members have equal rights concerning the provided good dependent on the neediness and deservingness.

Monitoring and self-responsibility:
- The group possesses a control capacity (= monitoring system).
- Group members act self-responsible.

The application of the features in the empirical part demonstrated that the assessment of the feature ‚group cohesion‘ remains unsatisfactory. Member States must recognise that they are in the same boat and have a common interest in finding a solution. I have assessed this feature by looking at specific wording in each piece of legislation, e.g. the emphasis on trust and the need to pursue a policy at the European level. This approach might be criticised since the recitals of secondary law are often coined by whitewashing. However, the formulation of the collective interest could further indicate whether group cohesion is present. Additionally, if e.g. the final vote was not made unanimously (i.e. not backed by all group members), it can be assumed that the group cohesion is less stable. Furthermore, this point underlines that a solidarity group goes beyond pure self-interest motivations even though this might be part of the initial motive to enter a solidarity group. The solidarity group rather develops a common perspective by jointly sharing the individual vulnerabilities. Therefore, joint perceptions are key for group cohesion. The point that the ‚collective interest takes precedence over the national interest‘ is a rather idealistic assumption, which is not only difficult to assess but also proved to be less relevant. Individual interests might always diverge from the collective interest, which is why the monitoring system – and the willingness to be monitored – is of importance. Rather, solidarity is expressed when Member States agree on a common approach despite national interests.

I analysed the feature 'reciprocity' by evaluating the resulting rights and obligations of a solidarity mechanism. Member States' agreement is dependent on a *clear and fair distribution of burdens and benefits as well as conditions*. Member States want to ensure the *exclusion of freeriding* which is only possible if common standards are implemented. To recall, this means that rules are accordingly implemented which clarify how the solidarity rights and obligations are carried out. Reciprocal compensation takes two forms. Either all Member States contribute to a fund, to which they have equal access based on pre-defined conditions; or Member States are direct-ly compensated for their contribution. The point of ‚deservingness‘ did not play any role in the discussion by the EU actors. Deservingness is the twin to responsibility; but it encompasses a moral judgement of the situation and in how far someone would be to blame to be in the situation. This approach, however, might be for the implementation of solidarity even more difficult to transform into measurable political tools. Under which conditions is a Member State directly to blame? Responsibility (agreeing on a set of obligations, which need to be fulfilled) is more expedient to transform into political guidelines. Even though ‚neediness‘ was not directly mentioned, ‚third-party responsibility‘ in form of a possible supply crisis, was a reason in speech acts to call for solidarity. The pressure to act in solidarity increases with normative arguments from the demanding state.

The group's monitoring capacity was the determining factor as to whether "institutionalised" solidarity was present. This aspect referred to the entitlement of the Commission (or another agent) to evaluate and control the implementation of solidarity mechanisms. This means that Member States need to agree on a monitoring system, which is crucial for an agreement on solidarity (compare the failed institutionalisation of solidarity in the IGA decision). If there was no such control mechanism in place, solidarity remained toothless. One additional factor, which was in the case of institutionalised solidarity significant, was self-responsibility. Self-responsibility reflects solidarity, since it keeps other group members out of harm. After all, solidarity is dependent on the individual contribu-tion, which means taking care of one's own situation for the good of the group. Member States supported ‚responsibility‘ as necessary feature, since only then there would be reassurance that all Member States exhausted their possibilities to protect themselves. Self-responsibility is key for the Member States to accept institutionalised solidarity. Responsibility repre-sents a process of putting in place different objectives (e.g. diversification and unbundling) to guarantee that every Member State is fully prepared in case of supply difficulties. Self-responsibility is as such a demand of the solidarity provider balancing the normative pressure which arises from neediness. This due diligence builds confidence over time that all systems are equally effective. Trustworthiness increases when Member States are not only willing to act self-responsibly but also to be monitored accordingly by others (compare credible commitment theory). Additionally, self-responsibility is easier to monitor and to control than deservingness. Responsibility is one of the main pre-conditions for solidarity between Member States, which has to be guaranteed. My research showed also that trust – in response to self-responsibility – plays an important part for the insertion of institutionalised solidarity. Trust develops over time when Member States are ensured that other Member States apply and comply with the common rules and when Member States have a platform for enhanced dialogue, which contributes to information-sharing (e.g. Gas Coordination Group).

The application of the concept of solidarity:

Solidarity takes different forms within the documents as aim, prerogative, esprit or mechanism, which is why solidarity needs to be carefully examined. The application of my concept showed that even though all legislative acts included solidarity as policy outcome (the term was mentioned either in the recitals or article(s)), institutionalised solidarity was hardly inserted. I looked at four different legal acts, which have been all revised after the Treaty of Lisbon came into effect. The application of the concept showed that all but one of the legislative acts had features of solidarity, however, this is the point where accurateness is obliged. Only the implementation of solidarity in the SoS regulation of 2017 is fulfilling the conditions for institutionalised solidarity.

The analysis of the principle of solidarity has shown, that there are *two main forms of solidarity* implemented in secondary energy law:

A. Solidarity as insurance mechanism.
B. Solidarity as behavioural norm.

Both forms of solidarity have occurred in the legislative acts. Form A – solidarity as insurance mechanism – was implemented by the SoS regulation and the internal market decision. In this case, Member States are interested to build a solidarity community in order to guarantee a certain good, which is in this case security of supply. Form B – solidarity as behavioural norm – was underlined by intergovernmental agreements and the TEN-E regulation. In both cases Member States were expected to behave according to the spirit of solidarity, i.e. to take into account the interests of neighbouring states and/or not to harm the others. A similar interpretation (solidarity as behavioural norm) has been issued by the Court. This analysis corresponds to the interpretation by Calliess that solidarity is, on the one hand, a general request to the Member States to take into account the interests of other Member States and, on the other hand, the specific demand to support each other in single situations (Calliess and Ruffert 2016).

To what extent are the two reflections on solidarity similar and divergent? Solidarity as insurance mechanism mirrors a popular understanding of solidarity. Group members have an interest in building a solidarity community when the group members profit from a joint provision of the good. However, solidarity exceeds the self-interest since its institutionalisation also refers to a joint responsibility which implies a normative reference. Rules can be established to clarify rights and obligations or burdens and benefits. The implementation of this form of solidarity usually requires further reflection on principles such as fairness and justice, which can be seen as a counterbalance to solidarity.

The second form of solidarity is different since the solidarity action is inherently difficult to apply. Solidarity corresponds in this case to a principle of action. Under which circumstances and up to which point do Member States need to investigate the consequences of their actions on neighbouring states? How is reciprocity ensured? The Court has not explained to what extent the interests need to be balanced or considered, so further clarification will be necessary.

Both forms of solidarity implicate a normative understanding of solidarity. *Group members are expected to make a sacrifice in order to serve the interest of the group.* This can be understood as the essence of solidarity, which is present in both forms of solidarity.

Solidarity as a particular phenomenon of integration

The application of my concept of solidarity demonstrated that it serves its purpose, which is to uncover whether declarative or institutionalised solidarity has been implemented. The implementation of *institutionalised solidarity* is according to my research – based on the cases under consideration – dependent on the question if the different features of solidarity can be translated into concrete mechanisms, as it has been the case with the solidarity mechanism in the SoS regulation (solidarity as insurance mechanism). Neofunctionalism – as presented by Niemann (2006) – has provided a theoretical framework, which is useful to research decision-making processes at EU level. In particular the inclusion of supranational actors – such as the Court – widened the research scope so that the evolvement of solidarity could be better assessed. The use of a process-tracing design was helpful in order to track back the developments in detail and thus to reveal how political processes and functional pressures are intertwined. Nevertheless, functional spill-over effects remain difficult to assess since the institutional environment is not sufficiently modelled. Niemann tried to bypass this problem with help of discourse analysis of the decision-makers. Only if a functional pressure is perceived as such, it is influential. Additionally, I connected the perception of functional pressure by the decision-makers with the acceptance of solidarity as policy solution. Cultivated spill-over puts supranational actors at the centre and explains that those actors are interested in more power, which is why they push for more integration. I argued that the implementation of solidarity serves as strategy to gain competences. Decision-makers eventually agree since supranational entrepreneurs convincingly presented that solidarity is necessary.

The most critical point is that solidarity between Member States *per se* cannot be sufficiently explained by neofunctionalism. I anticipated this limitedness of neofunctionalism, which is why this study is also an exploratory research endeavour. The aim was to identify the conditions, which lead to declarative or institutionalised solidarity and to reflect if those observations can be usefully fed into the theoretical framework of neofunctionalism. I found that solidarity implies that Member States are willing ,to give something up' in favour of the community. Even if there are different forms of solidarity as described above, the willingness to sacrifice something for the sake of the common good is the abstract meaning of solidarity.

I deduct from my observations that solidarity is a particular phenomenon of integration, which does not necessarily include a power shift to supranational actors but constitutes the trade-off between national and European interests in the course of integration. „The need for coordination" as expressed in one interview (Interview 8, DG Energy). The implementation of solidarity between Member States is thus dependent on three consecutive steps:

1) Entering negotiations

Member States are obliged to enter negotiations due to institutional but also factual reasons of interdependence (Scharpf 1991: 18). Member States want to „enhance their problem-solving capacities in an era of globalization, while indemnifying each other against the risks and losses implicit in integration" (Sangiovanni 2013: 241). Therefore, the EU faces a situation similar to that of federal states: constituent units need to cooperate to resolve collective action problems (Trein 2020: 979; Kneuer 2017: 19).

2) Problem-solving decision style

However, when it comes to distributional issues, federal systems risk blundering into the „joint decision trap" as the EU's problem-solving ability – just as in federal systems – is rather limited (Scharpf 1988; Kaiser 2012). One possible escape route from this trap is „(...) always to consider the interests of all those affected by the negative externalities of the policy decision too (...)" (Piattoni 2017: 282). Consequently, the implementation of solidarity demands a *cooperative interaction mode*, which estimates the overall benefits higher than the individual burdens. This is expressed by a ‚problem-solving' decision style (Scharpf 1988: 261 and 1991: 40). Scharpf argues that such a decision style might evolve due to a common identity or a common vulnerability. Although – as discussed in ch. 2.1.2 – identity might not be a stable source for European solidarity, Member States unite in their political allegiance and joint risk perception/interest. As such the introduction of solidarity between Member States in primary law entails normative expectations between co-equal governments. This reflects a certain federal spirit between the Member States (Arban 2017). However, the development of joint perceptions of vulnerability, risk or interests is no simple undertaking. Only if Member States are aware of and agree on what constitutes the joint interest, the commitment to solidarity increases.

3) Institutionalising solidarity

Eventually, this problem-solving decision style leads to the formation of appropriate institutions to guarantee solidarity. Consequently, trust, fairness and reciprocity as well as self-responsibility and monitoring remain crucial for the implementation of solidarity and their absence can lead to the abandonment of solidarity (compare also Scharpf 1988: 262). Therefore, in order to evaluate the implementation of solidarity between Member States it is necessary to look in detail at those features. From this it follows that wide-scoped rational choice assumptions are crucial to understand the implementation of institutionalised solidarity. Nevertheless, the collective thought is the bone of contention. Solidarity visions are divided between those who favour more contributions between Member States and those who want more self-responsibility in the sense of the group.

If solidarity, however, means to consider the interests of other Member States by adapting the own behaviour accordingly (solidarity as behavioural norm), Member States are much more hesitant to insert solidarity. Solidarity means in this case not to harm others even if it is at one's own expense (compare discussion on NS2). Group solidarity thrives on reciprocity which does not only mean that every group member can access common goods. But every group member needs to think about how its decisions would affect the group. Solidarity remains in this case primarily a normative demand. The reason for this is that this interpretation of solidarity is difficult to translate in conditions or in concrete mechanisms which hampers reciprocal commitments. This point underlines again that normative solidarity appeals need specification in order to achieve a clear policy design.

5.2. Synopsis of work: synthesis of findings

In the following, I will present the research results in an integrative manner in order to outline the empirical, comparative findings on the causal mechanisms. Both hypotheses have rendered limited explanatory power. Hypothesis 1 serves as sufficient explanation for the general implementation of solidarity as result of the gas crises but fails to explain why institutionalised solidarity was inserted in 2017. Hypothesis 2 contributes primarily to the understanding how solidarity was implemented, and the underlying causal mechanism is partly valid. The Commission and the Court proved to be the game changer.

Hypothesis 1 linked functional pressure with the implementation of solidarity. Integration of the internal gas market took place over time. However, this has not led automatically to functional pressures on security of supply. Member States did neither want nor expect that solidarity would lead to an increasing shift from the subsidiarity to the solidarity principle in energy policy, when it was introduced in primary law. Originally, the Member States agreed to the introduction of solidarity only to soothe new Member States and to demonstrate cohesion to the outside world. As of 2007, the Member States agreed to implement a European energy policy, which is why positive dynamics developed regarding the overall integration of the policy field.

There is evidence from interviews but also due to the proximity of cause and effect that the crises have had a crucial influence on the general acceptance of solidarity (inclusion of solidarity in internal market directive

2009 and security of gas supply regulation 2010). Functional pressures occurred with the gas crises in 2006 and 2009 which happened since the integration of the internal market and security of supply are functionally interdependent, but security of supply was not yet integrated. The further inclusion of solidarity was encouraged by the crises since the perception of Member States changed as they became aware of joint vulnerabilities (compare ch. 4.1.1). Directly after the gas crisis in 2009 there has been a change of thoughts, since the consequences of the interdependence became obvious, which convinced sufficiently the Member States to reorganise security of supply at the European level and to implement solidarity, as proposed by the Commission. Additionally, Eastern European states feared that Russia would use energy supply as geopolitical weapon, which is why there has been the general support for solidarity. The greater support of those states has been expressed in Council Conclusions. The European Council referred to solidarity mostly concerning security of supply, but solidarity is also connected with the necessity to create infrastructure in order to make solidarity operational. However, this was not sufficient to insert institutionalised solidarity. For this reason, this observation must be treated with caution. Functional reasons were underlined mainly by the Commission, which argued that the integration of the internal gas market necessitates solidarity since national measures alone would result in damage for the whole internal gas market.

Figure 8: Frames used by European Parliament

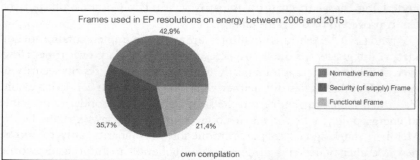

The Parliament had a tendency for normative frames in its resolutions underlining the obligations arising from the Treaty and the normative character of solidarity as behavioural norm. Functional frames were comparatively rare in use.

The Council's perception of possible functional pressures is difficult to evaluate since the arguments were not openly exchanged. However, most of the references to solidarity – in council presidency conclusions or press statements – were made in relation to security of supply. Furthermore, interviews revealed that it is difficult for actors to be openly against solidarity (Interview 7, EP; Interview 8, DG Energy), which underlines the normative function of solidarity (logic of appropriateness). But Member States were still hesitant about the integration of security of supply. The interviews further clarified that there was general agreement that Member States were pressured after the gas crisis to act and that there were functional needs arising from the unfinished market and insufficient infrastructure. Solidarity, however, was only implemented as political notion at that moment. The Council was very reluctant concerning the implications of solidarity when the SoS regulation and the internal gas market directive were negotiated.

Member States have agreed to introduce institutionalised solidarity once the impact of the solidarity mechanism has been sufficiently clarified. It has been important for the Member States to 1) make crises avoidable by further finalisation of the internal market, similar security of supply standards on the national level and by putting the necessary infrastructure in place. And 2) to clarify the content of solidarity. Only when responsibility, avoidance of freeriding and solidarity as measure of last resort were sufficiently refined, the Member States were finally willing to agree. Point 1 was also a trust-building exercise since Member States needed to be equally prepared in order to avoid crises and to act self-responsibly, which reduced the problem of freeriding. This had an additional impact on the adoption of solidarity as measure of last resort. Further points concerned the compensation of solidarity (no charity) and expectations arising from solidarity (rules and obligations).

But this evaluation is only true for the SoS regulation of 2010. When solidarity means to act upon a European interest and to respect the national interests of other Member States, Member States remained very reluctant. The TEN-E regulation (the financial support of infrastructure projects can be interpreted as expression of solidarity) showed that solidarity is inserted since it has a nice ring to it, but there is no intention behind. The IGA decision on the other hand expressed the unwillingness of Member States to let the Commission assess the solidarity principle.

The causal mechanisms as predicted have been partly present, however, it is necessary to recall the following points: The vulnerability of the system was highlighted by the gas crises, which led to a general agreement among Member States to revise the legislation and introduce solidarity mechanisms (in regulation 994/2010 and the internal market directive from 2009). However, ‚declarative' solidarity was implemented, i.e. solidarity could still only be expected to be voluntary depending strongly on the will of Member States. ‚Institutionalised solidarity' was introduced with the revision of the SoS regulation of 2017. There are three explanations for the implementation of institutionalised solidarity. First, the Russia-Ukraine conflict and the resulting pressure to have another gas crisis were perceived as pressures to further integrate. This situation reminded the Member States of the gas crisis in 2009 and the severe consequences ‚to be in the cold' in the middle of winter when it was difficult to operationalise solidarity due to the lacking infrastructure and the technological progress of bi-directional (reverse) flow. Second, solidarity became avoidable over time due to the increased security of supply standard. Member States were ensured that the market could function even in the event of a crisis since gas could be directed to the place where it was needed. Functional pressure changed over time since Member States were building the necessary inter-connectors, which means that the market became operational. Third, Member States had to agree on the conditions, under which they should provide solidarity. The clarification of the notion of ‚protected customers' helped to reassure Member States that they do not have to show disproportionate solidarity and that solidarity is equally given to each Member State as a last resort. Even though functional pressure serves as valid explanation for the general integration process of security of supply, and thus the insertion of solidarity in secondary law, it is no sufficient explanation for institutionalised solidarity. ‚Institutionalised solidarity' was introduced at the moment, when Member States hardly had to fear that its application would be actually needed.

Hypothesis 2 focused on the causal mechanisms between policy entrepreneurship and implementation of solidarity. I configured the causal mechanism based on the theoretical assumptions that supranational actors have a decisive role in the policy formulation process.

The Commission was early on interested in implementing a European approach to security of supply. Already in 2002, it proposed a Council directive on security of gas supply. At that time, both the Council and the Parliament rejected the need for a too strong involvement of the Commission and underlined the national competence for security of supply. Solidarity was nevertheless part of this first directive even though it remained a political notion only. All legislative acts, which included solidarity as outcome of the policy formulation process, included solidarity already in the proposal by the Commission. The interviews revealed that the Commission did not pursue a strategic application of solidarity but used solidarity as keyword, which was inserted whenever it suited. Solidarity was as such perceived as a buzzword similar to ,participation', ,subsidiarity' or ,citizenship' (Interviews 1 and 8, DG Energy). Certainly, it also reflected the spirit of the time, when the principle was also inserted at several points in the Constitutional Treaty. The Commission and the Parliament were both frequently endorsing the principle of solidarity in their reports after 2006. The Commission used mainly functional arguments to underline that solidarity is an answer to external political pressure and a way of action to embrace a coherent foreign energy policy. Solidarity was presented as policy solution to the gas crisis but also as necessity to create coherence in energy policy. In order to achieve the general objective of an integrated security of supply policy, the Commission used solidarity not only in its strategic papers but included solidarity also in the legislative proposals. The Commission followed a pragmatic approach aiming to finalise the internal energy market. Therefore, the Commission underlined in different ways the importance of solidarity as *one* policy solution. Alternative solutions in this regard were not presented – solidarity topped off the EU energy security strategy.

Figure 9: Frames used by Commission

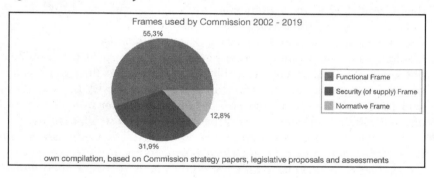

Until 2010, the Commission could not provide a clear vision of solidarity but was not convinced of solidarity as obligation to help. It took until 2014 that the Commission first envisioned a clearer definition of solidarity, when the Commission started to evaluate the solidarity mechanism as applied in the SoS regulation of 2010. The Commission's aim was to upload security of supply on the European level and solidarity was seen as necessary feature to guarantee security of supply. The vision of the

Commission aimed at defining ,solidarity as insurance mechanism'. The Commission hedged the term solidarity as a reaction to the concerns of the Member States, which regarded solidarity and responsibility as two sides of the same coin. The interpretation of solidarity as behavioural norm (,not to harm others' or ,taking others' interests into account') was hardly advocated by the Commission.

Institutionalised solidarity was only implemented in the SoS regulation of 2017 (Case 1). In the long-run, the Commission tried to get an agreement by Member States with the help of trust-building measures, such as dialogue. The Commission transformed successfully the Gas Coordination Group into a crisis response group. Thus, the GCG provided a platform to discuss sensitive issues and to exchange information in case of crisis. „In the gas sector we have really built a solid relationship where the people trust each other, they are talking the truth, they are saying what are the problems" (Interview 3, DG Energy).

But the Commission also followed a strategic move in 2014, when ENTSOG published a study on risk preparedness where it presented two scenarios of gas disruption: cooperative and non-cooperative behaviour of Member States were simulated. The Commission reframed the results of the study by replacing cooperation with solidarity. Based on this proof on the necessity of a ,solidarity mechanism', the Commission could gain support because it could illuminate the added value of putting the policy on the EU level. Hence, the Commission used the uncertain security of supply situation caused by the Russian-Ukraine conflict in order to stimulate the need of solidarity as response to the crisis (*strategic framing*).

Additionally, the Commission was aware that Member States could not block a general embracement of solidarity. The aim of the Commission was to promote the juridification of solidarity. However, the Commission remained open as to the possible implementation of solidarity by offering different options on its implementation. Most importantly, the Commission clarified that solidarity is no charity. The Commission left the concrete design of the solidarity mechanism open to the decision by the legislators by presenting different options how to apply responsibility (e.g. by requesting certain security of supply standards that each Member State had to fulfil), and that any improper advantage would be avoided by clear standards for each Member State (solidarity protected customers) and that solidarity would not be charity (compensation). The Commission understood that Member States needed to reflect on the different features of a solidarity mechanism and to agree on the rules of implementation.

The Parliament underwent a solidarity transformation after the Eastern enlargement. The majority of speeches in favour of solidarity has come from Baltic and Eastern European Member States. The Parliament not only supported the Commission in its legislative proposals on solidarity, but it was pushing for more solidarity. The request for more solidarity was mainly implemented by own-initiative reports and highlighted during debates. Solidarity was used by the Central and Eastern European MEPs mainly to support the Eastern Member States' desire to improve security of supply and create the necessary infrastructure. In general, the Parliament developed a normative perspective of solidarity. The Parliament was morally supporting solidarity by underlining solidarity as EU value and its possible role as positive narrative for EU integration. The principle of solidarity was not only called upon as particular principle of energy policy but also as basis of EU membership. When the Treaty of Lisbon came into force, the Parliament requested the application of solidarity since the Treaty obliged all Member States to act accordingly. MEPs highlighted the importance of European interests in contrast to national interests. At the same time, the Parliament did less insist on solidarity obligations (e.g. self-responsibility) but rather understood solidarity as value to help others in times of need. MEPs (again in particular from Eastern European countries and the Baltic states) emphasised also their fear that Russia would use energy as geopolitical weapon. The Parliament underlined that solidarity is a behavioural norm, which has been already early emphasised due to Nord Stream 1. For this reason, solidarity served as normative guideline on different levels within the EU: 1) to speak with one voice vis-a-vis external suppliers, 2) to support each other in crisis situations and 3) not to harm each other by pursuing national interests only. Nevertheless, this evaluation has to be treated with caution. MEPs from Eastern European Member States had a strong interest in the implementation of solidarity since this also served their ultimate interest of energy security. Therefore, those MEPs have acted as 'norm entrepreneurs' (Saurugger 2010): solidarity was demanded in a calculated political manoeuvre.

Therefore, the Parliament and the Commission supported each other, even though they used different arguments to substantiate the reasons for solidarity. The interviews confirmed the point that the Parliament was supportive – or even more ambitious — concerning the new legislation. The normative frame was powerful since it put pressure on Member States to take solidarity seriously into account.

However, the Commission and the Parliament were not the only actors responsible for the inclusion of solidarity on the political agenda. The

European Council made several references to solidarity and highlighted the need to connect *responsibility and solidarity* thus underlining the need that every Member State is self-responsible for its security of supply situation. This reflects the positions of the Member States, which were divided into supporting more regulation (solidarity) or more market (responsibility) (Interview 9, WP on Energy). Baltic and Eastern European Member States supported solidarity as moral obligation to help each other and underlined the need to speak with one voice. This became evident with Tusk's idea of an Energy Union. The other Member States, in particular Germany, the Netherlands and Scandinavian countries opposed these ideas and demanded market-based solutions. This division was further reflected in the Council discussions, which revealed that the Member States needed to clarify their understanding of solidarity. The European Council has been a general driver of solidarity, but never gave a clear order how to exactly implement solidarity. Freeriding had to be limited, but at same time solidarity should not be optional. Interviews confirmed that Member States were reluctant to embrace solidarity as long as there would be uncertainty of its scope of application. The aim was to produce clear rules for solidarity in security of supply, which each Member State had to implement, in order to avoid freeriding.

Furthermore, Member States agreed to solidarity because the need for solidarity was almost excluded due to strong preventive and emergency mechanisms. Solidarity could only be evoked as last resort. Both the Parliament and the Council have implemented the details of the Solidarity Article in the framework of informal contacts in order to achieve agreement at first reading. However, it was the Commission's careful preparation of different options on the implementation of solidarity, that paved the way for *institutionalised solidarity*. The Commission wanted to gain more competences and was definitely a driver for solidarity since it worked towards a concrete design of the solidarity mechanism which corresponded to the requests by the Member States.

The Court of Justice had a particular role since it was until 2019 very hesitant concerning the provision of a definition of solidarity although solidarity played already a certain role in other cases. The Court would have had the possibility to provide a judgment on solidarity already on the case C-226/16 concerning the consideration of protected customers. Advocate-General Mengozzi underlined the importance of solidarity as principle of EU law in general, and of energy policy in particular. It remains unclear why the Court chose to upload the principle of solidarity as legal principle when the case Poland vs. Commission was discussed.

The Court observed that solidarity permeated energy policy in general, which is why it became a legal principle in the making. However, the Court's ruling is not sufficient to provide clarity for the principle of solidarity. Further judgements are needed in order to clarify its aspects and to see if solidarity will be applied in a coherent form in different policy fields. The Court provided new impetus for European integration with this judgement and it proves that expectations of solidarity can turn into legal claims (Habermas 2014: 27). The judgement of the Court increased the impact of solidarity since solidarity is not only applicable to security of supply but to EU energy policy in general. To recall, the Court stated that „(...) *the principle of solidarity also entails a general obligation on the part of the European Union and the Member States, in the exercise of their respective competences, to take into account the interests of the other stakeholders*" (OPAL Judgement, emphasis added). The judgement might create further tension between solidarity and subsidiarity, i.e. between the common good and the individual freedom (cf. ch. 2.1.3 on subsidiarity). Art. 194(2) TFEU underlined the sovereignty of Member States to determine the choice of national energy sources. The judgement puts emphasis on the European dimension and the limits to this choice. The interpretation that the interest of other Member States must be taken into account has been a surprising development for the Member States and apparently also for the Commission. The Court proved that it has a particular role in the determination of the EU principles. The juridification of solidarity corresponds to Durkheim's argument that law is the objective crystallisation of solidarity (cf. ch. 2.1.2 on the interdependence source). A functionally differentiated society is not only connected by norms, but rights and duties are secured by law. According to the interviews, the Court was not obliged to focus its judgement on the principle of solidarity. It would have been sufficient to state that the Commission needed to assess the impact of the exemption decision on the security of supply situation of the concerned Member States. This conduct underlines the judicial activism of the court.

Solidarity was used as push button to further integration in the energy sector. The Commission has been particularly successful in the implementation of solidarity in secondary law. However, this depended on a clear vision of solidarity, which has been lacking in most cases. The reasons to include solidarity were 1) as response to the gas crises and 2) to promote policy coherence both internally and externally. The Commission presented solidarity as unavoidable policy option for an optimally functioning market and secure gas supply by using the ENTSOG study to underline the functional need for solidarity. Additionally, the Commission responded to the needs of the Member States by portraying different palatable options of solidarity, which ensured the Member States that solidarity comes with self-responsibility. But the role of the Parliament can also not be under-estimated. The Parliament used a strong normative frame on solidarity (as founding principle of the EU; as Treaty obligation), which could not be tackled by the Member States. The normative function of solidarity sufficiently pressured Member States to agree to a general insertion of solidarity. The study illuminates also that there is no meta-narrative of solidarity but that solidarity as guiding principle evolves in the discourse. Member States and the institutions struggle about the meaning and im-plications of solidarity which is difficult since solidarity covers so many different phenomena. Both causal mechanisms contribute to our under-standing why solidarity was implemented. The original cause of solidarity is more convincingly explained by functional spill-over and the normative pressure, but the supranational institutions are mainly responsible for the actual insertion of solidarity in secondary law.

5.3. The solidarity concept and further research avenues

The study has shown that solidarity has been coming slowly into existence between EU Member States. Solidarity is not only a normative appeal, but it is institutionalised on the European level and develops a legal character. These observations open up future research avenues.

First, my research focused on a specific set of similar cases, which is why the research results might be treated with caution regarding their generalisation. There has been only one of the legislative acts, which included institutionalised solidarity. Declarative solidarity has been imple-mented in all other legislation. For this reason, the assumption that self-re-sponsibility and monitoring capacities are sufficient to convince Member States to implement institutionalised solidarity must be further assessed. Additionally, the interpretation of the Court that Member States need to take into account the interests of other Member States will probably continue to cause strife between Member States. It remains to be seen how this decision will impact future legislation and eventually the behaviour of Member States. It is therefore necessary to identify other cases where institutionalised solidarity has been introduced. A comparison of those cases might reveal further reasons under which conditions Member States are willing to institutionalise solidarity. This is why the concept should be also transferred to other policy sectors. The concept of solidarity could be applicable for future research endeavours both in the same field (e.g. security of electricity supply; climate policy) and in other policy fields (migration; foreign policy; terrorism; Euro; health). Recently implemented instruments such as the Just Transition Mechanism and the temporary recovery fund *NextGenerationEU* are also promising research objects regarding the conditionality and deservingness of solidarity. A comparison between cases of institutionalised solidarity might be helpful to investigate why and under which conditions institutionalised solidarity is implemented. Furthermore, a comparison of cases, when solidarity was actually (not) applied, might provide further insights on the applicability and practical implications of solidarity mechanisms. This is relevant in order to see in how far applications differ and if the design of solidarity mechanisms determines its successful application. Additionally, solidarity might be implemented without being named. Therefore, a number of cases might exist where solidarity is actually the underlying principle.

Also, refugee and migration policies are still intensely debated at the EU level, but a solidarity approach seems out of reach. A wide-scoped rational choice approach of solidarity can be helpful in order to disentangle normative expectations and national concerns which is why it is necessary to have a closer look at how Member States perceive and experience the Schengen area. The wide-scoped RC approach focuses not only on the question how distribution is reached under fair conditions, but also how every Member State can contribute to the group's joint interest. Therefore, this approach is able to cover mechanisms of diffuse reciprocity in a heterogenous group. Nevertheless, the question of group cohesion remains significant so that Member States are willing to follow a problem-solving decision style. The group's interest to guarantee free movement in the Schengen area and to secure the external borders is less contested than to fairly distribute refugees between Member States. The strengthened support of the external border but also the increased internal security standards can be interpreted as a solidarity answer of the Member States on how to ‚protect' the joint space but demonstrate also how EU Member States externalised their internal problems. It might be helpful to consider a ‚solidarity linkage' between different issues: The protection of the Schengen area and the distribution of refugees and asylum seekers must be tackled together for a solidarity-based solution.

Second, the application of the solidarity principle, as described in the SoS regulation, is hardly imaginable. The de-facto demand for solidarity would only occur under very extreme circumstances. The security of supply situation of the EU is sufficiently strengthened to avoid such an event.

Member States have been certainly aware of this unlikelihood that solidarity would be actively demanded. Therefore, it is necessary to look also at the risk perceptions of Member States. The agreement to solidarity may not be based on a high risk perception but on the certainty that everyone is doing their utmost to reduce risks. Self-responsibility is linked to the dimension of trust. The Area of Freedom, Security and Justice represents another policy field where there is a lack of trust between Member States, as Member States are not properly applying secondary law and some Member States have deficiencies in their system of justice.

Third, energy policy – even though it is of strategic political interest and Nord Stream 2 might have stirred up the matter – is a rather technical policy field, which encloses less ethical and normative considerations than e.g. migration and refugee policies. Further cross-case comparison is necessary in order to shed light on the question which conditions influence the implementation of solidarity in secondary law – concerning both declarative and institutionalised solidarity. In particular, theoretical contributions of postfunctionalism could provide interesting insights into the solidarity relationships in different policy fields. Postfunctionalism underlines above all the exclusive effect of solidarity within societies but remains unspecific about competing solidarity relationships (Schimmelfennig and Winzen 2019: 1180). Moreover, differentiated integration might have an impact on the solidarity relationship. Different sub-groups exist in the EU, such as the Euro-Group. As consequence, Member States might equally face different competing solidarity relationships (Michailidou and Trenz 2019). Also, opt-outs might contribute to the feeling of cherry-picking, which could even signify the end of solidarity (Wessels and Wolters 2017: 94).

Fourth, further judgements will show how the principle of solidarity will be formed by the Court. However, it remains to be seen if the implications of solidarity are applicable to other questions of balancing national interests vs. the interests of other Member States. One possible solution would be to enhance the dialogue between Member States (cf. Interview 8, DG Energy). Although dialogue would not guarantee that Member States change their decision, it might be helpful to provide information and to exchange views on sensitive issues and to enhance the understanding of joint risks and vulnerabilities. In order to create horizontal solidarity, it is necessary to highlight commonalities and not the divisive elements. Both Member States and the Commission need to develop instruments how such a consideration might look like and how negative impacts might eventually be compensated.

Beyond that, further discussion on the contested term will contribute to a level playing field in terms of expectations and possible consequences. An imprecise use of solidarity might lead to misconceptions since research results are vague and the political implementation might be obscure. This is why this study contributed to raise awareness on the use of solidarity in politics and academia by providing a concept of solidarity and practical insights into the development of solidarity as a political tool.

Overall, uncertainty remains how the principle of solidarity will develop. The evolvement of solidarity as a legal principle depends on further interpretations of the Court. Clarifying judgements are needed in order to understand the scope and depth of the legal principle. Nevertheless, the principle of solidarity will have an impact on the development of political and legal decisions in the years to come. Solidarity might have been originally a political buzzword, but this study showed that it transformed into a valid principle in energy policy.

List of Literature

Aalto, Pami and Korkmaz Temel, Dicle (2014) 'European Energy Security: Natural Gas and the Integration Process', JCMS: Journal of Common Market Studies, 52(4), pp. 758–774.

ACER (2015) European Gas Target Model – review and update, Ljubljana – Slovenia: Agency for the Cooperation of Energy Regulators.

AFET (2006) Opinion Committee on Foreign Affairs of the Committee on Foreign Affairs for the Committee on Industry, Research and Energy on a European Strategy for Sustainable, Competitive and Secure Energy – Green paper (2006/2113(INI)), PE376.582. Brussels, 12.10.2006: Committee on Foreign Affairs.

Allen, Kieran and O'Boyle, Brian (2017) Durkheim: A Critical Introduction. London: Pluto Press.

Andoura, Sami (2010) 'Energy Cooperation under the Aegis of the Weimar Triangle- Springboard for a Common European Energy Policy', Friedrich Ebert Stiftung – International Policy Analysis, October 2010.

Andoura, Sami (2013) 'Energy Solidarity in Europe – From Independence to Interdependence', Notre Europe.

Andoura, Sami (2014) 'Energy solidarity: cohesive force or structural weakness?', College of Europe – Newsletter, 1.

Andreosso-O'Callaghan, Bernadette (2002) 'The Centrality of the Solidarity Concept in the Process of European Integration', An Irish Quarterly Review, 91(362), pp. 134–143.

Aoun, Marie-Claire and Rutten, Daan (2016) 'EU Security of Gas Supply: Solidarity Runs Through the Pipelines', Institut francais des Relations Internationales Clingendael International Energy Programme, pp. 1–7.

Arban, Erika (2017) Exploring the Principle of (Federal) Solidarity, Review of Constitutional Studies, Vol. 22, No. 2.

Austria (2016) Reasoned opinion on the application of the Principles of Subsidiarity and Proportionality, 7563/16. Brussels, 11.4.2016: President of the Austrian Bundesrat.

Bach, Maurizio (2018) 'Die institutionelle Dynamik Europas' in Bach, Maurizio and Hönig, Barbara (eds.), Europasoziologie – Handbuch für Wissenschaft und Studium. Baden-Baden: Nomos, pp. 57–68.

Bachtler John and Mendez Carlos (2020) 'Cohesion and the EU Budget: Is Conditionality Undermining Solidarity?' in Coman, Ramona, Amandine Crespy, and Vivien A. Schmidt, (eds.), Governance and Politics in the Post-Crisis European Union. Cambridge: Cambridge University Press.

Badanova, Ielyzaveta (2019) 'Making Sense of Solidarity in International Law-Input from the Integration of the European Gas Market', European Journal of Legal Studies, 11(2), pp. 105–142.

Barbier, Jean-Claude (2012) Les frontières de la solidarité dans l'Union européenne. In: B. Muller, J.-C.B.e.M.B. (ed.) Les solidarités à l'épreuve des crises. L'Harmattan.

Barnier, Michel, Speech (2002) Michel Barnier European Commissioner responsible for Regional Policy and Institutional Reform Presentation of the final report of the working group "defence" European Convention European Parliament Brussels, 20 December 2002: SPEECH/02/643.

Barosso, José Manuel (2010) Barroso demands solidarity on Greece. Financial Times: John Thornhill, Quentin Peel, Joshua Chaffin. Available at: https://www.ft.com/content/4da90494-35f0-11df-aa43-00144feabdc0 (Accessed: 12.02.2020).

Barroso, José Manuel (2009a) Political guidelines for the next Commission. Brussels, 3.9.2009: https://sbe.org.gr/newsletters/eflashnews/2009_21/Barroso_Political_Guidelines_2009.pdf.

Barroso, José Manuel (2009b) Statement of President Barroso on the resolution of the Ukraine-Russia Gas Dispute, Press point, SPEECH/09/12. Brussels, 20.1.2009: European Commission.

Bast, Jürgen 2014. Solidarität im europäischen Einwanderungs- und Asylrecht. In: aktualisierte Fassung eines Vortrags beim XI. Walter- Hallstein-Kolloquium an der Goethe-Universität Frankfurt, z.v.f.i.S.K.H., Solidarität als europäisches Rechtsprinzip?, Baden-Baden 2014 (ed.).

Bauböck, Rainer (2017) 'Citizenship and Collective Identities as Political Sources of Solidarity in the European Union', in Banting, K. and Kymlicka, W. (eds.) The Strains of Commitment: The Political Sources of Solidarity in Diverse Societies. Oxford: Oxford University Press.

Bauder, Harald and Juffs, Lorelle (2019) ''Solidarity' in the migration and refugee literature: analysis of a concept', Journal of Ethnic and Migration Studies, 46(1), pp. 46–65.

Baurmann, Michael (1999) 'Solidarity as a Social Norm and as a Constitutional Norm', in Bayertz, K. (ed.) Solidarity: Springer Netherlands.

Baute, Sharon, Abts, Koen and Meuleman, Bart (2019) 'Public Support for European Solidarity: Between Euroscepticism and EU Agenda Preferences?', JCMS: Journal of Common Market Studies, 57(3), pp. 533–550.

Bayertz, Kurt (1998) Solidarität: Begriff und Problem. Frankfurt am Main: Suhrkamp.

Beach, Derek and Pedersen, Rasmus Brun (2013) Process-Tracing Methods: Foundations and Guidelines. Ann Arbor: University of Michigan Press.

Beckert, Jens, Eckert, Julia, Kohli, Martin and Streeck, Wolfgang (2004) Transnationale Solidarität: Chancen und Grenzen. Frankfurt am Main: Campus Verlag.

Benson, David and Russel, Duncan (2015) 'Patterns of EU Energy Policy Outputs: Incrementalism or Punctuated Equilibrium?', West European Politics, 38(1), pp. 185–205.

Beutler, Bengt (2017) 'Solidarity in the EU: A Critique of Solidarity and of the EU', in Grimmel, A. and Giang, S.M. (eds.) Solidarity in the European Union: A Fundamental Value in Crisis. Cham: Springer International Publishing.

Bieber, Roland and Maiani, Francesco (2012) 'Sans solidarité point d'Union européenne. Regards croisés sur les crises de l'Union économique et monétaire et du Système européen commun d'asile,' Revue trimestrielle de droit européen, 2, pp. 295–328.

Bieling, Hans-Jürgen. and Lerch, Marika (2012) Theorien der europäischen Integration. Wiesbaden: Springer Fachmedien.

Biondi, Andrea, Dagilytė, Eglė and Küçük, Esin (2018) 'Introduction: European solidarity – what now?', in Biondi, A., Dagilytė, E. and Küçük, E. (eds.) Solidarity in EU Law: Legal Principle in the Making. Cheltenham: Edward Elgar Publishing Limited.

Blair, Tony (2005) Blair calls for stronger EU energy policy co-operation: Euractiv. Available at: https://www.euractiv.com/section/science-policymaking/news/blair-calls-for-stronger-eu-energy-policy-co-operation/ (Accessed: 30.09.2019).

Blanquet, Marc (2009) 'L'Union européenne en tant que système de solidarité: la notion de solidarité européenne', in Hecquard-Théron, M. (ed.) Solidarité(s) : Perspectives juridiques. Toulouse: Service des Presses de l'Université Toulouse.

Blatter, Joachim and Haverland, Markus (2014) 'Case Studies and (Causal-) Process Tracing', in Engeli, I. and Rothmayr, C. (eds.) Comparative Policy Studies. Conceptual and Methodological Challenges: Houndsmills Basingstoke: Palgrave Macmillan.

Blatter, Joachim, Langer, Phil C. and Wagemann, Claudius (2018) Qualitative Methoden in der Politikwissenschaft. Wiesbaden: VS Verlag für Sozialwissenschaften.

Bochkarev, Danila (2018) Commission's gas market proposal is an attempt to gain more control of energy policy. 6.6.2018: energypost.eu. Available at: https://energypost.eu/commissions-gas-market-proposal-is-an-attempt-to-gain-more-control-of-energy-policy/ (Accessed: 3.2.2020).

Börner, Stefanie (2014) 'Die Konstruktion transnationaler Solidarität durch EU-Sozialpolitik', in Knodt, M. and Tews, A. (eds.) Solidarität in der EU. Baden-Baden: Nomos.

Börzel, Tanja A. and Risse, Thomas (2018) From the euro to the Schengen crises: European integration theories, politicization, and identity politics, Journal of European Public Policy, 25(1), pp. 83–108.

Boudant, Joël (2010) 'La solidarité européenne entre dépendance énergétique et stratégies commerciales', in Barbato, J.-C. and Mouton, J.-D. (eds.) Vers la reconnaissance de droits fondamentaux aux États membres de l'Union européenne? Réflexions à partir des notions d'identité et de solidarité. Bruxelles: Bruylant.

Boutayeb, Chahira and Laurent, Sébastien (2011) La solidarité dans l'Union européenne: éléments constitutionnels et matériels pour une théorie de la solidarité en droit de l'Union européenne. Dalloz.

Bowen, Glenn A. (2009) 'Document Analysis as a Qualitative Research Method', Qualitative Research Journal, 9(2), pp. 27–40.

Brunkhorst, Hauke (2002) Solidarität – Von der Bürgerfreundschaft zur globalen Rechtsgenossenschaft. Frankfurt: Suhrkamp Taschenbuch.

Brutschin, Elina (2017) EU Gas Security Architecture – The Role of the Commission's Entrepreneurship. London: Palgrave Macmillan.

Bundestag (2006) Die Energieaußenpolitik der Europäischen Union. Berlin: Deutscher Bundestag – Wissenschaftliche Dienste.

Bundestag (2019) Antwort der Bundesregierung: Auswirkungen des EUGH-Urteils über die Reduzierung von OPAL-Kapazitäten, Drucksache 19/15684. Berlin, 3.12.2019: Deutscher Bundestag.

Burgess, Michael (2006) Comparative Federalism: Theory and Practice. New York: Routledge.

Burgess, Michael (2013) In Search of the Federal Spirit: New Comparative Empirical and Theoretical Perspectives. Oxford: Oxford University Press, 2012. Oxford Scholarship Online.

Buschle, Dirk and Talus, Kim (2019) 'One for All and All for One? The General Court Ruling in the OPAL Case', Oil, Gas & Energy Law Intelligence.

Calliess, Christian (1996) Subsidiaritäts- und Solidaritätsprinzip in der Europäischen Union: Vorgaben für die Anwendung von Art. 3b EGV am Beispiel der gemeinschaftlichen Wettbewerbs- und Umweltpolitik. Baden-Baden (Dissertation, Universität des Saarlandes, 1995).

Calliess, Christian (2011) 'Das Europäische Solidaritätsprinzip und die Krise des Euro – Von der Rechtsgemeinschaft zur Solidaritätsgemeinschaft?', Vortrag an der Humboldt-Universität zu Berlin, 18.01.2011 (Forum Constitutionis Europae).

Calliess, Christian and Ruffert, Matthias (2016) EUV, AEUV: das Verfassungsrecht der Europäischen Union mit Europäischer Grundrechtecharta: Kommentar. 5 Edn. München: C.H. Beck.

Cameron, Fraser (2007) The Nord Stream Gas Pipeline Project and its Strategic Implications, PE 393.274. Brussels: European Parliament.

Case (T-883/16) Judgment of the General Court (First Chamber, Extended Composition), (Internal market in natural gas — Directive 2009/73/EC — Commission Decision approving the variation of the conditions for the exemption from EU requirements of the rules governing the operation of the OPAL pipeline in regard to third party access and tariff regulation — Article 36(1) of Directive 2009/73 — Principle of energy solidarity). 10 September 2019: General Court of the European Union.

Case (C-848/19 P) Judgment of the Court (Grand Chamber), Appeal – Article 194(1) TFEU – Principle of energy solidarity – Directive 2009/73/EC – Internal market in natural gas – Article 36(1) – Decision of the European Commission on review of the exemption of the OPAL pipeline from the requirements on third-party access and tariff regulation following a request by the German regulatory authority – Action for annulment), 15 July 2021: Court of Justice of the European Union.

Checkel, Jeffrey T. (2005) 'It's the Process Stupid! Process Tracing in the Study of European and International Politics', ARENA Working Paper, 26.

Circolo, Andrea, Hamuľák, Ondrej and Lysina, Peter (2018) 'The Principle of Solidarity between voluntary commitment and legal constraint. Comments on the Judgment of the Court of Justice of the European Union in Joined Cases C-643/15 and C-647/15', Czech Yearbook of Public & Private International Law, 9, pp. 155–173.

CJEU (1973) Judgment of the Court of 7 February 1973. Commission of the European Communities v Italian Republic. Premiums for slaughtering cows. Case 39–72.: Court of Justice of the European Union.

CJEU (1988) Judgment of the Court of 20 September 1988. Kingdom of Spain v Council of the European Communities. Common organization of the market in the milk and milk products sector – Declaration that Council Regulations Nºs 1335/86 and 1343/86 are void – Reduction of the total guaranteed quantities. Case 203/86: Court of Justice of the European Union.

CJEU (2016) Action brought on 16 December 2016 — Republic of Poland v Commission (Case T-883/16). Luxembourg, 16.12.2016: General Court.

CJEU (2019) Judgment in Case T-883/16, Poland v Commission, PRESS RELEASE n° 107/19. Luxembourg, 10.9.2019: General Court of the European Union.

Closa, Carlos and Maatsch, Aleksandra (2014) 'In a Spirit of Solidarity? Justifying the European Financial Stability Facility (EFSF) in National Parliamentary Debates', JCMS: Journal of Common Market Studies, 52(4), pp. 826–842.

Collier, David and Levitsky, Steven (1997) 'Democracy with Adjectives. Conceptual Innovation in Comparative Research', World Politics, 49, pp. 430–451.

Commission (2000) Commission Decision of 16 November 2000 defining the specifications of projects of common interest identified in the sector of the trans-European energy networks by Decision No 1254/96/EC of the European Parliament and of the Council (2000/761/EC). Brussels, 16.11.2000: European Commission.

Commission (2002a) Press Release: Internal energy market: Commission proposes strengthening security of oil and gas supplies, IP/02/1288. Brussels, 11.9.2002: European Commission.

Commission (2002b) Proposal for a Directive of the European Parliament and the Council concerning measures to safeguard security of natural gas supply, COM(2002) 488 final. Brussels,11.11.2002: European Commission.

Commission (2003a) Commission Staff Working Paper, Decision of the European Parliament and of the Council laying down guidelines for trans-European energy networks and repealing Decisions No 96/391/EC and No 1229/2003/EC, Extended Impact Assessment, SEC(2003) 1369. Brussels, 10.12.2003: European Commission.

Commission (2003b) Communication: Energy Infrastructure and Security of Supply, COM(2003) 743 final. Brussels, 10.12.2003: European Commission.

Commission (2003c) Proposal for a Decision of the European Parliament and of the Council laying down guidelines for trans-European energy networks and repealing Decisions No 96/391/EC and No 1229/2003/EC, COM(2003) 742 final. Brussels, 10.12.2003: European Commission.

Commission (2003d) Report from the Commission "Better Lawmaking 2003" pursuant to Article 9 of the Protocol on the application of the principles of subsidiarity and proportionality (11th REPORT), COM(2003)770 final. Brussels, 12.12.2003: European Commission.

Commission (2003e) Trans-European Networks – 2001 Annual Report, COM(2003) 442 final. Brussels, 7.8.2003: European Commission.

Commission (2006a) COM(2006)105 final. Green Paper on a European Strategy for sustainable, competitive, and secure energy. Brussels: European Commission.

Commission (2006b) Commission Staff Working Document, Summary report on the analysis of the debate on the green paper "A European Strategy for Sustainable, Competitive and Secure Energy", SEC(2006) 1500. Brussels, 16.11.2006: European Commission.

Commission (2006c) An external energy policy to serve Europe's energy interests S160/06. Brussels: Paper from Commission/SG/HR for the European Council.

Commission (2006d) External energy relations – from principles to action, COM(2006) 590 final. Brussels: European Commission.

Commission (2006e) GREEN PAPER: A European Strategy for Sustainable, Competitive and Secure Energy, COM(2006) 105 final. Brussels, 8.3.2006: European Commission.

Commission (2007a) Commission response to text adopted in plenary, (SP(2007)5763). A6–0312/2007 / P6-TA-PROV(2007)413: European Commission.

Commission (2007b) Commission staff working document – Accompanying the legislative package on the internal market for electricity and gas – Impact Assessment, SEC(2007) 1179. Brussels, 19.9.2007: European Commission.

Commission (2007c) Communication: An Energy Policy for Europe, COM(2007) 1 final. Brussels, 10.1.2007: European Commission.

Commission (2007d) Proposal for a Directive of the European Parliament and of the Council amending Directive 2003/55/EC concerning common rules for the internal market in natural gas, COM(2007) 529 final. Brussels, 19.9.2007: European Commission.

Commission (2008a) Communication from the Commission to the European Parliament, the Council, the European Economic and Social Committee and the Committee of the Regions, Second Strategic Energy Review An EU Energy Security and Solidarity Action Plan: COM(2008) 781 final.

Commission (2008b) Communication on the Directive 2004/67/EC of 26 April 2004 concerning measures to safeguard security of natural gas supply, COM(2008) 769 final. Brussels, 13.11.2008: European Commission.

Commission (2008c) Green Paper: Towards a secure, sustainable and competitive European Energy Network, COM(2008) 782 final. Brussels, 13.11.2008: European Commission.

Commission (2008d) Second Strategic Energy Review – An EU Energy Security and Solidarity Action Plan, COM(2008) 781 final. Brussels, 13.11.2008: European Commission.

Commission (2009a) Accompanying document to the Proposal for a Regulation of the European Parliament and of the Council concerning measures to safeguard security of gas supply and repealing Directive 2004/67/EC – Impact Assessment (SEC(2009) 979 final). Brussels, 16.7.2009: European Commission.

Commission (2009b) Accompanying document to the Proposal for a Regulation of the European Parliament and of the Council concerning measures to safeguard security of gas supply and repealing Directive 2004/67/EC: The January 2009 Gas Supply Disruption to the EU: An Assessment, SEC(2009) 977 final. Brussels, 16.7.2009: European Commission.

Commission (2009c) Communication concerning the common position of the Council on the adoption of a directive of the European Parliament and of the Council repealing Directive 2003/55/EC concerning common rules for the internal market in natural gas, COM(2008) 907 final. Brussels, 12.1.2009: European Commission.

Commission (2009d) The January 2009 Gas Supply Disruption to the EU: An Assessment, SEC(2009) 977 final. Brussels, 16.7.2009.

Commission (2009e) Memo: Q&A: Greater EU coordination of measures to improve the security of gas supplies, MEMO/09/337. Brussels, 16.6.2009: European Commission.

Commission (2009f) Press Release: Gas Coordination Group: Solidarity works and the EU's gas market adapts to challenges of gas crisis, IP/09/75. Brussels, 19.1.2009: European Commission.

Commission (2009g) Proposal for a Regulation of the European Parliament and of the Council concerning measures to safeguard security of gas supply and repealing Directive 2004/67/EC, COM(2009) 363 final. Brussels, 16.7.2009: European Commission.

Commission (2010a) Energy 2020: A strategy for competitive, sustainable and secure energy, COM(2010) 639 final. Brussels, 10.11.2010: European Commission.

Commission (2010b) Energy infrastructure priorities for 2020 and beyond – A Blueprint for an integrated European energy network, COM(2010) 677 final. Brussels, 17.11.2010: European Commission.

Commission (2010c) Report on the implementation of the trans-European energy networks in the period 2007–2009, COM(2010)203 final. Brussels, 4.5.2010: European Commission.

Commission (2010d) Stock taking document; Towards a new Energy Strategy for Europe 2011–2020. Brussels, May 2010: European Commission.

Commission (2011a) Proposal for a Decision of the European Parliament and of the Council setting up an information exchange mechanism with regard to intergovernmental agreements between Member States and third countries in the field of energy, COM(2011) 540 final. Brussels, 7.9.2011: European Commission.

Commission (2011b) Proposal for a Regulation of the European Parliament and of the Council on guidelines for trans-European energy infrastructure and repealing Decision No 1364/2006/EC, COM(2011) 658 final. Brussels, 19.10.2011: European Commission.

Commission (2014a) Communication on the short term resilience of the European gas system. Preparedness for a possible disruption of supplies from the East during the fall and winter of 2014/2015, COM(2014) 654 final. Brussels, 16.10.2014: European Commission.

Commission (2014b) European Energy Security Strategy, COM(2014) 330 final. Brussels, 28.5.2014: European Commission.

Commission (2014c) Press release: Energy security: Commission puts forward comprehensive strategy to strengthen security of supply, IP/14/606. Brussels, 28.5.2014: European Commission.

Commission (2014d) Q&A on Gas Stress Tests, MEMO/14/593. Brussels, 16 October 2014: European Commission.

Commission (2014e) Report on the implementation of Regulation (EU) 994/2010 and its contribution to solidarity and preparedness for gas disruptions in the EU, SWD(2014) 325 final. Brussels, 16.10.2014: European Commission.

Commission (2015a) Consultation on the review of the Intergovernmental Agreements Decision. Brussels, 17.7.2015, https://ec.europa.eu/energy/consultations/consultation-review-intergovernmental-agreements-decision_en?Redir=1: European Commission.

Commission (2015b) A Framework Strategy for a Resilient Energy Union with a Forward-Looking Climate Change Policy, COM(2015) 80 final. Brussels, 25.2.2015: European Commission.

Commission (2015c) State of the Energy Union 2015, COM(2015) 572 final. Brussels, 18.11.2015: European Commission.

Commission (2016a) Commission Staff Working Document Impact Assessment, Accompanying the document, Proposal for a Decision of the European Parliament and of the Council on establishing an information exchange mechanism with regard to intergovernmental agreements and non-binding instruments between Member States and third countries in the field of energy and repealing Decision No 994/2012/EU, SWD(2016) 27 final. Brussels, 16.2.2016: European Commission.

Commission (2016b) Impact Assessment – Accompanying the document, Proposal for a Regulation of the European Parliament and of the Council concerning measures to safeguard security of gas supply and repealing Council Regulation 994/2010, SWD(2016) 25 final. Brussels, 16.2.2016: European Commission.

Commission (2016c) Press release: Energy Union – Commission presents energy security package, AGENDA/16/272. Brussels, 16.2.2016: European Commission.

Commission (2016d) Press Release: Towards Energy Union: The Commission presents sustainable energy security package, IP/16/307. Brussels, 16.2.2016: European Commission.

Commission (2016e) Proposal for a Decision of the European Parliament and of the Council on establishing an information exchange mechanism with regard to intergovernmental agreements and non-binding instruments between Member States and third countries in the field of energy and repealing Decision No 994/2012/EU, COM(2016) 53 final. Brussels, 16.2.2016: European Commission.

Commission (2016f) Proposal for a Regulation of the European Parliament and of the Council concerning measures to safeguard the security of gas supply and repealing Regulation (EU) No 994/2010: COM(2016) 52 final.

Commission (2017a) Nord Stream 2 – Divide et Impera Again? Avoiding a Zero-Sum Game. Brussels: European Political Strategy Centre.

Commission (2017b) Press release: Energy Union: Commission takes steps to extend common EU gas rules to import pipelines. Brussels, 8.11.2017: European Commission.

Commission (2017c) Press release: New rules to secure gas supplies in Europe bring more solidarity, IP/17/3203. Brussels, 12.9.2017: European Commission.

Commission (2017d) Energy union. Brussels. Available at: https://ec.europa.eu/ene rgy/topics/energy-strategy/energy-union_en (Accessed: 03.03.2020).

Commission (2018) Evaluation of the TEN-E Regulation and Assessing the Impacts of Alternative Policy Scenarios. Rotterdam, 27.2.2018: Trinomics B.V., Mr. Koen Rademaekers.

Commission (2019a) The Energy Union five years on: Infrastructure map of a resilient Energy Union. Brussels, April 2019: European Commission.

Commission (2019b) The Energy Union five years on: the Juncker Commission delivers on its Energy Union priority. Brussels, April 2019: European Commission.

Commission (2019c) Migration: Solidarity within the EU. Brussels, October 2019: European Commission.

Commission (2019d) Press release: Energy Union: Commission welcomes tonight's provisional political agreement to ensure that pipelines with third countries comply with EU gas rules, IP/19/1069. Brussels, 12.2.2019: European Commission.

Commission (2019e) Quarterly Report on European Gas Markets. Brussels: Market Observatory for Energy, DG Energy.

Commission (n.d.) EU Solidarity Fund: European Commission. Available at: https://ec.europa.eu/regional_policy/en/funding/solidarity-fund/#5 (Accessed: 03.02.2020).

Conclusions (2001) Presidency Conclusions European Council meeting in Laeken 14 and 15 December 2001, DOC/01/18. Laeken, 15.12.2001: European Council.

Conclusions (2006a) Brussels European Council, 15/16 June 2006, Presidency Conclusions 10633/1/06 REV 1. Brussels: European Council.

Conclusions (2006b) Brussels European Council, 23/24 March 2006, Presidency Conclusions 7775/1/06 REV 1. Brussels: European Council.

Conclusions (2007) Brussels European Council, 8/9 March 2007. Presidency Conclusions, 7224/1/07 REV 1. Brussels: European Council.

Conclusions (2008a) Brussels European Council, Council Conclusions, 14368/08 CONCL 4. Brussels, 15 and 16 October 2008: European Council.

Conclusions (2008b) Extraordinary European Council, Presidency Conclusions, 12594/2/08 REV 2. Brussels, 1.9.2008: European Council.

Conclusions (2009) Brussels European Council, Presidency Conclusions, 7880/1/09 REV 1. Brussels, 19/20 March 2009: European Council.

Conclusions (2011) European Council Conclusions, EUCO 2/1/11 REV 1. Brussels, 4.2.2011: General Secretariat of the Council.

Conclusions (2014a) European Council Conclusions, 20/21 March 2014, EUCO 7/1/14 REV 1. Brussels, 21 March 2014: European Council.

Conclusions (2014b) European Council, 26/27 June 2014, Conclusions. Brussels, 27 June 2014: European Council.

Convention (2002) Final report of Working Group VIII – Defence. Brussels: The European Convention – The Secretariat.

Costello, Rory and Thomson, Robert (2013) 'The distribution of power among EU institutions: who wins under codecision and why?', Journal of European Public Policy, 20(7), pp. 1025–1039.

Council (1977) Council Decision of 7 November 1977 on the setting of a Community target for a reduction in the consumption of primary sources of energy in the event of difficulties in the supply of crude oil and petroleum products, 77/706/EEC.

Council (2003a) 2507th Meeting of the Council (Transport/Telecommunications/Energy), 9317/03. Brussels, 14.5.2003: Council of Ministers.

Council (2003b) 2554th Council meeting – Transport, Telecommunications and Energy, 15988/03 (Presse 370). Brussels, 15.12.2003: Council of Ministers.

Council (2004) Council Directive 2004/67/EC of 26 April 2004 concerning measures to safeguard security of natural gas supply: Council Directive 2004/67/EC.

Council (2007) Press Release, 2782nd Council Meeting, Transport, Telecommunications and Energy, 6271/07 (Presse 24). Brussels, 15.2.2007: Council of the European Union.

Council (2008a) Energy Council, MEMO/08/770. Brussels, 8 December 2008.

Council (2008b) Internal Energy Market – General Approach, 9968/08. Brussels, 3.6.2008: Presidency.

Council (2008c) "Second Strategic Energy Review – An EU energy security and solidarity action plan"= Presentation and policy debate, 16345/08. Brussels, 5 December 2008: Council of the European Union.

Council (2009a) 2983rd Council meeting Transport, Telecommunications and Energy, 17165/09 (Presse 369). Brussels, 7.12.2009: Council of Ministers.

Council (2009b) Common position adopted by the Council on 9 January 2009 with a view to the adoption of a Directive of the European Parliament and of the Council concerning common rules for the internal market in natural gas and repealing Directive 2003/55/EC – Draft statement of the Council's reasons, 14540/2/08 REV 2 ADD 1. Brussels, 9.1.2009: Council of the European Union.

Council (2009c) Press Release, 2924th Council meeting, Transport, Telecommunications and Energy, Energy, 6670/09 (Presse 43). Brussels, 19.2.2009: Council of Ministers.

Council (2009d) Proposal for a Regulation of the EP and of the Council concerning measures to safeguard security of gas supply and repealing Directive 2004/67/CE – Progress report, 16000/09. Brussels, 16.11.2009: General Secretariat of the Council.

Council (2009e) Proposal for a Regulation of the European Parliament and of the Council concerning measures to safeguard security of gas supply and repealing Directive 2004/67/EC – Policy debate = Contribution from Denmark. Brussels, 16.12.2009: General Secretariat of the Council.

Council (2009f) Proposal for a Regulation of the European Parliament and of the Council concerning measures to safeguard security of gas supply and repealing Directive 2004/67/EC – Policy debate = Contribution from Greece, 17473/09 ADD 1. Brussels, 15.12.2009: General Secretariat of the Council.

Council (2009g) Proposal for a Regulation of the European Parliament and of the Council concerning measures to safeguard security of gas supply and repealing Directive 2004/67/EC – Policy debate = Contribution from Hungary, 17473/09. Brussels, 11.12.2009: General Secretariat of the Council.

Council (2010a) 3017th Council meeting Transport, Telecommunications and Energy (Telecommunications and Energy items), 10418/10, PRESSE 146. Brussels, 31.5.2010: Council of Ministers.

Council (2010b) 3035th Council meeting Competitiveness (Internal Market, Industry, Research and Space), 14426/1/10 REV 1, PRESSE 263, PR CO 23. Luxembourg, 11 – 12.10.2010: Council of Ministers.

Council (2010c) Communication from the Commission to the European Parliament, the Council, the European Economic and Social Committee and the Committee of the Regions – Energy 2020: A strategy for competitive, sustainable and secure energy, General overview of reactions by Member States, 18014/10. Brussels, 16.12.2010: General Secretariat of the Council.

Council (2010d) Proposal for a Regulation of the European Parliament and of the Council concerning measures to safeguard security of gas supply and repealing Directive 2004/67/EC – Outcome of the European Parliament's first reading, (Strasbourg, 20 to 23 September 2010), 13748/10. Brussels, 29.9.2010: General Secretariat.

Council (2010e) Proposal for a Regulation of the European Parliament and of the Council concerning measures to safeguard security of gas supply and repealing Directive 2004/67/EC – Progress report, 9817/10. Brussels, 19.5.2010: General Secretariat of the Council.

Council (2010f) Proposal for a Regulation of the European Parliament and of the Council concerning measures to safeguard security of gas supply and repealing Directive 2004/67/EC (First reading) – preparation of the final informal trialogue on 22 June, 8304/6/10 REV 6. Brussels, 4.6.2010: General Secretariat of the Council.

Council (2010g) Proposal for a Regulation of the European Parliament and of the Council concerning measures to safeguard security of gas supply and repealing Directive 2004/67/EC, 5338/10 ADD 1. Brussels, 22.1.2010: General Secretariat of the Council.

Council (2010h) Proposal for a Regulation of the European Parliament and the Council concerning measures to safeguard security of gas supply and repealing Directive 2004/67/EC (First reading) – Presidency briefing on the outcome of the informal trilogue – Analysis of the final compromise text with a view to agreement, 11136/1/10 Rev 1. Brussels, 24.6.2010: General Secretariat of the Council.

Council (2010i) Voting result, 3035th meeting of the Council of the European Union, 14877/10. Brussels, 12.10.2010: Council of Ministers.

Council (2012a) Preparation of Presidency Compromise for Informal Trilogue, 9137/12. Brussels, 3.5.2012: General Secretariat of the Council.

Council (2012b) Proposal for a Decision of the European Parliament and of the Council setting up an information exchange mechanism with regard to intergovernmental agreements between Member States and third countries in the field of energy – Preparation of the informal trilogue, 7404/12. Brussels, 16.3.2012: General Secretariat of the Council.

Council (2012c) Proposal for a Decision of the European Parliament and of the Council setting up an information exchange mechanism with regard to intergovernmental agreements between Member States and third countries in the field of energy – Provisional text of the Council compromise offer, 9653/12. Brussels, 11.5.2012: General Secretariat of the Council.

Council (2012d) Proposal for a Decision of the European Parliament and of the Council setting up an information exchange mechanism with regard to intergovernmental agreements between Member States and third countries in the field of energy (first reading) – Adoption of the legislative act (LA + S) =Statement, COMMON GUIDELINES, 13790/12 ADD 1. Brussels, 21.9.2012: General Secretariat of the Council.

Council (2012e) Proposal for a Regulation of the European Parliament and of the Council on guidelines for trans-European energy infrastructure and repealing Decision No 1364/2006/EC – Orientation debate = Contribution from the Greek delegation. Brussels, 13.2.2012: General Secretariat of the Council.

Council (2012f) Proposal for a Regulation of the European Parliament and of the Council on guidelines for trans-European energy infrastructure and repealing Decision No 1364/2006/EC, 13746/12. Brussels, 21.9.2012: General Secretariat of the Council.

Council (2013) 3188e session du Conseil de l'Union Européenne (Emploi, Politique Sociale, Santé et Consommateurs), tenue à Luxembourg le 4 octobre 2012, 14655/12 ADD 1. Brussels, 29.1.2013: Council of the European Union.

Council (2016a) Analysis of the final compromise text with a view to agreement, 13444/3/16 REV 3. Brussels, 14.12.2016: General Secretariat of the Council.

Council (2016b) Outcome of the Council Meeting, 3472nd Council meeting, Transport, Telecommunications and Energy and Transport issues, 9736/16. Luxembourg, 6/7 June 2016: Press Office, Council of Ministers.

Council (2016c) Proposal for a decision of the European Parliament and of the Council on establishing an information exchange mechanism with regard to intergovernmental agreements and non-binding instruments between Member States and third countries in the field of energy and repealing Decision No 994/2012/EU – examination of draft amendments, 12998/16. Brussels, 13.10.2016: General Secretariat of the Council.

Council (2016d) Proposal for a Decision of the European Parliament and of the Council on establishing an information exchange mechanism with regard to intergovernmental agreements and non-binding instruments between Member States and third countries in the field of energy and repealing Decision No 994/2012/EU, 6301/16. Brussels, 22.3.2016: General Secretariat of the Council.

Council (2016e) Proposal for a decision on establishing an information exchange mechanism with regard to intergovernmental agreements and non-binding instruments between Member States and third countries in the field of energy and repealing Decision No 994/2012/EU – Preparation for the second informal trilogue, 12998/2/16 REV 2. Brussels, 9.11.2016: General Secretariat of the Council.

Council (2016f) Proposal for a Regulation of the European Parliament and of the Council concerning measures to safeguard the security of gas supply and repealing Regulation (EU) No 994/2010 – Examination of Presidency compromise, 9739/16. Brussels, 9.6.2016: General Secretariat of the Council.

Council (2016g) Proposal for a Regulation of the European Parliament and of the Council concerning measures to safeguard the security of gas supply and repealing Regulation (EU) No 994/2010 – Examination of Presidency revised compromise, 9739/5/16 REV 5. Brussels, 8.12.2016: General Secretariat of the Council.

Council (2016h) Proposal for a Regulation of the European Parliament and of the Council concerning measures to safeguard the security of gas supply and repealing Regulation (EU) No 994/2010 – Policy debate, 9163/16. Brussels, 20.5.2016: European Commission.

Council (2016i) Proposal for a Regulation of the European Parliament and of the Council concerning measures to safeguard the security of gas supply and repealing Regulation (EU) No 994/2010 – Policy debate. 14226/16. Brussels, 23.11.2016: General Secretariat of the Council.

Council (2016j) Proposal for a Regulation of the European Parliament and of the Council concerning measures to safeguard the security of gas supply and repealing Regulation (EU) No 994/2010 – Presidency conclusions on the proposal for a Regulation on Security of Gas Supply, 15273/16. Brussels, 5.12.2016: General Secretariat of the Council.

Council (2016k) Transport, Telecommunications and Energy Council (Energy issues), Brussels, 6.6.2016: Press office – General Secretariat of the Council, https://www.consilium.europa.eu/media/22761/background-energy.pdf.

Council (2016l) Transport, Telecommunications and Energy Council, Public session. Brussels, 5.12.2016: Council of the European Union, https://europa.eu/!Pf9 8qu.

Council (2017a) Closer cooperation and reinforced solidarity to ensure security of gas supply, PRESS RELEASE 217/17. Brussels, 17.4.2017: Council of the EU.

Council (2017b) Information from the Presidency on the state of play, 5807/17. Brussels, 13.2.2017: General Secretariat of the Council.

Council (2017c) Proposal for a Regulation of the European Parliament and of the Council concerning measures to safeguard the security of gas supply and repealing Regulation (EU) No 994/2010 – Examination of Presidency revised compromise, 9739/6/16 REV 6. Brussels, 6.1.2017: General Secretariat of the Council.

Council (2017d) Proposal for a Regulation of the European Parliament and of the Council concerning measures to safeguard the security of gas supply and repealing Regulation (EU) No 994/2010 – Preparation of the second informal trilogue, 6345/17. Brussels, 16.2.2017: General Secretariat of the Council.

Council (2017e) Regulation of the European Parliament and of the Council concerning measures to safeguard the security of gas supply and repealing Regulation (EU) No 994/2010 – Analysis of the final compromise text with a view to agreement, 8734/17. Brussels, 5.5.2017: General Secretariat of the Council.

Court (2020) Orders of the General Court in Cases T-526/19 and T-530/19, Nord Stream 2 AG and Nord Stream AG v Parliament and Council, Press Release No 62/20, Luxembourg.

Crasnow, Sharon (2012) 'The Role of Case Study Research in Political Science: Evidence for Causal Claims', Philosophy of Science, 79(5), pp. 655–666.

Crasnow, Sharon (2017) 'Process tracing in political science: What's the story?', Studies in History and Philosophy of Science Part A, 62, pp. 6–13.

Crisan, Adina and Kuhn, Maximilian (2017) 'The Energy Network: Infrastructure as the Hardware of the Energy Union', in Andersen, S.S., Goldthau, A. and Sitter, N. (eds.) Energy Union Europe's New Liberal Mercantilism?: Vol. International Political Economy Series. 2nd ed. 2017. Ed: Springer ebooks.

Cyr, Hugo (2014) 'Autonomy, subsidiarity, solidarity: Foundations of cooperative federalism', Constitutional Forum, 23(4), pp. 20-40.

De Búrca, Gráinne (2005) 'Rethinking law in neofunctionalist theory', Journal of European Public Policy, 12(2), pp. 310–326.

De Jong, Jacques, Glachant, Jean-Michel, Hafner, Manfred, Ahner, Nicole and Tagliapietra, Simone (2012) 'A new EU gas security of supply architecture?', European Energy Journal, 2(3), pp. 32–40.

De Micco, Pasquale (2014) A cold winter to come? The EU seeks alternatives to Russian gas. European Parliament study, Brussels.

De Witte, Floris (2012) 'Transnational Solidarity and the Mediation of Conflicts of Justice in Europe', European Law Journal, 18(5), pp. 694–710.

Decision (No 1364/2006/EC) Decision No 1364/2006/EC of the European Parliament and of the Council of 6 September 2006 laying down guidelines for trans-European energy networks and repealing Decision 96/391/EC and Decision No 1229/2003/EC. 22.9.2006: Official Journal of the European Union.

Delors, Jacques (1995) Biographie: Jacques Delors: Toute l'Europe. Available at: https://www.touteleurope.eu/actualite/biographie-jacques-delors.html (Accessed: 05.03.2020).

Denninger, Erhard (2009) 'Solidarität als Verfassungsprinzip- Ideengeschichtlicher Hintergrund und moderne Deutungsversuche', Kritische Vierteljahresschrift für Gesetzgebung und Rechtswissenschaft, 92(1), pp. 20–30.

Detterbeck, Klaus (2011) ‚Idee und Theorie des Föderalismus‘, in Detterbeck, Klaus, Renzsch, Wolfgang and Schieren, Stefan (eds.), Föderalismus in Deutschland, München: Oldenbourg Wissenschaftsverlag, 2011, pp. 31–51.

Devuyst, Youri (2000) 'The European Unions Constitutional Order – Between Community Method and Ad Hoc Compromise', Berkeley Journal of International Law, 18(1), pp. 1–52.

Dictionary, Oxford English (n.d.) Solidarity. Available at: https://www.oed.com/vie w/Entry/184237?Redirectedfrom=solidarity#eid (Accessed: 26.02.2019).

Díez Medrano, Juan, Ciornei, Irina and Apaydin, Fulya (2019) 'Explaining Supranational Solidarity', Everyday Europe. Social transnationalism in an unsettled continent: Policy Press.

Directive (2004/67/EC) COUNCIL DIRECTIVE 2004/67/EC of 26 April 2004 concerning measures to safeguard security of natural gas supply. Brussels: Official Journal of the European Union.

Directive (2009/72/EC) Directive 2009/72/EC of the European Parliament and of the Council of 13 July 2009 concerning common rules for the internal market in electricity and repealing Directive 2003/54/EC (Text with EEA relevance). Official Journal of the European Union, L 211/55.

Domurath, Irina (2012) 'The Three Dimensions of Solidarity in the EU Legal Order: Limits of the Judicial and Legal Approach', Journal of European Integration, pp. 17.

Druckman, James N. and Lupia, Arthur (2000) 'Preference Formation', Annual Reviews Political Science, 3, pp. 1–24.

Duden (n.d.) Solidarität. Available at: https://www.duden.de/node/167951/revision /167987 (Accessed: 26.02.2019).

Durkheim, É. (1964) The Division of Labor in Society. Translated by: Simpson, G.: Free Press of Glencoe.

Dziedzic, Lukasz (2019) Einige Reflexionen zum Begriff der Solidarität in der Europäischen Union. Solidaritäts!?-Debatte: Theorieblog. Available at: https://w ww.theorieblog.de/index.php/das-team/ (Accessed: 05.10.2019).

ECON (2006) OPINION of the Committee on Economic and Monetary Affairs for the Committee on Industry, Research and Energy on a European strategy for sustainable, competitive and secure energy – Green paper (2006/2113(INI)), PE376.670. Brussels, 3.10.2006: Committee on Economic and Monetary Affairs.

EEAS (2016) Shared Vision, Common Action: A Stronger Europe. A Global Strategy for the European Union's Foreign and Security Policy. Brussels, June 2016: European External Action Service.

Ehricke, Ulrich and Hackländer, Daniel (2008) 'Europäische Energiepolitik auf der Grundlage der neuen Bestimmungen des Vertrags von Lissabon', zeus, 2008(4), pp. 579–600.

Eising, Rainer (2006) 'Europäisierung und Integration. Konzepte in der EU-Forschung', in Jachtenfuchs, M. and Kohler-Koch, B. (eds.) Europäische Integration. 2 ed. Wiesbaden: Springer VS.

Energy Community, Secretariat (2018) The State of Gas Market Integration in the Energy Community, Sofia: Energy Community.

Engler, Marcus (2016) Zur Entstehung europäischer Solidarität: Eine soziologische Analyse der Gewerkschaften bei Airbus im Konflikt. Wiesbaden: Springer VS.

ENTSOG (2014) Annual Report 2014: Securing Europe's energy future – implementing the internal market for gas, Brussels.

ENTSOG (2017) Gas Regional Investment Plan, Baltic Energy Market Interconnection Plan, Main Report, Brussels.

Euractiv.com (2010) Oettinger defends European vision on energ. 15.1.2010. Available at: https://www.euractiv.com/section/eu-priorities-2020/news/oettinger-defe nds-european-vision-on-energy/ (Accessed: 03.02.2019).

Federico, Veronica and Lahusen, Christian 'Solidarity as a Public Virtue?: Law and Public Policies in the European Union'. Transnational Perspectives on Transformations. Baden-Baden: Nomos.

Fernandes, Sofia and Rubio, Eulalia (2012) Solidarity within the Eurozone: how much, what for, for how long?: Notre Europe.

Ferreira-Pereira, Laura C. and Groom, John (2010) ''Mutual solidarity' within the EU common foreign and security policy: What is the name of the game?', International Politics, 47(6), pp. 596–616.

Fischer, Severin (2009) 'Energie- und Klimapolitik im Vertrag von Lissabon- Legitimationserweiterung für wachsende Herausforderungen'.

Fischer, Severin (2017a) Die Energiewende und Europa – Europäisierungsprozesse in der deutschen Energie- und Klimapolitik. Wiesbaden: Springer.

Fischer, Severin (2017b) 'Lost in Regulation: The EU and Nord Stream 2', Policy Perspectives, Vol. 5/5.

Fleming, Ruven (2019) 'A legal perspective on gas solidarity', Energy Policy, 124, pp. 102–110.

France (2008) French Presidency of the Council of the European Union. Work Programme, 1 July – 31 December 2008, Europe taking action to meet today's challenges.: French Government.

Garlick, Madeline (2014) 'Strengthening refugee protection and meeting challenges: The European Union's next steps on asylum', Policy Brief Series, (5), pp. 1–11.

Gazprom (n.d.) Nord Stream: Gazprom.eu. Available at: https://www.gazprom.com/projects/nord-stream/ (Accessed: 29.8.2020).

Geden, Oliver (2009) 'Wie solidarisch ist Europa?', Berliner Republik, 3, pp. 15–18.

Gelissen, John (2000) 'Popular support for institutionalised solidarity: a comparison between European welfare states', International Journal of Social Welfare, 9: 285–300.

George, Alexander L. and Bennett, Andrew (2005) Case Studies and Theory Development in the Social Sciences. Cambridge, MA: MIT Press.

Gerhards, Jürgen, Lengfeld, Holger, Ignácz, Zsófia, Kley, Florian K and Priem, Maximilian (2020) European Solidarity in Times of Crisis. London: Routledge.

Gerring, John (1999) 'What Makes a Concept Good? A Criterial Framework for Understanding Concept Formation in the Social Sciences', Polity, 31(3), pp. 357–393.

Gerring, John (2004) 'What Is a Case Study and What Is It Good for?', The American Political Science Review, 98(2), pp. 341–354.

Gerring, John (2006) Case Study Research – Principle and Practice, Cambridge University Press.

Giuli, Marco (2016) 'The energy security package: significant overhaul or business as usual?', EPC Commentary, 24 February 2016.

Goertz, Gary (2006) Social Science Concepts: A User's Guide. Princeton/Oxford: Princeton University Press.

Goldthau, Andreas (2016) 'Assessing Nord Stream 2- regulation, geopolitics & energy security in the EU, Central Eastern Europe & the UK', Department of War Studies & King's Russia Institute.

Gotev, Georgi (2019a) Nord Stream 2 takes unusual legal step against the Commission. Available at: https://www.euractiv.com/section/energy/news/nord-stream-2-takes-unusual-legal-step-against-the-commission/ (Accessed: 04.04.2020).

Gotev, Georgi (2019b) Russia and Ukraine finalise gas deal just ahead of New Year deadline: euractiv.com. Available at: https://www.euractiv.com/section/energy/news/russia-and-ukraine-finalise-gas-deal-just-ahead-of-new-year-deadline/ (Accessed: 26 May 2020).

Götz, Roland (2005) 'Die Ostseegaspipeline: Instrument der Versorgungssicherheit oder politisches Druckmittel?', SWP-Aktuell 2005/A 41, September 2005.

Greer, Scott L. (2006) 'Uninvited Europeanization: neofunctionalism and the EU in health policy', Journal of European Public Policy, 13(1), pp. 134–152.

Greer, Scott L. and Löblová, Olga (2017) 'European integration in the era of permissive dissensus: Neofunctionalism and agenda-setting in European health technology assessment and communicable disease control', Comparative European Politics, 15(3), pp. 394–413.

Grimmel, Andreas (2020) '"Le Grand absent Européen": solidarity in the politics of European integration', Acta Politica.

Große Kracht, Hermann-Josef (2017) Solidarität und Solidarismus – Postliberale Suchbewegungen zur normativen Selbstverständigung moderner Gesellschaften. Edition Politik Bielefeld: transcript.

Grybauskaitė, Dalia 2013. European energy policy – towards greater solidarity. Brussels: European Policy Centre.

Gschwend, Thomas and Schimmelfennig, Frank (2007) Forschungsdesign in der Politikwissenschaft: Probleme – Strategien – Anwendungen. Frankfurt am Main: Campus Verlag.

Haas, Ernst B. (1958) The Uniting of Europe: Political, Social, and Economic Forces, 1950–1957. Stanford University Press.

Haas, Ernst B. (1961) 'International Integration: The European and the Universal Process', International Organization, 15(3).

Haas, Ernst B. (1976) 'Turbulent fields and the theory of regional integration', International Organization, 30(2), pp. 173–212.

Habermas, Jürgen (2013) 'Democracy, Solidarity and the European Crisis', in Grozelier, A.-M., Hacker, B.r., Kowalsky, W., Machnig, J., Meyer, H. and Unger, B. (eds.) Roadmap to a Social Europe: Social Europe Ltd.

Habermas, Jürgen (2014) 'Im Sog der Technokratie- Ein Plädoyer für Europäische Solidarität', University of Brasilia Law Journal, 1(2), pp. 11–32.

Haghighi, Sanam S. (2008) 'Energy security and the division of competences between the European Community and its member states', European Law Journal, 14(4), pp. 461–482.

Hamer, Jens (2015) 'Rn. 10', in von der Groeben, H., Schwarze, J. and Hatje, A. (eds.) Europäisches Unionsrecht: Vertrag über die Europäische Union – Vertrag über die Arbeitsweise der Europäischen Union – Charta der Grundrechte der Europäischen Union. Baden-Baden: Nomos.

Haroche, Pierre (2020) 'Supranationalism strikes back: a neofunctionalist account of the European Defence Fund', Journal of European Public Policy, 27(6), pp. 853–872.

Härtel, Ines (2012) § 82 Kohäsion durch föderale Selbstbindung – Gemeinwohl und die Rechtsprinzipien Loyalität, Solidarität und Subsidiarität in der Europäischen Union. Handbuch Förderalismus – Föderalismus als demokratische Rechtsordnung und Rechtskultur in Deutschland, Europa und der Welt Berlin Heidelberg: Springer Verlag.

Härtel, Ines (2014) Solidität, Austerität, Solidarität: Staatsverschuldung und die (verfassungs-)rechtliche Verankerung von Schuldenbremsen im föderalen Mehrebenensystem (USA und Deutschland). Tübingen: Eberhard-Karls-Uni Tüb. Europ. Zentrum f. Föderalismusforsch.

Hartleb, Florian (2011) 'Wie entsteht ein gutes politikwissenschaftliches Konzept?', Zeitschrift für Politikberatung (ZPB), 4(3), pp. 109–118.

Hartwig, Ines and Nicolaides, Phedon (2003) 'Elusive Solidarity in an Enlarged European Union', Eipascope, 2003(3), pp. 19–25.

Haversath, Peter (2012) 'Solidarität im Recht. Gegenseitige Verbundenheit als Grund und Grenze hoheitlichen Handelns', Berliner Online-Beiträge zum Europarecht, 76.

Hayward, Jack (1959) 'Solidarity: The Social History of an Idea in Nineteenth Century France', International Review of Social History, 4(2), pp. 261–284.

Hayward, Jack and Wurzel, Rüdiger (2012) European Disunion: Between Sovereignty and Solidarity. London: Palgrave Macmillan UK.

Hechter, Michael (1988) Principles of Group Solidarity. California Series on Social Choice and Political Economy: University of California Press.

Hechter, Michael (1990) 'The Attainment of Solidarity in Intentional Communities', Rationality and Society, 2(2), pp. 142–155.

Heinkelmann-Wild, Tim and Zangl, Bernhard (2019) 'Multilevel blame games: Blame-shifting in the European Union', Governance, pp. 1–17.

Héritier, Adrienne (2017) 'Conclusion: European Governance in a Changing World: Interests, Institutions, and Policy-Making', International Journal of Public Administration, 40(14), pp. 1250–1260.

Hermes, Georg (2014) 'Die Solidarklausel in der europäischen Energiepolitik', in Kadelbach, S. (ed.) Solidarität als Europäisches Rechtsprinzip? Schriften zur Europäischen Integration und Internationalen Wirtschaftsordnung. 1 ed. Baden-Baden: Nomos.

Hilf, Meinhard and Schorkopf, Frank (2019) 'EUV Art. 2 Grundlegende Werte', in Grabitz, E., Hilf, M. and Nettesheim, M. (eds.) Das Recht der Europäischen Union. München: C.H. Beck.

Hilpold, Peter (2007) 'Solidarität als Rechtsprinzip – völkerrechtliche, europarechtliche und staatsrechtliche Betrachtungen', 55. Jahrbuch des öffentlichen Rechts, pp. 195–214.

Hilpold, Peter (2015) 'Understanding solidarity within EU law: An analysis of the 'islands of solidarity' with particular regard to Monetary Union', Yearbook of European Law.

Hix, Simon and Høyland, Bjørn (2013) 'Empowerment of the European Parliament', Annual Review of Political Science, 16(1), pp. 171–189.

Holesch, Adam (2021) 'Measuring solidarity: towards a survey question on fiscal solidarity in the European Union'. Acta Polit 56, pp. 376–394.

Hondrich, Karl and Koch-Arzberger, Claudia (1992) Solidarität in der modernen Gesellschaft. Frankfurt am Main: Fischer Taschenbuch.

Hooghe, Liesbet and Marks, Gary (2019) 'Grand theories of European integration in the twenty-first century', Journal of European Public Policy, 26(8), pp. 1113–1133.

House of Commons, Ministers (2008): House of Commons, European Scrutiny Committee.

Howarth, David and Roos, Mechthild (2017) 'Pushing the Boundaries New Research on the Activism of EU Supranational Institutions', Journal of Contemporary European Research, 13(2), pp. 18.

IEA (2006) Natural Gas Market Review 2006: Towards a Global Gas Market, Paris: OECD/IEA.

Immerfall, Stefan (2016) 'Mehr Solidarität durch „Mehr Europa"?', in Aschauer, W., Donat, E. and Hofmann, J. (eds.) Solidaritätsbrüche in Europa: Konzeptuelle Überlegungen und empirische Befunde. Wiesbaden: Springer VS, pp. 49–71.

Jachtenfuchs, Markus and Kasack, Christiane (2017) Balancing sub-unit autonomy and collective problem-solving by varying exit and voice. An analytical framework, Journal of European Public Policy, 24(4), pp. 598–614.

Jacqué, Jean-Paul (2015) 'Rn. 1–18', in von der Groeben, H., Schwarze, J. and Hatje, A. (eds.) Europäisches Unionsrecht: Vertrag über die Europäische Union – Vertrag über die Arbeitsweise der Europäischen Union – Charta der Grundrechte der Europäischen Union. Baden-Baden: Nomos.

Jegen, Maya (2014) 'Energy policy in the European Union: the power and limits of discourse', Les Cahiers Européens de Sciences Po, 2014/02.

Juncker, Jean-Claude (2016) State of the Union 2016. Brussels, 14.9.2016: European Commission.

Juncker, Jean-Claude (2017) "Avec une vue sur l'extérieur" – Discours du Président Juncker auprès du European University Institute à l'occasion de la State of the Union conference: Building a people's Europe, Florence.

Kadelbach, Stefan 'Solidarität als Europäisches Rechtsprinzip?'. Schriften zur Europäischen Integration und Internationalen Wirtschaftsordnung. Baden-Baden: Nomos.

Kaiser, André (2012) ‚§ 6 Politiktheoretische Zugänge zum Föderalismus'. In: Härtel, Ines (eds) Handbuch Föderalismus – Föderalismus als demokratische Rechtsordnung und Rechtskultur in Deutschland, Europa und der Welt. Springer, Berlin, Heidelberg.

Kannellakis, Marinos, Martinopoulos, Georgios and Zachariadis, Theodoros (2013) ‘European energy policy – A review', Energy Policy, 62, pp. 1020–1030.

Kapeller, Jakob and Wolkenstein, Fabio (2013) 'The grounds of solidarity', European Journal of Social Theory, 16(4), pp. 476–491.

Karagiannis, Nathalie (2007) 'Solidarity within Europe/Solidarity without Europe', European Societies, 9(1), pp. 3–21.

Keating, Michael (2009) 'Social citizenship, solidarity and welfare in regionalized and plurinational states', Citizenship Studies, 13(5), pp. 501–513.

Keating, Michael (2017) Europe as a multilevel federation, Journal of European Public Policy, 24:4, 615–632.

Kellermann, Florian (2019) EUGH-Urteil zu Gaspipeline Opal: Niederlage für Gazprom: Deutschlandfunk. Available at: https://www.deutschlandfunk.de/e ugh-urteil-zu-gaspipeline-opal-niederlage-fuer-gazprom.1773.de.html?Dram:artic le_id=458505 (Accessed: 15.10.2019).

Keohane, Robert O. (1986) 'Reciprocity in International Relations', International Organization, 40(1), pp. 1–27.

Keukeleire, Stephan and Delreux, Tom (2014) The Foreign Policy of the European Union. Palgrave Macmillan UK.

Kiljunen, Kimmo (2004) 'EU Constitution in the making', Centre for European Policy Studies.

Kim, Sunhyuk and Schattle, Hans (2012) 'Solidarity as a unifying idea in building an East Asian community: Toward an ethos of collective responsibility', Pacific Review, 25(4), pp. 473–494.

Kingdon, John W. (1995) Agendas, Alternatives, and Public Policies. New York: Longman.

Klamert, Marcus (2014) 'Solidarität als Rechtsprinzip der Europäischen Union', in Knodt, M. and Tews, A. (eds.) Solidarität in der EU. Baden-Baden: Nomos.

Kleger, Heinz and Mehlhausen, Thomas (2013) 'Unstrittig und doch umstritten – europäische Solidarität in der Eurokrise', Politische Vierteljahresschrift, 54(1), pp. 50–74.

Kleider, Hanna and Stoeckel, Florian (2019) 'The politics of international redistribution: Explaining public support for fiscal transfers in the EU', European Journal of Political Research, 58(1), pp. 4–29.

Kneuer, Marianne (2017) Im Kern solidarisch -Politik auf dem Prüfstand, in: Horster, D. and Martinsen, F. (eds.), Welches Europa wollen wir? Solidarität in der Politik, Weilerswist: 12–27.

Knodt, Michèle and Tews, Anne (2014) Solidarität in der EU. Baden-Baden: Nomos.

Knodt, Michèle and Tews, Anne (2016) Boundaries of European Solidarity – Lessons from Migration and Energy Policy, Mainz: Johannes Gutenberg Universität Mainz (2193–6684, 13).

Knodt, Michèle and Tews, Anne (2017) 'European Solidarity and Its Limits: Insights from Current Political Challenges', in Grimmel, A. and Giang, S.M. (eds.) Solidarity in the European Union: A Fundamental Value in Crisis. Cham: Springer International Publishing.

Kocak, Konur Alp and De Micco, Pasquale (2016) 'The quest for natural gas pipelines: EU and Eastern Partner energy policies: Security versus transit benefits', EPRS | European Parliamentary Research Service and Directorate-General for External Policies.

Koeck, Heribert Franz (2019) 'Solidarity in the European Union', La Albolafia: Revista de Humanidades y Cultura, 16.02.2019, pp. 85–92.

Konstadinides, Theodore (2013) 'Civil Protection Cooperation in EU Law: Is There Room for Solidarity to Wriggle Past?', European Law Journal, 19(2), pp. 267–282.

Kontochristou, Maria and Mascha, Evi (2014) 'The Euro Crisis and the Question of Solidarity in the European Union: Disclosures and Manifestations in the European Press', Review of European Studies, 6(2).

Kotowski, Christoph (2009) 'Revolution: untangling alternative meanings', in Collier, D. and Gerring, J. (eds.) Concepts and Method in Social Science: The Tradition of Giovanni Sartori: Routledge.

Kotzur, Markus (2017) 'Solidarity as a Legal Concept', in Grimmel, A. and Giang, S.M. (eds.) Solidarity in the European Union: A Fundamental Value in Crisis. Heidelberg: Springer.

Kraxberger, Sabine 2010. Solidaritätskonzepte in der Soziologie. Hallstatt: Momentum 10: Solidarität.

Kreppel, Amie and Oztas, Buket (2017) 'Leading the Band or Just Playing the Tune? Reassessing the Agenda-Setting Powers of the European Commission', Comparative Political Studies, 50(8), pp. 1118–1150.

Kreppel, Amie and Webb, Michael (2019) 'European Parliament resolutions—effective agenda setting or whistling into the wind?', Journal of European Integration, 41(3), pp. 383–404.

Kuhn, Theresa, and Nicoli, Francesco (2020) 'Collective Identities and the Integration of Core State Powers: Introduction to the Special Issue', JCMS: Journal of Common Market Studies, 58, pp. 3- 20.

Küçük, Esin (2016) 'Soliarity in EU Law: An Elusive Political Statement or a Legal Principle with Substance?', Maastricht journal of European and comparative law, 23(6), pp. 965–983.

Lahusen, Christian and Grasso, Maria (2018) 'Solidarity in Europe–European Solidarity: An Introduction', pp. 1–18.

Lais, Martina (2007) Das Solidaritätsprinzip im europäischen Verfassungsverbund. Schriften des Europa-Instituts der Universität des Saarlandes – Rechtswissenschaft, Europa-Institut Sektion Rechtswissenschaft Baden-Baden: Nomos.

Lang, Kai-Olaf and Westphal, Kirsten (2017) 'Nord Stream 2 – A Political and Economic Contextualisation', SWP Research Paper, pp. 1–39.

Langford, Lillian M. (2013) 'The Other Euro Crisis- Rights Violations under the Common European Asylum System and the Unraveling of EU Solidarity', Harvard Human Rights Journal, 26, pp. 217–264.

Larousse (n.d.) Solidarité. Available at: https://www.larousse.fr/dictionnaires/francais/solidarité/73312?Q=solidarité#72484 (Accessed: 26.02.2019).

Lauth, Hans-Joachim, Pickel, Gert and Pickel, Susanne (2015) Methoden der vergleichenden Politikwissenschaft: Eine Einführung. Wiesbaden: VS Verlag für Sozialwissenschaften.

Leonard, Mark and Shapiro, Jeremy (2019) 'Strategic sovereignty: How Europe can regain the capacity to act', European Council on Foreign Relations.

Liebsch, Burkhard (2007) 'Originäre Solidarisierung versus Pseudo-Solidität. Kritische Anmerkungen zur aktuellen Theorie-Diskussion um Solidarität', Jahrbuch für Christliche Sozialwissenschaften, 48, pp. 143–180.

Lindberg, Leon N. (1963) The Political Dynamics of European Economic Integration. Stanford University Press.

Lindberg, Leon N. and Scheingold, Stuart A. (1970) Europe's Would-be Polity: Patterns of Change in the European Community. Prentice-Hall.

Lippert, Barbara, Ondarza, Nicolai von and Perthes, Volker (2019) 'European Strategic Autonomy – Actors, Issues, Conflicts of Interests', SWP Research Paper, 4 (March 2019).

Lithuania (2015) Reply from Lithuania to the Public consultation on the Intergovernmental Agreements (IGAs) Decision. 22.10.2015: European Commission.

Loh, Wulf and Skupien, Stefan (2016) 'Die EU als Solidargemeinschaft', Leviathan: Berliner Zeitschrift für Sozialwissenschaft, 44(4), pp. 578–603.

Łoskot-Strachota, Agata (2014) 'Central European problems with Russian gas supplies', Centre for Eastern Studies, Analyses, 17.9.2014.

Łoskot-Strachota, Agata and Kardaś, Szymon (2019) 'Gazprom's interests hit by CJEU judgment on OPAL pipeline', OSW COMMENTARY.

Mahoney, James (2015) 'Process Tracing and Historical Explanation', Security Studies, 24(2), pp. 200–218.

Maichel, Gert (2005) 'Das Energiekapitel in der Europäischen Verfassung – mehr Integration oder mehr Zentralismus für die leitungsgebundene Energiewirtschaft Europas?', in Hendler, R., Ibler, M. and Soria, J.M. (eds.) "Für Sicherheit, für Europa". Festschrift für Volkmar Götz zum 70. Geburtstag. Göttingen: Vandenhoeck & Ruprecht.

Mair, Peter (2014) On Parties, Party Systems and Democracy: Selected Writings of Peter Mair. ECPR Press.

Maltby, Tomas (2013) 'European Union energy policy integration: A case of European Commission policy entrepreneurship and increasing supranationalism', Energy Policy, 55(100), pp. 435–444.

Mandil, Claude (2009) 'Mandil: Energy solidarity 'still just words'', Euractiv.

March, James G. and Olsen, Johan P. (1989) Rediscovering Institutions: The Organizational Basis of Politics. New York: Free Press.

Marcinkiewicz, Kazimierz (2006) 'Europe's energy musketeers must stand together', Financial Times.

Martens, Stephan (2008) 'Europa, eine Schicksalsgemeinschaft?', in Koopmann, M. and Martens, S. (eds.) Das kommende Europa – Deutsche und französische Betrachtungen zur Zukunft der Europäischen Union, Baden-Baden: Nomos, pp. 39–53.

Mau, Steffen (2008) 'Europäische Solidaritäten', Aus Politik und Zeitgeschichte. Available at: http://www.bpb.de/apuz/31218/europaeische-solidaritaeten (Accessed: 08.06.2020).

Mayring, Philipp (2010) 'Qualitative Inhaltsanalyse', in Mey, G. and Mruck, K. (eds.) Handbuch Qualitative Forschung in der Psychologie. Wiesbaden: VS Verlag für Sozialwissenschaften, pp. 601–613.

Merkel, Angela (2020) Regierungserklärung von Bundeskanzlerin Merkel. Berlin. Available at: https://www.bundeskanzlerin.de/bkin-de/aktuelles/regierungserkla erung-von-bundeskanzlerin-merkel-1762594 (Accessed: 19.06.2020).

Metz, Karl H. (1999) 'Solidarity and History. Institutions and Social Concepts of Solidarity in 19th Century Western Europe', in Bayertz, K. (ed.) Solidarity: Vol. 5. Dordrecht: Springer.

Michailidou, Asimina and Trenz, Hans-Jörg (2019) 'European Solidarity in Times of Crisis - Towards differentiated integration', in: Bátora, J. and Fossum, J.E. (eds.) Towards a Segmented European Political Order: The European Union's Post-Crises Conundrum (1st ed.), Routledge.

Miller, Bernhard (2007) 'Making Measures Capture Concepts: Tools for Securing Correspondence between Theoretical Ideas and Observations', in Gschwend, T. and Schimmelfennig, F. (eds.) Research Design in Political Science: How to Practice what they Preach: Palgrave Macmillan UK.

Miller, David (2017) 'Solidarity and Its Sources', in Banting, K. and Kymlicka, W. (eds.) The Strains of Commitment: The Political Sources of Solidarity in Diverse Societies. Oxford: Oxford University Press, pp. 61–79.

Müller, Andreas Th. (2010) 'Solidarität als Rechtsbegriff im Europarecht', in Sedmak, C. (ed.) Solidarität: Vom Wert der Gemeinschaft. Darmstadt: wbg Academic.

Müller, Jan-Werner. and Scheppele, Kim Lane (2008) 'Constitutional patriotism: An introduction', International Journal of Constitutional Law, 6(1), pp. 67–71.

Myrdal, Sara and Rhinard, Mark (2010) 'The European Union's Solidarity Clause: Empty Letter or Effective Tool? An Analysis of Article 222 of the Treaty on the Functioning of the European Union', Occasional UI Papers, Swedish Institute of International Affairs.

Natorski, Michal and Herranz Surrallés, Anna (2008) 'Securitizing Moves To Nowhere? The Framing of the European Union Energy Policy', Journal of Contemporary European Research, 4(2), pp. 71–89.

Nettesheim, Martin (2018) 'Überdehnt der EuGH den Grundsatz gegenseitigen Vertrauens?', EUZ – Zeitschrift für Europarecht, 20(1), pp. 4–21.

Nettesheim, Martin (2020) 'Konzeptionen und Dimensionen von Solidarität im Recht der Europäischen Union', in Becker, P. and Lippert, B. (eds.) Handbuch Europäische Union. Berlin: Springer.

Nicoli, Francesco (2019) 'Crises, Path Dependency, and the Five Trilemmas of European Integration: Seventy Years of 'Failing Forward' From the Common Market to the European Fiscal Union', Amsterdam Centre for European Studies, Research Paper No. 2019/05.

Nicoli, Francesco, Kuhn, Theresa, and Burgoon, Brian (2020) 'Collective Identities, European Solidarity: Identification Patterns and Preferences for European Social Insurance', JCMS: Journal of Common Market Studies, 58, pp. 76-95.

Niemann, Arne (2006) 'Explaining Decisions in the European Union', Explaining Decisions in the European Union. Cambridge: Cambridge University Press.

Niemann, Arne and Ioannou, Demosthenes (2015) 'European economic integration in times of crisis: a case of neofunctionalism?', Journal of European Public Policy, 22(2), pp. 196–218.

Niemann, Arne and Schmitter, Philippe C. (2009) 'Neofunctionalism', in Wiener, A. and Diez, T. (eds.) European Integration Theory. Oxford: Oxford University Press.

Niemann, Arne and Speyer, Johanna (2018) 'A Neofunctionalist Perspective on the 'European Refugee Crisis': The Case of the European Border and Coast Guard', JCMS: Journal of Common Market Studies, 56(1), pp. 23–43.

Obradovic, Daniela (2017) Cases C-643 and C-647/15: Enforcing solidarity in EU migration policy: European Law Blog: News and Comments on EU Law. Available at: https://europeanlawblog.eu/2017/10/02/cases-c-643-and-c-64715-enforcing-solidarity-in-eu-migration-policy/ (Accessed: 25.02.2018).

Oettinger, Günther (2013) Answer given by Mr Oettinger on behalf of the Commission, (2014/C 197/01). Brussels, 6.11.2013.

Oettinger, Günther (2014) Speech: Is delivery of the Internal Energy Market on time? SPEECH/14/476. Brussels, 18.6.2014: European Commission.

Øhrgaard, Jakob C. (1997) ''Less than Supranational, More than Intergovernmental': European Political Cooperation and the Dynamics of Intergovernmental Integration', Millennium, 26(1), pp. 1–29.

Ondarza, Nicolai von, Rudloff, Bettina and Tokarski., Pawel (2020) 'Corona-Krise: Italien braucht jetzt europäische Solidarität', SWP: Kurz gesagt.

Ottmann, Juliane (2008) 'The Concept of Solidarity in National and European Law: The Welfare State and the European Social Model', International Constitutional Law, 36(48), pp. 36–48.

Parliament (2003) Report on the proposal for a directive of the European Parliament and the Council concerning measures to safeguard security of natural gas supply (COM (2002) 488 – C5-0449/2002 – 2002/0220(COD)), A5-0295/2003. Brussels, 9.10.2003: European Parliament.

Parliament (2004) Report on amendment of the legal basis and on the 'general orientation' of the Council with a view to adoption of a directive of the European Parliament and of the Council concerning measures to safeguard security of natural gas supply (15769/2003 – C5-0027/2004 – 2002/0220(COD)), A5-0213/2004. Brussels, 22.3.2004: European Parliament.

Parliament (2005) Debate: Trans-European energy networks. Strasbourg, 6.6.2005: European Parliament.

Parliament (2006a) Debate, A European strategy for sustainable, competitive and secure energy, CRE 14/12/2006 – 3. Strasbourg, 14.12.2006: European Parliament.

Parliament (2006b) Debate: Guidelines for trans-European energy networks, CRE 03/04/2006 – 10. Strasbourg, 3.4.2006: European Parliament.

Parliament (2006c) European Parliament resolution on a European strategy for sustainable, competitive and secure energy – Green paper (2006/2113(INI)), P6_TA(2006)0603. Strasbourg, 14.12.2006: European Parliament.

Parliament (2006d) European Parliament resolution on security of energy supply in the European Union, P6_TA(2006)0110. Brussels, 23.3.2006: European Parliament.

Parliament (2006e) A European strategy for sustainable, competitive and secure energy – Biomass and Biofuels – Nuclear Safety and Security Assistance (debate), CRE 14/12/2006 – 3. Strasbourg: European Parliament.

Parliament (2006f) Security of energy supply in the European Union (debate) CRE 22/03/2006 – 12. Brussels, 22 March 2006: European Parliament.

Parliament (2007a) European Parliament resolution of 26 September 2007 on towards a common European foreign policy on energy (2007/2000(INI)), P6_TA(2007)0413. Strasbourg: European Parliament.

Parliament (2007b) Report on towards a common European foreign policy on energy (2007/2000(INI)): Rapporteur: Jacek Saryusz-Wolski, Member of European Parliament.

Parliament (2007c) Towards a common European foreign policy on energy (debate), 2007/2000(INI), CRE 25/09/2007 – 15. Strasbourg, 25.9.2007: European Parliament.

Parliament (2008a) Debates: Conditions for access to the natural gas transmission networks – Internal market in natural gas – European strategic energy technology plan, CRE 08/07/2008 – 12. Strasbourg, 8.7.2008: European Parliament.

Parliament (2008b) Position of the European Parliament adopted at first reading on 9 July 2008 with a view to the adoption of Directive 2008/.../EC of the European Parliament and of the Council amending Directive 2003/55/EC concerning common rules for the internal market in natural gas (EP-PE_TC1-COD(2007)0196). Brussels, 9.7.2008: European Parliament.

Parliament (2008c) Report on the proposal for a directive of the European Parliament and of the Council amending Directive 2003/55/EC concerning common rules for the internal market in natural gas, A6–0257/2008. Brussels, 13.6.2008: Committee on Industry, Research and Energy, Rapporteur: Romano Maria La Russa.

Parliament (2009a) An Assessment of the Gas and Oil Pipelines in Europe, IP/A/ITRE/NT/2009–13, Brussels: European Parliament.

Parliament (2009b) Debate: Gas supplies by Russia to Ukraine and the EU. Strasbourg, 14.1.2009: European Parliament.

Parliament (2009c) Debates – Internal market in natural gas, CRE 21/04/2009 – 17. Strasbourg, 21.4.2009: European Parliament.

Parliament (2009d) European Parliament resolution of 3 February 2009 on the Second Strategic Energy Review (2008/2239(INI)), P6_TA(2009)0038. Strasbourg, 3.2.2009: European Parliament.

Parliament (2009e) Recommendation for second reading on the Council common position for adopting a directive of the European Parliament and of the Council concerning common rules for the internal market in natural gas and repealing Directive 2003/55/EC, A6–0238/2009. Brussels, 3.4.2009: Committee on Industry, Research and Energy.

Parliament (2010a) European Parliament legislative resolution of 21 September 2010 on the proposal for a regulation of the European Parliament and of the Council concerning measures to safeguard security of gas supply and repealing Directive 2004/67/EC (COM(2009)0363 – C7–0097/2009 – 2009/0108(COD)), P7_TA(2010)0322. Strasbourg, 21.9.2010: European Parliament.

Parliament (2010b) European Parliament resolution of 25 November 2010 on Towards a new Energy Strategy for Europe 2011–2020 (2010/2108(INI)). Brussels, 2511.2010: European Parliament.

Parliament (2010c) Report on the proposal for a regulation of the European Parliament and of the Council concerning measures to safeguard security of gas supply and repealing Directive 2004/67/EC (COM(2009)0363 – C7–0097/2009 – 2009/0108(COD)), A7–0112/2010. Brussels, 29.3.2010: Committee on Industry, Research and Energy, Rapporteur: Alejo Vidal-Quadras.

Parliament (2010d) Security of gas supply (debate), CRE 21/09/2010 – 3. Strasbourg, 21.9.2010: European Parliament.

Parliament (2011a) Debate: Energy infrastructure priorities for 2020 and beyond (short presentation). Strasbourg, 4.7.2011: European Parliament.

Parliament (2011b) European Parliament resolution of 5 July 2011 on energy infrastructure priorities for 2020 and beyond (2011/2034(INI)), P7_TA(2011)0318. Strasbourg, 5.7.2011: European Parliament.

Parliament (2011c) Report on energy infrastructure priorities for 2020 and beyond (2011/2034(INI)), A7–0226/2011. Brussels, 14.6.2011: Committee on Industry, Research and Energy; Rapporteur: Francisco Sosa Wagner.

Parliament (2012a) Intergovernmental agreements between Member States and third countries in the field of energy (debate), CRE 12/09/2012 – 14. Strasbourg, 12.9.2012: European Parliament.

Parliament (2012b) REPORT on Engaging in energy policy cooperation with partners beyond our borders: A strategic approach to secure, sustainable and competitive energy supply (2012/2029(INI)), A7–0168/2012. Brussels, 16.5.2012: Committee on Industry, Research and Energy; Rapporteur: Edit Herczog.

Parliament (2012c) REPORT on the proposal for a decision of the European Parliament and of the Council setting up an information exchange mechanism with regard to intergovernmental agreements between Member States and third countries in the field of energy, A7–0264/2012. Brussels, 30.7.2012: Committee on Industry, Research and Energy, Rapporteur: Krišjānis Kariņš.

Parliament (2013a) Debate: Trans-European energy infrastructure, CRE 11/03/2013 – 20. Strasbourg, 11.3.2013: European Parliament.

Parliament (2013b) Report on the proposal for a regulation of the European Parliament and of the Council on guidelines for trans-European energy infrastructure and repealing Decision No 1364/2006/EC (COM(2011)0658 – C7–0371/2011 – 2011/0300(COD)), A7–0036/2013. Brussels, 8.2.2013: Committee on Industry, Research and Energy; Rapporteur: António Fernando Correia De Campos.

Parliament (2015a) 2014/2153(INI) European energy security strategy, PE 541.614v02–00. Brussels, 18.5.2015: European Parliament.

Parliament (2015b) European Parliament resolution of 15 December 2015 on Towards a European Energy Union (2015/2113(INI)), P8_TA(2015)0444. Strasbourg, 15.12.2015: European Parliament.

Parliament (2016a) Report on the proposal for a decision of the European Parliament and of the Council on establishing an information exchange mechanism with regard to intergovernmental agreements and non-binding instruments between Member States and third countries in the field of energy and repealing Decision No 994/2012/EU, PE 583.986v02–00. Brussels, 18.10.2016: Committee on Industry, Research and Energy; Rapporteur: Zdzisław Krasnodębski.

Parliament (2016b) REPORT on the proposal for a regulation of the European Parliament and of the Council concerning measures to safeguard the security of gas supply and repealing Regulation (EU) No 994/2010 (COM(2016)0052 – C8–0035/2016 – 2016/0030(COD)), A8–0310/2016. Brussels, 20.10.2016: European Parliament.

Parliament (2017a) Briefing, EU Legislation in Progress, New rules on security of gas supply. Brussels, November 2017: European Parliamentary Research Service.

Parliament (2017b) Debate: Information exchange mechanism with regard to intergovernmental agreements and non-binding instruments in the field of energy, CRE 01/03/2017 – 23. Brussels, 1.3.2017: European Parliament.

Parliament (2017c) Measures to safeguard the security of gas supply (debate) CRE 12/09/2017 – 4. Strasbourg: European Parliament.

Parliament (2019) Debate: Common rules for the internal market for natural gas CRE 03/04/2019 – 13, Brussels: European Parliament.

Pech, Laurent and Scheppele, Kim Lane (2017) 'Illiberalism Within- Rule of Law Backsliding in the EU', Cambridge Yearbook of European Legal Studies, pp. 3–47.

Petit, Yves (2010) 'La solidarité énergétique entre les Etats membres de l'Union européenne: une chimère?', Revue des affaires européennes, 17(4), pp. 771–783.

Piattoni, Simona (2017) 'Federal Power-Sharing in the European Union' in: Ferdinand Karlhofer, Günther Pallaver (eds.) Federal Power-Sharing in Europe, pp. 265 – 288.

Pickel, Susanne and Pickel, Gert (2018) Empirische Politikforschung. Oldenbourg: De Gruyter.

Piebalgs, Andris (2006) A Common Energy Policy for Europe, SPEECH/06/161. EU Energy Policy and Law Conference, Brussels, 9.3.2006: Brussels.

Piebalgs, Andris (2007a) EU's response to the global energy challenges, SPEECH/07/623. Speech at the Vilnius Energy Security Conference, Vilnius, 11 October 2007: European Commission.

Piebalgs, Andris (2007b) Speech: Energy for a Changing World: The New European Energy Policy, SPEECH/07/38. EU Energy Law and Policy conference, Brussels, 25.1.2007: European Commission.

Pirani, Simon, Henderson, James, Honoré, Anouk, Rogers, Howard and Yafimava, Katja (2014) 'What the Ukraine crisis means for gas markets', Oxford Energy Comment, (March 2014).

Pirani, Simon, Stern, Jonathan and Yafimava, Katja (2009) 'The Russo-Ukrainian gas dispute of January 2009: a comprehensive assessment', Oxford Institute for Energy Studies, February 2009, NG 27.

Pointvogl, Andreas (2009) 'Perceptions, realities, concession—What is driving the integration of European energy policies?', Energy Policy, 37(12), pp. 5704–5716.

Presidency (2008) Draft report to the European Council on energy security – Presidency briefing, 13827/1/08 REV 1. Brussels, 8.10.2008: Council of Ministers.

Presidency (2015) The programme of the Latvian Presidency of the Council of the European Union. Eu2015.lv: Latvian Government.

Presidency (2016) Programme of the Slovak Presidency of the Council of the EU, 1.7.-31.12.2016, www.eukn.eu/fileadmin/Files/Presidencies/2016_Slovakia/SK_P rogramme.pdf.

Presidency (2017) Programme of the Maltese Presidency of the Council of the European Union, 1 January 2017 – 30 June 2017: Maltese Government.

Press Release No 129/21 (2021) Judgment in Case C-848/19 P Germany v Poland, Court of Justice of the European Union, Luxembourg.

Princen, Sebastiaan (2011) 'Agenda-setting strategies in EU policy processes', Journal of European Public Policy, 18(7), pp. 927–943.

Puetter, Uwe (2012) 'Europe's deliberative intergovernmentalism: the role of the Council and European Council in EU economic governance', Journal of European Public Policy, 19(2), pp. 161–178.

Putnam, Robert D., Leonardi, Robert and Nanetti, Raffaella Y. (1993) Making Democracy Work: Civic Traditions in modern Italy. Princeton: Princeton University Press.

Rebhahn, Robert (2015) 'Solidarität in der Wirtschafts- und Währungsunion: Grundlagen und Grenzen'. Baden-Baden: Nomos.

Regulation (EU) No 347/2013 'Regulation (EU) No 347/2013 of the European Parliament and of the Council of 17 April 2013 on guidelines for trans-European energy infrastructure and repealing Decision No 1364/2006/EC and amending Regulations (EC) No 713/2009, (EC) No 714/2009 and (EC) No 715/2009'.

Regulation (EU)2017/1938 (2017) Regulation (EU) 2017/1938 the European Parliament and of the Council of 25 October 2017 concerning measures to safeguard the security of gas supply and repealing Regulation (EU) No 994/2010.

Reykers, Yf and Beach, Derek (2017) 'Process-Tracing as a Tool to Analyse Discretion', in Delreux, T. and Adriaensen, J. (eds.) The Principal Agent Model and the European Union. Cham: Springer International Publishing, pp. 255–281.

Rhinard, Mark (2010) Framing Europe: The Policy Shaping Strategies of the European Commission. Dordrecht: Republic of Letters.

Riley, Alan (2019) The 'principle of solidarity': OPAL, Nord Stream, and the shadow over Gazprom: Atlantic Council. Available at: https://www.atlanticcouncil.org/blogs/energysource/the-principle-of-solidarity-opal-nord-stream-and-the-shadow-over-gazprom/ (Accessed: 03.01.2020).

Rittberger, Berthold, Schwarzenbeck, Helena and Zangl, Bernhard (2017) 'Where Does the Buck Stop? Explaining Public Responsibility Attributions in Complex International Institutions', Journal of Common Market Studies, 55(4), pp. 909–924.

Rocco, Andrea (2019) 'The Impact of the Post Lisbon Energy Policy on EU Natural Gas Supplying Countries', EUTIP, Working Paper 01/2019.

Rohlfing, Ingo (2012) Case Studies and Causal Inference. Palgrave Macmillan UK.

Roth, Mathias (2011) 'Poland as a Policy Entrepreneur in European External Energy Policy: Towards Greater Energy Solidarity vis-à-vis Russia?', Geopolitics, 16(3), pp. 600–625.

Saldaña, Johnny (2012) The Coding Manual for Qualitative Researchers. Thousand Oaks, CA: SAGE Publications.

Sánchez-Bordona, Campos (2021) 'Opinion of General Advocate Campos Sánchez-Bordona delivered on 18 March 2021', Case C-848/19 P.

Sandholtz, Wayne and Stone Sweet, Alec (2010) 'Neo-functionalism and Supranational Governance', in Jones, E., Menon, A. and Weatherill, S. (eds.) The Oxford Handbook of the European Union. Oxford.

Sangiovanni, Andrea (2013) 'Solidarity in the European Union', Oxford Journal of Legal Studies, 33(2), pp. 213–241.

Sangiovanni, Andrea (2015) 'Solidarity as Joint Action', Journal of Applied Philosophy, 32(4), pp. 340–359.

Saracino, Daniele (2019) Solidarität in der Asylpolitik der Europäischen Union. Wiesbaden: Springer VS.

Sartori, Giovanni (1984) Social Science Concepts: A Systematic Analysis. SAGE Publications.

Sartori, Giovanni (1970) 'Concept Misformation in Comparative Politics', The American Political Science Review, 64(4), pp. 1033–1053.

Sartori, Giovanni (2009) 'Guidelines for concept analysis', in Collier, D. and Gerring, J. (eds.) Concepts and Method in Social Science: The Tradition of Giovanni Sartori: Routledge.

Saurugger, Sabine (2010) 'The social construction of the participatory turn: The emergence of a norm in the European Union', European Journal of Political Research, 49: 471–495.

Saurugger, Sabine and Terpan, Fabien (2013) 'Resisting EU Norms. A Framework for Analysis', Sciences Po Grenoble working paper, 2.

Scharpf, Fritz W. (1988) ‚The Joint-Decision Trap: Lessons from German Federalism and European Integration', in: Public Administration 66(3), pp. 239 – 278.

Scharpf, Fritz W. (1991) ‚Koordination durch Verhandlungssysteme: Analytische Konzepte und institutionelle Lösungen am Beispiel der Zusammenarbeit zwischen zwei Bundesländern', MPIfG Discussion Paper, No. 91/4, Köln.

Scharpf, Fritz W. (2016) 'De-constitutionalization and majority rule: A Democratic Vision for Europe', MPIFG Discussion Paper, 16(14), pp. 1–39.

Schiek, Dagmar (2020) 'Solidarity in the case law of the Euro-pean Court of Justice – opportunities missed?', in Krunke, H., Petersen, H. and Manners, I. (eds.) Transnational Solidarity. Concept, Challenges and Opportunities: Cambridge University Press.

Schimmelfennig, Frank (2018) 'European integration (theory) in times of crisis. A comparison of the euro and Schengen crises', Journal of European Public Policy, 25(7), pp. 969–989.

Schimmelfennig, Frank and Winzen, Thomas (2019) 'Grand theories, differentiated integration, Journal of European Public Policy', 26(8), pp. 1172–1192.

Schmale, Wolfgang (2017) 'European solidarity: a semantic history', European Review of History: Revue européenne d'histoire, 24(6), pp. 854–873.

Schmälter, Julia (2018) 'A European response to non-compliance: the Commission's enforcement efforts and the Common European Asylum System', West European Politics, 41(6), pp. 1330–1353.

Schmitter, Philippe C. (2005) 'Ernst B. Haas and the legacy of neofunctionalism', Journal of European Public Policy, 12(2), pp. 255–272.

Scholz, Sally (2008) 'Political Solidarity', Penn State University Press, University Park, Pennsylvania.

Schuman, Robert (1950) The Schuman Declaration. Paris, 9.5.1950: European Commission. Available at: https://europa.eu/european-union/about-eu/symbols/europe-day/schuman-declaration_de (Accessed: 26.8.2020).

Sedmak, Clemens (2010) Solidarität: vom Wert der Gemeinschaft. Grundwerte Europas Darmstadt: WBG.

Šefčovič, Maroš (2016) Speech by Vice-President Maroš Šefčovič on "Nord Stream II – Energy Union at the crossroads", SPEECH/16/1283. Brussels, 6.4.2016: European Commission.

Sharpston, Advocate General (2019) Case C-715/17 European Commission v Republic of Poland Case C-718/17 European Commission v Republic of Hungary Case C-719/17 European Commission v Czech Republic: Case C-715/17.

Siebold, Angela (2017) 'Open borders as an act of solidarity among peoples, between states or with migrants: changing applications of solidarity within the Schengen process', European Review of History: Revue européenne d'histoire, 24(6), pp. 991–1006.

Single European Act (1987). OJ L 169: Official Journal of the European Communities.

Smith, Nicholas H. and Laitinen, Arto (2009) 'Taylor on Solidarity', Thesis Eleven, 99(1), pp. 48–70. doi: 10.1177/0725513609345374.

Stein, Daniel D. (2019) Impact of the European Court of Justice's Opal decision: Atlantic Council. Available at: https://www.atlanticcouncil.org/blogs/energysour ce/impact-of-the-european-court-of-justices-opal-decision/ (Accessed: 3.11.2019).

Steinvorth, Ulrich (2017) 'Applying the Idea of Solidarity to Europe', in Grimmel, A. and Giang, S.M. (eds.) Solidarity in the European Union: A Fundamental Value in Crisis. Cham: Springer International Publishing.

Stephenson, Paul (2010) 'Let's get physical: the European Commission and cultivated spillover in completing the single market's transport infrastructure', Journal of European Public Policy, 17(7), pp. 1039–1057.

Stern, Jonathan (2006) 'The Russian-Ukrainian gas crisis of January 2006', Oxford Institute for Energy Studies.

Stjernø, Steinar (2005) 'Solidarity in Europe: The History of an Idea'. Cambridge: Cambridge University Press.

Stoffaës, Christian (2010) La sécurité gazière de l'Europe: De la dépendance à l'interdépendance: Centre d'analyse stratégique.

Stone Sweet, Alec (2010) 'The European Court of Justice and the judicialization of EU governance', Living Reviews in European Governance, 5(2), pp. 1–50.

Streinz, Rudolf and Bings, Sophie (2012) EUV, AEUV: Vertrag über die Europäische Union und Vertrag über die Arbeitsweise der Europäischen Union. Beck'sche Kurz-Kommentare 2 edn. München: Beck.

Summit (2002) EU-Russia Summit, 13970/02 (Presse 347). Brussels, 11.11.2002: Council of the European Union.

Szulecki, Kacper, Fischer, Severin, Gullberg, Anne Therese and Sartor, Oliver (2016) 'Shaping the 'Energy Union': between national positions and governance innovation in EU energy and climate policy', Climate Policy, 16(5), pp. 548–567.

Szulecki, Kacper and Westphal, Kirsten (2014) 'The Cardinal Sins of European Energy Policy: Nongovernance in an Uncertain Global Landscape', Global Policy, 5(11), pp. 38–51.

Tagliapietra, Simone (2017) 'The EU energy, climate and environmental policies: An overview', PONT Working Europe Seminar, Brussels, 27 March 2017.

Tallberg, Jonas (2000) 'The Anatomy of Autonomy- An Institutional Account of Variation in Supranational Influence', Journal of Common Market Studies, 38(5), pp. 843–864.

Talus, Kim (2013) EU Energy Law and Policy: A Critical Account. Oxford: Oxford University Press.

Tarabella, Marc (2013) Written question E-010039/13 Marc Tarabella (S&D) to the Commission. Definition of energy solidarity. Publications Office of the EU.

Taylor, Ashley (2015) 'Solidarity: Obligations and Expressions', Journal of Political Philosophy, 23(2), pp. 128–145.

Terhechte, Jörg (2014) 'EUV Art. 3 Rn. 57', in Grabitz, E., Hilf, M. and Nettesheim, M. (eds.) Das Recht der Europäischen Union: EUV/AEUV. München: C.H. Beck.

Thaler, Philipp and Pakalkaite, Vija (2020) 'How EU external energy policy has become 'supranationalised' – and what this means for European integration', LSE European Politics and Policy (EUROPP) Blog, 30.6.2020.

Thielemann, Eiko (2018) 'Why Refugee Burden-Sharing Initiatives Fail- Public Goods, Free-Riding and Symbolic Solidarity in the EU', Journal of Common Market Studies, 56(1), pp. 63–82.

Thielemann, Eiko (2003) 'Between Interests and Norms: Explaining Burden-Sharing in the European Union', Journal of Refugee Studies, 16(3), pp. 253–273.

Thompson, Evan (2015) 'The European Union's energy policy: Two-track development', in Witzleb, N., Arranz, A.M. and Winand, P. (eds.) The European Union and Global Engagement: Institutions, Policies and Challenges. Cheltenham UK: Edward Elgar Publishing, pp. 176 – 194.

Tramountana, Chrysanthi (2019) 'What is the scope of the EU external competence in the field of energy today?', Notre Europe Jacques Delors Institute, pp. 1–9.

Trampusch, Christine and Palier, Bruno (2016) 'Between X and Y: how process tracing contributes to opening the black box of causality', New Political Economy, 21(5), pp. 437–454.

Tranholm-Mikkelsen, Jeppe (1991) 'Neo-functionalism: Obstinate or Obsolete? A Reappraisal in the Light of the New Dynamism of the EC', Millennium, 20(1), pp. 1–22.

Tranow, Ulf (2012) Das Konzept der Solidarität: Handlungstheoretische Fundierung eines soziologischen Schlüsselbegriffs. Wiesbaden: Springer VS.

Trein, Philipp (2020) 'Federal dynamics, solidarity, and European Union crisis politics', Journal of European Public Policy, 27:7, pp. 977–994,

Tsourdi, Evangelia and De Bruycker, Philippe (2015) 'EU Asylum Policy: In Search of Solidarity and Access to Protection', EUI Policy Brief – Migration Policy Centre, 6, pp. 1–12.

Turmes, Claude (2018) Press Release: Special Treatment for Nord Stream II must end. 21.03.2018: Greens / EFA. Available at: https://www.greens-efa.eu/en/article/press/special-treatment-for-nord-stream-ii-must-end/ (Accessed: 04.04.2020).

Tusk, Donald (2014) 'A united Europe can end Russia's energy stranglehold', Financial Times.

Umbach, Frank (2014) 'Russian-Ukrainian-EU gas conflict: who stands to lose most?', NATO Review.

UN (n.d.) International Human Solidarity Day: United Nations. Available at: https://www.un.org/en/observances/human-solidarity-day (Accessed: 23.3.2020).

Van Cleynenbreugel, Pieter (2014) Market Supervision in the European Union: Integrated Administration in Constitutional Context. Leiden: Brill | Nijhoff.

Van Cleynenbreugel, Pieter (2018) 'Typologies of solidarity in EU law: a non–shifting landscape in the wake of economic crises', in Biondi, A., Dagilytė, E. and Küçük, E. (eds.) Solidarity in EU Law: Legal Principle in the Making. Cheltenham: Edward Elgar Publishing.

Van Oorschot, Wim and Komter, Aafke (1998) 'What is that ties...? Theoretical perspectives on social bond', Sociale Wetenschappen, 41(3), pp. 4–24.

Van Renssen, Sonja (2016) Gasland EU: upcoming energy security package is all about gas. Energypost.eu, 11.1.2016. Available at: https://energypost.eu/gasland-eu-upcoming-energy-security-package-gas/ (Accessed: 17.2.2020).

Vanheule, Dirk, van Selm, Joanne and Boswell, Christina (2011) The implementation of Article 80 TFEU on the principle of solidarity and fair sharing of responsibility, including its financial implications, between the Member States in the field of border checks, asylum and immigration, Brussels.

Vanhoorn, Lenhard and Faas, Henryk (2009) 'Short and long-term indicators and early warning tool for energy security', European Commission; JRC – Institute for Energy; Energy Security Unit, pp. 2–28.

Verhaegen, Soetkin (2018) 'What to expect from European identity? Explaining support for solidarity in times of crisis', Comparative European Politics, 16(5), pp. 871–904.

Viehoff, Juri and Nicolaidis, Kalypso (2015) 'Social Justice in the European Union- the Puzzles of Solidarity, Reciprocity and Choice', in Kochenov, D., de Búrca, G. and Williams, A. (eds.) Europe's Justice Deficit? Oxford: Hart Publishing, pp. 277–294.

Vinois, Jean-Arnold (2008) Security of gas supply: Gas Coordination Group. Brussels, 27.2.2008: European Energy Forum Dinner Debate.

Vinois, Jean-Arnold (2017) 'The Future of Gas in the Energy Union: Managing Its Decline?', in Hafner, M. and Tagliapietra, S. (eds.) The European gas markets: Challenges and opportunities, pp. 393–414.

Vinois, Jean-Arnold and Bros, Thierry (2019) 'Russian Gas Pipelines and the European Union- Moving from a Love-Hate Relationship "with Adults in the Room"?', Jacques Delors Energy Centre, 247, pp. 1–18.

Wallaschek, Stefan (2019) 'The Discursive Construction of Solidarity- Analysing Public Claims in Europe's Migration Crisis', Political Studies, pp. 1–19.

Weale, Albert (2016) "Political Legitimacy, Credible Commitment, and Euro Governance." In Beyond the Crisis: The Governance of Europe's Economic, Political and Legal Transformation, edited by Mark Dawson, Henrik Enderlein, and Christian Joerges. Oxford: Oxford University Press, 2015. Oxford Scholarship Online, 2016.

Wessels, Wolfgang and Wolters, Johannes (2017) "Chancen und Risiken von Aufbau- und Abbauflexibilisierung: Der Europäische Rat vor einem Trilemma." Integration 40, no. 2, 89–100.

Wessels, Wolfgang and Wolters, Johannes (2019) 'Der Europäische Rat', in Becker, P. and Lippert, B. (eds.) Handbuch Europäische Union. Wiesbaden: Springer VS.

Wessels, Wolfgang (2016) The European Council. London: Red Globe Press.

Westphal, Kirsten (2009) 'Russian Gas, Ukrainian Pipelines, and European Supply Security – Lessons of the 2009 Controversies', SWP Research Paper, RP 11.

Westphal, Kirsten (2020) ,Strategische Souveränität in Energiefragen: Überlegungen zur Handlungs- und Gestaltungsfähigkeit Deutschlands in der EU', SWP-Aktuell, Nr. 46.

Whist, Bendik Solum (2008) 'Nord Stream: Not Just a Pipeline – An analysis of the political debates in the Baltic Sea region regarding the planned gas pipeline from Russia to Germany', Fridtjof Nansen Institute, FNI Report 15/2008.

Wilde, Lawrence (2013) Global Solidarity. Edinburgh: Edinburgh University Press.

Wilde, Lawrence (2007) 'The Concept of Solidarity: Emerging from the Theoretical Shadows?', The British Journal of Politics & International Relations, 9(1), pp. 171–181.

Wildt, Andreas (1999) 'Solidarity: Its History and Contemporary Definition', in Bayertz, K. (ed.) Solidarity: Springer My Copy UK.

Wildt, Andreas (2017) 'Historisches Wörterbuch der Philosophie online', Solidarität. Basel: Schwabe Verlag.

Willer, David, Borch, Casey and Willer, Robb (2002) 'Building a model for solidarity and cohesion using three theories', in Lawler, E. and Thye, S. (eds.) Advances in Group Processes. Bingley: Emerald Group Publishing Limited.

Wolf, Dieter (2012) 'Neo-Funktionalismus', in Bieling, H.J. and Lerch, M. (eds.) Theorien der europäischen Integration. Wiesbaden: Springer Fachmedien.

Wydra, Doris (2010) 'Ein kritischer Blick auf den Solidaritätsdiskurs in der europäischen Union', in Sedmak, C. (ed.) Solidarität: vom Wert der Gemeinschaft Grundwerte Europas. Darmstadt: WBG.

Yafimava, Katja (2017) 'The OPAL Exemption Decision: a comment on CJEU's ruling to reject suspension', Energy Insight, pp. 1–11.

Annex

Annex 1: Definitions of Solidarity

Author	Definition of Solidarity
Baurmann (in Bayertz 1999: 243)	„By acting in solidarity I mean the voluntary transfer of goods or services to another individual or to a group of individuals whenever this transfer is not the object of an explicit contract. A transfer of this kind is *unconditional* in the sense that it is *not* contingent on the enforceable duty of the beneficiary to provide a specified equivalent for the gains he or she obtains. Acting in solidarity with a single individual means to contribute voluntarily and unconditionally to an *individual* good. Acting in solidarity with a group of individuals means to contribute voluntarily and unconditionally to a *public* good".
Casini (2013)	„solidarity as a form of action (or non-action) performed by certain actors to assist (or to not damage) other actors, so as to achieve a common goal".
Dictionary N.d.	„1a. The fact or quality, on the part of communities, etc., of being perfectly united or at one in some respect, esp. In interests, sympathies, or aspirations; spec. With reference to the aspirations or actions of trade-union members. Also attributive and in other combinations. B. Const. Of (mankind, a race, etc.). C. Const. Between or with (others). Also transferred. 2. Community or perfect coincidence of (or between) interests. 3. Civil Law. A form of obligation involving joint and several responsibilities or rights".
Duden (n.d.)	„Solidarität": „1. Unbedingtes Zusammenhalten mit jemandem aufgrund gleicher Anschauungen und Ziele. 2. (besonders in der Arbeiterbewegung) auf das Zusammengehörigkeitsgefühl und das Eintreten füreinander sich gründende Unterstützung".
Engler (2016: 35)	„Zusammenfassend kann festgehalten werden, dass Solidarität eine besondere soziale Norm ist, die für ein bestimmtes Kollektiv gilt, von den Mitgliedern reziprok anerkannt wird, sich in bestimmte Praktiken der Kooperation und des gegenseitigen Verzichts übersetzt und durch Sanktionsmechanismen abgesichert ist.
Hestermeyer (in Hestermeyer and Wolfrum 2012: 49)	„At the core of the concept is the idea of the interdependence of members of a self-identified and legitimate group who expect and are willing to help each other in need to some extent. In international law that group is the community of states".
Karagiannis (2007: 5)	„(S)olidarity is a recurrent specification of social bonds with a political view. In other words, it brings together, without disentangling them, a (often a posteriori) description of a certain social reality at a certain time, and a (often a priori) political project".
Kim and Schattle (2012: 467)	We „(...) define solidarity as an ethos of collective responsibility that sets up suitable background conditions for policy decisions that not only affirm pragmatic interests among a set of governments or stakeholders, but also, in some cases, extend from common normative values that can be

Author	Definition of Solidarity
	identified among cooperating regional political and economic actors in an interdependent world".
Klamert (2014: 40)	„Solidarity, thus, is a principle guiding the conduct of Member States in their relation with each other. As such, it is rather a political than a legal concept, important exceptions aside".
Knodt and Tews (Preuß 1998, 399 zitiert aus Webster's Wörterbuch, in Knodt and Tews 2014: 10)	Knodt and Tews follow the definition by Preuß, who understands solidarity as „Einheit (z.B. einer Gruppe oder einer Klasse), die auf einer Gemeinschaft von Interessen, Zielen und Maßstäben basiert oder diese hervorbringt".
Koroma (in Hestermeyer and Wolfrum 2012: 103)	„(...) the concept of solidarity in current international law represents (...) an emerging structural principle which in many cases creates negative obligations on States not to engage in certain activities, and in an increasing number of contexts establishes concrete duties on States to carry out certain measures for the common good".
Lahusen and Federico (2018: 15)	„First, solidarity is a relationship of support tied to (informal or formal) rights and obligations; second, solidarity might have universalist orientations but is most of the time conditional; and third, solidarity is institutionalised at several interdependent levels of aggregation".
Larousse N.d.	„1. Rapport existant entre des personnes qui, ayant une communauté d'intérêts, sont liées les unes aux autres : Il existe une solidarité entre les membres de cette profession. 2. Littéraire. Rapport d'interdépendance entre les choses : Solidarité entre deux phénomènes. 3. Sentiment d'un devoir moral envers les autres membres d'un groupe, fondé sur l'identité de situation, d'intérêts : Agir par solidarité. 4. Modalité d'une obligation s'opposant à la division d'une créance ou d'une dette divisible par nature et permettant à chaque créancier d'obtenir l'entier paiement (solidarité active) ou obligeant chaque débiteur à payer la totalité de la dette (solidarité passive)".
Loh and Skupien (2016: 578f.)	Es „(...) lässt sich die Diagnose formulieren, dass sich.postkonventionelle Solidarbindungen essentiell auf eine Gegenseitigkeitserwartung, das heißt eine „latente Reziprozität [...], die allen Solidaritätsbeziehungen zu eigen ist" gründen. Gerade diese Reziprozität unterscheidet die Solidarität von anderen Formen der Hilfeleistung, seien sie spontan (Barmherzigkeit) oder gewohnheitsmäßig (Wohltätigkeit). Anders als letztere ist solidarisches Handeln immer auch an den Gedanken einer Solidargemeinschaft geknüpft, in der jeder für den anderen einsteht".
Mau (2008)	„Solidarität bezeichnet einen Zusammenhang zwischen Individuen oder gesellschaftlichen Gruppen, der sich durch eine besondere Form von Verbundenheit und wechselseitiger Verpflichtung auszeichnet. Er steht für spezifische Formen sozialer Kooperation, die auf Bindungen innerhalb eines kollektiven Zusammenhangs und daraus hervorgehenden Gemeinwohldefinitionen zurückgehen".
Miller (2017: 62)	„Solidarity among members of a social group must be distinguished from solidarity with outsiders. It has four main components: 1) distinguishing features that bind members together; 2) mutual concern and mutual aid within the group; 3) acknowledgement of collective responsibility; 4) limits on inequality among members".

Author	Definition of Solidarity
Parsons (1951: 97–101)	„Solidarity action is defined as collectivity-oriented action, which contrasts with self-oriented actions."
Sangiovanni (2015: 343)	„I act in solidarity with you when: 1. You and I each (a) share a goal (b) to overcome some significant adversity; 2. You and I each individually intend to do our part in achieving the shared goal in ways that mesh; 3. You and I are each individually committed (a) to the realisation of the shared goal and (b) to not bypassing each other's will in the achievement of the goal; 4. You and I are disposed (a) to incur significant costs to realise our goal; and (b) to share one another's fates in ways relevant to the shared goal. 5. Facts 1.-4. Need not be common knowledge".
Steinvorth (in Grimmel and Giang 2017: 10)	„Solidarity is the virtue of equals who help one another in misfortunes they are not responsible for".
Stjernø (2005: 1)	Solidarity is „the preparedness to share resources with others by personal contribution to those in struggle or in need and through taxation and redistribution organised by the state".
Taylor (2015: 129)	„Solidarity is a kind of cohesive bond, seen in the capacity to affect the individuals related to that bond".
Tranow (2012: 54)	„Solidarnormen bringen die Erwartung eines Normgebers zum Ausdruck, dass bestimmte Akteure einen kompensationslosen Transfer privater Ressourcen bestimmten Umfangs zugunsten bestimmter anderer individueller Akteure oder einer bestimmten Gruppe leisten sollen".
Van Cleynenbreugel (2018)	„(T)he human desire to share particular burdens and advantages creates a framework of mutual support and responsibility entitlements that are captured by the notion of solidarity".
Van Oorschot and Komter (1998: 9)	„Solidarity behaviour means that one conforms to the solidarity obligations of one's role. The actual degree to which a collectivity can have its interests served by its members (i.e. the de facto internal level of solidarity) is thus a function of the degree to which the collectivity succeeds in imposing solidarity obligations on its members".
Wilde (2007: 171)	„In essence, solidarity is the feeling of reciprocal sympathy and responsibility among members of a group which promotes mutual support".
Wildt (2017)	„Solidarität (neulat. Solidaritas, von solidus dicht, gediegen, fest, ganz; engl. Solidarity; frz. Solidarité; ital. Solidarietà). ‹S.› [1] bedeutet die Bereitschaft, sich für gemeinsame Ziele oder für Ziele anderer einzusetzen, die man als bedroht und gleichzeitig als wertvoll und legitim ansieht, bes. die engagierte Unterstützung eines Kampfes gegen Gefährdungen, vor allem gegen Unrecht, im weiteren Sinne auch: Zusammenhalt, soziale Bindung, Zusammengehörigkeitsgefühl. ‹S.› meint im engeren, umgangssprachlichen Sinne immer ein praktisches oder jedenfalls emotionales Engagement für gemeinsame, meistens kooperative Ziele, vor allem im Kampf gegen Unrecht [2]. ‹S.› hat ursprünglich eine rein juristische Bedeutung, die sich im Deutschen – im Unterschied zum Frz. Und Engl. – nur noch in Zusammensetzungen erhalten hat, bes. in ‹Solidarobligation› (unbegrenzte Haftung jedes Schuldners für eine Gesamtschuld, die bei Zahlung durch einen für die anderen erlischt) und, in komplexerer Weise, in ‹Solidargemeinschaft› (Gemeinschaft, in der Lasten und

Author	Definition of Solidarity
	Schäden eines jeden in gleichem Maße, aber von jedem gemäß seiner unterschiedlichen Leistungsfähigkeit getragen werden, z.B. In der Sozialversicherung) [3]. Jene Bedeutung ist abgeleitet von der Rechtsfigur der Schuld oder Verpflichtung 'in solidum' (fürs Ganze) aus dem römischen Recht. ‹S.› erweitert sich dann vor allem zu einer Bedeutung, die man als 'politisch-soziale Brüderlichkeit' umschreiben kann".

Annex 2: Code Book – Concept of Solidarity

Codes as implemented in MAXQDA.

This code book provides an overview of the interpretation of the different features of solidarity based on my conceptualisation. The coding is an interpretative process, which was conducted multiple times in order to increase the consistency of the interpretations and to ensure that the evaluation of the single features was coherent.

1. Group cohesion

Group cohesion determines why the group sticks together to provide solidarity. It comprises the importance of joint solutions on the one hand and the feelings of trust and responsibility between the group members on the other hand.

Collective interest/renounce national solution
Code: Group cohesion/collective interest/renounce national solution
Collective interests refer to announcements which underline that the group has a shared goal. Group members renounce national solutions in favour of the collectivity. This might be expressed by references to the need to find European solutions, shared objectives of the Treaties or interdependence.

Trust building and Responsibility
Code: Group cohesion/Trust building and Responsibility
Trust and responsibility are two important features of solidarity. The evolvement of trust is necessary so that group members can rely on each other and that they are willing to put solidarity in place. Group members are confident that the group will share burdens. Responsibility on the other hand exists between group members which feel that they are interconnected and that are interested in the well-being of the group.

2. Reciprocity

Reciprocity refers to the mechanisms in place to ensure solidarity. It has two subgroups, which are access to solidarity and obligation to provide solidarity. The main feature of reciprocity is that it entails a mutual relationship. Every group member must participate even though the form of participation can vary.

Obligation to provide good
Code: Reciprocity/Obligation to provide good
The obligation to provide solidarity entails all references which underline that group members must put in place mechanisms which make reciprocity possible. The feature comprises calls to action but also clear rules how to provide solidarity. This category covers the obligations of solidarity.

Access to the good
Code: Reciprocity/Access to the good
The access to the good is also important to make solidarity work. The access must be regulated in so far that it is clear what can be actually demanded. The feature entails also the rules under which conditions access is provided. This category covers the benefits of solidarity.

3. Monitoring and Self-responsibility

Monitoring and Self-responsibility describes the category, which denotes the control function of the group to ensure solidarity. This feature of solidarity guarantees that solidarity mechanisms exclude free-riders, that the implementation of solidarity mechanisms is monitored and that there are control capacities.

Self-Responsibility
Code: Monitoring and Self-responsibility/Self-Responsibility
Self-responsibility describes the willingness of group members to ensure that they don't need help. Group members carry through all possible measures in order to prevent a situation where they need help. Therefore, they agree to a set of measures, which have to be applied individually. This is important to stabilise trust between group members and to exclude free-riders.

Control capacity
Code: Monitoring and Self-responsibility/Control capacity
The group puts in place different mechanisms to monitor that all group members follow the common rules. This might be an agent (e.g. the Commission) to monitor the implementation of certain mechanisms (including opinions), but also control functions, such as information sharing.